"This is a must-read for anyone looking to take their game of life to the pro level!! The wisdom from Brian in this book is unmatched and it will unequivocally change your life!"

— **Sean Casey**, New York Yankees hitting coach,
3x Major League Baseball All-Star

"Mark my words: Brian Johnson is going to change the world, and this book is his ultimate manifesto. I've seen it over and over—when people connect with the Heroic movement they flourish. And flourishing is contagious. One purpose-driven hero impacts others, and within just a few iterations, the world. The science is solid; the history goes deep. *Areté* will elevate us all."

— **Susan Peirce Thompson, PhD**, professor of brain and
cognitive sciences, *New York Times*
bestselling author of *Bright Line Eating*

"From the beginning of this book Brian Johnson sets up incredibly high expectations, promising us the best, most heroic version of ourselves. And then, with each word, metaphor, story, and research, Brian proceeds to overdeliver on his promise. You have in your hands a life-changing masterpiece."

— **Tal Ben-Shahar, PhD**, *New York Times* bestselling author of
Happier, taught largest class at Harvard

"As a close friend and mentor, Brian's insights and guidance have had a profound impact on my own personal growth. His unwavering dedication to making a positive impact on the world motivates me to be a better human being each day. Brian's burning passion for living life through the concept of *Areté* makes his noble mission a cause to relentlessly support. We all want a better world for our kids and future generations. Many of Brian's tenets of character and leadership have been woven into the very fabric of our world-class warriors in Naval Special Warfare during their basic training phase. Brian has been extremely gracious to the families of our fallen heroes, for which I will always be grateful. Brian Johnson is an exceptional individual that comes along once in a lifetime who possesses the wisdom, leadership qualities, and love of humanity that are necessary to make a lasting difference in our world."

— **Mike Magaraci**, former Force Master Chief of the Naval Special Warfare Community

"In *Areté*, Brian Johnson masterfully integrates time-honored wisdom with contemporary science, creating a road map for increased well-being. This will sound cheesy, but it's more than just a book—it's a call for all of us to unearth our untapped potential. Brian offers practical, tangible tools for turning our greatest challenges into fuel for resilience and personal transformation. His new book is essential reading for anyone seeking to harness their heroic potential and influence the world in a positive way."

— **Sonja Lyubomirsky, PhD**, Distinguished Professor of Psychology at the University of California, Riverside, bestselling author of *The How of Happiness*

"Every hero needs a guide. But when they hand you the play-book to leading a life of meaning… it's the ultimate gift! This book won't leave your nightstand."

— **Todd Herman**, bestselling author
of *The Alter Ego Effect*

"This book is your next read AND your training template for a life well-lived. Philosophy, ethics, and morality in our modern world have devolved into relativism and opinion, with little action to back up the blather. It wasn't always this way. In ancient Greece and Rome, the Stoics understood that a personal philosophy not backed by powerful action and habituation of virtues simply displayed a lack of character. Brian Johnson is a Stoic reincarnate. Not only does he have a deep love for marrying ancient with modern wisdom, but also has a passion for embodying such wisdom in his own life—through daily discipline and effort. In short, he is willing to do the work of self-examination and character refinement espoused by the Stoics, Yogis, Taoists, and other philoso-pher-practitioners of the past. In *Areté: Activate Your Heroic Potential*, Brian shares this wisdom with us so that we, too, can be men and women of character and deep integrity. It is a message that is both timely and urgent. Thank you Brian for this important work."

— **Mark Divine**, Retired Navy SEAL Commander,
New York Times bestselling author of
Unbeatable Mind and *The Way of the SEAL*

"I have followed Brian Johnson's work for over a decade. He is the coach of coaches. The impact he's had on me and, as a result, those I coach, is immeasurable. If you're looking to level up every aspect of your personal and professional life, this is a must-read."

— **Brian Cain**, mental performance coach for
MLB, UFC, NFL, PGA & NCAA champions

"Brian is the most Stoic guy I know. When I'm in a jam, when the universe is turning my life upside down, Brian is the man I call. Every Spartan in the world should read *Areté*."

— **Joe De Sena**, CEO and founder of Spartan

"Most of us have read our share of self-improvement books. *Areté* is something else entirely—a self-illumination book. Each page sheds light on the undiscovered capacities that have been too-long hidden away within each of us. Brian's genius lies in holding out these golden finds for us to recognize as our own, while simultaneously unleashing the untapped stores of purpose-driven energy we need to wield them well. This book will serve as a daily devotional for many. For those willing to dig deeper, it will serve as a treasure map, dog-eared pages and highlighted passages marking a clear trail back to our own best gifts."

— **Pilar Gerasimo**, award-winning health journalist,
podcaster, and author of *The Healthy Deviant*

"This book is a life-changing masterpiece that will leave a lasting impact on anyone who reads it. If you're searching for a roadmap to a meaningful life, look no further. The wisdom Brian shares in *Areté* is the compass that will guide you towards a life of purpose, happiness, and the realization of your true potential."

— **Brandon Guyer**, Los Angeles Angels
mental toughness coach,
founder of Major League Mindset

"This book threatens to be one of the all-time best and most timeless masterpieces of personal productivity and self-development. From ancient wisdom to modern science, training the body, mind, and soul, optimizing energy, love, sleep, work, and beyond, it is a profoundly thorough treatise on everything you need to live as a full and complete human. Shove aside any books you've been planning to read and move *Areté* to the front of the line. You'll thank yourself forever if you do."

— **Ben Greenfield**, founder of Kion,
bestselling author of *Boundless*

"Brian Johnson's virtues of zest, service, and optimism are only matched by his kindness, generosity, and love. These virtues were embodied in Brian making Heroic available to the corps of cadets at the United States Military Academy at West Point. These future Army officers now have access to tools to assist them in leadership development, self-mastery, and antifragility. The beauty of this is not just the self-development aspect of cadets using Heroic, but that upon graduation and commissioning, they will take these virtues and skills to their platoons of America's finest young women and men. This book gives heroic leaders from all walks of life access to Brian's wisdom. I highly recommend it."

— **Scott Parsons, PhD**, Assistant Vice Chancellor for
Character and Ethics Development at Texas Tech,
former Character Development Integrator at the
United States Military Academy at West Point

"I've known Brian Johnson for over twenty years, and I've never met anyone more focused and dedicated to making a difference in the world. He lives an authentically heroic life by constantly challenging himself to grow and learn, by unapologetically eliminating all distractions, and by never giving up on his dreams. With Heroic, Brian has created a powerful and inspiring company to help us all live our lives to the fullest. *Areté* is a must-read for anyone who wants to be a hero."

— **Kelly Perdew**, general partner of Moonshots Capital,
winner of *The Apprentice* Season 2, West Point graduate,
Airborne/Ranger trained, JD/MBA

"No one is doing more in our time to bring practical wisdom to the world than Brian Johnson. He searches through ancient philosophy, modern science, and the best thought of our day to find the insights and tools we all need to propel our lives upward and forward with true excellence. He finds all the best stuff and brings it to us in a powerfully actionable form in this new book.

It's an amazing achievement. I'm hoping that millions of people will benefit from Brian's great work in these pages. We need it now like never before."

— **Tom Morris, PhD**, public philosopher and author of over thirty books, including perennial bestsellers *True Success*, *If Aristotle Ran General Motors*, *The Oasis Within*, and *Plato's Lemonade Stand*

"Brian has alchemized the wisdom and teachings from the greatest thinkers on the planet. His teachings have created a framework for my own peak performance and leadership."

— **John Herdman**, Head Coach, Toronto FC, former Head Coach of the Canadian Men's National Soccer Team

"There is arguably no book more capable of accelerating your path to fulfilling your potential than *Areté* and no person more qualified to write it than Brian Johnson. Brian is a true modern-day philosopher who has distilled and consolidated wisdom from the greatest minds in history so that you can use it to create the life you desire and deserve."

— **Hal Elrod**, international bestselling author of *The Miracle Morning*

"Prepare to have your mind expanded and your heart opened by Brian Johnson's remarkable new book. *Areté* is a masterpiece that is certain to be read and revered by millions, and passed down from generation to generation. In a world where shallow superficiality seems supreme, Brian's book is a beacon of deep truth, wisdom, and inspiration—a call to arms for anyone with the courage to pursue their dreams, no matter how audacious they may seem. Put every other book away and dive headfirst into the pages of *Areté*. You'll emerge with a renewed sense of purpose, a deeper understanding of yourself, and the tools you need to make a lasting impact on the world."

— **Jim Huling**, Executive Coach, former Global Managing Consultant for FranklinCovey, bestselling author of *The 4 Disciplines of Execution*

"Brian is an exemplar of humility and stewardship. He's given us an innovative platform to optimize our internal work across the foundational human pillars of mind, body, and spirit to create balance and optimal performance. I highly recommend *Areté* for everyone looking to activate their Heroic potential."

— **Hugh Wyman Howard III**, Retired U.S. Navy Rear Admiral, former Commander of U.S. Naval Special Warfare and Naval Special Warfare Development Group

ARETÉ

ARETÉ

ACTIVATE YOUR HEROIC POTENTIAL

BRIAN JOHNSON

HEROIC
BLACK
STONE
PUBLISHING

For information about special discounts or bulk purchases,
please email arete@heroic.us.

Printed in the United States of America on acid-free paper

First edition: 2023
ISBN 979-8-212-41407-4
Personal Growth, Social Psychology, Leadership

Version 1

Heroic Blackstone Publishing
31 Mistletoe Rd.
Ashland, OR 97520

www.Heroic.us
www.BlackstonePublishing.com

This book is dedicated to YOU,
the hero we've been waiting for.

And ...

To my wife, Alexandra,
our kids Emerson and Eleanor,
and your families and kids.

Heroic families unite.
It's time to raise the next
generation of heroes
and change the world together.

451° IDEAS
TO ACTIVATE YOUR HEROIC POTENTIAL

OBJECTIVE II
FORGE ANTIFRAGILE CONFIDENCE

OBJECTIVE VII
ACTIVATE YOUR SUPERPOWER

✈

PHIL STUTZ SAYS...
FOREWORD

I've been a psychiatrist for forty-five years. That's a long time doing the same thing. Many of my colleagues have retired, worn down by the grind. What keeps me going is my patients. I've been fortunate enough to have a practice comprised of unusual people. They are not unusual because they've succeeded in conventional terms—even though most of them have.

They're unusual because they refuse to be defined by any single accomplishment. Their identity is based on a process of endless possibility. They don't stop creating. Working with these people can be profound but it's also a lot of fun.

Because I live in L.A., many of them are in show business—which also means they are famous. Eventually that rubbed off on me and I was designated as the "shrink to the stars." I cringe when I hear that phrase. Yes, I have treated a lot of actors but I've treated a lot of others in business, politics, the arts, medicine, etc. They all wanted the same thing: to unleash as much hidden potential as possible.

Just the way a seed holds inside it the potential to become a tree, every human being has a soul that holds inside it a vision of a future self. But that vision won't emerge by itself. Your soul has to be trained until it is strong enough to have an impact on the world. My job is to guide and encourage my patients as they move through this soul training. Rather than being the shrink to the stars it would be more accurate to call me the "shrink to the soul."

You're about to read an extraordinary book written by an extraordinary person: Brian Johnson.

I say that without hesitation because I have worked with Brian every week for years. At each meeting, I poured into him the totality of everything I had learned over forty-five years on any topic. I had done this with many others but no one even approached his ability to absorb information at dizzying speed and then make it his own.

But that's only half the story. Training the soul is mostly a process focused on the individual. Brian is also a genius at connecting people and nurturing a collective soul force.

In short, I know greatness when I see it and Brian's greatness just keeps on growing.

Brian has a profound impact on everyone who crosses his path. In today's digital media world he's considered an "influencer." But when I hear that term I think of someone with a lot of Twitter followers or someone who is plugged into the design and fashion worlds. The driving force for that kind of person is the fear of not being "cool," which is ultimately the fear of being left out.

Brian had no interest in working on this superficial level—it barely scratches the surface of what a human being is capable of. He would accept nothing less than the unlocking of the hidden potential in each human being. And just the way this potential goes unexpressed in each of us, the entire human race has its own hidden potential.

Brian's goal was to uncover this collective potential. Without it our survival as a planet is severely compromised.

But to guide our whole species to its highest potential is a daunting task. It requires no less than the ability to inspire every single human being. This may sound grandiose, even impossible, when you read it in the pages of this book. But when you're in Brian's physical presence you can feel a boundless, almost supernatural enthusiasm that makes anything seem possible.

Brian is a dreamer and he dreams big. What sets him apart is that he is disciplined and practical in pursuit of those dreams. Most self-help books are products waiting to be sold. They have little ambition beyond catching the attention of potential readers. We read them to give ourselves a non-specific sense of hope. Brian doesn't criticize others but he would never publish a book with such modest goals.

Especially now. Because right now we face a challenge so all-encompassing that it puts our very existence at risk.

The challenge comes from an enemy that wants to destroy us. This enemy is invisible but its effects stare us right in the face. Take a hard look at the institutions that form the foundation of modern society.

Government, education, the church, science, finance, media, medicine, the judiciary, etc. In every area there is a lack of discipline, leadership, and transparency.

This is a picture of a world that is falling apart. A world of chaos, fear, and darkness. And only if we put that world back together again will we be strong enough to defend ourselves. Sounds bleak and overwhelming. Enter: Brian Johnson.

He didn't know it, the world didn't know it, but he had been preparing for this moment all his life. The moment when the two sides of his soul, his two major talents, would work in harmony to defeat the enemy that had turned our world into a living hell. A force that could overcome evil.

Here are the two sides of Brian Johnson.

1. His drive to bring out the HEROIC potential of the individual. The state of functioning you'll need to reach if you want to do anything big and frightening. He presents this as a modern form of the hero. In a war the hero runs toward the battle. The more conflict around him (or her) the more inspired the hero becomes.

2. His drive to UNIFY the human race. As a unified whole the human race is capable of anything. The problem is that evil works to prevent unification. It focuses on the differences between us, not the common ground.

Brian has proven to me (and to his thousands of followers) that you can stay focused on the unique path toward your personal potential and at the same time live within a structure that applies to all human beings. He calls the values and habits that have this universal relevance "Virtues." The cardinal virtues Brian leans on have been present throughout all cultures across all time, including: Love, Courage, Wisdom, and Discipline.

This is only the foreword, not the book. I couldn't begin to cover all that you'll find as you read further. But understand the opportunity that you (and I) have been given. We are present at the inception of a new way to work with human beings that is exactly what is needed right now. Its timeliness comes from the extraordinary amount of conflict, confusion, and fear spreading without resistance over our world.

What Brian has developed is much more than a bunch of coping mechanisms for the over-stressed modern person, although that would be an improvement for most of us. He's developed a training program for the soul.

Commit to this training and you will gain the ability to transmute your biggest problems, your darkest days, into unstoppable courage, endless enthusiasm, and an unshakable faith in the future.

This book will change your life. And, if enough of us commit, it will change the world.

PHIL STUTZ, MD
Los Angeles, California

NICE TO MEET YOU
IT'S DAY 1. LET'S GET TO WORK!

Hi, this is Brian. I appreciate you taking the time to open this book. I wish we could spend some time together so I could get to know you more.

What I do know is that we're both busy and I like to share more wisdom in less time, so let's get straight to work.

I want to start by telling you a little story.

But... First, let me briefly introduce myself and give you a little context.

In addition to being the Founder & CEO of a company called Heroic Public Benefit Corporation (which I'll tell you more about), I'm the proud dad of a couple of kids (Emerson and Eleanor) and married to my best friend, Alexandra.

We live on a little ranch in the country outside Austin, Texas with three dogs (Zeus, Zap, and Wags—two of which adopted us), a cat (Heroic the Stoic, who also adopted us), and nine chickens (including Happy the Rooster and his hens).

Now... My ten-year-old son Emerson recently got into chess. And, when I say got into chess, I mean he REALLY (!) got into chess.

Less than a year ago we were introduced to a great website called ChessKid.com that features one of my all-time favorite teachers (Mike Klein, also known as FunMasterMike) who has figured out a way to teach chess while helping kids have fun and fall in love with the game.

We home-school Emerson so he has a lot of time to spend studying chess. And… Over the last ten months, he's spent HUNDREDS and HUNDREDS (!) of hours playing and practicing and all that.

To put it in perspective, he watches the Chess World Championships with the same enthusiasm I watched Major League Baseball's World Series when I was ten!

In short: He absolutely (!) loves everything about chess. He won the Texas Chess State Championship for his division and his current big dream is to become a chess Grandmaster.

That's the context.

I'm writing this on a Saturday afternoon. I'm putting the final touches on the book and thinking about how I want to introduce you to the concept of *Areté*.

I think THIS little sequence of events from this morning might just be the THE best possible way I can bring this wisdom to life.

So… Without further ado… Let's get to work.

P.S. Before I forget and so you know… The word *Areté* (we'll define it in a moment!) is pronounced "ARE-uh-tay."

Say it with me now:

Areté
=
ARE-uh-tay

P.P.S. Speaking of spending time together and getting to know one another more, I'd love to connect with you on our Heroic social training platform.

You can connect with me (and the rest of our Heroic community!) and get a bunch of other goodness by visiting:

HEROIC.US/ACTIVATE

ARETÉ
EXPLAIN IT LIKE I'M 10

I'm a pretty disciplined guy and have a pretty structured way I approach every day of the year.

This morning, I cut my normal morning work protocol short to focus on my love protocol.

The special occasion?

A chess tournament with Emerson at the Austin Grandmaster Chess Academy.

So… I leave my office early and step into the kitchen all fired up about the day ahead.

And… Emerson tells me he doesn't want to go.

Me: "Really? What's up, buddy?!"

Emerson's wilted-flower posture response: "I don't know. I just don't want to go."

Me: "Hmm. Interesting. How about we go on a quick walk and talk about it?!"

Emerson: "Okay."

We head out to hit the trail on our property.

Eleanor and Mommy follow.

Before heading the opposite direction on our little trail, Mommy says: "He says he doesn't want to go because he doesn't think he will win! You might want to talk about that."

Me to myself: "Fascinating. We'll definitely want to talk about that."

I reach out to hold Emerson's hand as we start our walk.

I squeeze it tight and tell him "I love you" in our little made-up language we call squeeze-eze.

He tells me he loves me back via a little squeeze.

Me: "So, Mommy says you don't want to go because you're not going to win the tournament?!"

Emerson: "Yah."

Me with a chuckle: "Dude. OF COURSE you're not going to win the tournament. You're going to play against guys that are INSANELY GOOD."

"Remember what Nick [his coach] said yesterday when he was invited to play at an elite tournament that HE knew he wouldn't win?"

Emerson: "Yah. He said he was super excited because he KNEW he'd be playing REALLY good players that would challenge him and help him get better."

Me: "EXACTLY. Win or learn. And learning is winning so let's go, right?!"

Emerson: "Yep."

Now...

That part of our chat was on the first half of our loop. Right after we established the opportunity to win or learn, we ran into Mommy and Eleanor who were headed the other direction.

We give them a high five and then continue our chat.

Me: "Hey buddy. You know that voice in your head that was telling you all the reasons you DIDN'T want to go to the chess tournament?"

Emerson: "Yes."

Me: "Well…"

And I stop walking and get down on a knee and look him straight in the eye as I say…

"We ALL have that voice in our head."

"And… I want you to listen really closely right now…"

"If you run your life making decisions based on what THAT voice in your head tells you, then…"

Pause.

"You will NOT create the life you want."

"PERIOD."

"Your Grandpa Phil calls that 'Part X.' We ALL have that voice. It's NEVER (!!!) going to go away."

"And… One of THE most important things you will ever do is learn how to deal with that voice."

Emerson: Eyes big. Focused. Locked in. Fully registered.

I stand up. We continue our walk.

I grab his hand again.

Me via squeeze-eze: "I love you."

Him via squeeze-eze: "I love you, too."

Me: "Now… Here's how you deal with that voice."

"First, you need to recognize that Part X is talking to you. You'll usually know because you will be whining or complaining or making up stories about why you don't want to do something you kinda know you actually DO want to do."

"Just notice the voice is there."

"Then practice Targeted Thinking by asking yourself, 'WHAT DO I WANT?!'"

We make eye contact. He's fully present and tracking.

Me: "So… What do you want in your life?"

Emerson: "Well… I want to be happy and…"

Me: "Exactly."

I pull up the sleeve on my sweatshirt and show him the (one-inch-tall, five-inch-wide!) tattoo on my left forearm.

"You want to be HEROIC and show up as your best self and create a great, joyful life in which you're giving your gifts to the world."

He nods his head and says: "Yah!"

Me: "And… You know HOW you will do that?"

Him: "By helping people?"

Me: "GREAT answer. Yes. Exactly. And… In this situation, you need to…"

Then I pull up the other sleeve on my sweatshirt to show him the (one-inch tall, four-inch wide!) tattoo on my right forearm.

"You need to live with *ARETÉ.*"

"You remember what that means?!"

Him: "Sort of…"

Me: "It's an ancient Greek word. We translate it into English as 'virtue' or 'excellence,' but it has a deeper meaning. Something closer to 'expressing the best version of yourself moment to moment to moment.'"

Then I stop again and hold up my right hand about eye level so it's parallel to the ground.

Me: "You see that line? That's you being your absolute best self."

Then I hold up my left hand about a foot below that, also parallel to the ground.

Me: "You see THIS line? That's you *not* being your best self."

"Now… You see that GAP between THIS line and THAT line?"

Emerson nods his head.

"Well… You know how you feel when there's *that* big of a gap?"

Emerson: "Not very good?!"

Me: "EXACTLY."

"Now… What if we CLOSED THE GAP between who we are capable of being and who we are actually being as we show up as the best version of ourselves?! How do you think *that* feels?!"

Emerson: "It feels good!!"

Me: "NO! It feels GREAT!!

"And THAT is the ultimate game we're all playing all day every day. When we close the gap and choose to do the things that help us show up as the best version of ourselves, we feel a deep sense of joy."

"The ancient Greek and Stoic philosophers had a word for that as well. They called it *eudaimonia*."

Emerson nods his head, letting me know he gets it.

We continue walking.

Me: "And guess what?! Remember that voice that was telling you all the reasons why you shouldn't go to the tournament today?"

Emerson: "Yah!"

Me: "He wasn't helping you make the best decision, was he?"

Emerson: "No!!"

Me: "And THAT is why I have this HEROIC tattoo and this *ARETÉ* tattoo."

Me via squeeze-eze: "I love you."

Him via squeeze-eze: "I love you, too."

And that, my fellow Hero in training, is one way to teach a kid the power of *ARETÉ*.

Helping you operationalize THAT wisdom so you can activate YOUR Heroic potential is what this book is all about.

HOW TO CLOSE THE GAP
INTRODUCING TARGETED THINKING

N ow that I've introduced you to my family and to the ultimate game of life, I want to introduce you to THE most powerful practice we can engage in to close the gap and live with *Areté* as we activate our Heroic potential.

It's called Targeted Thinking.

Let's go back to the trail and continue our chat with Emerson...

That part of the conversation we just discussed took us about ten minutes to complete—one half-mile loop on our property.

Here's how we started our second loop.

Me: "Alright. Living with *Areté* so we can be Heroic is the ultimate game of life. Now it's time to talk about chess."

I smile and look at him.

He smiles back.

Me: "Tell me... What do you want when it comes to chess?!"

Emerson: "I want to be a Grandmaster."

Me: "I know. I love it. And I think you can do it."

I squeeze his hand yet again. He squeezes mine back.

Me: "So... If you want to become a Grandmaster in chess, what do you need to do?"

Emerson: "Keep on practicing hard!"

Me: "Definitely! And... What ELSE do you need to do?"

Emerson thinks for a minute then says (as a light bulb goes on): "Play in a lot of tournaments!"

Me: "EXACTLY!"

Wink and a squeeze from me. Smile and a squeeze right back from E.

Me: "Now… When that voice in your head was telling you all the reasons why you shouldn't go to the tournament today, was he helping you do what you need to do to achieve what you want to achieve?"

Emerson: "No!!"

Me: "EXACTLY!"

Wink and a squeeze from me. Smile and a squeeze right back from E.

Me: "That's what we call Targeted Thinking. You've gotta know what you want and what you need to do to get it AND you need to pay attention to when Part X takes over your brain and tries to take you in the wrong direction."

I look at Emerson.

"Right?"

He looks back and says…

"YES!"

Me: "So… Ready to dominate the tournament and win or learn today?"

Emerson: "YES!"

Me: "LET'S GO, HERO!!"

Of course, none of this is about my son.

It's about YOU.

What do YOU want in your life?

Remember the ultimate game.

Hint: *ARETÉ* = HEROIC.

And…

Remember Targeted Thinking.

Know what you want.

Know what you need to do to get it.

Tell Part X to settle down.

And go do what you're here to do.

Close the gap.

Give us all you've got.

TODAY.

FEAR & LAZINESS
WISDOM FROM GRANDPA PHIL

I'm kind of enjoying this time together on our trail so let's walk another loop together.

So far, we've used Emerson's resistance to going to a chess tournament as the context to chat about *Areté* and closing gaps and Targeted Thinking and how to be Heroic.

I skipped an important early part of our chat.

Before we got to the whole *Areté* = Heroic, close-the-gap goodness, we talked about the TWO things that Phil Stutz (my spiritual godfather and Emerson's god-grandfather!) says gets in our way of experiencing all the joy we want to feel in this precious life of ours.

Pop quiz...

What do YOU think the TWO things are?

(Insert *Jeopardy* music here.)

Answer...

Phil Stutz, citing *his* favorite teacher, Rudolf Steiner, says that FEAR and LAZINESS are the two biggest obstacles to activating our Heroic (!) potential.

I repeat...

The two primary obstacles that are getting in the way of YOU activating YOUR Heroic (!) potential are very very very simple.

FEAR and **LAZINESS**.

With that in mind, if you feel so inspired, pause for a moment. Think about all that you want to create in your life.

Who are you at your best?

See it. Feel it.

Now… What's getting in the way of you closing the gap and BEING that best version of yourself?

If you're honest with yourself, you'll see that, more often than not, it's not the stuff outside of yourself that is limiting you.

It's your own fear and laziness.

Can you see that?

Know this: Heroes have strength for two.

Our secret weapon is love.

So… For whom will YOU do the hard work to conquer YOUR fear and laziness so you can give us all you've got?

Seriously.

For whom will YOU do the hard work to conquer YOUR fear and laziness so you can give us all you've got?

I'm committed to working hard and conquering MY fear and MY laziness for my wife, my kids, my friends, my team, our community, and…

YOU.

Day 1. All in.

Let's go, Hero.

CHARACTER VS. DESIGN FLAWS
HOW TO PLAY THE GAME OF LIFE

Now that we've mined some wisdom gems out of my morning with Emerson, how about one more gem from the evening and then we'll carry on?

For curious souls, Emerson wound up having a great day of chess. He won two games and "won" two more via lessons he learned in a couple of losses to some superior players.

We decided to stop at the laser tag place on the way home as a little celebration of the day and as a celebration of a milestone he hit on Chess.com.

So… We show up at Blazer Tag in Austin excited to have some fun.

And… we just miss getting into the group that's about to start. Eek.

The start time for the next group is so late that we won't be able to make it.

The guy running the show says he'll get us in, but we'll be missing part of the briefing in which everyone is told how to play the game.

Emerson had played earlier that week and he knew how to play. I haven't played laser tag in roughly forty years.

I'm thinking: "It's laser tag. Can't be that hard."

I say: "Perfect. Thank you!"

We head in to the final part of the briefing. Then we put on the gear. Then we head into the laser tag arena.

And …

I'm *absolutely* TERRIBLE.

(Laughing.)

As in, I'm really *really* **really** bad.

To put it in perspective, earlier in the week, Alexandra played with Emerson and she was so bad that she got a -99 score.

The guy who runs it said he'd NEVER seen anyone do that bad. We'd laughed about it as a family that night.

And …

Ten minutes into the twenty-minute game, I have a -100 score.

Facepalm.

My mental toughness is eroding quickly.

(Laughing.)

Self-talk: "Wow. I'm really bad at this. I think I should just quit playing and find the exit. This is embarrassing."

Then I look a little closer at the little stats dashboard on the laser thing.

Right above my Hall-of-Shame-worthy "-100" score, I see some data on my ammo. I have 1,000 units of laser tag ammo.

Now, that's a little weird because I'm pretty sure I started with 1,000 units of laser tag ammo and, trust me, I've been trying to use those laser tag ammo units. My trigger finger is sore from squeezing that thing so hard.

Then …

Somehow, as I fiddle with everything, I stumble upon a little button at the end of the laser.

I press it while squeezing the trigger and …

A laser fires.

I hear it!!

A sound has never been so beautiful.

Long story slightly shorter, now I get to work channeling my inner SEAL and start having a ton of fun. I end the game with 400-and-something points—right behind Emerson.

And…

You know what I thought of?

I thought of BJ Fogg.

As you may know, BJ runs the Behavior Design Lab at Stanford University.

He's done some of the research that inspired James Clear's *Atomic Habits* and Charles Duhigg's *Power of Habit*.

And, he wrote his own book called *Tiny Habits*.

I'm going to walk you through some of the best, most life-changing ideas from all those books as we turn you into a habit-installing (and -deleting!) ninja, but for now I want to emphasize the distinction from his book that I was thinking about as I took my laser tag gear off.

In short, BJ tells us that if you've struggled with changing your behaviors in the past, you might want to consider the fact that it wasn't a CHARACTER flaw, but a DESIGN flaw.

In other words, nothing was wrong with YOU per se, you simply didn't know HOW to effectively change your behavior.

Laser tag is a LOT easier and a LOT more fun when you know how to play the game. So is life.

It's time for the "How to play the game of life" briefing we never got.

P.S. Alexandra told me that I need to tell you that the week before, *she also* missed the part of the briefing in which they teach people how to shoot a laser, because she was chasing Eleanor at the time. Which meant that she had the *exact* same experience of not knowing how to shoot a laser. Haha. #soulmates

OVERLOAD
WHEN IN DOUBT, DO THIS

A dmiral William H. McRaven is one of my heroes.

As a Four-Star Admiral, his final assignment was as Commander of all U.S. Special Operations Forces.

You may have seen his commencement speech at the University of Texas at Austin called "Make Your Bed."

He's written a number of great books including one based on that talk (*Make Your Bed*), a memoir called *Sea Stories*, and another great book called *The Hero Code*.

In his most recent book on leadership, *The Wisdom from the Bullfrog*, Admiral McRaven shares eighteen military aphorisms that have guided his life.

One of them is called "When in Doubt, Overload."

Let's set some context and then we'll connect the wisdom from *that* book to the structure of *this* book.

As you may know, when aspiring U.S. Navy SEALs want to see if they have what it takes to join one of the most elite military forces in history, they have to go through what's known as BUD/S.

BUD/S is short for Basic Underwater Demolition/SEAL training.

Of course, that training is an extraordinarily challenging mental and physical trial. Only twenty percent of those who start finish.

Now… A little more context …

On June 6, 1944, General Dwight D. Eisenhower led the invasion of Normandy that turned the tide of World War II.

According to the Eisenhower Library: "The invasion force included 7,000 ships and landing craft manned by over 195,000 naval personnel from eight allied countries. Almost 133,000 troops from the United States, the British Commonwealth, and their allies landed on D-Day."

Pause for a moment and imagine the extraordinary commitment of all those troops AND their families—willing to make the ultimate sacrifice to protect the freedoms that we enjoy today.

And, if you feel so inspired, pause for another moment and feel into the equally extraordinary commitment of military servicemen and women AND their families who are *currently* protecting the freedoms that we enjoy today.

Note: It's easy to take those freedoms (and the warriors who protect them) *for* granted rather than *as* granted.

As we'll discuss, the wisest among us (and each of us in our wisest moments) appreciate the sacrifices these loving and courageous men and women make for us as we strive to give back in equal measure.

Now… Before the troops could get their three thousand landing craft on the five beaches of Normandy, you know who showed up in the darkness of the previous nights to clear the way?

Some of the very first U.S. Navy SEALs.

They were underwater demolition experts who found and destroyed the underwater barriers that had been set up to prevent that landing.

All of which leads us to McRaven's sixteenth leadership principle from his great book and one more question...

You know what U.S. Navy SEALs are taught as they calculate how much explosives they need to use to blow up the underwater obstacles they're tasked with destroying?

As McRaven puts it: Whenever they were in doubt about the amount of explosives to use, they were told to "*always overload*. Always put more energy, more focus, more power into the situation than seemed necessary. It was the only way to guarantee success in the face of uncertainty and doubt."

That's what I had in mind as I decided how I would structure this book.

I could have delivered a standard 200- to 300-page book with a few dozen (or even one hundred) potentially life-changing ideas.

I decided to OVERLOAD and give you a 1,001+ page book with 451 potentially life-changing ideas.

I want you to FEEL the explosive power of the ideas in this book as we get to work blowing up everything that may be in the way of us actualizing our potential so we can win the ultimate war between vice and virtue we are ALL waging all day every day.

Remember: When in doubt, we overload.

It's time to activate our Heroic potential.

451°
ACTIVATION ENERGY

H ave you ever heard of "activation energy?"

It's a chemistry thing. The dictionary tells us that it's "the minimum quantity of energy that the reacting species must possess in order to undergo a specified reaction."

Mundane examples: Water only boils once it reaches its activation energy point of 212° Fahrenheit. 100° certainly won't do it. 200° won't do it. Not even 210° or 211° will do it.

Simmering but not boiling.

Want to boil? Then you need to get the heat all the way up to 212°. Then you'll undergo the "specified reaction" and boil.

Same rules apply with fire.

Carbon and hydrogen atoms are hanging out in paper all day every day. And, of course, oxygen is hanging out in the air all day every day.

But… They won't combine to set the paper ablaze until a certain threshold is reached. We need 451° of heat to create enough energy to catalyze the magical dance that is fire.

400°? Nothing. 449°? Nothing. 450°? Nope. Nothing. 451°? BAM! Let there be fire.

That's activation energy.

And that's why this book has 451° ideas—any one of which might help you go to the next level. In aggregate? If all goes as planned, we'll activate your Heroic potential.

READY AT HAND
YOUR PHILOSOPHICAL ARMAMENTARIUM

E pictetus is my favorite teacher.

He was a former slave who taught (and practiced!) Stoic philosophy in ancient Rome. He trained the guys who trained the emperor-philosopher Marcus Aurelius. He's also the primary influence for the guys who created the modern cognitive behavioral therapy movement.

One of his students took really good lecture notes (thanks, Arrian!) and captured his wisdom in a manual called the *Enchiridion*.

The Greek word *enchiridion* is translated as "handbook." But it's important to note that the word literally means "within" (*en*) + "hand" (*kheir*).

To put it in perspective, the word was used to describe a hand dagger.

Epictetus's wisdom (and the wisdom of *all* great ancient philosophers) was less like a *guidebook* you held in your hand and more like a *sword* (or a tool) (or a Navy SEAL's explosive!) you held in your hand—wisdom that was *ready at hand* and could be used to meet life's inevitable challenges.

As we'll discuss, the Stoic philosophers told us that we needed to be WARRIORS of the mind, not mere librarians of the mind cataloging interesting ideas. They had an entire collection of weapons/tools in what was known as their "armamentarium."

That's how I'd like us to think about this book.

451° ideas to help us move from Theory to Practice to Mastery Together—closing the gap between who we're *capable* of being and who we're *actually* being as we activate our Heroic potential and give the world all we've got.

Not someday.

TODAY.

LEARNING 101
INTERLEAVING & SPACED REPETITION

As a professional philosopher for the last fifteen years, I've distilled over five hundred of the absolute best books on ancient wisdom and modern science into what I call "Philosopher's Notes."

I've also created over fifty hour-long master classes in which I distill the best ideas from those great books to help you optimize every facet of your life.

In the Heroic app, we have classes on everything from Purpose 101, Productivity 101, and Confidence 101 to Nutrition 101, Sleep 101, and Love 101.

We also have a class on Learning 101 in which I share the best ideas from some of the best books on learning including *Make It Stick*, *A Mind for Numbers*, and *How We Learn*.

In *that* class, we talk about a concept scientists call "interleaving." The basic idea is simple: If you want to learn something, you're better off varying your practice rather than grooving one identical rep after another.

For example, they've done research on baseball players. If you throw someone fifteen curveballs in a row then fifteen fastballs, they'll FEEL like they're doing really well, but they won't actually be improving the skills they need for an actual game when they won't know what's coming.

Scientists call that the "fluency illusion" and it's actually one of the greatest threats to effective learning.

The interleaving approach?

A random assortment of fastballs and curveballs that keeps the batter constantly guessing and, thereby, developing the ACTUAL skills he or she will need come game-time.

Of course, that doesn't always *feel* as good as the easier (more common) approach when you know what's coming. But, alas, that's where the learning occurs.

That's one of the things I had in mind as I mapped out how to best deliver these 451 potentially life-changing ideas. As you'll see, we're going to deliberately interleave different themes within the chapters in our seven objectives.

We're ALSO going to focus on *another* key aspect of Learning 101 called "spaced repetition."

The basic idea with that is exactly what it sounds like—we want to create a little space between our deliberate repetition of the stuff we REALLY want to make stick.

Speaking of repetition, here's how Dan Coyle puts it in *The Little Book of Talent*: "Repetition has a bad reputation. We tend to think of it as dull and uninspiring. But this perception is titanically wrong. Repetition is the single most powerful lever we have to improve skills, because it uses the built-in mechanism for making the wires of our brains faster and more accurate."

Interleaving and spaced repetition. They do a Hero good.

P.S. You know what else helps us master a concept? Explaining it to someone else. If you feel so inspired, share what you're learning as you go.

P.P.S. I created this book with two other books in mind: *The War of Art* by Steven Pressfield and *War and Peace* by Leo Tolstoy.

Pressfield is one of my all-time favorite writers. His incredibly inspiring and equally practical prose is an inspiration. It's very much how I love to write.

You can read one of the potentially life-changing microchapters in his nonfiction books in a minute or three.

That's exactly what I had in mind as I created this book.

Yet...

In addition to creating a SUPER-readable, open-the-book-up-to-any-page-and-potentially-change-your-life-in-a-few-minutes kinda book, I ALSO wanted to make sure the book had a density and gravitas to it.

And, of course, I'm committed to doing everything I can to deliver on Phil's promise from the foreword of the book in which he boldly says: "This book will change your life."

Plus...

We received thousands of notes from our Heroic community about why they were excited about this book—which were remarkably humbling and inspiring. I wanted to do my best to create a book worthy of comments like this...

"Brian is one of the great philosophers of our time. If this book is the distillation of his life's work then it will be worth its weight in gold."

"Humanity's greatest wisdom for living a prosperous life condensed into ONE book—how could anyone not be excited to buy this?!"

"This book will be a classic handbook such as 7 *Habits* and *How to Win Friends*. Timeless principles."

"This will be the best book in modern history for personal development. Period."

(No pressure no diamonds, right? Hah.)

As I stepped back and felt into what the book needed to be to have a shot at delivering on those expectations, I realized that I wanted to create a book that is basically *The War of Art + War and Peace*.

Pithy microchapters + dense brick of a book.

You can start from the first page and systematically work your way through the seven objectives (with the interleaving and spaced repetition!).

Or you can open up to any page and, hopefully, get inspired by one of the 451° Ideas in a minute or three.

Choose your own adventure, Hero.

LET'S GO!

THE 7 OBJECTIVES
TO ACTIVATE YOUR HEROIC POTENTIAL

All that's nice and warm and fuzzy, eh?

And ... It begs the question: "HOW are we going to activate your Heroic potential?!"

Before we get into the details, I'd like to step back for a moment and tell you a little bit about me ...

As I briefly mentioned, I'm the Founder & CEO of a company called Heroic Public Benefit Corporation. Our mission is to help create a world in which 51% of humanity is flourishing by the year 2051.

I've spent half of the last 25 years as a Founder/CEO and the other half as a philosopher.

As a Founder/CEO, I've raised over $25 million, made crowdfunding history, and built and sold two social platforms.

As a philosopher and teacher, I've helped millions of people from around the world and created an app and a protocol that have been scientifically shown to change lives.

You may be wondering: "What is Heroic?"

My friend and mentor John Mackey, the co-founder and former CEO of Whole Foods put it succinctly when he graciously said, and I quote, that "Heroic is the best self-development platform in the world."

We've been fortunate to serve some of the most elite performers in the world—including bestselling authors, Fortune

100 executives, military officers, athletes, and coaches. We've also trained over 10,000 people from 100+ countries with our Heroic Coach certification program.

With the Basic Training program in our Heroic app and the Mastery Series that is the foundation of our 300-day Heroic Coach program, we integrate ancient wisdom, modern science, and practical tools into SEVEN objectives.

This book features 451 potentially life-changing ideas that are loosely organized into the seven objectives that are the foundation of our protocols that have been scientifically shown to change lives.

Let's take a quick look at how we frame the seven objectives when we're training our Heroes in the app and training Coaches going through our certification program.

OBJECTIVE I: KNOW THE ULTIMATE GAME

The first thing we need to do is step back and make sure we're playing the right game. Fact is, in such a profoundly sick society, we almost certainly aren't.

We'll invite the ancient Greek philosopher Aristotle and leading positive psychologist Martin Seligman to the party as proxies for ancient wisdom and modern science and ask them about the ultimate meaning of life.

We'll save the details for our discussion in a moment but know this: They'll give us the *exact* same single-word ANSWER.

By the end of our first Objective you'll know the ultimate game you want to be playing AND how to play it well.

If your experience is like the thousands of people I've personally trained, this may be life changing.

OBJECTIVE II: FORGE ANTIFRAGILE CONFIDENCE

Once we've established the ultimate game we're playing it's time to learn how to play it well—which leads us to our second Objective.

We're going to forge Antifragile Confidence.

By the time we're done working together, we'll move from being Fragile to Resilient to ANTIFRAGILE such that the more life kicks us around, the stronger we get.

That requires confidence.

Which leads us to another etymological pop quiz. Do you happen to know what the word *confidence* literally means?

It means "intense trust." Not that everything will go perfectly in your life but that it DOESN'T MATTER how things go because YOU have what it takes to deal with whatever arises.

That's Antifragile Confidence. Cultivating even 10% of your capacity here will change your life.

How do we build "intense trust" in ourselves? The same way we build trust in any relationship: We DO what we say we will do.

More specifically for our purposes, with the Heroic app we help you develop a protocol—a set of behaviors that you engage in on a day-to-day basis that keep you plugged in to that best version of yourself.

But … Here's the secret sauce: We're going to help you write a new algorithm for your life.

It goes like this: "The WORSE you feel, the MORE committed you are to your protocol."

What do most people do when they feel a little off or overwhelmed?

They STOP doing the very things that would have kept them plugged in and capable of showing up powerfully.

Not us. The WORSE we feel, the MORE committed we are to our protocols.

This is your ticket to invincibility. You'll still have ups and downs because you're human, but... Your highs will be higher AND your lows will be higher. And that's heroically awesome.

OBJECTIVE III: OPTIMIZE YOUR BIG 3

Once we've established the game we're playing and learn Rule #1 on how to play it well, it's time to simplify self-development.

That's what we'll do with our third Objective as we optimize what we call your Big 3: Energy, Work, and Love.

As you've almost certainly experienced if you've spent *any* time in the self-development world, it can very quickly get overwhelming.

There's SO much we can work on. Where do we begin?

Well, Freud tells us that a good life comes down to two things: Work and Love. This is one of the few things on which I agree with the dear doctor but...

If your ENERGY is sub-optimal because of poor lifestyle

choices, you're going to have a *really* hard time showing up powerfully in *either* your Work *or* your Love.

Enter the Big 3: Energy, Work, and Love.

We're going to systematically help you get more Energized than you've ever been, such that you can be more productive and do higher quality Work than you've ever done and, at the same time, be more Loving and connected (to yourself and to your loved ones) than you've ever been in your life.

That's how to simplify self-development so you can more consistently show up as the best, most Heroic version of yourself.

OBJECTIVE IV: MAKE TODAY A MASTERPIECE

From there, it's time to get the fact that TODAY'S THE DAY to move from Theory to Practice to Mastery.

We're going to help you become a master at creating Masterpiece Days.

We'll start with your AM and PM Bookends and we'll teach you the fact that, somewhat paradoxically, a great day begins with the END of your prior day.

We'll talk about the simple, key behavioral changes that can literally change your life overnight and then we'll systematically install the highest-leverage behavioral changes that will help you show up powerfully in your Energy, your Work, and your Love ALL DAY EVERY DAY.

That, my Heroic friend, is how we're going to help you become more energized, productive, and connected than you've ever been.

OBJECTIVE V: MASTER YOURSELF

All of which leads us to our fifth Objective in which we'll master the three disciplines of self-mastery: structural discipline, reactive discipline, and expansive discipline.

We'll also tap into the art and science of behavioral change so you can become a master at installing and deleting the behaviors that will help you become who you aspire to be.

The #1 thing to know? It's all about using your willpower wisely to install habits that run on autopilot via algorithms.

If you feel so inspired, now might be a good time to pause for a moment and ask yourself: What's the ONE thing I KNOW I could be doing that, if I started doing it TODAY would most change my life?

Seriously.

What is it? What's the ONE thing you could be doing that, if you started doing it consistently, would most positively change your life?

Fantastic.

Imagine your life with that habit installed. Then imagine your life with your #1 BAD habit deleted.

Then imagine having so much Self-Mastery that you can install and delete habits at will. That's what our fifth Objective is all about.

OBJECTIVE VI: DOMINATE THE FUNDAMENTALS

From there it's time for our sixth Objective. It's time to dominate our fundamentals.

We have seven: Eating, Moving, Sleeping, Breathing,

Focusing, Celebrating, and Prospering. Each fundamental has a core set of behaviors that we'll train together.

Why does this matter?

Well… If you want to see how tall a building is going to be, look at how deeply they're digging the foundation.

We need to really get the fact that greatness (and becoming the best, most Heroic versions of ourselves!) is all about consistency on the fundamentals.

We'll have a ton of momentum when we get to this point and, again, if you're like the thousands of people I've trained, you'll find that you're suddenly able to easily change some key behaviors across each of our fundamentals—stuff you may have been struggling with for years.

This is exciting, life-changing, and incredibly empowering.

OBJECTIVE VII: ACTIVATE YOUR SUPERPOWER

All of that leads us to our final Objective. It's time to activate your superpower. I call it Soul Force.

Gandhi named it. Martin Luther King, Jr. talked about it in his "I have a dream" speech. It's the force that changes the world.

It's also the ONE thing that ALL of your heroes have in common. And, it's the one thing WE ALL have in common with our heroes as well.

We just need to activate it.

There's a formula for it. We'll dive into the details soon.

For now, know this: When you can get your Energy Focused on What's Important Now CONSISTENTLY, you will activate your Heroic potential and tap into the infinite power of Soul Force as you win the ultimate game of life and fulfill your destiny.

I can't begin to tell you how fiercely committed I am to helping you do exactly that.

Why?

Because that's precisely how we're going to help you activate your Heroic potential.

And, that's precisely how we can change the world. One person at a time. Together. Starting with you and me.

TODAY.

YOU ARE THE HERO
WE'VE BEEN WAITING FOR

As you may have noticed, we're already well into the first Objective.

Before we continue, I'd like to ask you a quick question…

Do you happen to know what the word *hero* means?

(I didn't either until I read Christopher McDougall's great book *Natural Born Heroes*.)

It's another ancient Greek word.

Etymologically, the word *hero* doesn't mean "killer of bad guys" or "tough guy" or anything like that it.

It means "PROTECTOR."

A hero has strength for two. And, very importantly, a hero is willing to do the *hard* work to *have* that strength for two.

And do you know what the secret weapon of the ancient hero was?

LOVE.

It's love that fuels our commitment to *do* that hard work to *have* the strength for two. It's love that gives us the courage to be willing to act in the presence of fear. It's love that gives us the discipline to do what needs to get done whether we feel like it or not.

And…

If you haven't noticed, our world needs heroes today more than ever before.

We have pandemic levels of anxiety and depression and

diabetes and cancer and political polarization and social injustice and environmental degradation.

And the *only* possible way we are going to meet those *historically significant* challenges and create a more noble and virtuous world for ourselves and for our kids and for their kids is if each of us steps up and starts showing up as the best, most Heroic versions of ourselves.

To put it directly…

YOU ARE THE HERO WE'VE BEEN WAITING FOR.

We just need you to step up and start acting like it.

It's time to activate your Heroic potential.

THE DOJO DECISION
GOING FOR MASTERY VS. THROUGH THE MOTIONS

I magine walking into a dojo. You're going to study a martial art. This is your very first day studying this art.

You might already have a dozen black belts in other martial arts, or this might be your very first time ever in a dojo. Either way is great. And, either way, you start in this school with a white belt.

So...

Here's the question.

As you look around the dojo and feel the energy of the place, are you there *going through the motions* or are you there *going for mastery*?

That may not sound like a big distinction, but it is.

If you're satisfied with yourself for simply getting off the couch and showing up and plan to kinda sorta go through the motions of the class, then you're going to show up with a VERY (!!!) different energy than the version of you that's GOING FOR MASTERY.

If you KNOW that you want to be a black belt in x years, you're ALL IN. You're not just kinda sorta going through the motions. You're using EVERY SINGLE MOMENT of that class to get a little better. You're paying attention, standing up tall, and giving your best. Moment to moment to moment.

So... As we begin our journey together, I ask you...

Are you planning to just go through the motions by simply reading yet another self-development book?

Or…

Are you sitting up nice and tall, with a fierce look in your eye, as you commit to going all in to give the world all you've got?

Of course, either answer is technically fine. And you and I may not be on quite the same page, and/or you may not feel inspired to really commit to going all in with me on this journey—which, of course, is MORE than just fine.

But… Let's not kid ourselves.

THIS ISN'T A DRESS REHEARSAL.

It's time to wake up and give the world all we've got. It's time to quit going through the motions of our lives—mindlessly scrolling through social media feeds and doing what everyone else is doing. It's time to stand up, put the smartphones down and high five our inner souls as we activate our Heroic potential and give the world all we've got.

When?

How about…

TODAY.

SOUL OXYGEN
WHAT MUST YOU BE?

A braham Maslow studied the greatest people of his generation. People like Eleanor Roosevelt and Albert Einstein.

He's the guy who came up with the whole "Hierarchy of Needs" and taught us about the importance of actualizing our potential.

In fact, he said that: "What one *can* be, one *must* be."

This need to self-actualize is, at a certain stage of our development, as important as our need to breathe.

It's kinda like soul oxygen.

To put it directly while deliberately repeating myself…

To the extent you ARE NOT showing up as the best, most Heroic version of yourself and there is a GAP between who you are *capable* of being and who you are *actually* being, YOU WILL SUFFER.

Period.

Which begs the question…

What must YOU be?

DESTINY MATH
+1 OR -1

A braham Maslow also told us that in any given moment, we have a choice. We can step forward into growth, or we can step back into safety.

Forward into growth, or back into safety. Forward into growth, or back into safety. I like to think of this as +1 or -1.

Moment to moment to moment. We have a choice.

+1 or -1. +1 or -1. +1 or -1.

Step forward.

Or go backward.

Step forward.

Or go backward.

+1 or -1. +1 or -1. +1 or -1.

How we feel at the end of the day is largely determined by those micro-moments of decision. You let enough of those -1 moments trickle into your life and you're going to want to crack open a bottle of something when you get home.

Alternatively, sprinkle a ton of +1s into your day and you're feeling radiantly alive and in love with life.

What happens when you aggregate and compound those micro-moments into days and weeks and months and years?

That's your destiny.

So... Let's choose wisely.

+1. +1. +1.

P.S. Maslow also said: "If you deliberately plan on being less than you are capable of being, then I warn you that you'll be unhappy for the rest of your life."

ENTELECHY
ARISTOTLE ON THE FORCE

I f I had to summarize my entire philosophy in one sentence, Abraham Maslow's gem from our last +1° might do the trick. *"What one can be, one must be."*

As we discussed, at a certain stage of our development, our need to actualize our potential is as real as our need to breathe.

2,500 years before Maslow, Aristotle talked about the same idea. He actually coined a word for that force that's driving us to actualize our innate potential.

He called it *entelechy*.

Entelechy is made up of three Greek words: *en* ("within"), *telos* ("end, perfection") and *ekhein* ("be in a certain state").

Entelechy literally means "to be in a state of perfection."

Think of the force that is driving the acorn to express its full potential as a towering oak tree. Then think of the force within YOU that is demanding YOU to become in actuality that which you are capable of being. That's *entelechy*.

Rollo May, another renowned psychologist of the twentieth century, described the same force, only he adds an important distinction between the acorn and us.

Here's how he puts it in *The Courage to Create*: "The acorn becomes an oak by means of automatic growth; no commitment is necessary. The kitten similarly becomes a cat on the basis of instinct. Nature and being are identical in creatures like them. But a man or woman becomes fully human only by his or her choices and his or her commitment to them. People attain worth and dignity by the multitude of decisions they make from day to day. These decisions require courage."

Our +1°…

Can you feel the force of *entelechy* pushing YOU to become what you are capable of being?

So can I.

Now go actualize your potential.

Close the gap. Live with *ARETÉ*.

Activate your Heroic potential.

TODAY.

YOUR SOUL'S CRIES
CAPACITIES CLAMORING TO BE USED

A ristotle and Maslow agree.

Call it *entelechy* or *self-actualizing* (or whatever you'd like), but we'd be wise to recognize the fact that we have an impulse to become in actuality that which we are in potentiality.

Can you feel that drive?

Again, we don't need to wait a decade to "get there."

First of all, there's no *there* there. Our potential is asymptotic. We never arrive. There's *always* more we can become.

And, even more importantly, there's ONLY EVER a *single moment* in which we can actualize our potential.

THIS MOMENT.

Which is why this book is called *Areté* and why I will unapologetically repeat myself and encourage/admonish you: "Close the gap. Live with *Areté*. TODAY."

Now...

In *Toward a Psychology of Being*, Maslow gives us another hint at how to approach the ultimate game of life and activate our Heroic potential. He tells us that we have "capacities" that are "clamoring to be used."

Here's how he puts it: "The muscular person likes to use his muscles, indeed, has to use them in order to self-actualize, and to achieve the subjective feeling of harmonious, uninhibited, satisfying functioning which is so important an aspect of psychological health. People with intelligence must use their intelligence, people with eyes must use their eyes, people with the capacity to love have the *impulse* to love and the *need* to love in order to feel healthy. Capacities clamor to be used, and cease their clamor only when they *are* used sufficiently."

Our +1° is (deceptively) simple.

What capacities do you have within YOU that are clamoring to be used?

Seriously. Take a moment. Step back. Reflect.

What capacities do you have within YOU that are clamoring to be used? (Perhaps focus on just one for now.)

Think of a time in your past when you DID fully utilize that capacity. Now imagine your life with you rocking that capacity again and again and again.

And, before we send you on your way to close the gap by putting those capacities to good use, how about another quick etymology lesson?

The word *clamor* comes from the Latin word that literally means "cry out."

For our purposes, know this: Your soul is crying out to be used. Pleading with you to actualize *all* of your latent potential.

Let's do that.

Close the gap.

Live with *Areté*.

TODAY.

ARISTOTLE & SELIGMAN
AS PROXIES FOR ANCIENT WISDOM & MODERN SCIENCE

I n the Mastery Series that is the foundation for our Heroic Coach certification program, I like to tell a little story about two of my favorite teachers to introduce our prospective Coaches to the essence of all our work together.

It goes something like this…

Let's invite Aristotle (no last name necessary) and Martin Seligman (founder of the positive psychology movement) to the party for their wisdom on the ultimate meaning of life. They'll serve as proxies for Ancient Wisdom and Modern Science.

Us: "Gentlemen. Thanks for joining us. Let's jump straight in. What's the meaning of life?"

We notice Aristotle and Seligman share a knowing glance with one another. They both seem to have a twinkle in their eyes.

Aristotle speaks first.

He tells us that the *summum bonum* (or "highest good") of life is to live with what the ancient Greeks (and Stoics) called *eudaimonia*.

That beautiful word literally means "good soul."

We weakly translate it into English as "happiness" but *eudaimonia* has a deeper meaning—something closer to "experiencing the joy of fulfilling your highest potential" or, in a word, to "flourish."

We thank Aristotle and ask Professor Seligman for his thoughts.

He smiles, nods his head in approval, and holds up a copy of his most recent book.

It's called *Flourish*.

Fascinating coherence between Ancient Wisdom and Modern Science on that one, eh?

Our next question for our two sages is simple... *How* do we flourish/live with eudaimonia?!

Once again, they give the exact same answer.

Aristotle answers in a single word: *Areté*. (Pronounced, as we've discussed but it's worth repeating: "ARE-uh-tay.")

Important note: If we wanted to summarize this *entire* book (and my entire philosophy) into a single word, THAT word is it—which is precisely why I have *ARETÉ* tattooed on my right forearm and why you'll see that word emblazoned on the cover of the book.

Areté.

As I explained to Emerson on the trail, we translate *Areté* as "excellence" or "virtue" but it also has a deeper meaning—something closer to "expressing the best version of yourself moment to moment to moment."

When we live with *Areté*, we're closing the gap between who we're *capable* of being and who we're *actually* being.

You know how that feels?

Hint: It feels REALLY REALLY REALLY good.

It's almost as if we're high-fiving our inner soul/that best version of ourselves and...

Voilà!

We get to experience a deep sense of eudaimonic joy.

We've ALL experienced this.

Let's take a moment to reflect on a time in our lives when we showed up as that best, most Heroic version ourselves.

Think back to a time when you made yourself proud. Feel the wisdom and discipline and courage and love with which you showed up to meet an important challenge.

Now, look forward and imagine a life in which you show up as THAT version of yourself.

I repeat: Empowering you to more and more consistently be that best, most Heroic version of yourself is what this book is all about. Literally *everything* we do together will be with THAT ultimate goal in mind.

Here's another way to think about it.

Let's draw two parallel, horizontal lines. Say about an inch apart. Kinda like this:

_____ Capable

- Gap -

_____ Actual

The top line represents who you're CAPABLE of being in any given moment. The bottom line represents who you're ACTUALLY being in any given moment.

That gap?

That's where your regret, anxiety, disillusionment, and all the other ick exists.

Close the gap such that who you are *actually* being is who you are *capable* of being and there's simply NO ROOM for the negative stuff.

How does that feel? It feels G R E A T.

Which, again, is why the Greeks told us we need to live with *Areté*. Moment to moment to moment.

What happens when we close that gap and express the best version of ourselves more and more consistently?

We feel the ineffable sense of joy the ancient philosophers called *eudaimonia*.

Again: Helping you do THAT is what this book is all about. Back to Professor Seligman. Let's ask *him* how to flourish.

Seligman would, once again, nod vigorously in Aristotle's direction. Then he would tell us that, when he and his colleagues launched the positive psychology movement, they STARTED by studying all the ancient wisdom traditions across all cultures—from Judaism, Christianity, and Islam to the ancient Greek philosophers, Taoism, Confucianism, Hinduism, and Buddhism.

And... You know what they all said?

Live with virtue.

P E R I O D.

Seligman would tell us that he and his colleagues built their entire movement on the foundation of putting our virtues in action.

At this precise moment, a choir of angels descends from the

heavens and sings. (Can you hear them?)

Ancient Wisdom and Modern Science agree: The ultimate meaning of life is to flourish by putting our virtues in action. Or, if you prefer to go old school, to live with *eudaimonia* via *Areté*.

THE 2,500-YEAR-OLD CHALLENGE
HERCULES & ARJUNA TELL US...

I f it's so obvious that the ultimate purpose of life is to express the best version of ourselves (in service to the world) by putting our virtues in action, then why isn't that the ultimate aim of all of us living today?

That, my friends, is a VERY good question.

Alas, this challenge is NOT a new one.

In fact, it's (at least) a 2,500-year-old dilemma that ALL the great teachers across ALL the great wisdom traditions have tried to address across ALL time.

We could spend the rest of our time unpacking the parallels across various wisdom traditions. For now, let's look at a couple examples.

Open the *Bhagavad Gita*, the sacred text of Hinduism and Gandhi's bible. What you'll see is a reluctant warrior (Arjuna) on a battlefield being counseled by his God (Krishna) to go play his role (heroically!) well.

That *external* battle is a metaphor for the *internal* war waging within ALL of us—that battle between the best version of ourselves and the not-so-awesome version of ourselves.

It's *vice* vs. *virtue*. Your *daimon* vs. your *demon*. (Note: The word *demon* is just the diminutive of *daimon*.)

Winning THAT civil war is ALWAYS the most important thing we can do.

And, for the record, when Gandhi encouraged us to "be

the change we want to see in the world," he wasn't saying that in some woo-woo "oh that sounds nice" kinda way—he was saying it in a fiercely practical, *Heroic* kinda way in which each of us needs to do the hard work to win the civil war raging within so we have the strength to meet life's challenges head on and lead our families and communities and world to a better place.

Now, the *Gita* was written In India sometime between 2,200 and 2,400 years ago. Let's head a little west and back in time a bit. We're going to spend some time with Socrates in Athens.

One of the ancient Greek (and Stoic) philosophers' heroes was Hercules. They loved to tell a story about Hercules BEFORE he was *Hercules* that captures the essence of the dilemma we face in the twenty-first century.

So… Let's imagine young Hercules.

He's walking by himself on a path in a forest when he comes to a fork in the road. Two goddesses approach him.

One rushes in front of the other. Socrates tells us that this goddess is overly made up and walking a little too fancy-like, preening and looking around to see if anyone notices her. (He told the story 2,500 years ago, but you can almost see her ready to snap a selfie and post it to Instagram.)

She tells Hercules that her friends call her Happiness (or *Eudaimonia*). But… Her real name is Vice (or *Kakia*).

She promises Hercules a life of pure pleasure and luxury with no effort. If only he'll follow her, he'll have it all!

The other goddess listens patiently then steps forward. Socrates tells us that she has an understated, radiant beauty. She tells

Hercules that there's no such thing as a good life that is centered on easy luxury.

This goddess tells him that, if he chooses to follow *her*, his life will be extraordinarily challenging and demand the best from him. For this, the gods will favor him with a true sense of meaning and deep joy as he reflects on his noble deeds.

You know what that second goddess was called?

Areté.

Hercules, of course, chose wisely.

HEDONIC VS. EUDAIMONIC
A TALE OF TWO BUSES

W ondering how that ancient wisdom applies to our modern lives? Here's a fun story to bring the point home.

Quick context: A few years ago, I was driving to the venue where we were hosting the graduation for our inaugural Heroic Coach program.

It was a Saturday morning. I planned to tell that story about The Choice of Hercules right before 500+ of us hopped onto a fleet of buses to do a Spartan Race together.

So…

I'm driving to the hotel to give my pre-Spartan Race pep talk when a huge bus cruises by. The entire side of the bus is covered by a sign that says: "WELCOME TO FREEDOM."

I say to myself: "Wow. That's awesome." Then I look a little closer and I see that the bus is taking people to a CASINO.

I laughed.

The Heroic gods just blessed me with THE PERFECT modern take on the ancient dilemma.

Vice dressed up as *virtue*.

Gambling is my ticket to *freedom*? Really?

Know this: You can boil this whole discussion down to the two forms of "happiness": *hedonic* vs. *eudaimonic*.

Hedonic pleasure is, basically, what you feel when you do what "feels" good. Of course, a good life includes a certain amount of hedonic pleasure but …

As you may have noticed, society is CONSTANTLY (!) seducing us with the *hedonic* side of things while dressing up *vice* as *virtue*.

We need to have enough wisdom to SEE THAT and then, following the lead of our beloved hero Hercules, enough discipline to choose the right course of action.

The true rewards of life are found by following *Areté* on her path to *eudaimonic* joy.

P.S. The ancient Stoic philosopher Epictetus also revered the Heroic power of Hercules. I shared this passage (from his *Discourses*) with our Coaches as part of our pre-Race pep talk:

"What would have become of Hercules, do you think, if there had been no lion, hydra, stag, or boar?—and no savage criminals to rid the world of? What would he have done in the absence of such challenges? Obviously he would have just rolled over in bed and gone back to sleep. So by snoring his life away in luxury and comfort he never would have developed into the mighty Hercules. And even if he had, what good would it have done him? What would have been the use of those arms, that physique, and that noble soul, without crises or conditions to stir him into action?"

P.P.S. All those crises we are currently facing as a society? THAT's what we, as heroes with noble souls, train for.

INTRINSIC VS. EXTRINSIC MOTIVATION
WANT TO BE PSYCHOLOGICALLY STABLE? FOCUS HERE

E dward Deci is one of the world's leading scientists studying intrinsic vs. extrinsic motivation.

In *Why We Do What We Do*, he captures the essence of his life's work that has influenced a generation of scholars and practitioners.

Here's what we need to know.

When we are *extrinsically* motivated, we tend to be focused on things like fame, wealth, and hotness.

When we are *intrinsically* motivated, on the other hand, we tend to be focused on things like becoming a better person, deepening our relationships, and making a contribution to our families and communities.

Pop quiz…

Which motivation do *you* think leads to greater levels of happiness and flourishing?

We don't need a PhD in Positive Psychology to know that going after the intrinsic stuff is more likely to boost our sense of well-being, right?

Follow up question…

What are YOU primarily focused on these days?

Of course, we need to take care of our material needs and pay the bills and all that. And, we will never be, nor should we even try to be, *exclusively* focused on the intrinsic stuff, but KNOW THIS…

Research shows that, if you are *primarily* motivated by the extrinsic stuff, then EVEN IF you are successfully pursuing those things, you will STILL be "less psychologically stable" (that phrase always grabs me—"less psychologically stable"!) than people who are focused on becoming a better person, deepening relationships, and making a contribution.

That's a REALLY powerful scientific fact.

It's why people who get to the peak of what David Brooks calls the "First Mountain" look around and wonder why they don't feel fulfilled. They got all the stuff they were told would make them happy and… they're not.

Stephen Covey said that going after the wrong (extrinsic!) goals is like climbing a ladder and getting to the top then realizing you put your life-ladder up against the wrong wall. Oops.

So… Where's YOUR focus?

What's one little thing you can (and will!) do to become a better person?

What's one little thing you can (and will!) do to deepen your relationships?

What's one little thing you can (and will!) do to make a contribution to your family and/or community?

Focus on what matters.

Close the gap. Live with *Areté*.

Experience eudaimonic joy.

TODAY.

MEET YOUR NEW BFF
"HI, DAIMON!"

Alright. We're making some good progress.

To review: ancient wisdom and modern science agree. The ultimate game of life is to flourish (*eudaimonia*!) by living with virtue (*Areté*). Got it.

To operationalize that wisdom, we need to get REALLY good at high-fiving our inner souls. With that in mind, it's time to officially and formally introduce you to your inner daimon. It's time for you to meet your new BFF.

You guys have actually *already* spent a lot of time hanging out. We just need to make sure you're spending a LOT more time together. And, we need to figure out how to invite that Heroic-best version of ourselves to the party when we need it most.

Here's a fun way to think about it.

You know those montage scenes in a movie where they flash a bunch of pictures and there's someone in those pictures who's always kinda off to the side or behind the hero?

Well, think back to all the times YOU were at your absolute best. Those moments in your life when you just CRUSHED IT.

You know who was *always* right there with you during those highlight-reel moments? Your inner daimon.

And you know WHY you were such a superstar in those all-time best moments? In short, your best self took over.

Here are a couple more fun ways to think about it.

Imagine that you've entered a tennis tournament. It's a doubles tournament. Only, there's a wrinkle. You don't get to pick your partner. The tournament director assigns a playing partner to you.

But...

Lucky for you!!

Somehow you were lucky enough to get THE BEST PLAYER IN THE WORLD AS YOUR PLAYING PARTNER. (How *amazing* would that be?)

Now...

Let's imagine that the Heroic gods have given YOU the ABSOLUTE BEST PLAYER IN THE WORLD AS YOUR PLAYING PARTNER IN **LIFE**.

Because that's *exactly* what happened.

You just need to quit playing with your *demon* and start playing with your *daimon* more and more consistently.

Let's do that.

TODAY.

DAIMON MEET GENIUS
GENIUS, DAIMON

Here's another fun historical fact.

As we've discussed, the Greeks called that best part of ourselves our *daimon*.

You know what their Roman friends called it?

Your *genius*.

And, back in the day, when you did something amazing, they liked to say that YOU didn't do it.

Your GENIUS did.

Everyone was said to have their own inner genius. A guiding spirit. Kinda like a little mini-me only a SUPER-ME.

Our job?

To create the conditions such that we can more and more consistently connect with and express that best version of ourselves—which (echo!) is, of course, *precisely* what we're going to do together and HOW we will activate your Heroic potential.

+1° at a time, Hero.

THE ULTIMATE JIHAD
WINNING THE BATTLE WITH OURSELVES

Rumi was one of the greatest spiritual teachers in history. His beautiful poetry is beloved around the world.

He was a Sufi—which is, essentially, a Muslim mystic. He was born in the 13th century in what is now Afghanistan. He lived and taught in Konya, Turkey which was, at the time, the capital of the dominant Seljuk Empire.

I can still vividly remember studying Rumi and visiting his grave in Konya on my philosophical tour over twenty years ago (during which I also studied Socrates in Athens, Jesus in Jerusalem, and Marcus Aurelius near the Danube in Hungary).

So… What does Rumi have to say about living with *Areté* and activating our Heroic potential?

Let's take a quick look at some of my favorite passages and then we'll wrap it up talking about the ultimate jihad.

First, how's this for going all in?

Rumi tells us: "I am burning. If anyone lacks tinder, let him set his rubbish ablaze with my fire."

And this: "Travelers, it is late. Life's sun is going to set. During these brief days that you have strength, be quick and spare no effort of your wings."

Then there's this approach to getting antifragile…

He tells us: "If you are irritated by every rub, how will you be polished?"

Think about that.

If you want to be polished, how do you expect to get there if you're irritated by every little rub of life?

Guess what? It's those "rubs" (a.k.a. challenges!) that are MAKING YOU SO SHINY!

Rumi also tells us: "This discipline and rough treatment are a furnace to extract the silver from the dross. This testing purifies the gold by boiling the scum away."

Yep. That's the ticket. We need to embrace all the little rubs antifragile-style as we step into the furnace so we can burn the scum away.

With that wisdom in mind, let's talk about the ultimate jihad. First, we need to understand what the word "jihad" actually means.

The root of *jihad* means "to strive" or "to exert oneself" and has two manifestations: one internal and one external. Unfortunately, we have a very limited understanding of the word "jihad" in the Western world.

We tend to think of it as a battle against external oppressors. But, battling things *outside* of ourselves is actually known as the LESSER jihad. The GREATER jihad?

That has nothing to do with anyone or anything *outside* of us. It's all about "striving" and "exerting" ourselves to win the battle between our higher and lower selves.

Rumi tells us: "The lion who breaks the enemy's ranks is a minor hero compared to the lion who overcomes himself."

And, after returning from a battle, Muhammad told his followers: "This day we have returned from the minor jihad to the major jihad."

All the great wisdom teachers echo this truth.

The greatest battle?

It will ALWAYS be between our higher and lower selves. Let's win that battle.

Close the gap.

Live with *Areté*.

TODAY.

P.S. If Socrates and Rumi were alive today, they would be soul brothers.

Here's how Socrates, who, for the record, was also a renowned warrior, put it nearly a thousand years before Rumi: "I desire only to know the truth, and to live as well as I can … And, to the utmost of my power, I exhort all other men to do the same … I exhort you also to take part in the great combat, which is the combat of life, and greater than every other earthly conflict."

VIRTUE CONNOISSEURS
WISDOM + DISCIPLINE + LOVE + COURAGE

I f the ultimate game is won by putting our virtues in action, then we better figure out how to get REALLY good at doing that, eh?

Answer: YES!

With that in mind, it's time to become virtue connoisseurs. Here's a quick master class on virtue.

We'll start with a quick review of what the ancient Greek and Roman philosophers had to say about their *four* cardinal virtues, then we'll look at what modern scientists have to say about their *six* cardinal virtues, then we'll boil all that down into the *four* modern Heroic cardinal virtues.

4 + 6 + 4.

Here we go.

First, the ancient Greek and Stoic philosophers.

Think: Socrates, Plato, and Aristotle, plus Seneca, Epictetus, and Marcus Aurelius.

They all agreed on their four cardinal virtues: Wisdom + Temperance + Courage + Justice.

We'll talk about them more in a moment when we modernize them.

Now, for the modern scientists.

As we discussed, when Martin Seligman and his colleagues kicked off the positive psychology movement, they started by cataloging all the virtues of all the ancient wisdom and spiritual traditions.

Think: Judaism, Christianity, and Islam, plus the ancient Greek philosophers, Taoism, Confucianism, Hinduism, and Buddhism.

Of course, those traditions differed on cultural details, but the researchers found an *astonishing* coherence among all of them.

So, they took the four cardinal virtues we just discussed (Wisdom + Courage + Temperance + Justice) that showed up in ALL traditions and they added two more virtues to the mix: what they called "Transcendence" and "Humanity."

Then they split those six core virtues into twenty-four sub-virtues that we'll talk about in a moment.

Now, I love all that ancient wisdom and modern science virtue goodness.

And...

I think we can simplify things as we figure out how to APPLY this wisdom to our modern lives.

Here's how we're going to approach it.

First, we definitely start with *Wisdom*.

The ancient Stoics told us that Wisdom is, in fact, THE virtue of which all the other virtues are simply expressions.

Then we have *Temperance*.

That's a REALLY weak word for what all the ancient wisdom teachers were REALLY getting at. It's not so much that we don't *drink too much* or *eat too much* per se, it's that we have self-mastery or DISCIPLINE. So, that's our second virtue.

Then we have *Courage*.

We'll keep that one as is and talk about it a LOT.

Btw: Did you know the word *courage* comes from the word that means "heart"? Yep. Just as your heart pumps blood to your arms and legs and all your other vital organs, courage is the virtue that vitalizes all the other virtues—which is why Aristotle considered courage THE most important virtue.

Then we go to *Justice.*

Now…

If you study the Stoics, you know that their sense of "justice" is more appropriately called LOVE. These guys were ALL IN on serving humanity as profoundly as they could.

For example, here's the great emperor-philosopher Marcus Aurelius in his notes to himself: *"Let your one delight and refreshment be to pass from one service to the community to another, with God ever in mind."*

Note: If that isn't Heroic love, I don't know what is.

Circling back to the positive psychologists, I think we can (and should) mash up their (kinda weird/sterile) word "Humanity" with "Justice" and just call it what it is: LOVE.

Now, we have our four core Heroic virtues that show up in the virtue compass in our Heroic app and on the back cover of this book that will guide all of our work together:

WISDOM + DISCIPLINE + LOVE + COURAGE.

By the time we're done playing together, we will have the WISDOM to know the game we're playing and how to play it well. We will have the DISCIPLINE to *actually* play that game well today. And, we will have the LOVE to deeply and joyfully connect with others. And, we will have the COURAGE to be willing to act in the presence of fear.

WISDOM + DISCIPLINE + LOVE + COURAGE.

Operationalizing *those* virtues is, ultimately, what it's all about.

YOUR TOP 5 VIRTUES
WHAT ARE THEY?

Now that we've discussed the four cardinal virtues of ancient wisdom (and modern heroism!), let's head back to the lab to learn more about what SCIENCE has to say.

There are two sets of five virtues we're going to discuss: The UNIVERSAL top five most-highly-correlated-to-flourishing virtues AND the top five virtues that are (pretty much) UNIQUE to you.

We'll start with the virtues unique to you.

Remember how I mentioned the fact that positive psychologists identified six core virtues that they extrapolated to twenty-four sub-virtues?

Well, here are those twenty-four virtues:

Appreciation of Beauty and Excellence, Bravery, Creativity, Curiosity, Fairness, Forgiveness, Gratitude, Hope, Humility, Humor, Integrity, Kindness, Leadership, Love, Love of Learning, Open-Mindedness, Persistence, Perspective, Prudence, Self-Regulation, Social Intelligence, Spirituality, Teamwork, and Zest.

Positive psychologists call those twenty-four sub-virtues "Character Strengths."

They've found that people who use their top strengths often in their day-to-day lives are happier. They also created a powerful little survey to help us get more clarity on our Top Five virtue-strengths—which they call "signature strengths."

Cruise on over to VIAcharacter.org and join over 15 million people who have taken the survey. It'll only take you ten minutes and I promise (!) it will be some of the best time you've ever invested in yourself.

Here's a fun fact via Ryan Niemiec, who is the Education Director of the VIA Institute and one of the world's leading authorities on the science of virtue.

He wrote a great book called *The Power of Character Strengths* in which he tells us that there are over 5.1 million possible combinations in your top five strengths.

When you take the test, you'll get a list of your strengths ordered from one to twenty-four.

Get this: There are six hundred sextillion possible combinations. (That's a six followed by twenty-three zeroes!)

So...

Take the test and, if you feel so inspired, write down your Top Five signature strengths here.

1. _____

2. _____

3. _____

4. _____

5. _____

(For curious souls, here are my Top Five Signature Strengths: Creativity + Hope + Zest + Courage + Wisdom.)

Once we KNOW our top virtues according to the VIA survey, we want to see how we're *already* using them when we're at our best, *and* we want to figure out how to more deliberately and consistently express them in our day-to-day lives.

So, if you feel so inspired, take a moment to reflect on how you've embodied those virtues in the past. And think about how you can more and more consistently embody them TODAY.

Science says: You'll be happier.

P.S. If you *really* want to go to the next level in every area of your life, consider getting the Heroic app. We worked with one of *the* best product-development firms in the world (the same company that helped build Slack and Uber Eats) to help you put your virtues in action all day, every day.

Research shows that, if you're like the 1,000+ individuals who participated in our pilot study, you might just get 40% more energized, 20% more productive, and 15% more connected using the app for just a few minutes a day for just thirty days!

THE OTHER TOP 5 VIRTUES
MOST HIGHLY CORRELATED WITH FLOURISHING

I n addition to those UNIQUE Top Five Virtues, science *also* says that there's a UNIVERSAL Top Five set of virtues.

These virtues have been most robustly correlated to our eudaimonic flourishing:

Gratitude + Hope + Zest + Curiosity + Love.

I repeat...

And this is worth paying attention to if you want to activate your Heroic potential and win the ultimate game of life...

These virtues have been most robustly correlated to our eudaimonic flourishing:

Gratitude + Hope + Zest + Curiosity + Love.

We'll briefly discuss what science says about each virtue's power and we'll look at some practical tools we can use to move from Theory to Practice for each.

But first...

Let's step back for a moment and talk about Aristotle's Golden Mean.

THE VIRTUOUS MEAN
VS. THE VICES OF DEFICIENCY & EXCESS

A discussion of virtue is not complete without a discussion of Aristotle's concepts regarding the vice of excess and the vice of deficiency.

The short story: Virtue is found at the "golden mean" between two extremes.

Of course, you can have too LITTLE of a virtue. Aristotle called that a "vice of deficiency."

And (very important AND!), you can *also* have TOO MUCH of a virtue. Aristotle called *that* a "vice of excess." Too much of a good thing, no matter how good that thing is, is typically NOT a good thing.

For example, too little courage is cowardice. That's a vice of deficiency. But… Too much courage is rashness. That's a vice of excess.

Here are a couple other things to keep in mind.

Aristotle encourages us to remember that it's REALLY hard to hit the target of the virtuous mean.

Sometimes you've gotta settle for the "lesser of two evils." But the point is: You're TRYING to hit the virtuous mean and not unconsciously going through your life.

Aristotle also makes the point that the mean isn't simply the "mathematical"-like average of two points on a spectrum. It's more nuanced than that. And, it's more personal. YOUR mean will be different than mine.

He tells us: "We must notice the errors into which we ourselves are liable to fall (because we all have different natural tendencies…), and we must drag ourselves in the other direction; for we shall arrive at the mean by pressing well away from our failing—just like somebody straightening out a piece of wood."

So…

Here's to straightening ourselves out and hitting the virtuous target!

And now, let's explore the five virtues science says are *most* highly correlated to flourishing: Gratitude, Hope, Zest, Curiosity, and Love.

Then we'll step back and explore some other ideas to make sure we know the ultimate game and how to play it well…

GRATITUDE
HOW TO BOOST YOUR WELL-BEING BY 25%

R obert Emmons is the world's leading scholar on the science of gratitude. He's written some great books on the subject including *Thanks!* and *Gratitude Works!*

Short story here?

Gratitude is an *extraordinarily* powerful virtue.

Professor Emmons shares some "eye-popping" (his words) stats in his books, including the data from his seminal research that established the fact that simply keeping a journal in which you write down five things for which you're grateful once a week for ten weeks leads to a 25% (!) boost in your happiness.

Pause and think about that for a moment longer…

Simply writing down five things for which you're grateful once a week for ten weeks can boost your happiness by 25%!

He tells us that grateful people sleep thirty minutes more and exercise 33% more. And, well, they experience a boost in pretty much every other measure as well.

He also tells us that it's *really* difficult to be SUPER grateful *and* SUPER depressed at the same time.

(Don't believe me/him? Try it.)

Grateful people have a different way of seeing things and use a different vocabulary. They often talk about "blessings" and "gifts" in their lives.

And, rather than taking things "*for* granted," they take things "*as* granted." (That's a big distinction.)

If you feel so inspired and want to +1° your flourishing, write down five things for which you're grateful:

1. _____

2. _____

3. _____

4. _____

5. _____

If you want to +25° your flourishing, do that often.

Gratitude.

It does a Hero good.

GRATEFUL FLOW
THE ANTIDOTE TO NEGATIVITY

Here's another way to practice the magic of gratitude right in the moment when you need it most.

In *The Tools*, Phil Stutz and Barry Michels call it "Grateful Flow." It's one of their recommended approaches to deal with any negative feelings you might be experiencing—overwhelm, depression, etc.

Here's the quick take on how to put the tool into practice.

The *moment* (emphasis on *the moment!*) you're aware that a cloud of negativity is floating into your day, step back, take a deep breath, and simply look around you and notice things for which you can be grateful.

For example, right now I'm grateful for the computer I'm working on, the bottle of water I just drank from, my wife and kids, the beautiful land outside my window, my health, you, and so much more.

That's Grateful Flow.

Tiny little things in our life that we can either take *for* granted or *as* granted.

Note: It's impossible (!) to be in a state of gratitude AND be in a state of misery at the same time.

Don't believe me? Try it.

Better yet… Practice it right now…

TAKING THINGS FOR GRANTED
VS. AS GRANTED

Continuing our discussion of how to apply the "eye-popping" research done on the power of gratitude, let's chat about another brilliant idea from Robert Emmons.

This one is from his book *Gratitude Works!*

Professor Emmons tells us: "Think about and then write down those aspects of your life that you are prone to take *for granted*. Instead, take them *as granted*."

I just LOVE that distinction.

Ungrateful people tend to take things (and people!) *for granted*.

For example, we tend to take all of the astonishing modern benefits that make our lives possible *for granted*. Stuff like a warm house, a car, a smartphone, the internet, and all the other magical marvels of modern life.

Robert tells us we'd be wise to move from taking people and things *for granted* to seeing them *as granted*.

Let's think about that for a moment longer.

I repeat: We can take the amazing people and goodness in our lives **for granted** or see them **as granted**.

That may not seem like a big deal, but it's a *really* big distinction.

Our +1°… Think about and then write down ONE aspect of your life that you are prone to take *for granted*. Instead, take it *as granted*.

ENTITLEMENT
THE #1 OBSTACLE TO GRATITUDE

Question: What's the #1 obstacle to gratitude?

Answer: According to Robert Emmons, the biggest obstacle to gratitude is a sense of ENTITLEMENT—the belief that the world owes you something.

And, because you are entitled to all the awesome things in your life and "deserve" it all, there's no reason for you to feel grateful.

The remedy to entitlement?

HUMILITY.

The humble person appreciates the fact that life is a sacred gift. Do you?

ON HUMILITY
THINKING OF OURSELVES LESS

S peaking of humility…

In his great book *Leadershift*, John Maxwell talks about the importance of humility.

He quotes pastor and author Rick Warren who tells us: "Humility is not denying your strengths. Humility is being honest about your weaknesses."

I like that one but it made me think of another quote on humility that I really like.

This one: "Humility is not thinking less of yourself, it's thinking of yourself less."

Isn't that good?

I repeat: "Humility is not thinking less of yourself, it's thinking of yourself less."

Now… I was pretty sure that quote was from C.S. Lewis so I Googled it to be sure and found a thoughtful commentary on the fact that the wisdom is often misattributed to C.S. Lewis but…

You know who really said it?

Rick Warren. Small world!

Our +1°: Let's remember that humility is not so much about thinking less of ourselves. It's about thinking of ourselves LESS. Easiest way to do that? Focus on others.

Be kind. Be present. Be generous.

TODAY.

P.S. Here's what C.S. Lewis actually said: "Do not imagine that if you meet a really humble man he will be what most people call 'humble' nowadays: he will not be a sort of greasy, smarmy person, who is always telling you that, of course, he is nobody. Probably all you will think about him is that he seemed a cheerful, intelligent chap who took a real interest in what you said to him. If you do dislike him it will be because you feel a little envious of anyone who seems to enjoy life so easily. He will not be thinking about humility: he will not be thinking about himself at all.

"If anyone would like to acquire humility, I can, I think, tell him the first step. The first step is to realize that one is proud. And a biggish step, too. At least, nothing whatever can be done before it. If you think you are not conceited, it means you are very conceited indeed."

REMEMBER WHO DUG THE WELLS
& GIVE BACK IN EQUAL MEASURE

An ancient Chinese proverb tells us to remember those who dug the wells.

In other words, remember those who came before you and made your life possible. And be grateful.

Someone, some time ago, took the time to dig that proverbial well from which you're now drinking.

I like to practice this when I turn on the faucet to wash the dishes or take a shower. An extraordinary number of anonymous people I'll never meet (going back generations) were involved in making that water flow.

It only takes a moment to appreciate them but when I do it, I feel my soul expand.

(Note to self: Do it more often.)

Einstein put it this way: "Every day I remind myself that my inner and outer life are based on the labors of other men, living and dead, and that I must exert myself in order to give in the same measure as I have received and am still receiving."

Here's the +1°…

Look around you. See the objects you take for granted and see the anonymous souls who made them all possible.

And, silently say: "Thank you."

Then exert yourself to give back in equal measure to all that you have been blessed to receive.

CELEBRATORY LOVE
GRATITUDE'S GENEROUS COUSIN

Now that we've taken a quick look at gratitude, let's talk about something Barbara Fredrickson calls "gratitude's generous cousin."

First, quick context.

Barbara is one of the world's leading well-being researchers. She wrote a book called *Love 2.0* in which she tells us that, from a scientific perspective, love is really all about those moments in our everyday lives in which we connect with someone over a shared positive emotion.

She calls them "micro-moments of positivity resonance" and we'll be talking about them and her a lot more soon.

For now, I want to focus on two different types of love: compassionate love and celebratory love.

Compassionate love is when our hearts open up to feel someone's pain and we wish them a sense of well-being. Celebratory love is, as the name implies, when we see the awesomeness in someone else and CELEBRATE it with them.

Barbara calls celebratory love "gratitude's generous cousin." (I love that.)

We appreciate SOMEONE ELSE'S good fortune when we practice (yes, it's a practice!) celebratory love.

We can do this all day every day.

See someone with a spring in their step and a smile on their face?

Take a moment to celebrate their apparent happiness and beam them a silent, virtual high five! Barbara silently says to herself: "May your happiness and good fortune continue!"

And, perhaps most importantly, when a loved one (or a friend or a colleague or… anyone) shares a story about their success with you, CELEBRATE IT!!!

Barbara tells us that most therapists focus on helping couples and families deal with the *challenges* in their relationships.

But, she tells us, it's actually WAY more important to get REALLY good at celebrating the POSITIVE stuff. If we can't do *that,* she tells us that our relationship is *really* in trouble.

Celebratory love.

It does a Hero and all our relationships good.

Let's practice it.

TODAY.

HOPE
GOALS + AGENCY + PATHWAYS

Now that we've explored some ideas on gratitude, it's time to talk about HOPE! This is one of my favorite virtues. And not just because it's in my own Top Five.

First, let's pause and think about the *opposite* of hope.

What is it?

Hopelessness.

Of course, it's REALLY hard to live with eudaimonic, Heroic joy if we feel *hopeless*—which is why understanding and mastering the SCIENCE of how to cultivate a grounded, resilient sort of hope is so important.

We have Rick Snyder to thank for pioneering the scientific exploration of hope.

In his great book *The Psychology of Hope*, Professor Snyder walks us through the THREE key aspects of cultivating a grounded, resilient kind of hope.

First, we need a **Goal**. Second, we need a sense of **Agency**. Third, we need **Pathways**.

It all (always!) starts with a clear goal. We need a vision of a better future.

Aristotle tells us that we are teleological beings. *Telos* means "target." He tells us that we need to have goals or targets at which we're directing our life force.

Modern positive psychologist Sonja Lyubomirsky echoes that ancient wisdom.

In her great book *The How of Happiness*, she tells us that happy people have projects—whether that's cultivating a garden or raising your children or launching a rocket to Mars.

So... How about YOU?

What's YOUR #1 most inspiring Target Goal right now?

(Seriously. What goal makes you want to get out of bed and have an awesome day?)

Again: It all starts with seeing a better future and having a specific goal that fires you up.

But...

Having a Goal isn't enough. We need to believe we can actually turn that dreamt-for vision into reality.

That requires what scientists call "Agency."

Agency is, essentially, a belief in our ability to make things happen. A sense of self-efficacy or self-confidence. We're going to talk about THIS a lot as well.

Then we need to create a "Pathway" (or a plan!) to achieve that Goal. And, very importantly, we need to know that, as they say in the military, no plan survives first contact with the enemy.

In other words, we need to EXPECT to hit obstacles and be willing to explore MULTIPLE PATHWAYS.

Plan A doesn't work? Perfect. Alchemize the lessons into Plan B. That doesn't work? Perfect. Repeat.

That's "Pathways" thinking and THAT's a quick look at the three key aspects of grounded, resilient hope.

Now it's time to look at my all-time favorite way to boost our Hope...

WOOP! THERE IT IS
THE SCIENCE OF MAKING YOUR DREAMS A REALITY

G abriele Oettingen is a world-class researcher and Professor of Psychology at New York University. She's spent her career studying the science of making your dreams a reality.

In her great book *Rethinking Positive Thinking*, she tells us that it's not enough to simply visualize our ideal life vision-board style. Although it's super important to start with a vision of our ideal lives, we then need to "rub it up against reality."

She created something called "**WOOP**" to help us make our dreams a reality. Here's the quick take:

W is for **Wish**

O is for **Outcome** (or benefits—kinda like the "why")

O is for **Obstacles**

P is for **Plan**

So, start with the **Wish**. What do you want in life? If you could wave a wand and create anything (in general or specific to a particular goal/project) what would you hope to achieve?

Seriously. If you're feeling it, do it right now. Think of the most important goal in your life right now. What is it?

Wave a wand. Everything goes perfectly. What do you achieve? Capture that in a few words. That's your Wish.

Now, think about the **Outcomes** you will experience when that Wish is fulfilled.

Think of all the benefits achieving that Wish will bring to you. See it. FEEL IT. It's super important to get really fired up about it.

Once we've got our Wish and Outcomes dialed in, it's time to rub that vision up against reality.

So…

What **Obstacles** will you face?

You've gotta KNOW you're going to face Obstacles and KNOW you have what it takes to get over/under/across/through/whatever them.

Embrace reality so you can properly prepare for it and create the reality you want.

Once we've identified the Obstacles, we need to create our **Plan**. The heart of this is something called "implementation intentions"—which are a genius way to anticipate challenges and deal with them in advance. We'll talk about them more in a moment.

For now: If X happens, then I will do Y.

What's your Plan to deal with the Obstacles so you can experience the benefits of bringing your wish to life?

One more time…

WOOP = **W**ish. **O**utcome. **O**bstacles. **P**lan.

I WOOP everything—from big goals to my next meeting.

Science says: WOOP! There it is.

Here's to making our dreams a reality.

IMPLEMENTATION INTENTIONS
THE POWER OF "IF... THEN..."

L et's continue our discussion of Gabriele Oettingen and her scientifically validated WOOP process.

Wish.

Outcome.

Obstacles.

Plan.

To recap: We get clarity on our ideal goal or Wish. We get fired up about the Outcome or benefits we'd like to experience. Then we rub that hoped-for future up against reality by identifying potential Obstacles. And, finally, we make a Plan to rock it.

(WOOP is truly magical, btw. As I say to our Heroic Coaches, if you're not using it all day every day by the end of our work together, then I'm not doing my job!)

So...

Gabriele's *husband* is also a world-class researcher and he's the one who came up with the most powerful way to craft an effective "Plan" to meet the "Obstacles."

His name is Peter Gollwitzer.

He created something called "Implementation Intentions."

Two little words we need to keep in mind:

"If..."

and

"Then."

IF X happens, THEN I will do Y.

Odysseus: IF I am approaching the Sirens, THEN I will have my sailors tie me to the mast so I won't steer my ship into the rocks.

Me: IF I wake up in the morning, THEN I will meditate and do Deep Work before doing anything else. IF the sun goes down THEN all my electronics go off. IF I am feeling a little wobbly, THEN I will think about what tool I can use to eat the challenge like an energy bar.

How about…

YOU?

What are YOUR top If… Then's?

IF _____ …

THEN _____ .

Implementation Intentions.

Let's dominate them.

All day. Every day.

Especially…

TODAY.

P.S. We're going to come back to this again and again as we help you make today a masterpiece, master yourself, dominate your fundamentals, and activate your superpower!

SWIMMING RATS
HOW TO INCREASE YOUR ENDURANCE BY 240X (!)

Although I'm not a big fan of some of the drawbacks of animal testing, here's a study that is astonishing and worth knowing about.

Get this...

In the 1950s, a Harvard-trained researcher based out of Johns Hopkins named Curt Richter ran some fascinating experiments.

He wanted to see how long rats could swim in two different conditions.

In the first condition, he simply let them swim as long as they could before giving up and drowning. They lasted fifteen minutes.

Then, in the other condition, right before they were about to reach that threshold of fifteen minutes, he picked them up and dried them off and let them rest briefly before putting them back in.

Guess how long they were able to swim after that quick reprieve...

A few more minutes? Another fifteen minutes? Maybe thirty minutes?

Get this... After being saved, those little rats swam for sixty (60!) hours—an absolutely astonishing two hundred and forty (240!) times longer.

Fifteen minutes vs. *sixty hours*.

That's crazy. How is that possible?

Richter said it was because of one very simple thing: HOPE.

The rats that had been saved had "seen" a better future. They "knew" there was a chance to survive so they just kept going and going and going.

All of which begs the question …

How's YOUR hope?

Remember: The science of hope is simple.

To recap: When we have hope, we believe our future will be better than our present. When we don't believe our future will be better, we are, literally, hopeless.

To increase our hope we want to optimize the three facets of hope:

1. We need to see a better future and have inspiring GOALS. (What are YOUR inspiring goals?)

2. We need to have a sense of AGENCY and believe that we can make that future a reality. (Do you?)

3. We need to have a plan AND be willing to pursue multiple pathways to get there. (Do you have a Plan A and are you prepared to dominate Plans B to Z if necessary?)

Know this, Hero: Your future WILL be better than your present. Why? Because we're going to do whatever we need to do to make it so. Period.

Remember the swimming rats and the power of HOPE.

LEADERSHIP'S SECRET SAUCE
HOW TO INCREASE ENGAGEMENT FROM 1% TO 69%

While we're chatting about the science of hope, let's focus on a key leadership stat.

First, imagine yourself as a leader.

(Which, of course, you are.)

See yourself in the various contexts in which you lead—from your role at work and in your family to your relationships with your friends and your most important relationship: with yourself.

The fact is, in any given moment throughout your day, you ALWAYS have the potential to lead.

Here's the deal.

Your effectiveness as a leader will A L W A Y S be driven by your ability to do one very important thing...

Inspire hope.

Remember: Hope is simple. It's the belief that our future will be better than our present. Its opposite, hopelessness, is when we *don't* believe our future will be better than our present.

So, pop quiz...

If you're a leader who DOESN'T inspire hope, what percentage of the people you're leading do you think will be engaged in whatever it is you're trying to get them to do?

What would you guess?

How about...

ONE PERCENT?!

That's it.

1%.

No hope?

No engagement.

On the other hand, imagine that you've done a great job of inspiring hope. You and your team/family (and yourself!) believe the future will be better than the present.

Now...

What percentage do you think will be engaged?

69%!!

To repeat...

If you DO NOT inspire hope in those you lead, you will see 1% engagement.

If you DO inspire hope, you will create SIXTY-NINE TIMES MORE ENGAGEMENT.

1% vs. 69%.

Hope matters.

A lot more than you may think.

So...

How will *your* future be better than your present? Count the ways then go share them with your crew.

Today's the day to lead with hope, Hero.

CURIOSITY
FLASHLIGHTS & HAMMERS

Next up: Curiosity.

It might have killed the cat but it actualizes the Heroic optimizer.

At this stage in our work together, the key distinction we want to make with this virtue is the fact that, as David Brooks puts it in his great book *The Second Mountain*, we want to analyze the data in our lives by first bringing a *flashlight* to the process NOT a *hammer*.

So…

What do YOU do when you make a mistake or things aren't quite working in your life?

Do you beat yourself up with a metaphorical hammer or do you grab a flashlight and look into what might need a little bit of work?

The vice of deficiency with curiosity as it relates to our Heroic optimizing?

We avoid looking at the reality of our lives and numb ourselves with distractions. ("Hi, binge-watching and Instagram and liquor store!")

The vice of excess?

We beat ourselves up with that metaphorical hammer and perfectionistic tendencies, obsessively ruminating about all the things that are wrong with our lives. (Then we go numb ourselves with distractions!)

To be clear: Shame has no place in our journey—which is why we're going to talk about the science of self-compassion in our next objective and why I will repeatedly encourage you to have a win or learn/growth mindset.

In short...

See what's working. Celebrate that.

See what needs work. Get on that.

Repeat.

WIN OR LEARN
3 QUESTIONS TO ASK AFTER A PERFORMANCE

L anny Bassham won a gold medal in rifle shooting in the 1976 Olympics. But he didn't win that gold until AFTER he fell short in the 1972 Olympics where he took home a silver.

He used that disappointment to fuel his mental toughness training and bring home the gold in his next attempt. Since then, he's been teaching people how to show up as their best when it matters most.

He wrote one of my all-time favorite books on mental toughness called *With Winning in Mind*. Here's one of my favorite things he teaches his elite performers.

After any performance—ESPECIALLY the ones where you fell short of your goals—ask yourself these three questions:

What did I do well?

What did I learn?

How will I get better?

We win. Or, we learn. And learning IS winning so we win or we win.

Our +1°: Learn anything awesome lately?

Think about a recent disappointment and let's quickly run it through this process:

What did you do well? (ALWAYS start here!)

What did you learn? (Well, what did you learn?!)

How will you get better? (+1°, baby!!)

High fives and let's go, Hero!

HOW TO WIN OR LEARN
OPERATIONALIZING LEARNING-WINS

E merson's newfound passion for chess has given us an opportunity to go to the next level in our relationship.

It's hard to put into words just how fun it has been to use his passion for chess as the context to teach him everything from dominating the fundamentals to forging antifragile confidence.

Not too long ago, we went on a road trip to the Texas State Chess Championships. It was just the boys while the ladies got some girl time together. Five-hour drive on Friday. Games on Friday night, Saturday, and Sunday, then five-hour drive home on Sunday.

Before we get to the point of this +1°, I want to share a little more context.

As we've discussed, Emerson got *really* into chess less than a year ago.

He entered his first informal tournament and won something like three games and lost two. Then he entered another informal tournament and almost won it. Then he entered his first "real" tournament (the Texas Regionals) and won the Novice division.

Then we went to the State Championships.

So...

Emerson and I are DOMINATING our new chess tournament protocol. (That's like us!)

Of course, we did our best to get great nights of sleep. We packed all our food so we could eat well. We meditated to Mommy's seven-minute peak performance visualization-meditation and rocked out to her one-minute declarations before each match.

We even invented a new workout called "Skippy Ball" in which we side-skipped across a huge empty parking lot while tossing a little ball to one another as I tried to find a way to make our thirty-minute a.m. workout fun. (It worked. He LOVED it.)

Now...

It's Sunday afternoon.

Emerson is 6–0 as he heads into the FINAL match of the tournament.

If he wins...

He'll be the Texas State Champion for his JV division.

Note: I started sweating a bit just typing that (hah) (seriously) feeling into how I felt waiting for him in the car after sending him off with a hug after walking into the room whispering: "Breathe in through your nose... Chest up, chin down. Calm confidence... You've got this, buddy. LET'S GO!!"

So...

I got off a FaceTime call with Alexandra and reflected on how I would practice my philosophy and MAKE SURE that he felt REALLY (!!) supported whether he WON *or* he LEARNED.

Then it hit me.

Every time he lost before, we IMMEDIATELY 1-2-3'd it by

celebrating what he did well, reflecting on what he could have done differently, and making a commitment to use that wisdom to play differently next time.

And…

Every single time we did that after he lost a game, he TRULY did learn something meaningful, and the lessons he learned DIRECTLY led to him WINNING as a result of the learning opportunity.

I wanted him to SEE the connection and that it TRULY is "Win or Learn!"

So… I made a little note file thing on my iPhone.

Title: **"Chess: Top Learning-Wins."**

Then I typed: "We Win or we Learn and Learning is Winning so we LOVE the winning AND the learning. OMMS! Let's go!"

Here's a quick look at the Top 3 "Learning-Wins" we've experienced so far to help YOU turn losses into learnings and turn those learnings into wins!

Learning-Win #1:

Loss = Learn: Very first informal tournament. After accidentally touching a piece, his opponent said he had to move the piece. He didn't know the rule to say "Adjust." And, he didn't know the rule that if you and your opponent disagree during a game you could call the tournament director over. He lost the game. And he cried.

Learning-Win: On Saturday (and Sunday!) at the State Championships, an opponent said that he needed to move a piece that he didn't need to move. Now he knows the rules so they brought the tournament director over. Had zero fear. Was right. Won game. Celebrated.

Learning-Win #2:

Loss = Learn: He felt tired in the final game of second tournament. Had he won that match, he would have won the tournament. He lost the last game. Cried.

Learning-Win: We decided that we'd do our best to make sure that was the last time he'd be tired in his final match. Started dominating Fitbit and went beast-mode with our Energy protocol before, between, and during matches.

Learning-Win #3:

Loss = Learn: In his first official tournament (Regionals), an opponent badgered him to accept a draw—asking him over and over and over. He finally accepted the draw even though he was up a couple points and would have easily won the game. He cried. It was the only game he didn't win as he won the championship.

Learning-Win: In the very next tournament, an opponent offered a draw again and again. He refused. And won. Now he knows that an opponent offering a draw is showing weakness and a fear of losing. With rare exceptions, that's a trigger to be aggressive and win.

So...

As I experienced the wonderful eudaimonic joy of waiting to see how my beloved ten-year-old son did in his big match, I'm prepared to Win or Learn...

And...

Emerson comes out beaming.

He won the match.

Awesome.

We celebrated.

Then we MADE THE CONNECTION between each of his Losses and how they DIRECTLY led to his Learning-Wins.

THAT is how we moved from Theory to Practice to (aspirational) Mastery on one sacred weekend in which the game of chess gave us an opportunity to play the ultimate game of life.

And...

That's our +1°.

Got kids? Grandkids? Nieces? Nephews?

Or colleagues or clients or friends?

How can you practice *your* philosophy a little more in *your* life and help them practice it a little more in theirs?

Remember...

We Win or we Learn.

And Learning IS Winning so...

We WIN or we WIN.

PARENTING CHAMPIONS
THE QUESTION TO ASK

I n our last +1°, we mined some wisdom from my recent road trip with Emerson to the Texas State Chess Championships.

Today I want to talk about one of the things we talked about on the long, five-hour drive home.

But first, I want to talk about one of my all-time favorite authors who wrote one of the main books that is guiding how I'm striving to support Emerson in his quest for chess mastery.

The book is called *Parenting Champions*. It's by Lanny Bassham, who also wrote *With Winning in Mind*.

In *Parenting Champions*, Lanny gives us some *great* wisdom on everything from creating an empowered self-image to setting effective goals.

But the thing that most struck me was this wisdom from the first chapter of the book—which is called: "The Question."

Lanny asks us: "Concerning your kids, I have just one question for you. What is more important to you, what your children Accomplish or who they Become?"

Pause for a moment and ask yourself that question … Which is more important for you? Lanny has asked thousands of parents and they all give the same answer you did.

It is, of course, who they Become.

And THAT is why I'm so excited for this next phase of my relationship with Emerson.

We now have a wonderful context to use his current, intrinsic passion for chess as the *perfect* context to help him win the ultimate game of life by practicing his/our philosophy.

Now… Let's chat about that five-hour drive.

Thinking about the importance of gratitude and the "Remember who dug the wells" wisdom, I asked Emerson who we needed to thank for helping him do so well in the tournament. I asked what, specifically, each person did.

He said: "FunMasterMike is funny and made chess fun."

And, he said his coach Nick saw his potential and helped him prepare. Mommy made him healthy food and meditations. And Daddy paid for it and drove him there and coached him on mental toughness. (Hah.)

Then we talked about all the people who built the roads we drove on to get there, the people who worked at (and built) the hotel we stayed at, and who built the car we drove and got the gas to the gas station and…

I let him know we could spend our entire drive trying to thank all the people who made our weekend possible and we'd still barely scratch the surface.

That's our +1°.

As we bring forth the best within ourselves and our kids in whatever "game" we're playing these days, let's remember the ultimate game AND let's remember the people who help us accomplish our dreams and become who we're destined to be.

Day 1. All in.

It's time to raise the next generations of Heroes.

SACRED MOMENTS
FILLED WITH LOVE

Concluding our recap of wisdom gained from my adventure with Emerson to the Texas State Chess Championships.

We dominated our protocols and practiced our philosophy and had an AMAZING weekend—way before and independent of Emerson bringing home a very large trophy.

But winning the chess matches wasn't the highlight of the weekend. There were a number of other moments and one in particular I'd like to discuss that was much more powerful.

First, a little more context…

Emerson played his first game on a Friday night at 7:15 p.m.—literally his normal bedtime. (Hah. Perfect.)

We dominated the blue-light blocking glasses and then dominated the match then got back to the hotel to dominate a good night of sleep.

And…

After tucking ourselves in we noticed that, for some strange reason, the hotel designers thought it was an awesome idea to have the smoke alarm thing blinking in a remarkably bright green light five feet above our head—perfectly angled to bounce off the two thousand inch plasma TV screen near the foot of the bed. We laughed.

Then we tried to tape my underwear on the wall to cover that blinking. It worked.

Until…

The underwear fell off the wall and onto my face fifteen minutes after we were asleep. We laughed some more.

Then we went down to the lobby and got some extra-strong tape that did the job and I had a misty moment as we finally fell asleep holding hands after playing footsie in our king-sized bed.

But… That's NOT quite the point of this +1°.

Fast-forward twenty hours and Emerson has played his three games on Saturday. I decide that we'd celebrate by going to Dave and Buster's. He's never been to THAT big of an arcade and I knew he'd love it.

So…

We're walking the mile from the conference center to the arcade. He's using my phone to navigate us. We get into the little strip-mall place where the arcade is.

And…

We see a mom and dad and two kids playing their violins asking for money.

Emerson asks if we can give them some money.

I told him that we didn't have any cash.

He insisted.

Then I realized I DID have some cash stashed away in my wallet and gave him some money to give to the family.

He walked up and gave the mom $20.

The woman looked at him with an open heart and said: "Bless you. Thank you so much."

(I got tears in my eyes typing that now.)

It was impossible not to feel her gratitude.

I could tell Emerson felt it.

I asked him: "Hey, buddy. How did that feel?"

He said: "It felt amazing."

I asked him: "Think about how you felt winning all those games today."

He felt into that.

Then I asked him: "What felt better—winning all those games OR helping this family?"

He didn't hesitate for a second as he said: "This felt WAY better."

To which I said: "Exactly. Remember that. Helping people is why we do what we do."

THAT moment was the highlight of our weekend and something we have reflected on many times since.

And…

That's our +1°.

Here's to appreciating the blessings of our lives and creating as many micro-moments of Love as we can with our Loved ones and with our world.

TODAY.

YOU & AN ELEPHANT
A PARABLE ABOUT BLIND GUYS & PERSPECTIVE

Once upon a time, in a land far away, six blind guys had never seen an elephant before. They had no idea what an elephant was or what one looked like.

They each walked up to the elephant at a different spot.

The first blind guy touched the side of the elephant and declares: "This is like a wall!"

The second guy touches the tail and says: "No! This is like a rope!"

The third guy touches the trunk and declares: "This is like a snake!"

The fourth grabs the tusk and says: "This is like a spear!"

Our fifth fellow touches the ear and says: "This is like a fan!"

And, finally, our sixth blind guy touches a leg and says: "This is like a tree trunk!"

Here's what's interesting. All those blind guys are 100% sure that they're 100% right. Of course, they're not. Their perspectives are only *partially* true.

We laugh at this story.

But, guess what? Same rules apply for us and that last political debate we had. Or that little argument with a spouse or child or colleague.

We tend to think that we're 100% right and that the other person is 100% wrong.

But, as Ken Wilber says, NO ONE is smart enough to be 100% right about *anything.* Nor is anyone smart enough (or silly enough) to be 100% *wrong* about anything.

There's always a PARTIAL truth to every perspective. And, if we want to optimize our communication, we'd be wise to *start* our dialogues by trying to see the other person's perspective, finding a place of mutual agreement, and then (and only then) respectfully tiptoeing to the outer edges of potential disagreement.

So…

The +1°: The next time you feel a little frustrated during an interpersonal interaction, take a moment to see if you think you're 100% right. Then see if you can step back from your certainty and try to see the other person's perspective.

Remember the blind guys and their six different elephants as you embody a little more humility and curiosity today.

ZEST
THE #1 VIRTUE

Positive psychologists arm wrestle a bit on which of the virtues is the #2 most powerful virtue. Is it Hope or is it Gratitude? But they agree that ZEST is the #1 virtue most highly correlated with our eudaimonic flourishing.

"Zest" is bit of a weird word for what we're going to call "Energy." And, I repeat, THIS IS THE #1 PREDICTOR of your psychological well-being.

We're going to spend a LOT of time getting our Energy to Heroic levels so we can show up most powerfully in our Work and in our Love.

Of course, there's a growing body of research on the powerful effects of eating, moving, sleeping, breathing, and focusing.

For example, we know that, as leading neuroscientist and sleep researcher Matthew Walker says in his GREAT book *Why We Sleep*, getting a good night of sleep is like walking over a bridge from despair to hope.

Imagine that for a moment. Get a *bad* night of sleep and you risk going from hope to despair. Get a *great* night of sleep, and you give yourself a chance to walk over the bridge the other way from despair to hope.

We also know that our gut produces something like 80–90% of our body's serotonin. Think about *that* for a moment as well. Your GUT (!) produces more serotonin than your brain! Which is why optimizing our *nutrition* is one of the fastest ways to boost our mood.

And, we know that, as Harvard MD psychiatrist John Ratey puts it in *Spark*, movement is like taking a little bit of Ritalin and a little bit of Prozac. Or, as Kelly McGonigal tells us in *The Joy of Movement*, when we exercise, we release what scientists call "hope molecules."

And, did you know there's even a threshold daily step-count under which we're more likely to feel anxious and depressed? Yep.

As Kelly puts it: "The average daily step count required to induce feelings of anxiety and depression and decrease satisfaction with life is 5,649. The typical American takes 4,774 steps per day. Across the globe, the average is 4,961."

(How many steps are YOU getting these days?)

Again, this is all part of a longer chat we'll have throughout our time together. For now, know this…

Your PHYSIOLOGY is driving a LOT MORE of your PSYCHOLOGY than you may realize.

Which is why the wisest psychiatrists out there, like Harvard MD psychiatrist Dan Siegel, talk about "brain hygiene" and the importance of focusing on your nutrition, movement, and sleep.

I repeat: Science says that your Energy is the #1 predictor of your psychological well-being.

So… What's the #1 thing you KNOW you could be doing to boost your Zest/Energy?

Is TODAY a good day to get to work on that?

LOVE
0.0, 1.0, 2.0, 3.0, 8.0 & ∞.0

L ove.

Some scientists make a VERY strong case that LOVE is, in fact, THE most important virtue to cultivate.

In fact, Harvard psychiatrist and researcher George Vaillant (author of *Spiritual Evolution*) puts it succinctly when he tells us: "Happiness equals love—full stop."

We're going to have fun redefining Love by extending some ideas from Barbara Fredrickson's great book *Love 2.0*.

Barbara is another one of the world's leading positive psychologists. She tells us that Love 1.0 is, basically, love for our family and most intimate others. This is, of course, a critical aspect of love but...

Professor Fredrickson tells us that it's just *one* facet of our potential for Love.

She encourages us to find "micro-moments of positivity resonance" with people all day every day and describes the underlying neuro-psychological benefits of exiting our "cocoons of self-absorption" long enough to make authentic connections. She calls this Love 2.0.

I love it. And, I say, why stop there?

Let's start by loving ourselves via Love 0.0—remembering the fact that, as Ayn Rand said in *The Fountainhead*: "One cannot say 'I love you' without first saying the 'I.'"

How do we do that?

Well, we'll talk about it more, but two key ways are via self-compassion and practicing your #1 self-care habit.

(On that front: What's the #1 thing YOU do when you're at your best? Got it? Awesome. Now... How about we love ourselves enough to make that a non-negotiable?!)

Then we have Love 1.0 which is Love for our family.

How can we optimize that? Again, we'll talk about this a LOT as well.

For now, know that your greatest gift to your family is your PRESENCE and that the greatest obstacle to giving that gift of presence is your smartphone.

Therefore... Want soul connections? Put away your smartphone when you're with your loved ones.

Then we have those Love 2.0 micro-moments of positivity resonance we get by exiting our cocoons of self-absorption.

Again, show up. Be present. Put away your smartphone and do simple things like make eye contact and smile.

Then we're going to throw in Love 3.0 which, for us, will capture the power of ENCOURAGING others.

Aristotle said that courage is the #1 virtue. Therefore, if we want to love people, what better way than to *encourage* them?

Note: The word literally means to "inject someone with courage." (How awesome is that?!)

Then we have Love 8.0.

We need to bring Love to our Work. We'll talk about how to do THAT as well and bring more meaning and engagement to the Work we do by making the connection to the people we're *already* serving with what we *already* do.

Then we have Love ∞.0.

The practicing lover of wisdom? The philosopher? We love it ALL. The "good" and the "not so good."

It's all fuel for our Heroic fires.

Love.

Redefined.

Practiced.

All day, every day.

Especially…

TODAY.

ARISTOTLE'S "HAPPINESS"
MAY NOT BE WHAT YOU THINK

A ristotle was born in Greece on the border of Macedonia in 384 BC.

His father was the court physician to the Macedonian king. At the age of seventeen, he went to Athens where he studied with Plato in his Academy for twenty years until Plato's death.

Shortly thereafter, he was summoned to Macedonia by the king and became the tutor of the young Alexander the Great. Aristotle was forty-one. Alexander was thirteen.

Then Aristotle went back to Athens where he created his Lyceum and, essentially, spent the rest of his life studying and mastering every imaginable subject—from logic, ethics, history, and politics to anatomy, biology, and zoology. And, of course, psychology and philosophy.

His insights have shaped our world.

Side note: Did you know that his Lyceum survived for an astonishing *five hundred* years after his death?

Let's revisit his ideas on what it means to flourish.

This time, we're going to bring in Jonathan Barnes, editor of the Penguin Classic edition of the *Nicomachean Ethics* on which I created our Philosopher's Note.

In his introduction, Barnes goes to great lengths to establish the fact that Aristotle's sense of "eudaimonic happiness" is VERY different than our modern take on "happiness."

Here's how Barnes puts it...

"To call a man eudaimōn is to say something about how he lives and what he does. The notion of eudaimonia is closely tied, in a way in which the notion of happiness is not, to success: the eudaimōn is someone who makes a success of his life and actions, who realizes his aims and ambitions as a man, who fulfills himself."

In other words, the ultimate aim of life is not "happiness" as we know it, but more of a sense of ACTUALIZATION.

True happiness, in the Aristotelian sense, MUST include the successful actualization of our potential. THAT is the ultimate purpose of life. The highest good. The *summum bonum*.

Back to Barnes. He also tells us: "It will not do to replace 'happiness' by 'success' or 'fulfillment' as a translation of eudaimonia; the matter is too complicated for any such simple remedy, and in what follows I shall continue to employ the word 'happiness,' guarding it with a pair of inverted commas. But it is worth considering Aristotle's recipe for eudaimonia with the notion of success in mind. The Ethics, we are thus supposing, is not telling us how to be morally good men, or even how to be humanly happy: it is telling us how to live successful human lives, how to fulfill ourselves as men."

THAT is the type of "happiness" we're after—a deep sense of fulfilling ourselves and leading our best, most successful lives.

How do we do that?

We live with *Areté*.

HOW TO FLOURISH
SCIENCE SAYS: PERMA

Martin Seligman has written a number of seminal books on the science of well-being.

When he and his colleagues launched the Positive Psychology movement, he wrote a book called *Authentic Happiness*. A decade later, he updated his thinking with a book called *Flourish*.

Short story: A good life isn't just about maintaining a positive emotional state represented by that big yellow smiley face. A good life is about moving toward your highest potential (*flourishing*!) and that DOESN'T always feel like sunshine and rainbows.

(As we discussed, the ancient Greeks made a similar distinction with their two different types of "happiness": *hedonia* and *eudaimonia*.)

So, Seligman tells us that there are five key facets to the science of flourishing. He captures them in a handy-dandy acronym: **PERMA**.

Here's a quick look:

P is for **Positive Emotion**. Although experiencing a *permanent*, never-ending positive state isn't either necessary or possible, having a consistent level of positive emotional affect is a key aspect of well-being.

So, smile! Enjoy your life.

E is for **Engagement**. Want to feel great as you flourish?

ENGAGE with your life. Create more and more moments of flow as you stretch toward goals that matter and give your best self to the moment.

(Note: Want to feel *really* good? I repeat: Engage your core VIRTUES. The whole science of well-being is grounded on the universal virtues of all major religious and philosophical traditions.)

R is for **Relationships**. Science is unequivocal: Healthy relationships are a core component of a healthy, flourishing life. Invest your time here. Go create some micro-moments of awesome and deepen your connections with those you love.

M is for **Meaning**. We need to have a connection to a deep sense of purpose in our lives. What inspires you? Who benefits from the work you do and how you show up in the world? Bring that to mind each day and make your life an expression of that service.

A is for **Achievement**. Want to flourish? Then we need to have goals that challenge us and enable us to experience the joy of achievement. What's firing you up these days? Have clear goals, create micro-wins, and celebrate the process.

PERMA = Positive Emotion, Engagement, Relationships, Meaning, and Achievement.

Where are you strong? Celebrate! And what can use a little work? +1° it!

Here's to living with *Areté* and flourishing. TODAY.

LEARNED HELPLESSNESS
DON'T GIVE UP

I n our last +1°, we talked about Martin Seligman and the science of flourishing.

Quick recap: It's all about PERMA: Positive Emotion + Engagement + Relationships + Meaning + Achievement.

Before he got into all that, Seligman was the world's leading authority on how to learn optimism. But before he mastered *that*, he discovered something very interesting about how we learn HELPLESSNESS.

Here's the short story: Decades ago, Seligman was in a lab with dogs. He split them into a couple groups. One group of dogs was given shocks but they could figure out how to avoid them easily. The other group was given random shocks that they couldn't avoid. That was the first part of the study.

For the second part of the study, the dogs were given a shock again but this time it was super easy for all of them to learn how to avoid the shock. The group that easily escaped the shock the first time easily learned the second time.

But, get this.

The group that couldn't avoid the random shocks in the first part of the experiment, *didn't even try* to learn how to escape the shock in the second part—even though it was now super easy to learn.

They just curled up in a ball and let the shocks continue. They had LEARNED HELPLESSNESS.

Scientists have replicated that finding with other stimuli in studies with other animals, including humans.

But get this …

Not all people learn helplessness.

Some of them, even after being bombarded with "shocks," maintain an empowered response. Seligman wanted to understand what made THEM tick.

He distilled the essence of what he learned into another one of his great books called *Learned Optimism*.

He tells us that it all comes down to the 3 P's of Optimism— which we'll talk about in our next +1°.

Before we go there, you need to know why you should care about all this.

KNOW THIS: Learned helplessness is basically a one-way ticket to depression.

If you've been shocked by life and learned to curl up in a ball, you've given up your power and that leads to places we don't want to go.

Solution: LEARN OPTIMISM.

LEARNED OPTIMISM
THE 3 P'S

In our last couple +1°s, we spent some time with Professor Martin Seligman. We learned the PERMA model of flourishing and the perils of learning helplessness.

Now, it's time to LEARN OPTIMISM. Let's get to work.

In his classic book on the subject, appropriately called *Learned Optimism*, Seligman tells us that there are three "P's": Permanence, Pervasiveness, and Personalization.

Here's the quick look.

Permanence. This is all about whether something will be temporary or enduring.

Let's say something challenging happens.

The Optimist will say: "Bring it on. I'll do what needs to get done and then it will pass."

The Pessimist, on the other hand, says: "Gah. Yet *another* problem. Is life *always* going to be this terrible?"

Interestingly, when something GOOD happens, the Optimist and the Pessimist flip their orientations.

The Pessimist, who was sure the bad thing would be permanent, thinks the *good* thing will be fleeting. And, vice-versa with the Optimist who believes the good things will endure while the bad things will pass.

(How do *you* show up?)

Pervasiveness. This is all about whether the life situation "pervades" all aspects of your life or just that specific situation.

The Optimist is able to isolate the "bad" event into one compartment of their life. If they have a challenging discussion at work, they don't say: "My whole life sucks." They don't make it *pervasive* the way a Pessimist tends to do.

Again, the opposite happens with the good stuff. It's only a lucky break in one part of their life for the Pessimist and another sign of all the awesomeness for the Optimist.

(How do *you* show up?)

Personalization. This is all about whether or not we take personal responsibility for the situation.

It's a nuanced discussion but... If a bad thing happens, an Optimist is more likely to see the environmental circumstances that might've led to the event occurring while the Pessimist will take it all personally. Of course, the Optimist will have a healthy level of "needs work!" ownership when appropriate, but they won't beat themselves up unnecessarily.

And, again, the opposite happens with the good stuff. A Pessimist thinks they must have gotten lucky and the Optimist high-fives themselves for rockin' it.

(How do *you* show up?)

Those are the three P's of Optimism: Permanence, Pervasiveness, and Personalization.

Remember: We can learn helplessness. AND... We can learn optimism. How will you +1° today?

THE SPEED OF LIGHT
A LESSON IN PERSPECTIVE

Do you know how far away the sun is? It's a staggering 93 million miles away. You know how long it takes a ray of the sun's light to reach us? Eight minutes and twenty seconds.

I didn't know either of those things until I read Michael Singer's *Living Untethered*. He shares those stats and many others to help us gain some perspective on our lives by holding our existence in the context of the utter vastness of the universe.

Here's another fun fact.

The next closest star beyond our sun is called Proxima Centauri. It is 4.2 light-years away.

You know how far that is?

Imagine holding a very powerful flashlight above the Earth. Turn it on for ONE second. That light will go around the Earth SEVEN AND A HALF TIMES in a *single* second.

Soak that in for a moment. That's the speed of light.

Now, if you want to go from the sun to that next-closest star, you'd need to move at THAT speed for 4.2 YEARS.

You know how far that is?

A light-year is about SIX TRILLION miles, so, if my math is correct, the next closest star is about 2.5 QUADRILLION miles away.

My brain just exploded trying to comprehend that. (Yours?)

You know what exists between the sun and that next star?

ABSOLUTELY NOTHING.

You know how many stars are in the universe?

TWO HUNDRED BILLION.

You know what exists between the light-years separating EVERY ONE of those TWO HUNDRED BILLION STARS?

ABSOLUTELY NOTHING.

As Singer tells us, 99.999% of the entire, mind-bogglingly big universe is filled with ABSOLUTELY NOTHING BUT DARKNESS.

And...

Yet...

Here we are on planet Earth, failing to appreciate the miracle that is our existence—complaining about the weather on the way to work and the slow internet connection on our Zoom call and/or whatever other trivial things we're letting bother us.

That's our +1°.

If you feel so inspired, the next time you look up at the sun, look beyond it. Appreciate the vastness of our universe and the preciousness of our lives.

Then feel your feet on the Earth and say "Thank you!" to whatever power you believe created all this magic as you get back to work being your best, most Heroic self in service to something infinitely bigger than yourself.

All in. Day 1.

Let's go, Hero!

YOU'RE NOT A BIG DEAL
& THAT'S A LIBERATINGLY BIG DEAL

My friend Tripp Lanier is a very funny guy.

In his book *This Book Will Make You Dangerous,* he shares some of the wisdom he's acquired coaching (mostly) guys for the last fifteen-plus years.

If you (or the man in your life) like to laugh deeply (at some "irreverent" humor) while joyfully activating your Heroic potential, then I think you'll enjoy his "Irreverent Guide for Men Who Refuse to Settle."

Tripp tells us that we need to drop the nonsense and get to work experiencing the things we really want: more freedom, aliveness, love, and peace. NOW.

In a chapter entitled "Find the Fun," Tripp echoes Michael Singer's perspective-building wisdom in the microchapter "You're Not a Big Deal."

Here's how he puts it: "When we think of big—and I mean really big—we usually think of the sun. It's massive, right? In fact, you could fit 1.3 million Earths inside the sun. Let that sink in.

But according to astronomer and scientist Michelle Thaler, if you were to shrink the sun down to the size of the dot in this letter 'i' right here on the page—that tiny-ass little dot—if you made the sun that big, then the relative size of our galaxy, the Milky Way, would be the size of the Earth. Take a minute to visualize that.

But let's not stop there. A while back, astronomers found a tiny section of the night sky that appeared to be empty. And 'tiny' means the size of the head of a pin if you held it out at arm's length. If you were to hold that tiny pinhead up to the sky, then that little, tiny portion of the sky appeared completely void of celestial light. So they focused the Hubble Telescope up there, and let it absorb light for ten days.

And in that tiny, tiny dark part of the night sky, which looked completely empty, they ended up discovering three thousand galaxies.

So what does this all mean? You, me, all of us—our daily crises and dramas and getting pissed off because the barista forgot to put 3.5 soy vegan [ahem] sprinkles in our lattes—when we start to imagine this massive universal perspective, we start to see that no matter what we are thinking or doing, it's really just not that big of a deal. And it never will be."

Pause. Reflect.

That's our $+1°$.

We're not a big deal.

And, that's a really liberatingly BIG deal.

Let's zoom out far enough to see that all those "daily crises and dramas" just AREN'T a big deal. Period. Then, let's zoom back in and enjoy this precious life of ours.

TODAY.

100 QUESTIONS
AN EXERCISE TO CREATE A MEANINGFUL LIFE

Michael Gelb wrote a great book called *How to Think Like Leonardo da Vinci.* I can still vividly remember reading it shortly after selling my first business nearly twenty-five years ago. It was life-changing.

Michael has a bunch of great exercises and distinctions to help us tap into our potential. Here's one of my favorites.

It's called the One Hundred Questions Exercise.

It goes like this… Find a quiet place where you won't be disturbed for forty-five to sixty minutes. Bring your journal and a pen. Start writing down questions. We want one hundred of them.

Your questions can be about whatever comes to mind. Why is the sky blue? What's my purpose? Whatever you come up with is perfect. Just write them down. Again, we want one hundred of them.

If you're like me, the first dozen or two will come pretty easily. And then you'll need to dig a little deeper. Don't stop until you get to one hundred.

That's Part I.

Part II? Look at that list of questions and notice the themes that emerge. Maybe you had a bunch of questions about your health or relationships or purpose. Notice whatever categories and themes bubble up.

Part III? Now we're ready for showtime. Look at those one hundred questions and pull out the ten questions you find most powerful and meaningful.

(Note: It's not supposed to be easy. That's the point. No pressure, no diamonds!!)

Once you have those ten questions, RANK ORDER them from the most powerful question down.

I did this exercise on Saturday, June 8th, 2001 and my life is basically a reflection of my top ten questions from that day.

Which begs the question... What questions are guiding YOUR life?!

THE WAY
DOES NOT EXIST

I n his classic manifesto *Thus Spoke Zarathustra*, Friedrich Nietzsche's enlightened hero is asked: "What's the way?"

He replies: "'This is my way; where is yours?'—Thus I answered those who asked me 'the way.' For the way—that does not exist."

Carl Jung echoed this wisdom as well.

He told us: "The shoe that fits one person pinches another; there is no recipe for living that suits all cases."

To state the obvious as we embark on our Heroic quests together: We each need to find our own way.

So…

What's YOUR way?

Are you on it?

How can you live with an even deeper level of integrity with what YOU know is true? (While, very importantly, allowing others to do the same?)

Turn up the heat.

Close the gap. Live with *Areté*.

Activate your Heroic potential.

Play the ultimate game well.

On your terms.

TODAY.

THE HEALTHY DEVIANT
WHEN BEING WELL-ADJUSTED ISN'T A GOOD IDEA

P ilar Gerasimo is one of the wisest humans I know.

Among many other things, she created the award-winning *Experience Life* magazine and is the author of a GREAT book called *The Healthy Deviant: The Rule Breaker's Guide to Being Healthy in an Unhealthy World.*

You may be wondering…

What's a Healthy Deviant?

I'll answer that in a moment.

First, let's look at some stats from the first chapter called "The Crazy That Passes for Normal."

Get this…

- 50% of U.S. adults are diagnosed with a chronic illness
- 68% are overweight or obese
- 70% are taking at least one prescription drug (for folks over sixty, the average is FIVE)
- 80% are mentally or emotionally "not flourishing"
- 97.3% are not maintaining healthy habits (decent nutrition, adequate exercise, not smoking, healthy body composition)

Which leads us to Pilar's guess that 99% of us are not healthy, happy, or on track to stay that way.

Which leads us to one big sad face.

Which leads us to what she calls the "Unhealthy Default Reality" of our modern culture.

Which leads us back to the question…

What's a "Healthy Deviant?"

Good question.

Here's the answer…

Pilar says: "A Healthy Deviant is any person who willingly defies unhealthy norms and conventions in order to achieve a high level of vitality, resilience, and autonomy."

The lead quote in the book is the quote I come back to more than any other in our 300-day Heroic Coach program.

It's from Jiddu Krishnamurti.

He tells us: "It is no measure of health to be well adjusted to a profoundly sick society."

Yep. That's about right.

In a society in which the VAST majority of us are sick and tired and anxious and depressed and, well, blah…

IT IS NO MEASURE OF HEALTH TO BE WELL ADJUSTED TO THAT SICK SOCIETY.

(Right?)

That's our +1°.

Embrace your healthy deviance.

TODAY.

STOIC HOSPITALS
EPICTETUS & SENECA IN SURGICAL GOWNS

S eneca, Epictetus, and Marcus Aurelius are the three great Roman Stoic philosophers.

Seneca was a statesman, billionaire, and literary genius. Epictetus was a former slave turned philosopher-teacher to Rome's elite young noblemen who taught the guys who taught the emperor-philosopher, Marcus Aurelius.

Pop quiz: Do you know the #1 rule of Stoicism?

Pop answer: The Stoics tell us that some things are within our control and some things are not. Our job as *warriors* of the mind is to focus on the things (our thoughts and our behaviors!) that are within our control.

Easier said than done, but it *is* that simple.

Today we're going to talk about the fact that both Seneca and Epictetus used the metaphor of a hospital to make the point of how hard it is to live a noble life.

Whereas a lot of the popular self-help gurus of their day (called "sophists") liked to make you feel really good at the end of their lectures as they made themselves feel really good, basking in a standing ovation, Epictetus tells us that attending a lecture by a Stoic philosopher should feel more like a trip to the HOSPITAL than a trip to the SPA.

Epictetus considered effective philosophy (and certainly effective teaching of Stoic philosophy) to feel more than a little uncomfortable.

No standing ovation for the philosopher at the end of his lecture. Everyone leaves in a bit of shock from the fierce demand to embrace reality—which typically feels more like *surgery* than a *massage*.

I, of course, love that.

Continuing our surgery/hospital metaphor…

When offering advice to a friend, Seneca liked to say that he wasn't trying to deliver it from a stage/soapbox as if he knew it all.

It was much more like he was in a hospital with his friend, lying on the table next to him and simply offering some insights he'd picked up along the way as a fellow traveler and patient getting put back together in the visit to the Heroic hospital that is part of a virtuous, noble life.

I, of course, love that as well. A lot.

And… That's our +1°.

Is there anything in your life that could use a little surgical removal? How can YOU step up and practice your philosophy with a higher degree of grounded, fierce urgency?

I'm over here in a matching gown wishing you luck with your procedure as I engage in mine.

Day 1. All in.

LET'S GO, HERO.

MEMENTO MORI
WANT TO LIVE? REMEMBER DEATH

I magine the glory days of the Roman Empire.

Picture a huge crowd celebrating a victorious general returning from a successful battle.

The general is in his chariot, basking in the praise of an adoring crowd. He's feeling pretty good.

Now, look a little closer and what you'll see is an advisor sitting behind the general. That advisor has one job—to whisper something into the general's ear.

What does he whisper?

Here's a hint: It's not "You rock! Well done." The general is receiving enough praise from the world.

Our advisor's job? He whispers a variation on a couple themes—either saying *sic transit gloria* or *memento mori*.

Sic transit gloria?

That's Latin for "all glory is fleeting."

Memento mori?

That's Latin for "remember death." As in: Remember that YOU will soon die.

So, again, back to our parade. The crowds cheer. Our advisor reminds us that all glory is fleeting. It's time to remember death.

Why in the world would we want to do that?

Well, ancient philosophers (from the Stoics to the Buddha) didn't *run away* from death.

They EMBRACED the fact that we're going to die and even went so far as to encourage us to *rehearse* our own deaths.

Why?

In short: We contemplate death to fully embrace the preciousness of life.

Memento Mori.

P.S. I have Ryan Holiday's *Memento Mori* coin on my desk to remind me of the power of this practice.

TIME TRAVELING
HANGING OUT WITH THE FUTURE YOU

See that time machine over there? Yep. That one. Let's hop in. Please secure that seatbelt.

Ready? LET'S GO.

BOOM.

It's five years from now.

Unfasten that seat belt of yours. Step out of the time machine. And... Who do we see?

It's YOU!!

Only...

It's the most RADIANTLY ALIVE version of you that you can possibly imagine.

GASP.

Would you look at YOU?!?

You're clearly in the best energetic shape of your life. You're calm. Confident. Energized. Tranquil. You're HAPPY.

No... More than that. You're JOYFUL. You're alive and flourishing and clearly living in integrity with your deepest values. Amazing.

Now... You and your Heroic-Best You get to spend ONE MINUTE together.

What does THAT version of you have to tell the current version of you?

If you feel so inspired...

Pause. Reflect.

Imagine the most optimized, Heroic version of you five years from now. You're living in integrity with your deepest values and flourishing in every area of your life.

Here's the question: What does THAT version of you want THIS version of you to know?

What ONE thing does FUTURE YOU tell CURRENT YOU?

Got it?

Write that down.

And, most importantly…

Follow that advice.

TODAY.

A QUICK TRIP TO HELL
WAKE UP! THIS ISN'T A DRESS REHEARSAL

That last time-traveling reflection exercise was inspired by two of the world's leading positive psychologists.

In her book *The How of Happiness*, Sonja Lyubomirsky tells us that "best-selves exercises" like that one are some of the most robust ways to boost our hope and well-being.

Tal Ben-Shahar offers a time-traveling exercise of his own in his great book *Happier*, in which he tells us that we ALL ALREADY HAVE ALL THE WISDOM WE NEED—we just need to tap into it and then live in integrity with it.

It's time to invite another one of my all-time favorite positive psychologists to join us. Then we'll take another little trip in that time-traveling machine.

Hero, meet Caroline Adams Miller. In my opinion, Caroline is one of *the* most practical positive psychologists in the world.

In her *great* book *Getting Grit*, she walks us through the science of grit and helps us apply it to our lives.

One of the main lessons from her book is the fact that gritty people don't fear failure. They KNOW (!) that to do great things they will, inevitably, fail. A lot.

As she says: "They have to go outside their comfort zone over and over to get where they want, all the while with no guarantee of success. That doesn't stop them, though; they'd rather bet on themselves than accept a life in which they'll never know what might have been."

That last line about preferring to bet on themselves rather than accept a life in which they'll never know what they might have been reminds me of two things.

First, I'm reminded of Sonja Lyubomirsky's wisdom on the Science of Regret.

Short story: We have a weird ability to adapt to whatever hardships we face in our lives. So our failures don't actually wind up bothering us as much as we think they will.

We're poor "affective forecasters" as the behavioral economists like to say.

But…

The stuff we never *really* went for? *That* has the potential to create a bunch of regret over the course of our lives—which is one of the reasons why people on their deathbeds don't regret their failures as much as they regret the risks they didn't take.

All of which reminds me of this…

"Someone once told me the definition of Hell: The last day you have on earth, the person you became will meet the person you could have become."

Yikes.

With *that* in mind, it's time to take another trip in our time-traveling machine. This time it's not going to be as pleasant.

We're going to the very end of our lives.

Take a deep breath.

Hold on tight.

And…

We're there.

We get out of our magical time-traveling machine and ... We see you on your deathbed.

Only, gulp, something's not quite right ...

It's clear that you DID NOT listen to the advice you got from that heavenly Heroic version of you with whom we just spent some time.

Eek. You can feel the pain of regret that this version of you is experiencing.

It's heartbreaking.

Then ...

Right as you are about to take your last breath ...

The door to your room opens ...

And ...

In walks that best, most Heroic version of you. Aged, but just as vitally alive and joyful and loving as ever. *That* version of you looks at the *other* version of you with compassion and sadness.

Then ...

You're gone.

Some would say that that is one definition of Hell—to meet the version of you that you COULD have become right when it was too late to do anything about it.

Good news. It's NOT too late to do something about it.

It doesn't matter how long we might have allowed ourselves to get hypnotized by the power of poor choices and bad habits.

TODAY IS THE DAY for us to step up and decide to activate our Heroic potential.

Wake up!! This isn't a dress rehearsal, Hero.

THE ULTIMATE END
LET'S BEGIN WITH THIS IN MIND

W e're going to take ONE more trip in that time machine.

Before we do, let's take a nice, deep breath. In through your nose. Down into your belly. Back out through your nose—exhaling slightly longer than your inhale as you release any tension that might have arisen.

Sit up a little taller. Bring a smile to your face.

It's time for one more trip.

This one's sobering but beautiful.

We're going all the way to the end of your life again, only this time, you showed up more and more consistently as that best, most Heroic version of yourself.

Not perfectly, of course, as there ARE NO PERFECT HUMAN BEINGS.

But you did it.

You lived a great life you're proud of.

Step out of the time machine one last time. We're at someone's end of life celebration. And it's truly a celebration.

This person clearly lived a wonderfully Heroic life.

You look inside the casket and see…

That person is YOU.

People are laughing and crying and sharing memories of how you inspired them and changed their lives. It's time to pull up a chair and listen to the eulogies.

Who says what?

Seriously.

Pause for a moment and feel into being at your own memorial service.

WHO SAYS WHAT?

And what do you HOPE they have to say about you?

What virtues do you hope they think of when they talk about you?

Know this: The ultimate purpose of everything we will do together is simple...

We're going to help you be THAT version of yourself. Never perfectly, but more and more consistently.

When?

As always...

Starting TODAY.

P.S. Now that we know the ultimate game and how to play it well, it's time to learn Rule #1 of a good, noble life as we forge antifragile confidence in Objective II.

- (I) KNOW THE ULTIMATE GAME
- (II) **FORGE ANTIFRAGILE CONFIDENCE**
- (III) OPTIMIZE YOUR BIG 3
- (IV) MAKE TODAY A MASTERPIECE
- (V) MASTER YOURSELF
- (VI) DOMINATE THE FUNDAMENTALS
- (VII) ACTIVATE YOUR SUPERPOWER

RULE #1
IT'S SUPPOSED TO BE CHALLENGING

Welcome to Objective II.

Now that we know the ultimate game and how to play it well, it's time to forge some antifragile confidence.

We'll define "antifragile" and "confidence" in a moment. Then we'll enter the "forge" and give you a bunch of tools to get your mental toughness dialed in before giving you a ticket to invincibility.

But…

First, we need to start with Rule #1 of a good, Heroic life. Let's put it in bold and all caps to make sure we don't miss it…

RULE #1: IT'S SUPPOSED TO BE CHALLENGING.

I know that sounds obvious, but truly getting this can change your life.

In fact, the story you might be telling yourself about why you *shouldn't* have to deal with all those challenges in your life is, arguably, THE greatest obstacle to your deep, sustainable, eudaimonic happiness.

There are a bunch of ways to bring this point home.

Let's start with this…

What's your all-time favorite inspiring movie?

Maybe *Star Wars*? Or *Harry Potter*? Or perhaps *The Matrix, Black Panther,* or *The Shawshank Redemption*?

Or maybe it's *The Hunger Games*, *The Wizard of Oz*, *Apollo 13*, or *Schindler's List*?

What's the ONE thing *your* favorite inspiring movie and all those other inspiring movies have in common?

Quite simply...

All those movies feature a hero who faced extraordinary challenges. If they didn't, you would have gotten up and walked out of the movie theater. (Right?)

Well...

If you want to live a life that makes YOU feel inspired, you better learn how to get EXCITED about facing all of life's challenges.

I repeat Rule #1 of a good, noble, Heroic life: It's SUPPOSED to be challenging.

Period.

It's time to learn how to embrace that fact and turn every challenge into an opportunity to activate your Heroic potential.

It's time to forge your antifragile confidence.

THE SOUL GYM
STYROFOAM WEIGHTS VS. REAL WEIGHTS

Here's another way to think about Rule #1.

I got this metaphor from Steve Chandler—the brilliant coach and prolific author with whom I worked 1-on-1 for several years before I started working with Phil Stutz.

Let's say you want to get stronger. So, you go to the gym.

But, when you go to the gym, you don't lift any real weights. You decide to bang out some reps with STYROFOAM weights.

Sure, that's a lot easier than lifting real weights but, Captain Obvious here, we're not going to get any stronger if we don't actually challenge ourselves by lifting some REAL weights, eh?

Same with life.

If we want to build Heroic strength for two, we've gotta be willing to lift some real weights.

All those challenges in your life—from the little things to the bigger things?

Those are the weights in your Heroic soul gym.

We'd be wise to see them as such.

EXONERATION
PART II OF RULE #1

O ne more thing before we move on to define some key terms. You need to know that Rule #1 of a good, noble, Heroic life has two parts.

Part I: As we discussed, it's supposed to be challenging. And...

Part II: As my beloved coach Phil Stutz puts it, you're never going to be exonerated. In other words, you're *never* going to get to a place where you *don't* have challenges.

Now, that might sound like bad news but... again... When we *really* get this, it's the most liberating news imaginable.

Why? Because once we *really* get the fact that it's SUPPOSED to be challenging AND that we're *never* going to get to a place where it isn't, we can quit beating ourselves up and stop shaming ourselves for not being perfect.

We can see the fact that we're experiencing challenges (and inevitably feeling overwhelmed/etc. at times) not because something's wrong with us.

We're experiencing challenges because we're HUMAN.

In fact, when you *really* REALLY get this, you'll see all your challenges as "reverse indicators"—not that you're doing something wrong but that you're doing something right.

You're a hero battling the dragons that inevitably show up on our quests—striving to do so with more and more wisdom, discipline, love, courage, gratitude, hope, curiosity, and zest.

In a word... *Areté*.

Let's close the gap.

And activate your Heroic potential.

TODAY.

ANTIFRAGILITY
ARE YOU FRAGILE, RESILIENT, OR...

N ow that we've established Rule #1 of the ultimate game, it's time to define some key terms.

Let's start with one of my all-time favorite words: *antifragile*.

I picked this word up from Nassim Taleb.

He wrote a whole book on the subject, appropriately called *Antifragile*, in which he walks us through the fact that there's a big difference between being fragile, being resilient, and being antifragile.

Although Taleb focuses primarily on macroeconomic, technological, and cultural systems, we're going to focus on YOU and your life.

Here's the short story.

You can be *fragile* and break easily. You can be *resilient* and withstand more stress before breaking down (and then bouncing back a little quicker than most). OR ... You can be the OPPOSITE of fragile.

What would happen if, the MORE you got kicked around, the STRONGER you got?

Seriously.

What would that be called?

You'd be *ANTIFRAGILE*.

And, frankly, if there's ONE THING I hope you get from this book, it's THIS idea.

Those obstacles? When you view them from the right perspective, they can (and should!) make you stronger. Period.

Taleb gives us a great metaphor to bring the point home. Imagine the wind. It's a strong wind.

Now...

That strong wind will EXTINGUISH a candle.

But...

It will FUEL a FIRE.

The question is, when you face the inevitable (emphasis on INEVITABLE!) "winds" of life, are you showing up like a candle and getting blown out by the first breeze OR are you showing up with a HEROIC FIRE such that those winds FUEL your fire?

Helping you rub your hands together with a smile as you laugh with the Heroic gods and thank them for the challenges they've blessed us with is one of my primary intentions with this book.

Which is why the Heroic mantra isn't "OM." It's "OMMS." As in: "OBSTACLES MAKE ME STRONGER."

Chant it with me now: *"OMMS!"*

And, if you feel so inspired, chant it to YOURSELF every single time YOU face an obstacle in your life.

TODAY.

CONFIDENCE
WHAT IT REALLY IS & HOW TO CREATE IT

I t's time to define another one of my favorite words: *confidence.*

Etymologically, the word *confidence* comes from two little Latin words: *con* and *fidere*.

The word literally means "with intense trust."

Intense trust in WHAT? Not that everything will go perfectly. That, of course, is crazy.

We need to cultivate an intense trust in *ourselves* such that it DOESN'T MATTER what happens because we know that we are the type of people who can do what needs to get done whether we feel like it or not.

We need to INTENSELY TRUST ourselves, such that we KNOW that we can not only handle whatever life throws at us, but we can get STRONGER as a result.

Enter: Antifragile Confidence.

And guess what? That level of intense trust (and the true, grounded, Heroic, antifragile confidence that comes from it), is, like every other form of trust, earned.

You need to earn that trust in yourself all day every day. You know how you do that?

The same way you earn trust in ANY relationship.

You do what you say you will do.

THE SCIENCE OF CONFIDENCE
ALBERT BANDURA SAYS...

L et's talk about the science of confidence.

Albert Bandura is one of the most respected psychologists in the world. He studies the science of self-efficacy. Also known as: the science of confidence.

Here's a quick take on what we know.

A sense of self-efficacy—a belief that you can achieve what you set out to achieve—is, to put it in technical terms, SUPER important.

For example, if you want to predict who will win a wrestling match between equally talented competitors, find out which one has a stronger belief in his ability to win. And bet on them.

There's scientifically validated wisdom in Henry Ford's quip: "Whether we think we can or think we can't, we're right."

Bandura tells us that there are four primary ways we can build self-efficacy: mastery experience, vicarious learning, social persuasion, and physiology.

Let's briefly explore each.

Mastery Experience: In other words, past success. Small and big wins from the past are great ways to boost your current confidence.

Create those wins, feast on them as you build your self-image as someone who succeeds ("That's like me!"), and bring those past mastery experiences to mind when you're facing current challenges.

Vicarious Learning: In other words, seeing *someone else* achieve the success YOU would like to achieve. Basic idea here: If *they* can do it, YOU can do it. KNOW that.

Note: DO NOT get *envious* of their success. Celebrate it. And say: "If they can do it, I can do it."

Social Persuasion: In other words, someone *tells* you that you can achieve success. Like a coach. Or a supportive parent or a friend. (Or ME: "You've got this, Hero!")

You can also persuade *yourself* through positive self-talk and an antifragile, confident mindset. (And remember to be the one persuading *others* of their potential!)

Physiology: In other words, if you want to succeed, ACT like a successful person.

Flip the switch. Walk, talk, breathe and carry yourself as the best, most Heroic version of yourself.

The +1°…

With all that in mind, let's turn up the heat with a quick check-in…

What's a past success we can celebrate?

Who has achieved something you'd like to achieve?

Who's supported you and what did they say?

When you're at your best, how do you walk, talk (to yourself and others!), breathe and hold yourself?

There ya go. That's the quick 1-2-3-4 on the science of confidence. Here's to your self-efficacy, Hero!

"BRING IT ON!"
REVERSING YOUR DESIRE

Now that we know Rule #1 of this wonderful game of life and we've defined what it means to forge antifragile confidence, we need to understand the proper way to handle life's (inevitable!) challenges.

In short, we need to learn how to eat them like energy bars.

Let's explore *three* powerful ways to go about doing that. They can be summarized in three Heroic mantras: "Bring it on!," "I'm excited!," and "OMMS!"

Let's start with "Bring it on!"

Phil Stutz and Barry Michels wrote a great book called *The Tools*. There are five tools in the book that help us deal with the biggest challenges we all face in our lives.

The most important tool in the book is the first one. It's called "The Reversal of Desire" and helps us deal with THE most powerful challenge: Fear.

Phil and Barry tell us that most people like to live within their comfort zones.

Why is that?

Well, what does it feel like outside of our comfort zones? By definition, it's uncomfortable.

And most people hate feeling any level of discomfort so they pretty much do everything they can to avoid the pain of being outside their comfort zone.

Now, that's great if being mediocre is your goal, but not so great if you're serious about living your greatest life and activating your Heroic potential.

Here's the deal…

Your *infinite* (!) potential exists on the *other* side of your comfort zone.

And, again, what does it *feel* like when you exit your comfort zone and start exploring the zone of your infinite potential?

You feel fear. Doubt. Anxiety. Fill in the blank with the pain of your favorite sense of discomfort.

So…

Knowing that our infinite potential exists on the *other* side of our comfort zone *and* that we feel pain/discomfort/ etc. when we exit our comfort zone en route to our infinite potential, if we're serious about optimizing our lives to activate our Heroic potential, we need to REVERSE OUR DESIRE— rather than try to *avoid* pain, we need to learn to love it.

We need to see those moments when our heart skips a beat and our palms start to sweat as the gifts that they are—tickets to our destiny.

Which leads us to the tool. It's simple.

The next time you feel even an *inkling* of fear/doubt/etc., practice saying to yourself (more precisely, Phil and Barry tell us to *scream* to yourself), "BRING IT ON!"

Know that your *infinite* (!) potential exists *just* on the other side of your comfort zone.

And, very importantly, know that you don't need to (and shouldn't try to!) go a *mile* outside your comfort zone. Just get in the habit of going an *inch* outside your comfort zone.

Every. Single. Time you feel that *whisper* of fear, get in the habit of reminding yourself that *this* is the opportunity to get a little stronger as you say to yourself "BRING IT ON!"

Something magical happens when we do this.

In fact, science shows that we fundamentally change on a PHYSIOLOGICAL level. By INVITING the challenges into our lives, we move from what researchers call a "threat response" to a "challenge response" and, when we do that, our entire bodies change.

"Bring it on!"

Try it.

It works.

"I'M EXCITED!"
WHAT TO SAY WHEN YOU'RE NERVOUS

A lison Wood Brooks is a researcher at Harvard Business School. She's studied the most effective strategies for dealing with acute stress.

First, a little test: Imagine that you need to give a big presentation in front of a bunch of people. Your heart's been pounding for days at the mere thought of this talk. Palms are sweaty. All that.

What should you tell yourself? Should you try to calm down or should you try to feel excited?

When Alison asked that question to hundreds of people, the response was nearly unanimous: 91% said they thought the best advice was to try to calm down.

But…

That's not what her research shows is most effective.

Get this…

Alison brought people into her lab and gave them a super-stressful test. She made them give an impromptu speech—something that has been proven to do a *very* good job at eliciting a very high level of stress.

(Side note: Did you know that people are more afraid of public speaking than dying? Yep. That's why Jerry Seinfeld once joked that "If you have to go a funeral, you're better off in the casket than doing the eulogy." Hah!)

So, back to our study.

Everyone is told they have to give a speech. The normal stress response kicks in. She instructs half of them to say to themselves: "I am calm." The other half were instructed to say: "I'm excited!"

Guess what? The "I'm excited!" group *way* outperformed the group that tried to calm themselves down.

Why is that?

Because anxiety is what scientists call a "high-arousal state" while being calm is a "low-arousal state." It's almost impossible to shift from a high-arousal state of fear/anxiety/etc. *immediately* into a calm state. It's like cruising at eighty miles an hour and slamming on the brakes. Not a good idea.

Much wiser to take all that fear energy and simply reframe it as excitement—channeling it into a positive, constructive direction and, effectively, pressing go on the accelerator rather than stop.

Simply saying *"I'm excited!"* is a surprisingly powerful way to make that happen.

So…

If you feel so inspired, the next time YOU feel yourself getting energized before something important to you, remember to say…

"I'm excited!"

OMMS
THE HERO'S MANTRA

I love Spartan Races.

There's something about *paying* to face obstacles that so perfectly captures the spirit of everything we need to do to activate our Heroic potential.

Joe De Sena, founder of Spartan Race and grit exemplar extraordinaire, tells us that we want to become "immune to obstacles."

Imagine being IMMUNE to obstacles such that they have no effect on you. In fact, let's take it one step further and remind ourselves that, when properly framed, obstacles *literally* make us stronger.

Of course, the obstacle course is simply a physical representation of the mental and emotional and creative obstacles we all face every day.

We want to get immune to those obstacles. We want to see that they make us stronger. And we want to see that truth IN THE MOMENT the Heroic gods are blessing us with an unexpected challenge.

That's why I created the Heroic mantra to help me internalize this...

OMMS. Obstacles Make Me Stronger.

OMMS. The hero's mantra.

OMMS. Chant it with me now, with a fierce determination

in our souls and a smile on our faces, knowing we have what it takes to meet any and every challenge life throws at us.

OMMS. OMMS. OMMS.

All day. Every day.

Especially…

TODAY.

P.S. This isn't just a pom-pom waving, peak performance idea. The great spiritual teacher Sri Swami Satchidananda uses the same metaphor of an obstacle course in *his* brilliant book *The Golden Present.*

And, know this: His book is laid out as a series of daily inspirational readings one can enjoy throughout the year.

On January 1 (Day 1!), he tells us: "Life must be a challenge. Only then is it exciting. In an obstacle race, you are forced to surmount all the obstacles: to jump over the hurdles, go through the barrels, crawl under the rugs, climb over walls.

What would happen if, to avoid all that, you went around all the obstacles and asked for the winner's cup? Would they give it to you? No. They would say, 'You must go back and face all the obstacles.'

… Make your life as exciting as possible, but always think of it as fun. The adversities as well as the harmony should be enjoyable. Don't become sober and morose and have a castor oil face in the name of spirituality. Just be happy. Jump with joy. Even if you make a mistake, say, 'Hey, I did this? Great! What a wonderful lesson I learned!' If you really want to, you can make everything fun."

DALIO'S 5 STEPS TO SUCCESS
& MISTAKE-LEARNER'S HIGHS

Now that we have a few powerful tools to help us properly handle challenges, it's time to learn how to deal with what you call "failure."

Here's the short story with that one: IT'S ALL DATA!

When we properly frame our experiences in life, there's no such thing as "winning" or "losing." We either win or we learn and learning IS winning so...

We WIN or we WIN. Period.

Of course, there will be times when we don't hit the targets we set for ourselves, but that in no way implies we "failed" in the way we tend to think of that word as long as we're practicing our philosophy and using that data to get a little better.

Don't believe me? Perfect.

How about Ray Dalio?

As you may know, Ray Dalio is one of the most successful people alive. *Time* magazine says he's one of the one hundred most influential people on the planet while *Fortune* magazine says his company (Bridgewater Associates) is the fifth most important private company in the U.S. while *Forbes* tells us he's one of the one hundred wealthiest people alive.

How'd he achieve that extraordinary level of success?

In his book *Principles* he walks us through precisely how he does it. In fact, he shares a "Five-Step Process to Get What You Want in Life."

Before we take a quick look at that process, let's step back and look at a complementary framework Dalio shares.

He tells us that the whole point of life is to evolve, and he draws beautiful upward spirals to capture the essence of a good life.

In short: We start with an audacious goal. Then we FAIL. Then we learn. Then we improve. Then we set even more audacious goals. And we repeat the process. Forever.

(Did you notice that second step? Yep. We set audacious goals and THEN WE FAIL!! More on that in a moment.)

For now, back to our 5-Step Process to Get What You Want in Life that mirrors his higher-level process of evolving.

The five steps include Goals, Problems, Diagnosis, Design, and Doing. The process goes something like this:

Step 1. We need **Goals**. What do you want? Get clear. Visualize it. Know your why.

Step 2. Identify the **Problems** you're facing that are preventing you from reaching your goal. Most (unsuccessful) people (with a fixed mindset) like to pretend that they'll be able to achieve their goals without hiccups. The best among us, Dalio tells us, KNOW they will face obstacles and use them as fuel to evolve.

Step 3. **Diagnose** the problem. What's at the root of your problems? Get clear.

Step 4. **Design** a solution to the problem. What do you need to do to solve the riddle? As Dalio would put it, build a "machine" that will solve your problem.

Step 5. Get to work **Doing** what needs to be done.

Again: You start with an audacious goal. Then you fail. Then you figure out why you failed. Then you design a better solution to your challenge. Then you get to work on the solution.

Then you spiral up and repeat that process of evolving into a slightly better version of you.

For how long? E N D L E S S L Y.

Now, Dalio tells us that it's REALLY important to fall in love with that process. ESPECIALLY (!) the part most people shy away from—that whole failing part.

Question: "But can't I just evolve without all those mistakes?" (Insert laughter from all wise teachers ever.)

Answer: "No. You can't."

Therefore, the wisest among us tell us that we want to fall so deeply in love with the *process* of making mistakes and then getting a little better that we're kinda like a runner who hits a certain point during his or her run where the pain goes away and the "runner's high" takes over.

Dalio calls this a "mistake-learner's high."

You're so engaged in the dynamic process of optimizing that you learn to *LOVE* the mistakes—knowing that they're just part of the process of going after something audacious and the perfect data/fuel to activate your Heroic potential just a little more today.

MIS-TAKES
EMBRACE THEM AS YOU CREATE A MASTERPIECE

I n his great book *Spiritual Liberation*, Michael Bernard Beckwith redefines "mistakes" as "mis-takes."

He tells us to imagine ourselves as the director of a movie.
We have a huge budget, an amazing crew, the best actors in the
world and an impeccable script.

Question: Do you think you're going to film the whole movie
in one long, perfect take?

Even with decades of experience and the best of everything
you know that's ABSURD!!!

Of course (!) you're going to have to re-do most scenes.
Some *over* and *over* and *over* again until you get them right.
Those are all just *mis-takes*. No big deal. All part of the pro-
cess, right?

Well, guess what?

Same rules apply to that life of yours you're directing.
You WILL need to reshoot some scenes. A lot of them. Some
A TON of times.

Those mistakes you're making?

They're really just "mis-takes." Not a big deal. Just step back
and take another shot at it.

Science agrees on this point as well.

Robert Biswas-Diener wrote the book on the science of courage called *The Courage Quotient*. He tells us that courage is all
about being willing to act in the presence of fear.

One of the examples *he* uses in *his* book is from the movies as well. He quotes an Oscar-winning director friend of his who shoots HUNDREDS of hours of film to create a ninety-minute movie.

Only 1% of the stuff he shoots ever makes it into the final product. Was the other 99% a "failure"?

Of course not.

As Biswas-Diener says, the key "is to not treat mistakes as though they are barely acceptable but to embrace them as if they were your friends and also gateways to creativity, confidence, and spontaneity."

THAT is how to deal with what we call failure.

It's ALL data.

We win or we learn and learning IS WINNING so let's WIN or WIN.

When?

As always...

TODAY.

THERE ARE NO PERFECT HUMANS
& YOU AND I WON'T BE THE FIRST

I f we're looking for things that get in the way of our eudaimonic joy and antifragile confidence, thinking that we shouldn't be experiencing challenge-problems would be at the top of the list.

Closely related would be the sense that something must be wrong with *us* because we *are* experiencing those challenges.

When we forget Rule #1 and THEN tell ourselves we must be inherently flawed because our lives aren't perfect, we run the risk of cooking up a toxic brew of perfectionistic shame—which, of course, is not a wise idea.

Therefore, if we're serious about forging some world-class antifragile confidence, we better hit this whole shame thing hard as well.

Let's invite three of my favorite psychologists to share their wisdom on this subject: Abraham Maslow, Tal Ben-Shahar, and Kristin Neff.

First, Maslow.

As you may know, Abraham Maslow was a humanistic psychologist who came up with the whole "hierarchy of needs."

He basically said that as you take care of basic needs (like food and shelter and then a sense of belongingness and self-esteem), you get to a point where the need to actualize your potential is, as we discussed, as real as your need to breathe.

As part of his research, Maslow studied the greatest people of his generation—extraordinary humans like Albert Einstein and Eleanor Roosevelt. These were truly great people who, in his words, had "self-actualized" their potential and, in my words, had given their greatest gifts in Heroic service to the world.

But... Here's the deal.

These self-actualizing exemplars were NOT perfect.

Not even a single one of them.

Which is why Maslow said so unequivocally that there simply are NO perfect people.

Movers and shakers? Yep.

Truly great people? Yep.

Perfect people? Not even one.

It's INCREDIBLY important that we keep that in mind as we pursue our own vision of optimizing and actualizing. I repeat: There are no perfect humans.

And...

Newsflash...

You and I won't be the first.

PERFECTIONISM, SCIENCE OF
OPTIMALIST VS. PERFECTIONIST

T al Ben-Shahar taught one of the largest classes in Harvard's history—on the science of positive psychology.

In one of his great books called *The Pursuit of Perfect*, he tells us that there are two distinct forms of perfectionism—one of them is adaptive and the other is not.

He tells us they are so different that they need different names.

There's the unhealthy perfectionist who suffers from all the things you'd expect from perfectionism: anxiety, depression, etc. He calls them a "Perfectionist."

Then, there's the healthy, high-functioning perfectionist who uses those high standards to fuel their growth. He calls them an "Optimalist."

Perfectionist vs. Optimalist.

Here's the primary difference between the two.

The (unhealthy) Perfectionist fails to embrace reality. They actually think they can work for sixteen hours a day in pursuit of their great work while staying super healthy and being a great spouse and parent and being super active in the community and a great friend to dozens and… (I get stressed just typing that.)

The source of their misery is the fact that they fail to embrace the constraints of reality. They simply CAN'T do all of those things. Then, when they inevitably fall short of their expectations, they beat themselves up mercilessly and experience all the negative effects of unhealthy perfectionism.

The (healthy) Optimalist?

They have really high standards and want to be a great creator, spouse, parent, friend, and vital human, but they rub their vision up against reality. They see only so many hours in a day and construct their optimal life within the boundaries of those healthy constraints.

Note: The word "optimal" is derived from the Latin *optimus* which means the "best"—not the "perfect." In this case: The best within the constraints of our individual realities.

Spotlight on you…

Do you tend to be a Perfectionist or an Optimalist?

Remember: It's all about holding our high standards WHILE embracing the constraints of reality.

SELF-COMPASSION, SCIENCE OF
SELF-KINDNESS, COMMON HUMANITY & MINDFULNESS

As we go ALL IN on closing the gap and trying to activate our Heroic potential, it's easy to get overwhelmed.

That's when the science of self-compassion comes in. Here's what you need to know.

First, the science is unequivocal: Shame is super toxic. It does nothing but erode our ability to function at a high level and enjoy the process.

We need to learn how to cultivate self-compassion.

According to Kristin Neff—the world's leading Self-Compassion researcher who literally wrote the book on the subject—we need to embrace *three* things if we want to cultivate our self-compassion.

First, we need to be nice to ourselves.

She calls it "self-kindness." This is pretty straightforward but super important to keep in mind.

When you're facing a setback and feel yourself slipping into toxic rumination, talk to yourself the way you'd talk to a dear friend (or child).

In other words: BE NICE!!

Then, we need to embrace what Kristin calls "common humanity." We need to know that we're not alone.

We ALL experience challenging times.

The fact that you're anxious/upset/stressed/whatever isn't about *you* being *you* per se. It's about you *being human*.

Finally, we need to be mindful.

In short, we need to notice the negative emotions and negative self-talk that's arising, then simply label it without dropping into the ruminative chaos and move on with living the next moment of your life.

Self-kindness. Common humanity. Mindfulness.

Think of those as the key ingredients for your healing balm. And remember to apply that healing balm generously to the inevitable dragon scars you *will* get on your hero's journey.

DRAGON SCARS
WEAR THEM LIKE MEDALS

S peaking of dragon scars …

Paulo Coelho comes to mind. In one of his great books, he tells us: "I don't regret the painful times; I bare my scars as if they were medals."

Think about that for a moment.

Most of us try to hide all of our scars. But not the Heroic among us. The wise hero KNOWS that we can't go out fighting dragons for a living and not get clawed up on occasion.

The Heroic among us (and all of us at our Heroic Best) don't shamefully hide those scars. They (and we) proudly show them off.

"Yep. Got that one fighting that huge, mean dragon in the Andes."

"Oh, that one? Hah. Yah. Wow. That was a BEAST! Should have seen it. Almost took me out."

"Oh, man. Yah. That was another crazy one…"

Those scars?

They are the hero's MEDALS—badges of honor that prove that we've been willing to step up and enter the arena again and again.

All of which begs the question: Do you have any scars you've been hiding? Is now a good time to redefine them as medals earned as part of your hero training?!

Fantastic.

One more time: Let's remember that there are no perfect human beings and...

You and I won't be the first.

Let's embrace the constraints of our reality as good optimalists as we stock up on the healing balm and wear those scars like antifragile medals.

TODAY.

GRIT, SCIENCE OF
INTENSE PASSION & PERSEVERANCE

No conversation about forging antifragile confidence would be complete without a discussion of the science of grit—which leads us back to the University of Pennsylvania to hang out with one of Martin Seligman's colleagues: Angela Duckworth.

Angela is the world's leading researcher on what she calls "grit." She's dedicated her life to helping us all (especially our next generation of heroes!) cultivate this essential quality.

In her great (!) book, appropriately called *Grit*, she walks us through the origin story of her theories and then gives us a practical framework we can use to cultivate grit in our lives and in the lives of our families, communities, and world.

First, the origin story.

Angela visited the United States Military Academy—also known as West Point—where some of the brightest and most committed aspiring leaders go to prepare themselves to serve our country.

These young men and women spend years working hard to get into West Point.

Then … An astonishing number of them would drop out in the first seven weeks of training called "Beast Barracks."

"Beast," as it's known, is a deliberately challenging initiation designed to help them "make the transition from new cadet to Soldier."

But… The Army couldn't figure out WHY those who dropped out were dropping out.

Enter: Angela. She cultivated a simple ten-question test called the "Grit Scale." And… She figured it out.

Although the young cadets' "Whole Candidate Score" (which measures things like GPA, SAT, and leadership and athletic experience) did predict who would do well over the course of the four years at West Point, it DID NOT predict who would actually make it through those first seven weeks.

Angela's simple Grit Scale provided the most accurate prediction of who would make it through.

As she says: "Half of the questions were about perseverance. They asked how much you agree with statements like 'I have overcome setbacks to conquer an important challenge' and 'I finish whatever I begin.'

The other half of the questions were about passion. They asked whether your 'interests change from year to year' and the extent to which you 'have been obsessed with a certain idea or project for a short time but later lost interest.'"

In short, grit has two variables: Intense passion + intense perseverance.

We'll talk about the FOUR things you can do to build your grit in our next +1°. For now…

How's *your* passion and *your* perseverance?

Let's turn up the heat on both as we activate our Heroically gritty potential.

PSYCHOLOGICAL ASSETS
FOUR OF THEM TO BUILD GRIT

I n our last +1°, we talked about Angela Duckworth and her science of grit.

As you may recall, Angela defines grit as intense passion plus intense persistence.

Note #1: Notice the use of the word "intense." Remember our 451° activation energy point!

Note #2: The type of passion Angela is talking about is, she tells us, more like a COMPASS than a fireworks display. We're not getting fired up by one flashy thing after another. We get REALLY clear on who we are and what we're committed to and then we dedicate our lives to following that North Star.

In *Grit*, Angela walks us through the primary obstacles we all face in trying to cultivate our grit and she gives us four "psychological assets" we want to cultivate to meet those challenges.

Here they are: Interest + Practice + Purpose + Hope.

1. **Interest**. If we want to cultivate sustainable passion, we need to be intrinsically drawn to what we do. It needs to be what scientists call "self-concordant." It's not a "should." We need to love it.

Of course, we all have facets of our lives that aren't particularly awesome, but we're not going to put in the effort over the long run unless we, like the grit paragons, have an "enduring fascination and childlike curiosity" and "practically shout, 'I love what I do!'" (← Do you?)

2. **Practice**. Angela talks about Anders Ericsson's research on deliberate practice and juxtaposes/integrates it with Csikszentmihalyi's work on Flow in a powerful way.

She points out that one key aspect of perseverance is the ability to discipline ourselves to show up Every. Single. Day with an attitude of "Whatever it takes, I want to improve!" (← Do you?)

3. **Purpose**. Purpose is all about seeing that our work matters in the world. It's essential that we love what we do, but we're not going to sustain our interest over the long run if it's just about us. We need to make the connection to something bigger than ourselves.

Angela tells us that fully mature exemplars of grit invariably say things like: "My work is important—both to me and to others." As we would say, we need to have HEROIC strength for two! (← Do you?)

4. **Hope**. Angela tells us that hope defines every stage of grit. It's the "rising-to-the-occasion" kind of perseverance in which we KNOW that we have the ability to achieve what we set out to do.

Speaking of hope...

Do you remember the scientific 1 + 2 + 3?

Recall that we need to have a vision of a better future (a.k.a.: a Goal/Target) + a sense of Agency (or belief you can make it happen) and a plan plus a willingness to explore multiple Pathways (wisely doing whatever it takes for however long it takes to make that dream a reality). (← Do you?)

Finally, you know what else Angela says?

She tells us: "There's an old Japanese saying: 'Fall seven, rise eight.' If I were ever to get a tattoo, I'd get these four simple words indelibly inked."

Yep. Fall down seven times, rise eight. STRONGER. That's the essence of the Science of Antifragile Grit.

Let's cultivate it.

TODAY.

P.S. One of my all-time favorite teachers is a Stanford Professor named William Damon. His thinking on moral development and the power of purpose has influenced me and my thinking on the subjects profoundly.

I highly recommend his wonderful books *The Power of Ideals*, *Noble Purpose*, *A Path with Purpose*, and *A Round of Golf with My Father*.

In addition to being one of the world's leading scholars on purpose, he is an incredible human being and an inspiring demonstration of the wisdom and ideals to which he has dedicated his life to studying.

Also, for more on how to discover your purpose, check out Purpose 101 and Purpose 102 in the Heroic app, in which I share the Top 10 Big Ideas and 25 journal exercises/questions that have most shaped my life: Heroic.us/Activate.

RESPONSE-ABILITY
STIMULUS [GAP] RESPONSE

Now that we've defined antifragile and confidence and talked about some key practices, it's time to talk about one of our Heroic superpowers: Response-Ability.

Notice the two words there: "Response" and "Ability."

If we want to optimize our lives and activate our Heroic potential, we need to get really good at CHOOSING our response to any given situation.

As Viktor Frankl tells us, in that space between a stimulus and our response, there is a gap. In that gap is our freedom.

Remember that bus that said, "Welcome to Freedom"? (You know... The one that was taking people to a CASINO?!?)

Well, if Frankl had seen that, he would have winced and lectured us as well.

The REAL ticket to freedom? Being able to choose your response to any given situation.

Too many people (and most of us too often) think that how they respond to a given stimuli is determined by whatever it is that happened.

They miss the fact that it's our INTERPRETATION of that stimuli that determines our response.

It's stimulus → interpretation → response.

NOT stimulus → response.

Stephen Covey talks about this in his classic book *The 7 Habits of Highly Effective People*.

In fact, he tells us that this skill is so important that it's the #1 habit of highly effective heroes. He tells us that we need to "be proactive" rather than "reactive." That's EXACTLY what we're talking about here.

Why is being "proactive" his #1 habit? Because ALL the great teachers say the same thing. We need to be capable of choosing our response to any given situation.

Back to Viktor Frankl for a moment.

As you probably know, he experienced the horrors of the Holocaust during World War II. He lost his entire family—including his pregnant wife.

Yet… He REFUSED to give up what he called the last of the human freedoms—his freedom to CHOOSE his response to that situation.

He chose to show up and play his role as a psychiatrist in a concentration camp as well as he could—striving to give hope and meaning to others going through the same horrific ordeal as he used that experience to create the philosophy and therapeutic methodology (Logotherapy) he would later share with the world.

As you may *not* know, Frankl was deeply inspired by Epictetus and Stoicism. In fact, how he responded to the challenges in his life is the perfect modern exemplification of the core tenet of Stoicism: some things are within our control, others are not.

The wise person knows that, although we can't control the things that are happening to us, we CAN (and MUST!) control our responses to them.

THIS is another one of the hero's superpowers. We refuse to EVER give up our ultimate freedom.

That's Response-Ability—an essential component to forging Antifragile Confidence.

VICTIM VS. HERO
WHAT WILL IT BE?

N ot too long ago, we had a little chat about "The Dojo Decision" in which I challenged you to consider whether you're "going through the motions" or "going for mastery."

As we discussed, there's a BIG difference in how we approach life when we're ALL IN on being our best.

We also talked about The Choice of Hercules—and his decision to follow the Goddess of Virtue (*Areté!*) rather than the Goddess of Vice dressed up as Happiness.

Know this: Those decisions and choices aren't a "make it once and you're done forever" kinda thing.

We're CONSTANTLY being asked by life how we're going to show up and we need to CONSTANTLY recommit to being our best selves OVER and OVER and OVER again.

Which leads us to the ultimate choice we're going to make…

Are we going to be victims or are we going to be heroes?

Because, to state the obvious, the world has way more than enough victims complaining (and blaming and criticizing) and is in *desperate* need of more heroes who *refuse* to give up their last and ultimate freedom to choose to show up as powerfully as they can in the face of life's adversity.

So…

What will it be: Victim or Hero?

THAT is the ultimate question.

And, again, this is not an "I'm a HERO!!!" one-and-done kinda thing.

It's a moment to moment to moment all day every day kinda thing.

How do we make the shift from victim to hero?

One simple question will do the trick.

That's the focus of our next +1°.

TARGETED THINKING (PART II)
HOW TO MOVE FROM VICTIM TO HERO

O ne of the best little books you've probably never heard of is called *The Power of TED** by David Emerald.

It's a little fable with some big wisdom.

The basic idea goes something like this: There are two primary orientations with which we can show up in the world: as a Victim or as a Creator.

If you're a Victim, you perceive life's challenges (and challengers) as "Persecutors." Then you look for "Rescuers" to save you from life's challenges. David calls that the "Dreaded Drama Triangle" or "DDT" for short.

Victim-Persecutor-Rescuer.

We ALL spend WAY more time in that triad than we'd like to admit.

The other orientation? You can be a Creator.

When you're living from a Creator orientation, you see those *very same* challenges (and challengers) for what they are: "Challengers." Rather than try to get rescued (by someone or some addictive behavior), you seek "Coaches" who can support you in creating the life you want.

David calls that triad "The Empowerment Dynamic," or "TED" for short.

We could talk about that for a very long time.

For now, I want to focus on the ONE QUESTION that helps us IMMEDIATELY (!) move from Victim to Creator.

It's surprisingly simple and equally powerful.

Here it is: "What do I want?"

The Victim complains and complains and complains (and criticizes and blames and gossips and whines and …).

The Creator cuts through all that nonsense and asks: "WHAT DO I WANT?"

That's how we make the shift from Victim to Creator.

To go from Victim to Creator to HERO, we need to add a follow-up question.

Here it is: "Now what needs to be done?"

Put those two questions together and we have what I call Targeted Thinking.

Question #1: "What do I want?"

Question #2: "Now what needs to be done?"

Those two questions help us move from Victim to Creator to Hero while remaining grounded in reality AND getting us ready to focus on what needs to get done.

To recap: When facing ANY and EVERY challenge (that tempts you to get negative and start complaining, etc.), the first question to ask is: "What do I want?"

That provides a TARGET for our minds. When we get clarity on that target, the next question is simple and brings us to the task at hand: "Now what needs to be done?"

Life is challenging us? Perfect.

"What do I want?" Target set.

"Now what needs to be done?" Aim taken.

Then, most importantly, go do what needs to be done.

Targeted Thinking. Try it. It works.

CHICKEN POOP
YOUR STINKIN' THINKIN'

I n our last +1°, we chatted about Targeted Thinking.

I want to give you a couple of mundane, everyday examples of how I've applied this wisdom with our kids, then we'll go next level with it.

First, a little more context on how I came up with Targeted Thinking.

My framework for Targeted Thinking was inspired, in part, by a guy named Trevor Moawad, who wrote a book called *It Takes What It Takes*. He was NFL quarterback Russell Wilson's mental toughness coach.

The big idea from his book?

Something he called "neutral thinking."

Basic idea?

We can have "positive thinking" and ignore reality by only focusing on the "good" stuff. We can have "negative thinking" and ignore reality by only focusing on the "bad" stuff.

Neither of those are as effective as having "neutral thinking" in which we just allow whatever is to be what it is while we do what needs to get done to get what we want.

Today I want to bring that wisdom to life with a little story from the Johnson Ranch.

So… As I was reading that book a few years ago book, I took a break and explained this idea to Emerson.

Here's the example I used: Our chickens. And their poop.

Quick context: At the time, we had just moved to the country. We got some chickens because we thought they'd be awesome. They are. The kids love them, etc.

And…

Those gals (and guy) sure know how to poop! And, they seem to especially love to do their work under our beautiful back porch where I used to meditate in the morning as the sun was rising.

Let's just say that the meditation scene was slightly less idyllic with the smell of chicken poop wafting up. (Hah.)

So…

Back to the book.

I told Emerson that the guy who wrote the book had a dad who was really into all this stuff and taught him a bunch of these ideas when he was a kid. I smiled and rubbed his little head as I imagined what HE might have to say in a few decades.

Then we talked about the difference between negative thinking, positive thinking, and neutral thinking.

I gave him an example of my own negative thinking as it related to those chickens and their poop.

Note: That's *always* one of the best ways to deliver a message. Start with your own shortcomings—don't start with someone else's.

My negative thinking went something like this: "Those chickens! Their poop STINKS! Why do they need to hang out under the porch and then poop where they hang out? I think we might want to find them a new home."

(He might have heard me say something along those lines

more than once in my less-enlightened moments, so he quickly understood the example.)

Then I told him that the "positive" thinking would go something like this: "It's not so bad and the chickens are so great."

He immediately knew that that simply wasn't honest and/or true and wouldn't be the optimal approach.

Then I told him that *neither* of those approaches was as effective as neutral or TARGETED thinking.

Targeted thinking would go something like this: "The chickens are pooping under the patio. It stinks. The kids love them and we're going to keep them so we need to create a solution. Let's limit their access to that location and figure out a poop control protocol. Next step: Order some chicken wire for the bottom of the patio and install it."

Boom. Done.

Emerson got it immediately.

And, years later, he still has his chickens.

Our +1°... Got any chicken poop in your life?

If you feel so inspired, let's run it through a quick analysis. What's the negative thinking you might be running on it? How about the positive thinking approach?

And, most importantly, what would a targeted thinking approach look like? Take clear aim. Hit your Target, Hero.

All of which leads us back to Trevor's dad. You know what he taught him as a kid? To get rid of the "stinkin' thinkin'."

Let's do that. TODAY.

THE FLAT TIRE
& THE ULTIMATE QUESTION

In our last couple +1°s, we've been chatting about Targeted Thinking. I promised to share a couple of mundane, everyday family examples to bring the point home.

We visited the Johnson Ranch to discuss my relationship with our chickens and their poop. Now it's time for some flat bike tires.

Quick context.

The morning after I had that chat with Emerson about how to approach the chicken situation with either negative, positive, or Targeted Thinking, we were doing our family workout—which, at the time, featured me chasing the kids on their bikes as we have fun going around the half-mile trail loop we created around our property.

Only… This morning, Emerson's bike had a flat tire.

He immediately started crying—super bummed he wouldn't be able to ride his epic lime green (hah) bike around the trail, as planned.

So…

I cruised over and said: "Buddy! Your tire's flat. That's a bummer. I get it. And… Remember that chat we had last night about neutral thinking and targeted thinking?"

Emerson: "Yah."

Me: "Well, let's do some Targeted Thinking! Remember the question we need to ask? WHAT DO YOU WANT?"

He said: "I want to ride my bike."

I said: "Exactly. So what can we do to make that happen?"

He said: "Get the bike pump and fill up the tire."

I said: "Exactly."

So…

We cruised into the barn, found the bike pump, and filled up the tire. The air surprisingly held.

Boom. Done.

Tire was filled.

He was off to the trail races.

And, that's our +1°…

Spotlight on YOU…

Got any metaphorical flat tires in your life?

(Echo: Of course you do. You're human!)

How are you reacting?

With negative thinking or positive thinking or…TARGETED THINKING?

Take clear aim. Hit your Target, Hero.

TODAY.

TARGET PRACTICE
NEXT LEVEL TARGETED THINKING

In our last few +1°s, we talked about Targeted Thinking. Let's do a quick recap then we're going to go next level with it.

Step 1. Move from Victim to Hero by asking yourself a simple question: WHAT DO I WANT?

I repeat: Victims complain about what's not working in their lives. Heroes create what they want in their lives by asking THAT question.

Step 2. Once you've gotten even an *inkling* of clarity on what you want in any given moment, the follow-up question is simple: NOW WHAT NEEDS TO GET DONE?

We brought that wisdom to life with discussions about its efficacy in dealing with chicken poop and flat tires.

Today I want to hone our practice by adding a few more steps to the Targeted Thinking protocol.

Yes, knowing what you want is *essential* to the process of living Heroically and creating a better life. And, of course, taking action in pursuit of creating that ideal, is *also* essential.

And…

Before we even ask ourselves what we want, we need to step back an inch or three from the current challenge and ACCEPT REALITY EXACTLY AS IT IS.

This is what Byron Katie describes as "Loving What Is." Which is really just a modern take on the ancient Stoic practice known as "The Art of Acquiescence."

So… Step 0 in our updated Targeted Thinking protocol is simple: Acceptance—complete and utter acceptance of EXACTLY what is happening right now. Period.

That, of course, is much easier said than done but the wisest among us get the power of this practice.

Then… Once we've stopped arguing with reality (reminding ourselves that we will ALWAYS lose when we argue with reality!) we are ready for the first step in our protocol.

Step 1. Asking ourselves: WHAT DO I WANT?

Feeling energetically sluggish? Unproductive or lacking purpose at work? Disconnected from yourself and/or your loved ones?

Perfect. Accept that.

Now… What do you want?

To feel more Heroically Energized? More Heroically (and purposefully) Productive? More Heroically Connected?

Awesome. Spend THREE SECONDS (!) getting a little more clarity on that.

Note: We're not talking about a three months' worth of thirty-minute journaling sessions to get clarity.

SPEND THREE SECONDS RIGHT IN THE MOMENT YOU FEEL WOBBLY THINKING ABOUT WHAT YOU WANT.

Got it? Awesome. That's Step 1.

Step 2. Ask yourself: What can I do RIGHT NOW that would take me one step closer to getting more of what I want?

Again, to be clear…

We don't need a 101-page polished strategic plan you're going to submit to some higher authority for a grade here.

SPEND THREE SECONDS RIGHT IN THE MOMENT YOU FEEL WOBBLY THINKING ABOUT WHAT YOU CAN DO RIGHT NOW TO GET MORE OF WHAT YOU JUST DECIDED YOU WANT.

Got it? Awesome. That's Step 2.

Now we're ready for Step 3.

This is, unquestionably, the most important of all the steps but it's far less effective if you don't do the first ones.

Here it is...

Step 3. TAKE ACTION.

SPEND THREE SECONDS GETTING INTO ACTION DOING THE THING YOU DECIDED YOU NEED TO DO TO GET MORE OF WHAT YOU JUST DECIDED YOU WANT.

(Yes, that's a lot of ALL CAPS.)

To recap.

Step 0. Accept your current reality.

Step 1. Create a Target of what you want.

Step 2. Decide what you can do RIGHT NOW to move in the direction of your desired outcome.

Step 3. Take action.

Final step? REPEAT that process.

Take clear aim.

Hit your Target, Hero.

TODAY.

THINKING VS. DOING
LESSONS FROM A BEACH BALL

I n one of my coaching sessions with Phil Stutz, he told me to write something down. (He often does that.)

He said: "Draw a horizontal line. Above that line, put 'Thinking Space.' Below the line, put 'Work Space.'"

Then he asked me: "You know what the 'Thinking Space' is good for?"

I didn't have a very good answer.

He said: "NOTHING. Nothing happens in the Thinking Space."

Hah.

Obviously, stepping back and thinking about things is a vital skill but the fact is, nothing actually HAPPENS until we take action, use the tools and get to work on and in our lives. (And, for the record, most of us don't actually THINK, we ruminate—which, as we'll discuss, is not good. At all.)

Phil says we all tend to live in the Thinking Space. He says we need to force ourselves DOWN—out of (over)thinking and into the Work Space. How? Use one of our +1° tools, get to work, do ANYTHING but overthink (or indulge in our Kryptonites).

He tells us that it's kinda like a beach ball in water. You press it down and what does it want to do? Pop back up.

Well, we want to get REALLY good at keeping that ball down.

Do you (like me and most people on the planet), have a default tendency to spend too much time thinking about things and not enough time actually DOING things?

Remember the beach ball.

Push it down every time it pops back up.

THE STOCKDALE PARADOX
UTTER FAITH & BRUTAL FACTS

Vice Admiral James Stockdale was shot down during the Vietnam War.

He spent seven and a half years in a brutal prison camp. He spent four of those years in solitary confinement and two years in leg irons. He was tortured fifteen times.

Stockdale heroically embraced his role as the clandestine commanding officer of what became hundreds of prisoners.

In his book *Good to Great* Jim Collins tells us about what he called "The Stockdale Paradox."

Stockdale said that naïve optimism got you killed in those camps. Some guys thought they'd get out by Christmas. When Christmas came and went, they thought they'd get out by Easter. When Easter came and went, it was Thanksgiving.

Then... They lost hope. And died.

Stockdale told us the ones who survived did something different.

They KNEW (!!!) that they would eventually be free *and* they KNEW (!!!) it was not going to happen any time soon. Stockdale himself knew it would be at least five years. But, he knew the day would come.

The Stockdale Paradox.

Utter confidence in our inevitable success and utter eyes-wide-open humble embrace of the reality that it isn't going to happen immediately and/or be easy.

As Stockdale puts it: "This is a very important lesson. You must never confuse faith that you will prevail in the end—which you can never afford to lose—with the discipline to confront the most brutal facts of your current reality, whatever they might be."

That's the heart and soul of true confidence.

How's yours?

PUNCHED IN THE FACE LATELY?
WHAT TO DO THE NEXT TIME THAT HAPPENS

Brian Cain is one of the world's best mental toughness coaches.

His client list includes four Major League Baseball Cy Young Award winners, eight UFC world champion mixed martial artists, World Series and Super Bowl Champions and MVPs, Olympic medalists, and countless other elite athletes and coaches.

He's written a couple great little books: *The 10 Pillars of Mental Performance Mastery* and *One Percent Better.*

He's also a friend and longtime student of mine who has his clients read Philosopher's Notes to go to the next level. (Cainer: !!!)

I want to chat about one of his clients.

Quick context: Brian recently visited me and the Johnson fam out here in the country outside of Austin. The kids and wifey and I had fun learning how to eat fire and break an arrow with our necks and do other fun things we didn't think we could do.

There was a big UFC pay-per-view event a few weekends after his visit. Brian happened to be coaching one of the fighters in ALL THREE of the top three fights (two for championship belts). He invited me to go to the event but, me being me, I told him thank you but (laughing), I'm going to be in bed hours before the championship fights so...

Although I didn't go to watch the fights, I DID do a little research on his fighters. I read an article on one of the guys fighting for a title. His prior competitors talked about how much he freaked them out because he seemed to LOVE getting hit in the face. The harder they hit him the more he smiled as he asked them if that was all they had.

I share that story because, in my a.m. Heroic meditation, right after Epictetus tells me to practice my philosophy and to remember the Choice of Hercules, he often reminds me to remember that particular fighter—telling me that if HE can smile when he LITERALLY gets punched in the face, I can smile when *I* inevitably get metaphorically punched in the face.

Now, I understand that the whole "martial art" metaphor thing might not be your thing but it's been a handy philosophical teaching tool for thousands of years so…

If you feel so inspired, the next time you get metaphorically punched in the face (note: NOT *if* but *WHEN*!), I encourage you to remember Epictetus and his boxers and Cainer and his mixed martial artists and see if you can have fun flipping the switch and SMILING as you ask the Heroic gods if THAT is all they've got.

That very next challenge you're going to face sooner than you may like? That's PRECISELY what we train for.

A + S + GOYA = R
BREAK ANY ARROWS WITH YOUR NECK LATELY?

I n our last +1°, we talked about the fact that Brian Cain recently visited me and the Johnson fam out here in the country
outside of Austin.

I casually mentioned that the kids and wifey and I had fun
learning how to eat fire and break an arrow with our necks and
do other fun things we didn't think we could do.

Let's talk more about those broken arrows.

First, a little more context.

As we discussed, Brian is one of the world's leading mental
toughness coaches. He's also a longtime student of mine and easily
tied for first as one of the most inspiring, energized human beings
I know.

When he visited, he left a couple books with me as gifts:
The 10 Pillars of Mental Performance Mastery and *One Percent
Better*.

They're both super-quick-reading, inspiring fables packed
with a ton of wisdom. I read both of them in the same weekend.
They're fantastic.

Think: If Paulo Coelho wrote about mental toughness. And
kinda like Robin Sharma's *The Monk Who Sold His Ferrari* or
Dan Millman's *Way of the Peaceful Warrior*.

10 Pillars is all about the foundation of Brian's mental performance mastery program while *One Percent Better* is all about,
as per the sub-title: "How to Close the Gap from Where You Are

to Where You Want to Be." How? By getting ONE PERCENT BETTER. When? TODAY, Hero.

Now… In *One Percent Better*, Brian shares this little success formula with us: A + S + GOYA = R.

As the character in his book puts it, that acronym means "Ability + Strategy + Get Off Your Anatomy and do the work = Results."

Then she says: "Ability is not something you are lacking to be the optimal version of yourself. You are simply blocking it. How we unblock our ability is by giving you the right strategy… When you do that, you will see better results."

So… Want to activate your Heroic potential?

Know this: You're not necessarily lacking the Ability. The real issue might be that you don't have the right STRATEGY.

This was a lesson that Brian made vividly real for me and the kids when he visited. How he'd do it? He showed us how to break an arrow with our neck and eat fire.

What's breaking arrows with your neck and eating fire have to do with this idea? Everything.

Here's the short story.

Brian took a wooden arrow and placed one end against the wall and the other end against his neck. Then he took a deep breath, stepped forward, and SNAPPED THE ARROW in half.

Then he invited us to do it. To which we were all tempted to say: "Nope! We're good!" (Hah.) Then he told us: "You don't lack the ABILITY to break the arrow with your neck. You just lack the STRATEGY on how to easily do it safely."

Then he taught us how to do it. Then I did it. BOOM!

Same thing with eating fire. There's a STRATEGY on how to do it. Once you know it, it's EASY.

And, well, same thing with pretty much EVERYTHING in our lives.

BJ Fogg echoes this wisdom in *Tiny Habits*. He tells us: "We are not the problem. Our approach to change is. It's a design flaw—not a personal flaw."

Again, it's a STRATEGY issue, not an ABILITY issue.

Which brings us back to the equation A + S + GOYA = R.

Ability + Strategy + Get Off Your Anatomy and DO THE WORK if you want the Results!

You can't just know what to do. You have to DO IT.

So… GOYA!

Not someday.

TODAY.

1% BETTER
CLOSE THE GAP TODAY

I n our last couple +1°s, we spent some time hanging out with world-class mental toughness coach Brian Cain.

We broke some arrows, ate some fire, and got an invitation to a big UFC event where one of his fighters made Epictetus proud by smiling as he got punched in the face.

Today we're going to spend some more time with Cainer.

We're going to talk about getting 1% better.

Let's head back to his little fable (appropriately called *One Percent Better*) in which his characters Sunny and Mr. Big are having a little chat.

"'Good morning, Mr. Big! It's time to get juiced. Either we are going to dominate the day or the day will dominate us. Are you ready?' Sunny asked this with the excitement of a kid on Christmas Day.

As we began walking the halls to the scent of bacon and breakfast, Sunny started asking me about math. 'Mr. Big, there are twenty-four hours in a day and sixty minutes in each hour. How many minutes are there in a day?'

I quickly took out my phone and asked, 'Hey, Siri. How many minutes in a day?'

'There are 1,440 minutes in a day,' Siri chimed back.

Then she asked, 'What's 1% of 1,440?'

This is where I was stumped. I wasn't sure how to do the math. After all, I wasn't a math teacher. 'No idea,' I replied.

'1% of a day is fourteen minutes and twenty-four seconds,' she said emphatically. 'Everyone wants to get 1% better but they fail to intentionally invest 1% of their day because they don't even know that it's a strategy for success.'"

Quick context: Mr. Big is a burned-out teacher. Sunny is his mentor. She works in the cafeteria and "brings the juice!" every day. Her #1 lesson and the focal point of the book?

As Brian tells us: "The best place to start is to intentionally invest 1% of your day into yourself and become a better version of you today than you were yesterday. Then wake up tomorrow and do the same thing. Rinse and repeat. It's actually quite simple."

Let's review the math.

There are twenty-four hours in a day. Sixty minutes per hour. That's 1,440 minutes per day.

1% of that?

Fourteen minutes and twenty-four seconds.

1% of your day.

Here's the question: What's the #1 thing you KNOW you could be doing that, if you spent just 1% of your day doing it, would have THE most positive impact in your life?

Seriously. What is it?

1% of your day meditating is 14 minutes and 24 seconds of meditation.

Would that change your life?

How about 1% of your day training? Or 1% of your day with ZERO technology spent 101% focused on being present with your significant other and/or kids?

Would that change your life?

Or 1% of your day reflecting on your life purpose. Or LIVING more on purpose—doing the things you KNOW you could be doing for just fourteen minutes and twenty-four seconds TODAY?

Would that change your life?

+1%. +1%. +1%

Tiny investments that lead to tiny gains.

That add up.

Fast.

Here's to using 1% of our days to get 1% better.

TODAY.

WHY BE AVERAGE?
BEST OF THE WORST & WORST OF THE BEST

I n our last several +1°s, we've been having fun hanging out with world-class mental toughness and peak performance coach, Brian Cain.

And, trust me. Any time spent with Cainer is going to be fun. He is *easily* one of the most inspiring human beings on the planet. You can't help but feel energized being in his presence.

Let's chat about one of the lines in his fable, *The 10 Pillars of Mental Performance Mastery*, that jumped out and tattooed itself on my consciousness.

It's about being average. Coach Kenny is the guide in the fable. He's coaching a burned-out executive.

He tells him: "'You are like most people,' Coach Kenny said. 'And we call that average. Like I have said, I hate the word average. It means you are the best of the worst and the worst of the best. It's a terrible place to live.'"

Average.

It's the best of the worst and the worst of the best. Stuck in the middle of the rugged mountain of mediocrity.

Not where we want to hang out.

Brian has Coach Kenny say: "You are giving the world your B or C game and you don't even know it because you have never been trained on how to give your A game."

And: "The world needs you at your best. You can't be normal, you must be elite."

And: "If you don't have a plan, how are you getting better? The problem is when you stop getting better, you start getting bitter, and nobody likes being around people who are bitter all the time."

Lest you think that wisdom is just some rah-rah, pom-pom waving goodness from an overly ambitious peak performance coach, how about some parallel wisdom from one of the twentieth century's great spiritual teachers, Eric Butterworth?

Butterworth was Maya Angelou's spiritual teacher. And, apparently, Oprah considers his great book *Discover the Power Within You* to be one of her all-time favorite books.

Here's how Butterworth puts it in one of *my* all-time favorite books, *Spiritual Economics*.

He tells us: "Why be an average person? All the great achievements of history have been made by strong individuals who refused to consult statistics or to listen to those who could prove convincingly that what they wanted to do, and in fact ultimately did do, was completely impossible."

Average.

It's the best of the worst and the worst of the best. Stuck in the middle of the rugged mountain of mediocrity.

As Sylvester Stallone tells his son in *Rocky IV*: "THAT'S NOT YOU! YOU'RE BETTER THAN THAT!"

It's Day 1.

It's time to go all in.

It's time to activate our Heroic potential.

Let's go, Hero!

THE IMPOSSIBLE
IT'S WHAT'S FOR BREAKFAST

S teven Kotler wrote a great book called *The Rise of Superman* in which he features extreme sports athletes to demonstrate how we can all accelerate our performance gains.

Quick context.

The things snowboarders and skateboarders and other extreme athletes can do today were *literally* IMPOSSIBLE not too long ago.

Steven walks us through how, by consistently pushing ourselves JUST outside our comfort zone, we can make the impossible into something that's possible.

He says it's all about finding the sweet spot *just* outside of our comfort zone. Right at the edge of Csikszentmihalyi's Flow channel where our skills meet our challenges.

He tells us we don't need to go nuts and try to do the impossible tomorrow. We just need to go *slightly* outside our current capacities.

A 4% stretch to be precise.

And then do it again tomorrow. And the day after that. And the day after that. And...

Specifically, he says: "If we want to achieve the kinds of accelerated performance we're seeing in action and adventure sports, then it's 4% plus 4% plus 4%, day after day, week after week, months into years into careers. This is the road to real magic.

Follow this path long enough, and not only does impossible

becomes possible, it becomes what's next—like eating breakfast, like another day at the office."

Imagine that.

4%. 4% ...

Tiny little gains aggregated and compounded over an extended period of time and ...

The impossible becomes possible.

It's what's for breakfast.

THE RISE OF SUPERYOU
NEW MANTRA: "NO PRESSURE, NO DIAMONDS"

I 've interviewed a couple hundred people over the years and I could easily write a book (or three) featuring the wisdom from just those chats.

But…

The ONE (goosebumps) line that is *at least* tied for first as *the* most transformative response to any question I've ever asked came at the end of one of my chats with Steven Kotler.

I asked him: "What's ONE thing you would encourage us to have in mind as we strive to optimize our lives and activate our Heroic potential?"

He paused for a moment.

Looked up and to the right as he pondered the question.

Then he said: "No pressure, no diamonds."

I repeat: If we *truly* want to activate our Heroic potential, we need to be willing to exit our comfort zones and viscerally (!) *know* beyond a shadow of a doubt that our *infinite* potential exists on the *other* side of our comfort zone. We need to, as *all* the great peak performance and mental toughness coaches put it, get comfortable being uncomfortable.

Let's be willing to go 4% out of our comfort zones all day every day as we remember: "No pressure, no diamonds."

P.S. I've repeated this mantra to myself *thousands* of times:

"No pressure, no diamonds."
"No pressure, no diamonds."
"No pressure, no diamonds."
"No pressure, no diamonds."
"No pressure, no diamonds."
"No pressure, no diamonds."
"No pressure, no diamonds."
"No pressure, no diamonds."
"No pressure, no diamonds."
"No pressure, no diamonds."
"No pressure, no diamonds."
"No pressure, no diamonds."
"No pressure, no diamonds."
"No pressure, no diamonds."
"No pressure, no diamonds."
"No pressure, no diamonds."
"No pressure, no diamonds."
"No pressure, no diamonds."
"No pressure, no diamonds."
"No pressure, no diamonds."
"No pressure, no diamonds."
"No pressure, no diamonds."
"No pressure, no diamonds."
"No pressure, no diamonds."

ACRES OF DIAMONDS
GOT ANY PRICELESS GEMS IN YOUR BACKYARD?

I n our last +1°, we had fun with our new mantra: "No pressure, no diamonds."

Continuing the diamond theme, let's talk about Acres of Diamonds. It's a classic, old-school self-development story.

Have you ever heard it?

Super-short version: Diamonds are being discovered in Africa. A farmer decides he's going to head out in pursuit of his fortune so he sells his farm, leaves his family, and searches the continent for years. He finds nothing and, apparently, throws himself into a river and dies.

Lo and behold, the man who purchased his farm discovers a funny-looking rock on his new land. That rock turns out to be one of the biggest diamonds ever discovered. The farm is covered with funny-looking rocks like that. His farm becomes one of the most profitable diamond mines in the world.

Moral of the story: Before you head out in search of diamonds, check out your current situation. You might just be sitting on acres of diamonds.

Are you?

P.S. Thomas Edison comes to mind as well. He once said: "Opportunity is missed by most people because it is dressed in overalls and looks like work."

HOW TO MAKE A PEARL
TO GO WITH OUR DIAMONDS

D o you know how pearls are made?

It's a truly fascinating process and the *perfect* metaphor for the process of activating our Heroic potential—which is why I have a pearl on my desk as I type this.

Here's the short story.

The pearl-making process begins when an irritant gets inside a mollusk's shell. The irritant becomes the nucleus for a pearl as the mollusk releases a strong, iridescent substance known as "nacre" to protect itself from that irritant.

The mollusk coats the irritant with THOUSANDS and THOUSANDS of layers of nacre and, over a period of YEARS, the pearl slowly takes form.

So…

Do *you* have any "irritants" in *your* life?

(Of course you do. You're human.)

Will you turn those irritants into beautiful pearls?

(Of course you will. You're Heroic.)

Let's follow nature's lead and create some luminescent pearls as we release our own "strong and iridescent" nacre in the form of applying our favorite wisdom tools in the face of life's (inevitable) irritants.

How often should we release our nacre?

I repeat: THOUSAND AND THOUSANDS of times.

How long will it take to make our pearl?

Well, it depends on the growth rate (which is driven by how often we practice!) but expect it to take years—we're talking "horticultural time" not stopwatch time with this kind of creative work.

Here's to creating a collection of gemstones.

No pressure, no diamonds.

No irritants, no pearls.

SANDPAPER GRIT
SAND ON PAPER APPLIED TO YOUR LIFE

I n our last +1°, we talked about how to make a pearl. Recall that the first step was to introduce an "irritant."

We connected that gem origin story to another: No pressure, no diamonds.

We could say: No sand, no pearl. (And/or: No irritant, no pearl!)

Today I'd like to spend a little more time talking about sand. Only this time we're going to put it on some paper and talk about how to make some grit.

First, to be clear: I'm probably the least handy guy on the planet and I think I've used sandpaper precisely once in my adult life. (Hah!)

But…

I do love the latent metaphorical wisdom in everyday things, so here we go…

Of course, sandpaper comes in different flavors. I love how those flavors are measured on a "grit" scale.

As the How Stuff Works folks put it: "For heavy sanding and stripping, you need coarse sandpaper measuring 40- to 60-grit; for smoothing surfaces and removing small imperfections, choose 80- to 120-grit sandpaper. For finishing surfaces smoothly, use a super fine sandpaper with 360- to 600-grit."

That's our +1°.

Without going into the finer details of sandpaper and allowing for some metaphorical freedom, let's celebrate the fact that different projects require different levels of grit.

The rough work? Lower grit will do the trick. But as you advance to the stuff you want *super*-polished, you'll need ten times (!!!) more grit.

Yep. That sounds about right for our metaphorical optimizing.

So… What can use a little sandpaper in YOUR life?

Here's to a toolshed packed with (a variety of!) grit.

YOU VS. YOUR PROBLEMS
SIZE YOURSELF UP THEN STEP UP!

T. Harv Eker wrote a great little book called *Secrets of the Millionaire Mind*.

In it, he tells us that our "problems" are only problems in relationship to how we're showing up.

It goes something like this.

You can have a Size 1 problem. Or a Size 3. Or Size 5. Or even a Size 10 problem.

Let's say a Size 1 problem is someone cutting you off on the freeway. Or maybe stubbing your toe. A Size 10 problem is, let's say for the sake of discussion, you dying.

Now, how you *perceive* and RESPOND to any of the "problems" in your life will be determined by YOUR size.

You can be a Size 1 person or a Size 3 or a Size 5 or a Size 10 or whatever.

Now, let's look at what happens when you experience a Size 1 problem of someone cutting you off on the freeway. To be blunt, for that to be a big deal, you need to be a pretty small person (at least in that moment). For it to be a REALLY big deal (like, I'm road-raging kinda thing), you're being a flea-sized .01 version of your potential 10 Heroic self.

Can you see that?

Now, we can march up the scale of problem significance and see that if we're operating from a pretty high perspective, all those problems become less of a big deal.

Lose your job or face a creative challenge in your business? The Size 1 or 2 or 3 version of you freaks out then shuts down for months. The antifragile 7 or 8 or 9 version of you says: "Bring it on. I'm about to get better. Let's do this!!" The Size 10 you just laughs and says: "Yep. It's go time. No pressure no diamonds, baby!" and then shows up with more grounded power than ever before.

Of course, if you want to go really nuts with it, dial yourself up to a *Spinal Tap* 11 and now you don't have any problems. You just have life happening and you surfing the waves of life.

All of that to say…

Do you have a "problem" in your life these days?

(If you're human and alive, the answer to that question is, of course, "Yes.")

What size is that problem?

And, what size are YOU being?

And, most importantly, how can you +1° yourself just a little more today to see that problem from a higher vantage point?

KEEP SHOOTING
A TRUE STORY

Once upon a time (1938 to be precise) there was a pistol shooter. He was incredibly good. Had plans to be the best. Unfortunately, our Hero has his right hand blown off by a faulty grenade during combat training. (Gah.) That was his shooting hand. (Double gah.)

All hopes are lost.

Or… Are they?

After a depressing month in the hospital, our Hero decides that he will simply learn how to shoot just as well with his *left* hand. He starts secretly training.

He trains and trains and trains. He's now very good. He shows up at the 1939 World Championships. Everyone's shocked to see him there. They're even more shocked when he wins. His Olympic dreams are back on track.

Enter: World War II. The 1940 and 1944 Olympics are canceled. He waits.

He shows up at the next Olympics. He's now thirty-eight.

The world champion asks him what he's doing there. Our Hero tells him he's there to learn.

And… He wins.

His name is Károly Takács.

The moral of the (true) story?

Keep shooting.

APPROACH VS. AVOIDANCE
WHAT DO YOU DO WHEN YOU FEEL CHALLENGED?

What do you do when you feel challenged? Do you AP-PROACH the challenge? Or, do you AVOID it?

Psychologists tell us that this is one of the distinguishing variables between the healthiest and least healthy among us (and, of course, between our healthiest and least healthy moments).

Know this...

Healthy people APPROACH their challenges.

Less-than-healthy people AVOID them.

If you think you have what it takes to meet a given situation, you perceive it as a CHALLENGE to approach and to overcome.

If you think you *don't have* what it takes to deal with a given situation, you will perceive it as a THREAT and you'll try to avoid it.

What's fascinating is that our physiology will change depending on how we interpret the situation.

When we APPROACH it as a challenge, we get the necessary energy to rock it and we feel good.

When we try to AVOID it as a threat, we get a concoction of stress hormones we *don't* want and feel enervated, putting our health in jeopardy.

So...

Our +1°...

Got a challenge? Fantastic.

Quit avoiding it. APPROACH IT.

Say it with me now…

"BRING. IT. ON!"

THE INSTINCT CYCLE
MATTIS, STUTZ & OODA LOOPS

General Jim Mattis is the former Secretary of Defense and one of the most formidable strategic thinkers of the twenty-first century.

He wrote a GREAT book on leadership called *Call Sign Chaos: Learning to Lead*.

I want to combine Jim Mattis's wisdom on decision-making with Phil Stutz's wisdom on the same subject then combine both of them to the OODA Loop.

Let's get to work.

Here's how Mattis puts it: "When you are in command, there is always the next decision waiting to be made. You don't have time to pace back and forth like Hamlet, zigzagging one way and the other. You do your best and live with the consequences. A commander has to compartmentalize his emotions and remain focused on the mission. You must decide, act, and move on."

That's pretty much what Phil calls "The Instinct Cycle."

He tells us that when we need to make a decision, we need to trust our INSTINCTS on what the right next step is. Then we need to DECIDE what we're going to do. Then we need to take ACTION. Then we need to be prepared to accept the CONSEQUENCES of that decision.

Then we need to MAKE THE NEXT DECISION as we go through the process over and over and over again.

Phil says that the best decision maker is not the one who *gets the most decisions right*. It's the one *makes the most decisions*.

All of which reminds me of the OODA loop.

You know what that is?

As Wikipedia tells us: "The OODA loop is the cycle Observe-Orient-Decide-Act, developed by military strategist and United States Air Force Colonel John Boyd."

It was originally developed by a fighter pilot for fighter pilots. It's applicable to ALL OF US.

The basic idea? The fighter pilot (and/or aspiring Hero!) who can go through the Observe-Orient-Decide-Act steps of the OODA loop the FASTEST is the one most likely to win.

All that to say…

You are the commander of your life.

What is the next decision you need to make?

Get clear on what you think is the next best step and…

DECIDE.

Do your best.

Live with the consequences.

REPEAT.

All day every day.

Especially…

TODAY.

P.S. Teddy Roosevelt also comes to mind. He once said: "In any moment of decision, the best thing you can do is the right thing, the next best thing is the wrong thing, and the worst thing you can do is nothing."

HAGFISH ARE FREAKY
GOT ANY IN YOUR LIFE?

Have you ever heard of hagfish? They're pretty creepy.

I apologize in advance for the visual image here, but I think it's worth it.

Here's how Steve Chandler describes hagfish in *Time Warrior*: "To really live now there are two things I want to phase out of my life forever: (1) Resentments about the past and (2) Worries about the future."

These two activities, strengthened by repeated indulgence, are like hagfish. Hagfish? Many people don't know what hagfish are, but they are just like worries and resentments.

In the real, undersea world, hagfish are blind, slimy, deep-water eel-like creatures that dart into the orifices of their prey and devour them, alive, from the inside.

Kill the hagfish in your life. Then you can live now and maybe procrastinate later.

Um... Wow.

That's a heck of a way to kill your prey, eh? Dart into their orifices and then devour them, alive, from the inside? Yikes.

And...

That's our +1°.

Got any hagfish in your life? Any resentments and/or worries that are eating YOU from the inside out?

Today a good day to do some hagfishing?

REALLY HARD VS. IMPOSSIBLE
WANT TO GO FOR A BIKE RIDE TO MT. EVEREST?

I n *Spartan Up!*, Joe De Sena tells the *ridiculously* inspiring story of extreme adventurer Göran Kropp.

It goes like this…

Imagine your friend inviting you on an adventure.

He tells you: "Let's hop on our bikes from our homes in Sweden, ride to the base of Mount Everest, then hop off, ascend to the summit without oxygen or a sherpa and then come back down and ride back home! You in?!"

You might be tempted to say: "Dude. That's crazy!"

You might even be tempted to say that it's impossible. But…

Important note: it's not *impossible*.

It's just REALLY REALLY REALLY hard.

Know this: We'd be wise to recognize the fact that there's a *huge* difference between "really hard" and "impossible."

Our +1°…

Do YOU have any "impossible" dreams that need to be re-defined as simply really (really!) hard?

Yah? Which one?

What ONE big thing would you dare to dream (and do) if you knew you couldn't fail?

Think about it. Dream about it. Get fired up about it.

Then go WOOP it.

And, if you decide you're willing to pay the price, then go DO IT.

P.S. Might want to keep this wisdom from Seneca in mind: "It is not because things are difficult that we do not dare, it is because we do not dare that they are difficult."

JESUS, TOLLE & YOU
THE PARABLE OF THE WISE & FOOLISH BUILDERS

S hortly after COVID arrived on the scene, I ran into my friend
Michael on the trail.

Well, technically, we did a six-feet-apart virtual elbow tap.

He asked me if I'd seen Eckhart Tolle's recent talk on how to
deal with a crisis. I told him I hadn't. (I read books, folks!)

He told me Tolle read from the Bible and shared the story
about the guy who builds his house on the sand and it gets destroyed when the storms come in.

I thought: "Yep. That's exactly right."

Fast-forward a few months and I'm reading Tom Morris's
great book *Plato's Lemonade Stand*. It's all about using ancient
wisdom to turn life's (inevitable!) lemons into lemonade.

You know what story Tom uses to bring home the point about
the power of building our lives on unchangeable truths so we can
weather the inevitable storms of life?

The same passage from the Bible that Tolle referenced.

Enter: Google search.

Two of them.

First, to find Tolle's talk.

Second, to find the passage from the Bible.

It's known as "The Parable of the Wise and the Foolish Build-
ers." It's also known as "The House on the Rock."

You'll find it in Matthew 7:24–27.

Here it is:

"Therefore everyone who hears these words of mine and puts them into practice is like a wise man who built his house on the rock. The rain came down, the streams rose, and the winds blew and beat against that house; yet it did not fall, because it had its foundation on the rock. But everyone who hears these words of mine and does not put them into practice is like a foolish man who built his house on sand. The rain came down, the streams rose, and the winds blew and beat against that house, and it fell with a great crash."

Interpretative note: You are the builder. Your life is the house. Practicing (or not practicing!) the fundamental truths of your philosophy is the foundation.

So...

How's YOUR house?

Have you been building the foundation on the rock of your philosophy?

A.k.a. are you PRACTICING YOUR PHILOSOPHY?

It's in times of rain and floods and winds when we get a little (or a lot!) more clarity on the quality of our construction.

Here's to building our lives on solid rock.

TODAY.

EMOTIONAL STAMINA
WHAT TO DO WHEN YOU'RE HAVING A ROUGH DAY

W hat do you do when you're having a rough day?

Maybe it starts the moment you wake up and you just don't *feel* like doing your normal things?

Or maybe it kicks in a little later in the day after a disappointment or a challenging conversation.

Things aren't going your way.

What do you do?

Here's an ABSOLUTELY ESSENTIAL LESSON we must learn...

On those days when we feel the WORST, we need to be THE MOST committed to executing our protocol and dominating our fundamentals.

PERIOD.

I wish I could reach through the pages of this book and look you in the eye as I say: "There are few things that will *ever* be more life-changing than *really* getting this."

Phil Stutz calls that *emotional stamina*. I adapted that into what I call *antifragile confidence*. Same basic idea.

I repeat: On those days when we feel the WORST, we need to be THE MOST committed to executing our protocol and dominating our fundamentals.

I can still remember the very first time I heard the phrase

"emotional stamina." At the end of one of our very first sessions, Phil told me that I had a lot of it.

I had no idea what he was talking about so, at the beginning of our next session, I asked him: "What's emotional stamina?"

He told me that I bounce back from challenges/setbacks quickly. That requires emotional stamina.

Then he told me that we need to say *this* to ourselves in our most challenging times: "I don't feel good but I'm going to keep up with the protocol. In fact, I am MOST avid about sticking with the protocol when it's hardest."

I repeat.

Imagine being the MOST committed to doing the little things you *know* keep you plugged in when you LEAST feel like it.

The worse we feel, the *more* committed we are to doing the work. (Period!)

Of course, I repeat yet again, all of this presupposes that we HAVE a protocol.

What's YOURS?

Who are you and what do you DO when you're at your best? Life doesn't need to be so complicated and/or so hard. Know who you are and what you do when you're at your best.

THEN DO THAT.

ESPECIALLY (!) when you don't *feel* like it.

Here's to cultivating our emotional stamina and forging our antifragile confidence, Hero.

TODAY.

LEVITY + GRAVITY = BUOYANCY
TO SELL IS HUMAN & THE NEW ABCS

D an Pink tells us that *To Sell Is Human*.

Although only one in nine Americans is *technically* in sales, he says that the other eight in nine spend a ton of their time in "non-sales selling."

In fact, the research he commissioned shows that we spend around 40% of our time (or twenty-four minutes out of every working hour!) trying to move people to do things—whether that's pitching an idea to colleagues or trying to change someone's behavior.

Then there's the personal time we spend "selling" / "moving" others—from selling our kids on a philosophical idea ("mistakes are awesome!") or your spouse on how to optimize your nutrition ("sugar isn't awesome!").

In that context, he tells us we need some new ABCs of selling. As you may know, the "ABCs" of the old-school, hard-core sales approach are "Always be closing."

That, to say the least, is not where it's at. Now? Dan says it's all about "Attunement + Buoyancy + Clarity."

Here's the super-quick look.

Attunement is basically the ability to connect with others. We get there via three things: humility, trying to figure out what the other person is thinking (this is more effective, btw, than trying to figure out what they're *feeling*) and strategically mimicking their movements and words (but doing it subtly and acting like a human being without being weird about it).

Buoyancy is actually what I want to focus on today. More on that in a moment.

Then we have Clarity. We need to be able to concisely communicate the essence of our offer—finding the 1% of what really matters while asking good questions, etc.

So…

All that to arrive at Buoyancy.

Buoyancy is how we stay afloat in the "ocean of rejection" we all feel when we try to "sell" people on our ideas and/or products, etc. Dan offers us tips to stay buoyant before, during, and after our pitch.

Before: We want to make sure our self-talk is empowering.

During: We want to keep our positivity ratios optimized. 1:1 isn't going to do it. Nor will 2:1. Research shows that 3:1 is the sweet spot. (Note: 11:1 isn't going to work either.)

After: We want to make sure our "explanatory styles" are rocking a la Martin Seligman's wisdom on learned optimism.

Now, we're ready for the point of this +1°.

You know that positivity ratio? We want to target 3:1.

Too little positivity isn't going to work.

AND (very important and!)…

TOO MUCH positivity isn't going to work either.

I love the way Dan frames Barbara Fredrickson's wisdom on this: "Fredrickson sees the healthy positivity ratios… as a calibration between two competing pulls: levity and gravity. 'Levity is that unseen force that lifts you skyward, whereas gravity is the opposing force that pulls you earthward. Unchecked levity leaves you flighty, ungrounded, and unreal. Unchecked gravity leaves you collapsed in a heap of misery,' she writes. 'Yet when properly combined, these two opposing forces leave you buoyant.'"

Levity + Gravity = Buoyancy.

How's your levity?

How's your gravity?

Here's to your buoyancy!

ANTIFRAGILE BUOYANCY
HOW'S YOUR BARBELL?

I n our last +1°, we talked about the power of *buoyancy* and the optimal ratio of positive to negative.

Recall that, as per Barbara Fredrickson (the leading researcher on the subject), we want a positive to negative ratio of 3:1.

Not 1:1 or 2:1.

And… Not 11:1.

She says we want to balance "levity" with "gravity."

Too much of one or the other and we can fly away into an ungrounded fantasyland or… into a pit of despair.

Levity + Gravity = Buoyancy.

When I first read that, I thought about one of Nassim Taleb's ideas on how we can cultivate our antifragility. He tells us that we want to take a "barbell" approach to life.

Imagine a barbell with weights on either side of bar:

Taleb tells us that, in pretty much every aspect of our lives we want to find a way to be *simultaneously* both super **AGGRESSIVE** *and* super **CONSERVATIVE**.

Building a business? Awesome. As you swing for the fences make sure you do it without ever risking knocking yourself completely out of the game.

That's our antifragile barbell:

(Conservative)——————(Aggressive)

Notice that we can stand that barbell up and drop in levity and gravity. Like this:

(Levity)

(Gravity)

That's our antifragile buoyancy barbell.
How's YOURS?
Do you tend to lean one way or the other?
Too much levity?
Or…
Too much gravity?
What's one little way you can optimize today?
Here's to building your buoyancy biceps one rep at a time!

HOW TO BECOME AN ICONOCLAST
THE SCIENCE OF BREAKING ICONS

I n his great book on the neuroscience of being an *Iconoclast*, Gregory Berns tells us that there are, essentially, three things that make the iconoclast special.

Here they are.

First: An iconoclast sees the world differently.

If we want to create something new and heroically awesome for the world, the first step is to see things differently than everyone else.

And guess what?

If we're constantly flooding our consciousness with inputs and responding to every single push notification and checking out the latest breaking news without any quiet time to think, that's pretty much impossible.

(Are you creating this time or are you living in an echo chamber of the latest and greatest?)

Second: We need to get really good at taming our amygdala.

Once you've stepped back and seen the world differently and then proposed an alternative reality, you're going to get pushback. Fear will, inevitably, arise. The iconoclast has trained his/her brain not to respond like normal people.

Iconoclasts have a big toolbox to deal with fear. We do things like approach rather than avoid our challenges ("Bring it on!") and remind ourselves that obstacles make us stronger.

(How about you?)

Finally, as iconoclasts-in-training, we need to develop our social intelligence.

Gregory tells us that effective iconoclasts develop a reputation for fairness and, essentially, being a trustworthy, good human.

(Let's do that.)

To recap our Iconoclastic big three:

1. See the world differently.
2. Tame the amygdala.
3. Be a good person.

Quick inventory…
Where are you strong?
What needs work?
And, how will YOU break some icons TODAY?

REVERSE INDICATORS
REFRAMING YOUR ENCOUNTERS WITH DRAGONS

L et's say you've decided to embark on a Heroic quest.

(GOOD DECISION!)

Now, every good hero's journey has some pretty epic dragon battle scenes. (Right?)

And, those encounters are, pretty much by definition, pretty intense. (Right?)

I mean, you don't leisurely stroll up to a dragon in the middle of your quest and just hop on it for a ride. (At least not until you're a full-fledged dragon-taming master!)

So, the focus of this +1°…

When you encounter the inevitable dragons on that adventure of yours, know this: Those intense feelings of "OMG!!! What have I done to my life?!" and that desire to run away from it all and run right back to the comfort of your old life are NORMAL!!

In fact, in one of our coaching sessions, Phil dropped this wisdom gem on me: He said that those moments of terror are often "reverse indicators."

We tend to think that when we feel terrified we're doing something WRONG.

Phil says: "NO NO NO!!!"

Those moments of discomfort are often REVERSE INDICA-TORS. They aren't necessarily signs that something is WRONG. They're often signs that something is RIGHT.

Specifically, they're often signs that you're right where you need to be to grow: Outside your comfort zone—which, you'll recall, feels really uncomfortable.

Of course, as with all (partial) truths, too much of a good thing isn't a good thing. We need to find the proper balance of challenge and skill as we practice our philosophy while embodying the virtues of wisdom, discipline, love and courage—finding that virtuous mean right there between the vices of excess and deficiency.

With that in mind and, assuming you've WOOPed your goals and you're willing to pay the price as you take the next steps on your Heroic quest...

Question time:

Feeling uncomfortable lately?

That discomfort might just be a sign that you need to take a deep breath, get excited about the opportunity to practice your philosophy and get to work.

If you *haven't* felt uncomfortable lately, then perhaps you need to quit sidestepping lizards and be willing to go into the forest of the unknown and meet your dragons.

Here's to your Heroic growth and embracing the reverse in-dicators that point the way.

PERCUSSUS RESURGO
"STRUCK DOWN, I RISE AGAIN!"

Harvey Dorfman was one of the world's top mental training coaches. He earned World Series rings as the mental training coach for the Oakland A's and the Florida Marlins.

In his old-school bible called *Coaching the Mental Game*, Dorfman walks us through the A to Z's of getting mentally tough. (He prefers to call it "mentally disciplined.")

"R" is for "Relentlessness."

He tells us: "Relentlessness is the reciprocal of quitting—yielding—giving up. It is an aggressive, persistent, attack-mode attitude. It defines a warrior. The relentless performer gives himself intensely, entirely, and constantly to competition."

To bring the point home, he drops a fantastically Heroic Latin phrase on us: *Percussus resurgo.*

"Struck down, I rise again."

Our +1°...

Anything knock YOU down lately?

Remember: *Percussus resurgo.* Struck down, we rise again. And again. And again. And again.

All day, every day. Especially TODAY.

EXTREME OWNERSHIP
NAVY SEAL WISDOM ON LEADERSHIP

U.S. Navy SEALs Jocko Willink and Leif Babin were two of the most senior leaders on the ground in the most intense battles of Iraq.

They wrote a great book about how to lead called *Extreme Ownership*.

The #1 rule?

Quit making excuses.

Instead, take EXTREME ownership of EVERYTHING in your life.

Emphasis on EXTREME and EVERYTHING.

What would that look like? Well, in essence, with that level of ownership, you'd never (but only never!!!) make an excuse or blame anyone. About anything. Ever.

Not at work. Not at home. Not on the road between home and work.

You'd resolve to choose the most optimal response to any given situation, learning from whatever setbacks arise as you immediately focus on the next best step.

Period. Repeat. Forever.

At work. At home. On the road between home and work.

EXTREME ownership.

Hooyah!

ON A BAD TEAM?
SEALS SAY: NO BAD TEAMS, JUST BAD LEADERS

I n our last +1°, Navy SEALs Jocko Willink and Leif Babin told us that leadership is all about EXTREME ownership. No excuses. No blaming. Ever.

They tell us that, ultimately, *there are no bad teams* per se, *only bad leaders*. To bring the point home, they tell us a story about guys in boats.

Imagine Navy SEAL training. You're already exhausted from weeks of basic training. Now it's time for Hell Week.

One of the most brutal aspects of the training is when the aspiring SEALs are split into "boat crews"—each with seven guys. Each team gets an old-school World War II-era inflatable boat that weighs 200 pounds. They need to carry this boat up and over twenty-foot-high sand berms and run with it for miles. Then they get to paddle it out to the ocean, dump it over so everyone's out and freezing wet and then paddle it back in.

And...

They're always competing with everyone else. If you lose, you have to go through extra, bonus brutal stuff while the winners get to take the next race off. (The instructors constantly remind everyone: "It pays to be a winner!")

So, with that in mind, imagine Boat Crew II. These guys win every single race. They're simply crushing it. And, although they're physically hammered, they're actually smiling throughout the process.

Then we have Boat Crew VI. These guys are LOSING every single race. To put it mildly, they are simply NOT crushing it. And, as you can imagine, they're not too happy about it—cursing and blaming one another for all their problems.

So… Each crew has a leader. Boat Crew VI's leader is convinced that they're losing because his team sucks. He's certain that Boat Crew II is simply made up of the best guys and his team isn't.

Now, our wise instructor knows that there's no such thing as a bad team, just a bad leader.

So, he devises a little experiment. He commands the leaders to swap teams. The leader from the always-winning Boat Crew II would now switch places with the leader from the always-losing Boat Crew VI.

What happens?

The worst boat crew suddenly became the best. They went from losing nearly every race to winning nearly every race.

As Jocko and Leif remind us: There are NO bad teams. Only bad leaders.

Let's shine the spotlight on YOU.

Whether it's at home or at work, do you ever think you're on a "bad team?"

Guess what… You're the problem. (Hah. Seriously.)

Quit blaming and criticizing.

Start taking EXTREME OWNERSHIP.

Give us all you've got.

TODAY.

OWNISH VS. VICTIMESE
LEARNING A NEW LANGUAGE

In Steve Chandler's great little book called *Reinventing Yourself*, he makes a distinction between being an "Owner" or a "Victim."

It's very much like David Emerald's "Victim vs. Creator" paradigm from his book *The Power of TED**.

One of the things Steve points out is that the LANGUAGE of an Owner is *very* different from the language of a Victim.

Here's how he puts it: "Owners use the words 'I can' a lot, while victims favored 'I can't.'" Owners had goals, projects, and challenges, whereas victims had problems, hassles, and nightmares. Owners said they were busy, and victims said they were swamped.

Owners were 'designing a life,' while victims were 'trying to make a living.' Owners were psyched and excited about changes in the workplace, while victims were worried and ticked off. Owners looked to see what they could get from an experience, while victims tried to get through it. Owners would plan things and victims would wish things."

Pop quiz…

What's YOUR native language?

Know this: "This link I'd seen between language and performance was interesting, but what was even more exciting was how people's lives would change once they began practicing using new language."

We are all, shall we say, bilingual in both Ownish *and* Victimese.

But…

How about we practice our Ownish a little more today and become a lot more mindful of when we might be slipping into Victimese?!

Want to go ALL IN?

Learn Extreme Ownish a la the *Extreme Ownership* guys.

I repeat…

The keys to mastering *that* dialect?

NEVER make excuses.

NEVER complain.

NEVER criticize.

Period.

YES LIVES IN THE LAND OF NO
WANT A BIG YES FROM LIFE?! EMBRACE THE NO'S

I n our last +1°, we talked about mastering Ownish and noticing when we slip into Victimese.

We also talked about going all in and mastering the dialect of
Extreme Ownish—which, I'm told, is where it's *really* at.

It's time to talk about one of the things Victims dread the
most.

It's a very short word.

Two letters.

N + O.

As in "No."

I can vividly remember Steve Chandler teaching me this
lesson he so perfectly captures in *Reinventing Yourself*.

Here's the short story.

Victims fear the word no and will do whatever they can to
avoid ever hearing it. As Steve says: "To a victim, 'no' means rejection. Total, devastating rejection. 'No' doesn't just sound like 'no'
to the victim, it sounds like, 'No, no, NO, you are NOT WORTH
ANYTHING!'"

He continues by saying: "Victims spend the better part of
their lives trying to avoid hearing the word 'no,' because they've
made it mean rejection—total, thorough, and personal—rejection. It is little wonder they want to avoid it whenever possible.
The trouble is that by avoiding 'no,' they also avoid 'yes.' The two
go together. They live together."

And, finally, he says: "The primary reason that people don't get what they want in life is that they are afraid to ask for it. Afraid of the rejection they have made 'no' to mean to themselves."

So… Yes and no live together.

In fact, as Steve told me: "**Yes** lives in the land of **no**."

Let's visualize that for a moment.

Draw a big circle on a piece of paper. Then a little circle inside the big one.

The big circle? That's the land of "No." That little circle? That's the land of "Yes." Very important thing to notice: The "Yes" lives within the land of "No."

Therefore, Captain Obvious echo here: Let's remember that if we want to get to Yes we MUST be willing to go through the land of No.

Want success? We must be willing to experience failure.

Practically speaking, what big "YES!" are you hoping to get from life?

Got it? Fantastic. Now, lace up your hiking shoes and start your trek through the land of No.

See you at the summit of Mount Yes, Hero.

GOESWITH
OUR NEW WISDOM WORD

I n our last +1°, we talked about the fact that YES lives in the land of NO.

We drew two circles. A big one (for the land of No) and then a small one within that big one (for the land of Yes).

Moral of the story: *Yes lives in the land of No.*

Want a YES from life?! Be willing to get a lot of No's.

Be willing to get rejected. Be willing to experience a lot of failures. Be willing to make a lot of mistakes.

I repeat: *Yes lives in the land of No.*

Apparently, Alan Watts liked to say that some things so consistently "go with" other things that we should have a word for it: "goeswith."

For example, night *goeswith* day.

Light *goeswith* dark.

Success *goeswith* failure.

And…

Yes *goeswith* no.

That's just how it is.

Here's to embracing reality and remembering that everything *goeswith* everything else.

Then remember to say "YES!" to it all.

TODAY.

DEATH COOKIES
FUEL FOR THE JOURNEY TO YOUR INFINITE POTENTIAL

Continuing our discussion of how to forge antifragile confidence, let's look at another way to dominate it.

As we've discussed, science says that the healthiest and most Heroic among us (and all of us in our healthiest and most Heroic moments) APPROACH rather than AVOID our challenges.

Here's another way to look at that concept.

In my very first coaching session with Phil Stutz, he taught me that "Speed Is a Force." He told me that our confidence erodes the longer we wait to take action once we *know* what we need to do.

The solution?

Close the gap between conception and action. Do it now!

Phil told me that one of the best ways to CREATE that Speed is to "eat death cookies."

"Death cookies"?

Yes. Death cookies.

Short story: Phil tells us that we're all afraid to die. We're afraid of the big, jumbo-end-of-life kinda death AND we're also afraid of the micro-moments in which we fear our precious little ego might get killed.

But here's the deal.

Those little moments of fear are THE source of all our potential power.

If we consistently *avoid* them, we won't grow. If we consistently APPROACH them, we catalyze our growth.

Those little micro-moments of fear?

They're death cookies. Each little death cookie you eat makes you stronger.

In fact, Phil tells us that the cookie with the most fear is the one that is the most valuable. We just need to discipline ourselves to eat it.

The +1°...

What's freaking you out a bit these days?

More specifically, what's ONE thing you *know* should do but you're having a hard time getting yourself to do it?

Remember that your infinite potential exists on the other side of that discomfort.

Eat the death cookie.

Now.

VULNERABILITY HANGOVERS
EVER HAD ONE?

B rené Brown tells us that what we all *really* want from other people is for them to be authentic. And *that* means we need them to be vulnerable.

And… Guess what the *last* thing is that any of us actually *want* to be? Yep. You guessed it. Vulnerable.

Which (laughing) presents a little issue in our quest to create authentic relationships. The very thing we want (and need!) from one another is the thing we have the hardest time giving.

Which leads us to our +1°.

Have you ever *really* put yourself out there and boldly expressed the best version of yourself and then woke up the next day wondering what in the world you were thinking?

(Laughing. Me, too. Too many times to count.)

Brené calls that a "vulnerability hangover."

And, she tells us about one of her biggest hangovers. With beautiful irony, she tells us about the day she gave a little TEDx Talk on her research on shame and vulnerability. She really put herself out there, sharing her own challenges and struggles.

She felt pretty good as she was giving the talk but woke up the next day FREAKED OUT that she'd told the audience about her nervous breakdown and other personal details of her life.

The talk was, of course, filmed. She immediately started imagining calling the organizers and having them delete the talk. If that didn't work maybe she could somehow get it off the servers. There's no way, she thought, that she could endure having a couple hundred MORE people see her in such a vulnerable state.

Fast-forward a decade and nearly ONE HUNDRED MILLION people have benefited from Brené's willingness to dare greatly and share her authentic, vulnerable self.

Which leads us back to YOU and this +1°.

How can YOU be even more authentically alive today? Let's stay grounded (of course) and see if we can (wisely) be a little more vulnerable today.

And, if you wake up tomorrow with a little vulnerability hangover, remind yourself that the feeling is a REVERSE INDICATOR. It's a sign that something's RIGHT not wrong.

Here's to you being you.

All of you.

TODAY.

NEVER WASTE A MIS-TAKE
IT'S ALL AWESOME DATA

Have you ever made a mistake?

I just laughed out loud after typing that.

I've made a mistake or two million as well.

Here's the deal: When we approach it with the right mindset (that would be a growth, experimental mindset), we come to realize that those mistakes are P R E C I O U S.

The data we get on what *doesn't work* is priceless.

Therefore, never beat yourself up about a mis-take.

Simply remind yourself that we either win or we learn and learning is winning. Remind yourself that no movie was ever shot from start to finish without a ton of re-takes. Think of Emerson's chess learning-wins.

Then say to yourself "Needs work!" as you rewind your game film, see yourself executing the missed scene perfectly and then get back at it.

Repeat.

Forever.

Especially...

TODAY.

DWYSYWD
THE LAWS OF LEADERSHIP

Jim Kouzes and Barry Posner are two of the world's leading academic researchers on the science of leadership. They offer us a few Leadership Laws.

Here's their First Law of Leadership: "If you don't believe the messenger, you won't believe the message."

In short, people follow people they TRUST. Earning the trust and loyalty of those you aspire to lead is the first step in leadership. You do that by building a credible foundation.

Which leads us to their Second Law of Leadership—the way we actually earn that trust. It's very simple. Shockingly simple, in fact. Here it is: "Do What You Say You Will Do."

"DWYSYWD" for short.

Our +1° is simple: Do YOU do what you say you will do?

Notice how often you say you'll do things that you don't actually do (and perhaps never intended to do). Think about both the big things and the little things.

When you say you'll get back to someone tomorrow, GET BACK TO THEM tomorrow. When you say you'll play a game of chess with your kids, play a game of chess with your kids. When you say you'll show up and meditate/exercise/work tomorrow morning, show up and meditate/exercise/work tomorrow morning.

DWYSYWD.

Today.

MAKING NEW COMMITMENTS
WHAT TO DO WHEN YOU NEED TO ADJUST COURSE

Doing what you say you will do is Kouzes's and Posner's Leadership Law #2. It's the foundation of credibility and trust. I repeat: DWYSYWD.

Period.

And...

Sometimes life happens and data presents itself between the time you made a commitment and the time you intended to deliver on it.

In those situations when it no longer makes sense to follow through with our commitments, what do we do?

First, we step back and make sure that when we make a commitment we're REALLY committed to following through. We don't want our default to be constantly breaking commitments. We want to discipline ourselves to only say we're going to do something if we're *really* committed to actually doing it.

And, of course, we need to do everything in our power to HONOR those commitments and be appropriately (compassionately-ruthlessly) honest with ourselves when we're not doing our best.

With that practice of consistently doing what we say we will do in place and a fierce commitment to doing our best to honor the commitments we make, we're in a better position to change things up when the situation calls for it.

In those moments?

We get clear on what our *new* commitment will be and we communicate that change with whomever is involved—renegotiating whatever needs to be renegotiated with as much respect and grace as possible.

Easier said than done, of course.

For now…

Do you have any commitments you need to follow through on? Any that need to be renegotiated with a new set of commitments?

What's one little (or big!) thing you can do today to move toward a deeper level of integrity?

Get on that.

Close the gap.

Live with *Areté*.

TODAY.

CELEBRATE CONFUSION
YOUR GATEWAY TO CLARITY

Once upon a time, I was at a Tony Robbins event. Thousands of people. Fired up. And, literally, walking on fire.

I basically filled up an entire journal as I was learning how to unleash the power within. Here's one idea that has stuck with me over the last twenty years.

Imagine thousands of people in an auditorium. Someone stands up to ask a question.

They start with: "I'm confused…"

Then Tony interrupts them and has the entire audience stand up and give them a MASSIVE, extended, standing ovation.

And, EVERY SINGLE TIME someone starts one of their questions with "I'm confused…" everyone hops out of their seats to cheer.

The message: "You're confused? That's fantastic!!!"

Why?

Because that confusion is our gateway to clarity.

That confusion signifies our willingness to leave an old way of thinking and move toward a new way of thinking.

Now, as fate would have it, going from one way of thinking to a new way of thinking is rarely a super elegant process.

We like to THINK it should be a snap-your-fingers and you instantly have it all figured out kinda thing but, alas, that's not how it works. At all.

Growth is messy.

Wrapping our brains and our behaviors around new ways of seeing the world is messy.

Enter: Confusion.

And, enter: A standing ovation!

We need to discipline ourselves to associate confusion with AWESOME not with terror. Easier said than done which is why we need to practice it.

So…

How about you?

Feeling any confusion about anything lately?

Step back. Give yourself a standing ovation.

Remember that a good life is one hero's journey after another. And, by Joseph Campbell's definition, living heroically means being willing to leave the known world and venture into the forest of the unknown. Again. And again. And again. And THAT, by definition, can be a bit scary. It's supposed to be.

I repeat…

Let's get comfortable being uncomfortable.

I've heard that's the fastest way to activate our Heroic potential.

"Bring it on!"

"I'm excited!"

"Standing ovation!"

HEROIC REFRAMING
HOW TO BUILD ANTIFRAGILE, HEROIC CONFIDENCE

Here's a question we want to have ready at hand when we hit the inevitable challenges/glitches/dragon battles/etc.

"How can I use this to get even stronger?"

Our +1°…

Bring to mind something that might be stressing you out at the moment. Maybe it's a big creative challenge you're in the middle of or a recent setback you're recovering from.

Apply the Heroic reframing question to it.

"How can I use this to get even stronger?"

Well, how can you?

Pause. Reflect. Act.

Then do that again the next time you feel stress bubbling.

And again the next time.

Repeat. Forever.

Forge your Heroic, antifragile confidence one (micro-challenging) rep at a time.

Close the gap.

Live with *Areté*.

TODAY.

THE SECOND ARROW
QUIT SHOOTING YOURSELF WITH IT

In *No Mud, No Lotus,* Thích Nhất Hạnh tells us that suffering is a part of life.

You can't create a beautiful lotus flower without some mud. As he says, lotuses don't grow in marble.

And...

You can't create a happy, flourishing life without some suffering. That's just how it is. We need to embrace that reality.

In fact, Thầy (as he's known to his students) tells us that a big part of happiness is learning how to "suffer well." We want to quit making our suffering worse than it needs to be.

To bring the point home, the Buddha shared a story about two arrows. The first arrow strikes you and it hurts. But, if a second arrow hits you in the *exact* same spot, the pain won't just double, it'll go up TENfold. (Ouch!)

But, here's the deal. WE are the ones shooting *ourselves* with that second arrow. How? By complaining about it, wishing it didn't happen, moping around, etc.

In *Self-Compassion*, Kristin Neff tells us the same thing. She tells us that pain is inevitable in life but that suffering is a function of how much we resist that pain.

She shares an equation: Suffering = Pain x Resistance.

Pain happens. Our *suffering* is a function of how much we resist it. Shoot ourselves with that second arrow and suffering goes up exponentially. So, let's not do that.

Got any challenges in your life right now?

Are you shooting yourself with a second arrow?

If so, stop.

Let's accept that suffering is a part of life and remember: No mud, no lotus.

TOLLE ON FOOD POISONING
SAME RULES APPLY TO THOUGHTS

H ave you ever had food poisoning?

Me too. Not fun, eh? How'd you get yours?

Actually. Bad question. I'm having flashbacks of the time I got so sick in Bali I couldn't get out of bed for days. Yikes.

Seriously though.

My hunch is that you don't make a habit of doing whatever you did that led to the food poisoning.

Well, guess what…

Eckhart Tolle tells us that it's the same thing with our THOUGHTS.

Here's how he puts it in *The Power of Now*: "Once you realize that a certain kind of food makes you sick, would you carry on eating that food and keep asserting that it is okay to be sick?"

He makes that point in the context of people "accepting" certain things in their lives but then getting stuck there rather than moving all the way through that phase to a deeper sense of enlightenment.

He says: "It is certainly true that, when you accept your resentment, moodiness, anger, and so on, you are no longer forced to act them out blindly, and you are less likely to project them onto others. But I wonder if you are not deceiving yourself. When you have been practicing acceptance for a while, as you have, there comes a point when you need to go on to the next stage, where those negative emotions are not created anymore. If you don't, your 'acceptance' just becomes a mental label that allows your ego to continue to indulge in unhappiness and so strengthen your separation from other people, your surroundings, your here and now."

Our +1° has three parts.

First, are you eating any FOODS that you know don't work for you? Pick one. Is now a good time to let it go?

Second, are you eating any THOUGHTS that are making you sick? Is now a good time to stop nibbling and/or feasting on those thoughts?

Third, are you engaging in any BEHAVIORS that make you sick? Yah? Which one is ready to go?

Here's to ditching the stuff that makes you sick and indulging in the stuff that makes you feel great.

And, let's remember Seneca's wisdom that the *real* game of life is to get to a place where doing/eating the stuff that is *best* for us is what we *most* enjoy.

Close the gap.

Live with *Areté*.

Activate your Heroic potential.

TODAY.

ZIGS & ZAGS
EMERSON ON YOUR HEROIC VOYAGE

I have read Ralph Waldo Emerson's Heroic essay *Self-Reliance* at least a dozen times.

Among many other wisdom gems, Emerson tells us that: "The voyage of the best ship is a zigzag line of a hundred tacks. See the line from a sufficient distance, and it straightens itself to the average tendency."

Guess what? Same rules apply for our own lives.

We zig. And we zag.

Step back far enough and we can see a straight line from one version of ourselves to the highest versions of ourselves.

The challenge?

When we're in the midst of figuring things out it's easy to doubt ourselves and think that it SHOULD be one straight, unbroken up-and-to-the-right growth curve.

That's when we'd be wise to remember a couple other gems from our wise friend…

Emerson also tells us: "If I have lost confidence in myself, I have the universe against me."

Therefore, he says: "Trust thyself: every heart vibrates to that iron string."

Those zigs and zags? They're part of the process.

Trust thyself. Play the long game. Get back to work.

Close the gap. Live with *Areté*.

TODAY.

THE HOME RUN KING
IS ALSO THE STRIKE OUT KING

As you know if you're a baseball fan, Babe Ruth was his generation's great home run king.

He hit 714 home runs.

AND...

He struck out 1,330 times.

Note: For the non-math majors in the crowd, that's nearly TWICE as many times.

As you ALSO know if you're a baseball fan, Aaron Judge recently broke the American League single-season record for home runs.

He hit sixty-two (!) home runs in a single season.

Note: Even the great Babe Ruth maxed out at sixty (!) home runs in a single season.

And...

You know how many times Judge struck out in 2022?

He struck out 175 times in 2022 alone. (That's nearly THREE TIMES as many strikeouts to home runs!)

And...

When I was checking in on the 2022 playoffs, I noticed that our modern-day home run hero recently set ANOTHER record. He struck out FOUR times in a playoff game for the FOURTH time—the most of any player in Major League Baseball history.

I repeat: The greatest home run kings are ALSO the greatest strike out kings.

Which reminds me of some wisdom from another Yankees legend, Derek Jeter.

Derek Jeter once said: "To be able to hit the game-winning home run, you have to be willing to strike out in the same batter's box."

Our +1°…

Strike out lately?

Perfect.

Remember our home run king.

Work your protocol.

Get back in the batter's box.

Give us all you've got.

TODAY.

THE PARADOX OF FIRE
THE OBSTACLE IS THE WAY

Marcus Aurelius once wrote a reminder to himself that is as powerful today as it was when he reflected on it nearly two thousand years ago.

He told himself: "The impediment to action advances the action. What stands in the way becomes the way."

Ryan Holiday wrote a brilliant book inspired by that wisdom called *The Obstacle Is the Way*.

We need to know that, when we approach an obstacle with the necessary wisdom, what *stands in the way* BECOMES the way. The *impediment* to action ADVANCES the action.

Note: That's the essence of what it means to be antifragile.

We're always trying to make problems or "obstacles" go away. But what if we allowed them to *be* the way?

What if we trained ourselves to immediately accept (and love!) what is as we rubbed our hands together at the opportunity to create a better plan using those obstacles as fuel for the next level of our growth?

In *The Inner Citadel* (a book about Aurelius, recommended by Ryan, written by the great French philosopher Pierre Hadot), we learn about "the paradox of fire."

Here it is…

Fire "grows stronger the more things are brought to it which could smother it, or at least present an obstacle to it."

That's very much like Nassim Taleb's wind.

Recall that a strong wind *extinguishes* a candle but it FUELS the fire.

The question is ...

Which are you?

INVINCIBILITY
HERE'S YOUR TICKET

A ll of that leads us to what may be the most important part of this entire book.

It's time to make you invincible.

How? Via one simple formula. We'll get to that formula in a moment. First, let's go back to one of my very first coaching sessions with Phil Stutz nearly seven years ago.

As we discussed (and I am *deliberately* repeating myself here), Phil ended by saying "you have a lot of emotional stamina—maybe the most I've ever seen." I wrote that down on page five of that day's notes and I made a note to ask him what he meant by that mysterious phrase "emotional stamina" when we chatted next.

Of course, the first question in our next session the following week was: "What's emotional stamina?"

Phil's answer will be tattooed on my brain forever and, if you feel so inspired, I encourage you to consider tattooing it on YOUR brain as well.

He told me that, if you want to cultivate the ability to deal with life's challenges you need emotional stamina and, if you want emotional stamina, you need to run a certain algorithm in your life. This one: "The worse you feel, the MORE committed you are to your protocol."

Note: A choir of angels sang at that moment. (And might have just made another appearance for me.)

All of which begs the question: What do YOU do when you feel bad?

If you're like most people (and how I used to be), the WORSE you feel the WORSE you act—you stop doing the fundamentals that keep you plugged in.

You stay up late and watch stupid stuff past the time you know you should be asleep. You stare at your screen when you should be connecting with your kids. You pay less attention to what you're eating and let your training slip. And maybe you engage in a bunch of other more destructive behaviors.

But…

What if…

When you felt TERRIBLE, you (somehow!) got yourself to DO THE VERY THINGS you do when you're at your best with a FEROCITY that you didn't even know you had?

What if, when you typically tend to spiral DOWN into a circus because you're not feeling great and start engaging in sub-optimal behaviors, you spiral UP and recommit yourself with an even greater level of grounded intensity to being the change you want to see by doing the very things you know serve you best?

I'll tell you PRECISELY what happens when you do that because I know, firsthand, what happens.

Rather than spiraling down and out every time life gets hard, you're going to get STRONGER.

A lot stronger.

You're still going to have "highs" and "lows" because you're human.

But those highs are going to be HIGHER, and your lows are also going to be HIGHER. And that is a really, *really,* **really** empowering feeling.

In fact, we could call that Antifragile Confidence—when you know that you have what it takes to respond to whatever life throws at you and not only deal with it but use it as fuel to get better.

One simple algorithm, practiced repeatedly: "The worse you feel, the more committed you are to your protocol."

THAT, my dear Hero, is your ticket to invincibility.

Of course, as inspiring as that possibility is, before you can even work your protocol, you need to HAVE one—which is why we need to spend time helping you get REALLY clear on what you do when you're on.

Then we're going to challenge you to make your prior best your new baseline by DOING what you do when you're at your best more and more consistently while eliminating those kryptonites that derail our hard work.

It's time to take the first steps in creating that protocol. We'll start by simplifying self-development—which is the focus of our next objective.

THE BIG 3, AN ORIGIN STORY
COVEY + ROBBINS + FREUD

Stephen Covey's *7 Habits of Highly Effective People* was, literally, the *very* first self-development book I ever read.

Quick story…

It's the summer of 1995. I'm a twenty-one-year-old student at UCLA—studying Psychology with a minor in Business. At the time, there was no such thing as "Positive Psychology." I thought about getting my PhD, but I couldn't see how I'd study what I wanted to study.

Then, one day, I found myself behind a one-way mirror tracking the behavior of some kids. I was sitting next to the husband of the PhD student for whom I was working.

This guy worked for the old Arthur Andersen. We hit it off. Long story a little shorter, they wound up recruiting me to join them and sent me off to a global leadership event at their corporate headquarters.

THAT's where I was introduced to Covey and the idea that we could, with wisdom and effort, deliberately change our lives.

As a first-generation college student with hard-working but very conservative Catholic parents, this was a revelation to me.

My life changed that weekend. I could SEE that I had a LOT more power than I used to think.

I didn't know what I would do with that awareness yet, but simply KNOWING that we could deliberately strive to become the best version of ourselves (in service to the world) was an insight that profoundly influenced my life.

One of the things Covey taught was that we each have "Roles" in our lives and that we'd be wise to get clear on the "Goals" we have for each of those Roles and then architect our lives around them. He captured this idea in the phrase "Roles and Goals."

I loved that idea. Only, at least for me, I found that it was REALLY easy to get REALLY overwhelmed by ALL the Roles I play. These days, I'm a father and a husband and a philosopher and a CEO and a friend and a teacher and an athlete and … Where do I begin and where does it end and what should I prioritize and … ?

Fast-forward a few years.

It's now 1999. I can still vividly remember driving a U-Haul from the east coast to Los Angeles while listening to Tony Robbins's Personal Power II CDs after winning the business plan competition at UCLA's Anderson School of Management and getting ready to raise $5 million in the midst of the dot-com boom of the late 90s.

Tony had a similar framework to Covey.

Rather than Roles and Goals, he called them "Categories of Improvement." I diligently tried to master each of the "Categories" of my life but, again, quickly found myself overwhelmed. There were SO MANY areas of my life I wanted to dial in! They were basically near infinite.

Fast-forward another decade and a half.

I've dedicated my life to studying and teaching these ideas.

I encounter Sigmund Freud's quip that a good life is, essentially, all about two things: Work and Love.

A choir of angels sang at PRECISELY that moment.

"Work and Love."

YES!

That's it.

Only...

If we have a hard time getting out of bed in the morning because of poor lifestyle choices, we're going to have a REALLY hard time giving our best to our Work *or* to our Love.

Therefore, we need to *start* with ENERGY and then focus on Work and Love and ...

VOILÀ.

We have our Big 3: Energy, Work, and Love.

Get those right and we're *at least* 80% there.

That's Part I of the Big 3 origin story.

THE BIG 3 X 2
IDENTITY, VIRTUES & BEHAVIORS

I f we agree that a good life (essentially) comes down to getting our Energy, Work, and Love optimized, that begs the question…

How do we do that?

Knowing that the ultimate game we're playing is to express the best version of ourselves more and more consistently by living with *Areté* as we put our virtues in action, I propose that we need to get clear on *another* Big 3.

First, we need to know who we are at our best: Energy, Work, and Love wise. We'll refer to those best versions of ourselves as our "Identities."

Then we want to get clear on what Virtues that best version of ourselves embodies.

Then, most importantly, we need to DO the things that best version of ourselves would do. We'll call those "Behaviors."

Enter, our second Big 3: Identity, Virtues, and Behaviors.

We'll spend a little time unpacking each of those Big 3s then we'll embrace some Learning 101 interleaving and spaced repetition so we can go from Theory to Practice to Mastery Together TODAY.

SAWS VS. CHAINSAWS
IT ALL ALWAYS STARTS WITH ENERGY

L et's go back to Stephen Covey's 7 *Habits* for a moment. This time, we'll look at the very last habit of highly effective people.

After teaching us the importance of being proactive, beginning with the end in mind, doing first things first, thinking win/win, seeking first to understand and then leveraging the power of synergy (Habits #1–6!), Covey tells us that we need to make sure we take time to renew ourselves as we "Sharpen the Saw."

To bring the point home, he tells us to imagine walking in a forest. We see someone sawing down a tree. It's obvious to us that the blade is dull—which is making that person work *way* harder and longer than they would need to if they had a sharp blade.

So, we suggest that they sharpen their saw a bit. In response, the person tells us: "I'm TOO BUSY to take the time to sharpen my saw!"

Moral of the story: Don't be that saw person who thinks you're too busy to get your Energy dialed in or you run the risk of not having the vitality you need to give your best to your Work and Love!!

(Personal question: ARE YOU BEING THAT GUY OR GAL?)

Of course, I love that story.

And... I say, why just take the time to "sharpen the saw"?

If getting our Energy is SO ESSENTIAL to our flourishing (it is!), then I say we step back and take the time to BUILD A CHAINSAW!!!

Remember: Science says that ZEST (a.k.a. ENERGY!) is THE #1 predictor of our well-being and flourishing—which (echo!) is why a good, Heroic life *begins* with getting our energy to Heroic levels so we can show up most powerfully in our Work and Love.

Therefore, I repeat…

Let's make sure we're prioritizing our Energy.

Don't just sharpen your saw.

Build a chainsaw.

ENERGY, ETYMOLOGY OF
THE CAPACITY FOR WORK (& LOVE)

B efore we move on …

It's time for another etymological lesson. Do you happen to know what the word *energy* literally means?

The word *energy* comes from the ancient Greek word *energeia* which has two parts: *en + ergon*.

It literally means "in work."

My 2,084-page *American Heritage* dictionary defines the word as: "The capacity for work or vigorous activity."

Perfect.

Only, for our purposes, I think we should consider slightly modifying that to: "Energy is the capacity for Work and Love."

The next logical question is simple: How do we create Heroic levels of Energy?

To answer *that* question, let's bust out our favorite microscopes and see if we can find some little energy powerhouses within our bodies.

MEET YOUR MITOCHONDRIA
THE POWERHOUSES IN EVERY CELL

Look inside almost every single cell of your body and you'll find those little powerhouses of human energy.

We'll skip the details and the final exam but, as you may recall from your high school biology class, those powerhouses are called mitochondria.

Know this: The health of *those* little guys plays THE leading role in YOUR health and well-being. We'd die in seconds if our mitochondria stopped producing energy.

Fun fact: It's impossible to know the exact number with certainty, but, with hundreds to thousands of mitochondria in nearly every one of our forty or so TRILLION cells, we have as many as a QUADRILLION mitochondria in our body.

That's a one followed by sixteen zeroes. Add them all up and you get 10% of our total body weight.

All of that is fascinating. And it all begs the next question: How do we take good care of our mitochondria?

I just smiled as I typed that out. Why? Because even *asking* that question is a *huge* step forward.

If all we asked ourselves during the day was: "Is what I'm about to do going to help my mitochondria do their jobs as well as they can?" we'd *dramatically* improve our Energy and, by extension, the quality of our Work and our Love lives.

Details on how to go about doing that to follow in Objective VI on Dominating the Fundamentals.

For now, I'll ask you a simple question: What's the #1 thing you *already* know you *could* be doing to dial in your Energy?

And, perhaps even more importantly, what's the #1 thing you *already* know you could STOP doing that would most powerfully boost your Energy?

Maybe it's eliminating alcohol. Or sugar. Or late-night binge-watching or…

Whatever those #1s are, it's time to get ourselves Heroically Energized so we can show up most powerfully in our Work and in our Love.

TODAY.

P.S. One more fun fact: Did you know that your mitochondrial DNA are inherited exclusively via your mother? Yep. "Thanks, mom!"

DEEP WORK VS. SHALLOW WORK
AN EQUATION TO ACTIVATE YOUR SUPERPOWERS

Now that we've (hopefully!) established the fact that a great life starts with getting our Energy dialed in, it's time to focus all that Energy on our Work and on our Love.

I'm not going to need to sell you on the importance of Work as much as I'll need to make sure you're properly balancing and integrating all that Work time with the Love in your life.

But... I do want to make sure we're going to the next level together and doing GENIUS Work rather than Mediocre Work.

Quick note before we jump in: You have unique roles and quests in your life. HONOR them. Turn Pro and go ALL IN on being a world-class Mom or Dad (or whatever it is for you) if that's what you've decided you're here to do in this phase of your life.

And remember: We are NOT trying to optimize our Work with a primary focus on achieving all the extrinsic goals society tries to seduce us to pursue. The wealth and the fame and power and all that? It's fine. But let that be a BY-PRODUCT of (and fuel for) our commitment to growth and connection and making a meaningful contribution to our communities. THAT's how we eudaimonically flourish and serve heroically.

With that disclaimer, let's kick off our Genius Work discussion by inviting one of my favorite thinkers (and friends) to the party: Cal Newport.

Cal has a very big brain. He got his PhD from MIT and is a professor of Computer Science at Georgetown. He's also written a number of great books, including one of my all-time favorites: *Deep Work.*

In *Deep Work*, Cal tells us that we can either do Deep Work or we can do Shallow Work. Deep Work, he says, is becoming simultaneously more RARE *and* more VALUABLE. (In fact, he tells us that the ability to do Deep Work is a superpower in the twenty-first century.)

While most people flit around from one Shallow Work task (email/Slack message/reactive this or that) to another, very few of us are unplugging from technology and locking ourselves in a bubble of focus where we can do some truly impactful Deep Work.

But… *That's* where the real magic happens.

(Another personal question: How are YOU doing with that?)

Cal has a Deep Work equation that's worth internalizing before we extend it into what will become our Soul Force equation. He tells us:

High Quality Work Produced = Time Spent x Intensity of Focus

In other words: Want to produce some GREAT work in a very efficient period of time?

Increase the intensity (!) of your focus.

How? Deep Work.

Turn everything off. Give yourself a block of time to do nothing but Deep Work.

Repeat that tomorrow.

And then again. And again. And again.

We'll come back to this (again and again!) as we architect our Masterpiece Days and hone our ability to focus.

GENIUS WORK VS. MEDIOCRE WORK
OUR REAL JOBS

Deep Work is awesome. And, I say: "Why stop at Deep Work when we can go for GENIUS Work?"

Recall the fact that both the Romans and the Greeks had a word for our inner guiding spirit—that Heroic best within each of us.

The Greeks called it your *daimon*.

The Romans called it your *genius*.

As we discussed, WAY back in the day, the Romans believed we each had our own genius. It was kinda like a little mini-me only more like a SUPER-ME. If we ever did anything amazing, it was said our GENIUS had done it.

Note: This is one of the reasons why experts on creativity (from Steven Pressfield to Elizabeth Gilbert to Stephen King) tell us that OUR job in the whole creative process is to simply create the conditions such that we can more and more consistently connect with and express that best version of ourselves.

Again: If the ultimate game is to bring our best, most *eudaimonic* versions of ourselves to more and more moments throughout our day (it is!), then, when we succeed at doing that with our Work, we could say we're doing Daimon or Genius Work so… That's officially our target.

No more Mediocre Work. Let's go ALL IN on creating the conditions that will allow us to do Genius Work.

THE GENIUS WORK EQUATION
ENERGY X TIME X FOCUS

With that in mind, know this...

The FIRST and most important variable in our Genius Work Equation isn't actually "Time Spent."

It's ENERGY.

When we get our ENERGY dialed in and then consistently focus THAT Energy like a *chainsaw* on what's truly most important Work-wise, we might astonish ourselves with Genius Work.

I say: Let's!

Therefore, the Deep Work equation: **High Quality Work Produced = Time Spent x Intensity of Focus**

Becomes this Genius Work equation: **Genius Work Produced = ENERGY x Time Spent x Intensity of Focus**

Note: We'll optimize that even more in Objective VII when we activate your superpower known as Soul Force.

MEDIOCRITY VS. EXCELLENCE
SUMMIT THAT RUGGED MOUNTAIN

S peaking of "mediocre," now might be a good time for another quick etymology lesson and pop quiz ...

Do you happen to know what the word *mediocre* *literally* means?

It's from an ancient Latin word: *mediocris.*

Medius = "middle" + *ocris* = "rugged mountain."

So ... The word *mediocre* LITERALLY means to get stuck in the middle of a rugged mountain. Isn't that fascinating?

Mediocrity.

That's *definitely* not where we want to get stuck.

As always, that begs the practical question: How do we make it through that midway point and summit the peak of our potential?

Let's open up our thesaurus for some clues.

We'll start with synonyms for mediocre.

There are a lot of them: "ordinary, average, middling, middle-of-the-road, uninspired, undistinguished, indifferent, unexceptional, unexciting, unremarkable, run-of-the-mill, pedestrian, prosaic, lackluster, forgettable, amateur, amateurish."

Eek. Those are all great ways to get stuck.

But ... Guess what? There's only ONE antonym for mediocre. Can you guess what it is?

"Excellent."

Yep. That's the ticket.

EXCELLENCE.

When we hit those inevitable tough spots on the rugged mountain that is our Heroic quest, we need to show up with *excellence*. We need to do our best.

You may recall that the Greeks had a word for that as well.

Areté.

That's *always* the best way to high five our inner daimons as we joyfully summit those rugged mountains of life where our Genius resides.

See you at the summit, Hero!

EXCITING GOALS
CREATIVE HEROES NEVER RUN OUT OF THEM

S peaking of summits, Mihaly Csikszentmihalyi tells us that the most Heroic among us are ...

"Like the climber who reaches the top of the mountain and, after looking around in wonder at the magnificent view, rejoices at the sight of an even taller neighboring peak, these people never run out of exciting goals."

Yep.

That sounds about right.

What's *your* next peak, Hero?

And ...

Is TODAY a good day to take the next steps on your next quest?

See you at that summit as well, Hero!

HEROIC RELATIONSHIPS
ARISTOTLE +1°

A lright. We're on a roll.

We want to get our Energy optimized to Heroic levels so we can do Genius Work. Got it.

Then what? Then we want to make sure we're prioritizing the next critical facet of our Big 3: LOVE.

There are a lot of things we can discuss here. Let's start by bringing Aristotle back to the party to hear his thoughts.

This time, we'll be hanging out with him and a couple of the world's leading positive psychologists who also happen to be two friends who *also* happen to be the authors of another one of my all-time favorite books.

Hero, Meet James Pawelski and Suzie Pileggi Pawelski.

James and Suzie are two of the world's leading scholars on the science of virtuous relationships.

They wrote a great book called *Happy Together* in which they tell us that Aristotle told us that we can have one of a few different types of relationships.

Here's the quick take...

We can have a relationship based purely on having fun. This is hedonic in nature. When the fun ends, the relationship tends to end.

Nothing wrong with this, of course, but Aristotle tells us that this isn't the highest form of a relationship and that we can do better.

The next kind of relationship is based on making money together. These relationships are transactional. When the money dries up, the friendship tends to do the same.

Again, nothing inherently *wrong* with this type of relationship per se, but it's not the highest form of a relationship.

Aristotle tells us that the best relationships are *eudaimonic* in nature. In these relationships, we deeply care about the other person's well-being, and we truly want to see them and help them flourish.

THIS, he says, is the highest form of relationship.

James and Suzie call this an "Aristotelian relationship" and, in their book on intimate relationships, they wisely encourage us to become "Aristotelian lovers."

All of which is awesome.

And …

I think that there's *another* level to which we can all aspire to form relationships.

I say, let's form *HEROIC* relationships.

Let's have fun supporting one another in activating our Heroic potential so we can change the world together.

Day 1. All in.

Let's go, my dear Heroic friend!

WE SEE HEROES
IN THE FACES OF MEN & WOMEN

Walt Whitman once said: "In the faces of men and women, I see God."

You know what I see?

I see HEROES.

Imagine...

When you're out and about today (and, perhaps even more importantly, when you're in and hanging out with your family today), take a moment to step back and SEE the absolute best, most heroically awesome essence of the people with whom you're interacting.

And remember this important (and sobering) fact...

It's hard to see in others what we're not seeing in ourselves.

Therefore...

Let's make sure the first person in whom we see the Heroic tomorrow morning is that person looking back at us in the mirror.

I see you, Hero.

Day 1. All in.

LET'S GO.

COMPASSION VS. ENCOURAGEMENT
IT'S TIME TO HAVE COURAGE TOGETHER

Alll of that leads us back to our redefined sense of Love we chatted about in our first Objective.

We'll start integrating our Love practices as we architect our Masterpiece Days in our next objective.

For now, remember that it all starts with Love 0.0.

Quite simply: We're going to have a hard time giving others the love we aren't giving ourselves.

The fastest way to dial this in? Identify the #1 thing you do when you're at your best. Then make a 101% nonnegotiable commitment to yourself TO DO THAT every. single. day.

Love 1.0 is all about showing up powerfully for our friends and family.

The fastest way to dial *this* in? Put your phone away. Science says it's a distraction and will erode the depth of your connection. Show your loved ones you love them by focusing on *them* not on your phone.

Love 2.0 is all about those micro-moments of positivity resonance with various people throughout your day.

Again, the #1 obstacle here is your smartphone. Put it away. Exit your cocoon of self-absorption and be PRESENT.

Love 3.0 is what we call Heroic love. We're going to come back to this in a moment because I think it's so important and so rarely discussed.

Love 8.0 is love for our work.

We want to KNOW that, when we're doing it right, there's actually NO difference between our Work and our Love as our work IS an act of love. Bring meaning to your current role by seeing how you're making a difference in people's lives.

Love ∞.0 is the love of EVERYTHING.

We quit arguing with reality and learn to not only accept it but LOVE it. Byron Katie wrote a whole book on the subject called *Loving What Is,* while Nietzsche told us that's it all about Amor Fati—or loving our fate.

Now, let's go back to Love 3.0. I want to talk about what I consider to be the essence of Heroic love. We're going to talk about *compassion* vis-à-vis *encouragement* and we might even coin a new word: *comcourage.*

First, let's remember that Aristotle tells us that COURAGE is the #1 virtue that we need to make sure we express, because without it we can't express all the other virtues and win the ultimate game of flourishing by more and more consistently expressing the best version of ourselves.

If having courage is *the* most important thing we can do for *ourselves* to actualize our eudaimonic potential, wouldn't *giving others encouragement* to actualize *their* eudaimonic potential be the most loving thing we can do?

Sure seems like it—which is one of the reasons why I think ENCOURAGEMENT is a super-underrated virtue. It gets way less airtime than compassion yet, I'd say (without diminishing the importance of compassion), that it's *at least* as important as compassion—*especially* as we face historically significant challenges.

Again: YES. We need compassion.

And... We need to move beyond "suffering with" others in the middle of challenging times to HAVING COURAGE TO-GETHER during these extraordinarily challenging times.

Enter: Our new word... *Comcourage*. "To have courage to-gether." Let's compare and contrast *compassion* and *comcourage*.

Here's the definition for *compassion*: "sympathetic pity and concern for the sufferings or misfortunes of others: *the victims should be treated with compassion*."

Etymologically, *compassion* comes from the Latin *com* + *passio*. It literally means "to suffer with."

Here's my proposed definition for *comcourage*: "fierce belief in the strength of others to meet their challenges combined with a willingness to act together in the presence of fear to conquer and grow from those challenges: *the aspiring heroes facing chal-lenges should be treated with comcourage*."

Etymologically, our new word *comcourage* comes from the Latin *com* + *cor*. It literally means "to have heart with."

As you may recall, the word *courage* comes from the Latin word for heart. Just as the heart pumps blood to our arms and legs and other organs, COURAGE vitalizes all our other virtues.

So... Let's inject some courage into the lives of our loved ones and all those around us. Let's be willing to face challenges together. Heroically.

TODAY.

Remember...

"In the faces of men and women, we see HEROES."

START WITH WHO
YOU AT YOUR BEST =

W e've taken a quick look at the first Big 3: Energy, Work, and Love. Now it's time to take a quick look at the second Big 3: Identity, Virtues, and Behaviors.

Let's jump straight in on the Identity side of things with an important question...

WHO ARE YOU AT YOUR HEROIC BEST?

If you could wave a wand and activate that best, most Heroic version of yourself, WHO WOULD YOU BE?

If you feel so inspired, pause and think about that for a moment. Let's think about it in the context of our Big 3...

Who do you want to become Energy-wise? A world-class athlete? A healthy, fit, energized radiant exemplar?

Who do you want to become Work-wise? An iconoclastic artist or entrepreneur or leader? A super-productive person?

Who do you want to become Love-wise? A great husband/ wife, mother or father, friend and colleague?

Those versions of you at your Heroic best Energy, Work, and Love wise? That's what we'll call your "Identities."

With the Heroic app, we help you name those best versions of yourself as we create an Identity that will guide all our behaviors. Then we help you identify the Virtues that best version of yourself embodies. Then we help you get clarity on the specific Behaviors you dominate when you're at your best.

Identity → Virtues → Behaviors.

Showing up as that best, most Heroic version of ourselves more and more consistently (but never perfectly!) is how to win the ultimate game.

In short: Be that best version of yourself in your Energy, Work, and Love all day every day.

Start with who.

TODAY.

WANT BETTER HABITS?
START WITH WHO

In *Atomic Habits*, James Clear presents a couple different ways to approach habits. He calls one "Outcome-Based" and the other "Identity-Based."

Long story short, he tells us that we want to start with our Identity. Rather than start with thinking about WHAT we want to achieve, and HOW we're going to get there, James tells us that we want to start by thinking about WHO we are committed to *becoming*.

THAT'S the engine that drives the creation of the best habits and the destruction of the worst.

Start with *who*.

With that in mind…

Who do YOU want to become?

With *that* in mind…

Are your habits in line with that best version of you?

Pay attention because our identities and our habits go together.

Get this. James tells us: "The more you repeat a behavior, the more you reinforce the identity associated with that behavior."

In fact, he continues by telling us: "The word *identity* was originally derived from the Latin word *essentitas*, which means being, and *identidem*, which means repeatedly. Your identity is literally your 'repeated beingness.'"

Isn't that amazing?!

Your Identity? It's LITERALLY what you repeatedly do and who you repeatedly are.

What's interesting is that you can make a shift in your Identity by choosing to BE a different person and/or choosing to DO different things.

Want to be a leader? Lead.

Want to be a writer? Write.

Want to be a better father or mother or husband or brother? Act like one.

Want to be healthy? Act like a healthy person.

James actually shares a story about a friend of his who lost one hundred pounds by simply making decisions that a healthy person would make.

Our +1°...

Who do YOU aspire to be in this one precious journey of ours? Are you *repeatedly* BEING that version of you?

Here's to becoming all we're capable of being.

Let's close the gap.

And live with *ARETÉ*.

Today.

IDENTITY → BEHAVIORS → FEELINGS
VS. FEELINGS → BEHAVIORS → IDENTITY

H ere's another way to look at it.

We want our IDENTITIES to drive our behaviors rather than how we're *feeling* in any given moment to drive the show.

Most people follow this progression most of the time (and we ALL follow this progression at least some of the time):

FEELINGS → Behaviors → IDENTITIES

I don't (insert whiny voice) *feel* like doing x, y, or z awesome behavior so I don't do it and, as a result, I don't have an empowered Identity.

Important note: Letting your *feelings* drive your behaviors is a GREAT way to make sure you never sustainably activate your Heroic potential.

Here's what we want to do instead. Our *Heroic* Identity creation formula goes like this:

IDENTITIES → Behaviors → FEELINGS

I have committed to being the sort of person who does x, y, and z so I DO those things whether I *feel* like it or not and, interestingly, I often wind up feeling GREAT after engaging in the behavior I used to avoid *while* becoming the person I was always destined to be.

To recap: Don't let your **FEELINGS** drive your Behaviors. Start with your **IDENTITIES** and let *those* drive your Behaviors.

The result?

A deep sense of eudaimonic joy that's the byproduct of living with *Areté*.

THE OLD YOU?
THEY'RE ON PERMANENT VACATION

A nother word-phrase for "Identity" is "Self-Image."

Let's invite some of the leading thinkers on the subject to the party.

We'll start with Maxwell Maltz, author of the old-school classic *Psycho-Cybernetics*. Before he wrote that book, Maltz was a renowned plastic surgeon who discovered that, while some people's lives changed dramatically after he altered their appearance through plastic surgery, some people's lives didn't change at all.

He believed that the primary factor that differentiated these groups was their self-image—not what they saw in the mirror but the images they had of themselves in their MINDS.

As such, Maltz tells us that the most important thing we need to do is work on how we see ourselves. We need to work on our self-image.

Specifically, he says: "A human being always acts and feels and performs in accordance with what he imagines to be true about himself and his environment."

Gold-medal winning mental toughness coach Lanny Bassham says the same thing. In *With Winning in Mind*, he tells us that we'll never consistently outperform a poor self-image and that "Changing a Self-Image that is keeping you from reaching your goals may be the most important skill you will ever learn."

(Quick pop quiz: How's YOUR Self-Image? Is it helping or hindering you in reaching your goals?)

All of which begs the question: How do we optimize our self-image?

Here's Maltz's take: "Imagine how you would feel if you were already the sort of personality you want to be. If you have been shy and timid, see yourself moving among people with ease and poise—and feeling good because of it. If you have been fearful and anxious in certain situations—see yourself acting calmly and deliberately, acting with confidence and courage—and feeling expansive and confident because you are."

Let's combine that optimized self-image visualization with consistent ACTION via some scientifically proven ideas.

For that, it's time to welcome Richard Wiseman to the party. Professor Wiseman has both the best last name ever (right?) and the best job title ever. He's Britain's official professor in "the Public Understanding of Psychology."

In his great book *The As If Principle*, Wiseman takes a fascinating look at the power of BEHAVIORS driving FEELINGS rather than the other way around.

He leans heavily on some William James wisdom and tells us: "The notion of behavior causing emotion suggests that people should be able to create any feeling they desire simply by acting as if they are experiencing that emotion. Or as James famously put it, 'If you want a quality, act as if you already have it.' I refer to this simple but powerful proposition as the 'As If' principle."

I repeat, with emphasis: *"If you want a quality, act as if you already have it."*

Wiseman continues by saying: "This aspect of James's theory energized him more than any other. In one public talk, he described the potential power of the idea as 'bottled lightning' and enthusiastically noted, 'The sovereign voluntary path to cheerfulness … is to sit up cheerfully, to look round cheerfully, and to act and speak as if cheerfulness were already there … To wrestle with a bad feeling only pins our attention on it, and keeps it still fastened in the mind.'"

One of my favorite parts of the book is when he teaches us how to "Create a New You." How? Wiseman tells us to imagine the best version of ourselves and then to ACT LIKE THAT VERSION OF YOU all day every day.

I love this: "It might be helpful to think of your old personality as being on vacation for two weeks, so you have an opportunity to act like a different person. It is important, however, that you play out your new role twenty-four hours a day, even when you're alone. The 'As If' principle will cause you to feel like a new person, and the new you will soon become part of your actual identity."

Note: I've gotta say that I've always had a bit of an allergy to the way some self-help authors have run with the basic idea of "acting as if" into a "fake it until you make it" approach, so I found it particularly refreshing to read Wiseman's take on the *hundreds* of studies that prove the efficacy of the 'As If' approach without all the silly stuff that triggers an allergic reaction.

With that in mind: Let's VISUALIZE ourselves at our absolute best and then ACT like that version of ourselves.

The old you?

They're on a permanent vacation.

P.S. Check out Self-Image 101 and the Philosopher's Notes on these great books in the Heroic app for more.

ALTER EGOS
THE POWER OF SECRET IDENTITIES

Todd Herman is one of the world's leading high-performance coaches and mental game strategists.

He wrote a great book called *The Alter Ego Effect*. As per the sub-title, it's all about "The Power of Secret Identities to Transform Your Life."

Before we get into some of my favorite wisdom from that book, get this…

Did you know that you can bring people into a lab, test their vision, and find that people dressed up as (and pretending to be) Air Force pilots will LITERALLY SEE BETTER?

It's (goosebumps) crazy but true. Ellen Langer proved it.

In her great book *Counterclockwise*, she talks about that study and other mind-bogglingly powerful research she's conducted in her "Psychology of Possibility" lab at Harvard.

In *his* great book, Todd Herman helps us apply the science behind the power of "secret identities" to transform our lives.

It's truly remarkable stuff and one of the reasons I'm so bullish on the power of committing to and living in integrity with our "Identities" via the Heroic app.

Here's one of my favorite ideas from Todd's book…

Think about Superman and Clark Kent. We all know they're the same guy.

But… Which one is the "real" person and which one is the alter ego?

Alas, although 90% of the people to whom Todd asks this question say that Superman is the alter ego, they get it backward.

The REAL person is Superman. The fumbling Clark Kent is the alter ego.

With that in mind, I ask … Who is the REAL you?

The eudaimonically, soul-level inspired Superyou or the fumbling, fearful Clark Kent-ish you?

(Insert *Jeopardy* music here.)

To help us answer the question, let's bring Eric Butterworth back into the discussion. (Love that man.)

In *Discover the Power Within You*, he tells us: "You may say, 'But I am only human.' This is the understatement of your life. You are not only human—you are also divine in potential. The fulfillment of all your goals and aspirations in life depends upon stirring up and releasing more of that divine potential. And there is really nothing difficult about letting this inner light shine. All we must do is correct the tendency to turn off our light when we face darkness."

Our +1°…

Close your eyes.

Imagine *the absolute best, most Heroic version of yourself.*

Feel your power. See your radiance.

And… GO BE THAT BEST, MOST HEROIC VERSION OF YOURSELF.

The old you? They're on permanent vacation.

It's time for the *real* you to take over.

TODAY.

CHIEF MORALE OFFICER
THAT WOULD BE YOU

M ike Manazir is a Retired U.S. Navy Admiral and Top Gun
Fighter Pilot.

He wrote a GREAT book called *Learn How to Lead to Win*. I
got his book on the recommendation of a dear friend, U.S. Navy
Captain Daryle Cardone.

Daryle recommended Jim Mattis's book on leadership, *Call
Sign Chaos*. That book was so good that I asked him what *other*
books on leadership he recommended. Daryle told me I needed
to read Admiral Manazir's book—who's one of his cherished
mentors.

I immediately got it. And, after reading it, I could see why
Daryle admires him so much. He's a good human being.

The book is, as you'd expect from the title, all about helping us learn how to lead to win. It's part memoir, part leadership
manual—featuring thirty-three powerful stories from Admiral
Manazir's life and the lessons he gained along the way.

It reminds me of another memoir by another Admiral I
admire: William H. McRaven's *Sea Stories*.

In fact, as I typed that, I realize that this book is a bit of a
hybrid of McRaven's memoir AND his book *The Hero Code*.
Mash those two books up and swap out the SEAL stories for a
Top Gun Fighter Pilot/aircraft carrier Admiral's stories and you
get this book.

Here's my favorite Big Idea from the book …

Admiral Manazir tells us: "As I approached the day I was to take command of the Tomcatters of Fighter Squadron (VF) 31, I was starting to feel the upcoming burden of command—my first one. I was having a beer with a buddy at the Naval Air Station Oceana Officers' Club Bar, the scene of many junior shenanigans, and for once, I was deadly serious. The question had occurred to me and I asked out loud, 'Why is morale important?'

Seems easy to answer, but I was trying to figure out what the benefit of high morale would be beyond 'everyone is happy.' I mean, I can just order them to do the task, right?

Title 10 of the United States Code outlines the role of the US armed forces. In chapter 511, paragraph 5947, the Requirement of exemplary conduct of the Commanding Officer is enshrined in law, and says all commanding officers are required to 'promote and safeguard the morale, the physical well-being, and the general welfare of the officers and enlisted persons under their command or charge.'"

I find it ASTONISHINGLY inspiring to know that an Officer in the United States military is LEGALLY (!) required to "promote and safeguard the morale, the physical well-being, and the general welfare" of the individuals under their command.

And…

You know what I think of after I think of all the loving and courageous men and women serving our country who are protecting the freedoms on which our flourishing are so dependent?

I think of YOU.

You know what YOUR #1 job is?

Well, first, as Admiral Manazir tells us, you need to know that YOU ARE A LEADER.

Period.

Whether you're a parent or a grandparent or a coach or an executive or an addiction counselor or a teacher or ANYONE who has ONE person looking to them for guidance.

In fact, at the VERY least, you are the Commanding Officer of YOUR OWN LIFE.

So...

Start acting like it.

How?

Well, let's open back up to Title 10 of the United States Code outlining the role of the US armed forces as we recognize the fact that ALL of us are engaged in the eternal battle between vice and virtue—the "great combat" as Socrates put it 2,500 years ago.

Chapter 511, Paragraph 5947 clearly articulates the RE-QUIREMENTS OF EXEMPLARY CONDUCT (what a beautiful phrase!) for YOU, the Commanding Officer of your life.

You have a moral obligation to "promote and safeguard the morale, the physical well-being, and the general welfare" of everyone in your charge—starting with YOURSELF.

I salute you, Chief Morale Officer.

Take command. Lead to win the ultimate game.

TODAY.

THE RIGHT WHY
VS. THE WRONG WHY (YOURS?)

Michelle Segar is one of the world's leading researchers studying the science of how to consistently engage in healthy behaviors—stuff like eating well, exercising, getting more sleep and all that.

In her great book called *No Sweat*, she tells us that the reasons we choose to engage in these behaviors matter. Some people have the "Right Why." And, some people have the "Wrong Why."

Getting our "Why" right is super important. So, here's what you need to know.

Michelle can bring people into a lab and ask them WHY they would like to engage in a certain health behavior like exercising.

Some people tell her they want to exercise for *abstract, clinical* reasons like losing weight or generally getting healthier.

Very normal, "good" reasons but, as we'll discover, not very effective.

Other people will tell her that they want to exercise for very *concrete* reasons: They want to enhance the quality of their daily lives. They want to feel more energized NOW.

It's not some abstract, long-term thing. It's an immediate benefit and they know that engaging in a certain behavior like exercising (or eating well or sleeping) will give them that benefit.

As it turns out, MOST people choose abstract reasons. In fact, 75% of the people in her research came up with the fuzzy reasons while only 25% chose the concrete reasons.

But get this...

When Michelle tracks the exercise levels of the individuals in her studies, here's what she finds: The group that says they want to exercise for the fuzzy reasons exercises 30% LESS than the group that gave the "I want to feel better today!" reasons.

Why is that?

In short: We're wired to want IMMEDIATE gratification. Therefore, we want to choose the Right Why that delivers that immediate gain.

Spotlight on you: Why do YOU want to exercise more or eat better or get a better night of sleep?

Do you tend to have *abstract* ("I want to lose weight/live longer/get healthier") reasons or more *concrete* ("I want to feel great now!") reasons?

Optimize your why.

Make the connection to how you feel when you do what you know is best for you (both physiologically *and* psychologically) and *know* that choosing to engage in your desired health behaviors will make you feel better IMMEDIATELY.

That's the Right Why.

WHAT'S YOUR #1 SELF-CARE HABIT?
ONE OF THE MOST IMPORTANT QUESTIONS

As we've discussed in the last couple +1°s, Michelle Segar is one of the world's leading researchers studying the science of how to optimize our health behaviors.

Here's one more pro tip…

She tells us that one of THE most important things we can do is identify the *#1 thing* we do that keeps us energized and plugged in and ready to rock.

She calls this your #1 self-care habit.

Hers is sleep. So is mine. Her husband's is exercise. Alexandra's is time to meditate and journal and reflect.

Spotlight on YOU…

What's YOUR #1 self-care habit?

What's THE #1 thing you do when you're *most* on?

The thing that helps you ensure you have a great day?

And, perhaps even more directly: What's the thing that if you DON'T do it, you run the very high risk of having a very BAD day?

Is it getting a great night of sleep? Is it getting in a great work-out? Is it eating really well? Is it meditating? What is it?

THIS is my #1 self-care habit:_____.

Let's make that a non-negotiable keystone habit.

TODAY.

P.S. Don't stop there... Spend another moment or three identifying your *significant other's* (and/or kids') #1 self-care habit.

Fact is, great relationships are only created by two healthy people. 1 + 1 = !!!

If you want to optimize the love in your life, you'd be wise to (a) start by optimizing yourself and (b) support your partner (assuming they want the support!) in optimizing *their* lives.

And...

Our #1 self-care habit is a *really* good place to start.

As we discussed, my #1 is sleep. Alexandra knows this. And, she knows that she doesn't really want to be around me when I'm not meeting this fundamental need. So, we prioritize this to make sure I'm getting good sleep. (Thank you, Babes!)

Alexandra's #1 self-care habit is time alone every day to meditate/reflect/create/etc. Knowing this, we prioritize it to make sure she gets that time.

So... What's YOUR #1.

And... What's your PARTNER'S #1?

Find out. Help them rock it.

Activate your relationship's Heroic potential.

TODAY.

CHORES VS. GIFTS
THE RIGHT WHY HELPS

Quick question: Which activity do you prefer?

[ ] OPENING GIFTS
    or
[ ] DOING CHORES

OF COURSE we *all* like opening gifts a heck of a lot more than we enjoy doing chores, right?

Well… How do YOU approach eating, moving, sleeping, and dominating all your other fundamentals?

Are you approaching those behaviors like a grumpy person begrudgingly doing chores?

OR…

Are you dominating your eating, moving, sleeping and other fundies like a birthday kid opening a ton of presents?

Know this: Michelle Segar tells us that when we approach our healthy behaviors with the Right Why, we're *much* more likely to approach those same behaviors with a joyful enthusiasm.

We'd be wise to see our positive behaviors for precisely what they are: GIFTS we are giving to our future selves.

Let's do that.

Joyfully.

TODAY.

MARGINAL GAINS
HERE'S HOW TO WIN

O nce upon a time, no British cyclist had ever won the Tour de France. Over one hundred years of trying; precisely *zero* wins.

Then a guy named Sir David Brailsford stepped in and created Team Sky. He said that a British cyclist would win the Tour within five years. People thought he was crazy.

Until they won it in two years. Then, for good measure, they won four of the next five races as well.

How'd he do it? Marginal gains. He looked for all the *tiny* little places where he could optimize.

Things like making sure the riders' uniforms were always washed in the same skin-friendly detergent for a little more comfort.

Things like making sure the riders always slept on the same exact mattresses every night to give them the best shot at a good night of sleep.

Things like making sure the hotel rooms were always properly vacuumed to reduce potential infections.

TINY little things.

Any one gain wouldn't do a whole lot, of course.

But, as we know, when we aggregate and compound enough of those tiny little incremental optimizations, MAGIC happens. In this case, Tour de France victories.

As Brailsford puts it (via Matthew Syed in *Black Box Thinking*): "I realized early on that having a grand strategy was futile on its own. You also have to look at the smaller level, figure out what is working and what isn't. Each step may be small, but the aggregation can be huge."

Guess what?

The same rules apply to our lives. A grand strategy, although important, is futile on its own. We need to go granular and figure out what's working and what isn't. So...

What's working for you? Do more of it.

What's NOT working for you? Do less of it.

Specifically: Do you create more Masterpiece Days when you begin your day in a certain way? Do you have more energy when you eat less of x and more of y? Do you feel better when you exercise or go to bed by a certain time? What other data can you collect?

TEST!!! Get feedback. Look honestly at what's working and at what needs work and dial it in.

FIND THE MARGINAL GAINS.

Not complicated. Easy to overlook. But super powerful.

I REPEAT: When we aggregate and compound marginal gains over an extended period of time we get EXTRAORDI-NARY gains.

In cycling, that's what separates you from the pack and leads to Tour de France victories. In life, that's what separates us from our old selves so we can actualize our potential.

"THAT'S LIKE ME!"
HOW TO OPTIMIZE YOUR SELF-IMAGE

W hether you're an athlete, entrepreneur, teacher, parent, engineer, leader, or [fill in the blank here], what percentage of your performance do you think is mental?

"I think ___ % is mental."

When Lanny Bassham, our Olympic gold-medal-winning friend (who wrote *With Winning in Mind*) asks elite performers that question, they all say that elite performance is 90% mental.

90%!!!

Then he asks them what percentage of their training time and money they spend on their mental game. Their answer is almost always very little—nothing, or less than 10%.

As Lanny says: That makes no sense. If we want to show up as our best, we MUST train our minds.

How? Lanny tells us that one of the key variables to peak performance is fine-tuning our Self-Image. He tells us that how we behave will always be in accordance with how we see ourselves.

Our Self-Image is what "makes you act like you." If we have a poor Self-Image, we will never consistently perform better than that Self-Image.

The good news: We can optimize our Self-Image. And, Lanny tells us, we MUST optimize our Self-Image if we want to reach elite levels of performance.

Our current Self-Image has been formed by countless (!) "imprints." Therefore, if we want to change it, we need to bombard ourselves with a constant diet of positive imprints—removing the negative internal chit-chat and never talking about things we don't want to see in our lives while affirming all the things we do want to see come to fruition in our lives.

We want to rehearse our optimal performances and, each time we perform at our best—from the rehearsed visualized moments to the most mundane real moments—we want to affirm "That's like me!"

"That's like me to turn off my electronics to get a good night of sleep." "That's like me to wake up and meditate." "That's like me to follow my nutrition protocol and train like a world-class athlete." "That's like me to be creative before reactive." "That's like me to dominate another Deep Work time block." "That's like me to shutdown completely and transition to Deep Love time." "That's like me to respond to bids from my wife and kids and create micro-moments of awesome without my phone around."

REPEAT.

ALL DAY.

EVERY DAY.

That's like YOU to go from Theory to Practice to Mastery and create a truly Heroic Self-Image.

Day 1. All in.

LET'S GO, HERO!

"THAT'S NOT LIKE ME!"
PART II ON HOW TO OPTIMIZE YOUR SELF-IMAGE

As we just discussed, elite performers agree: 90% of our performance is mental.

90%!!!

Yet… For some very strange reason, very few of us dedicate an appropriate amount of our time to optimizing our mental game.

One key way to do that is to optimize our Self-Image. As Lanny says, our Self-Image is what "makes you act like you." A poor Self-Image drives poor performance. Therefore, we need to dial it in.

One key way to do *that* is to affirm "That's like me!" when you're on.

"That's like me to do what I say I'm going to do." "That's like me to approach my challenges rather than avoid them." "That's like me to have my phone out of sight and out of touch when I'm with my family."

"That's like me!" "That's like me!" "That's like me!"

All day every day as we live in integrity with our Big 3 Identities and forge a Heroic Self-Image.

Here's the follow-up question and practice…

What do you do when you INEVITABLY (!) fall short of your standards and leave that gap between who you were *capable* of being and who you were *actually* being and the voice of shame starts to creep in?

Well...

Here's what I do.

First, I shine a flashlight of curiosity on the situation before I bring the hammer.

I want to find the MOMENT RIGHT BEFORE things went sideways.

There's pretty much ALWAYS a single moment when we made a choice to listen to our *demon* rather than listen to our *daimon*. We just need to have the wisdom and curiosity and the discipline to take the time to look for it.

Then, rather than replay all the negative downstream consequences of our poor choice (while shaming ourselves in the process—further eroding our Self-Image), we go back to that choice-point moment and use the data as an opportunity to get better (while taking response-ability and creating a stronger Self-Image).

For example, the other day I was driving home with Alexandra and the kids after a long day out. We were twenty minutes into our forty-minute drive home and the kids went over the edge.

I found my impatience growing along with their craziness. I may have impolitely asked them to be quiet. (Hah.)

To which Emerson might have called me, and I quote: "Jerky Face." (Hah.)

I took a deep breath and let it go.

Then, ten minutes later as we got closer to home, Emerson asked if he could drive when we got to our mailbox—which is not too far from our property.

I KNEW that I should say, "Sure, buddy!" as we ALWAYS have a great time with him driving. He'd laugh. I'd laugh. Eleanor would roll the window down and stick her head out of it so she could feel the wind on her face—which is one of the cutest things ever, btw. Eyes closed, hair blowing back. Pure six-year-old joy.

But... What did I do?

I COMPLETELY IGNORED my daimon's wise counsel and, instead, let my demon take over the controls as I rudely replied: "NOT TODAY, BUDDY. I can't say I'm a huge fan of being called a JERKY FACE!"

(Facepalm.)

Enter: The Gap.

Emerson had already forgotten whatever had made us upset. But he's now slumped down in his seat and disappointed. Eleanor is now upset that her brother is upset.

And, let's just say that the REST of the evening followed that same sub-optimal trajectory.

So... As I reflected on the events the following morning, what did I do?

I said: "That's NOT like me."

Then I went back to the MOMENT when I could have made a better decision and imagined how the rest of the evening would have gone had I closed the gap.

Then I recommitted to doing a little better next time.

Then I did some damage repair with the kids as I shared what I just shared with you—using the entire experience as a fantastic opportunity to get a little better as a family.

"That's like me!"

"That's NOT like me!"

Two powerful mantras to forge a Heroic Self-Image.

"NEEDS WORK!"
MAKE A MIS-TAKE? SAY THIS TO YOURSELF

W hat do YOU say to yourself when things don't go as planned?

It could be in the middle of a big game or a creative project or… a drive home with your kids after a long day.

As you may have noticed, it's *really* easy to ruminate on that gap we created and turn a "bad shot" into a bad day (or series of bad days or weeks or months or… life).

As we've discussed, Lanny Bassham is one of the best mental toughness coaches in the world. He's also one of the best rifle shooters in history.

He tells us we need to "re-load" after every shot.

Shoot and hit your target perfectly?

Lanny tells us to FEAST on that success. "That's like me!" "That's like me!" "That's like me!" All day every day as you build your self-image as a world-class performer.

Kinda sorta hit your target?

That gets an "OK."

Miss your target completely?

Like "OOPS! I just acted like an idiot and really wish I could have that shot back!" kinda thing? Then we *re-load* by simply saying to ourselves: "Needs work."

We DO NOT (I repeat, we DO NOT!) ruminate on all the different ways we screwed up and how we messed up all hopes for the future.

Nope.

A simple "Needs work!" will do.

Then we quickly go back to the moment we erred and think about what we *could* have done to execute the moment perfectly.

Then we replay THAT moment in our heads.

The benefit?

Rather than groove the negative outcome into our consciousness over and over, we thwart that negative self-image building AND we use the opportunity to LEARN something.

Remember: We win or we learn and learning IS winning so we WIN or we WIN.

I *love* to use this. It's literally one of the most powerful tools in my tool box.

How about you?

Make any mistakes lately?

Bring a recent moment in which you fell short of your standards and failed to show up as your best self.

Let's re-load it.

Replay the scene in your mind and go to the MOMENT in which you made that sub-optimal choice. Imagine making a better choice. Got it? Awesome. Now let it go.

That's like you to win or learn.

All day every day.

Especially TODAY.

THE PUZZLE OF LIFE
& HOW TO BUILD IT

W hen Emerson was younger, we got *really* into puzzles.

We started with a 100-piece, little kids' puzzle of The World. Then we went to a little older kids' 100-piece puzzle featuring Dinosaurs. From there we rocked a 200-piece puzzle featuring A Pirate's Battle.

From there, it was time for a 300-piece Underwater Adventure. Then we stepped up our puzzle game and went for a 500-piece (adult puzzle) featuring an animal scene from the Serengeti.

THEN…

We walked into the little family-run toy store in town and told our friend Joe we were ready for a 1,000-piece puzzle. This one featured The Cove complete with an underwater scene of various fish, beautiful blue skies, and matching blue water.

And…

We got to work.

I'm not a big puzzle guy but everyone knows how you start a puzzle right?

Q: After finding the right place to actually work on your puzzle, what's the recommended first thing to do? (Yes, I Google-studied this as we ramped up the difficulty level.)

A: You find the edge pieces. (Right?)

Guess what?

The SAME thing holds true with building the puzzle that is our lives.

We need to START with the edge pieces.

We need to find the basic fundamentals that hold the whole puzzle together.

I repeat: When you're starting a 1,000- (or 10,000-!) piece puzzle, you don't start with the hardest part of the puzzle.

Right?

(You know what I'm talking about—those sections of pure, identical sky blue that make you want to pull your hair out. Hah.)

You save the super-crazy-tricky parts for the VERY END after you've systematically hammered the easier parts.

Right?

Again…

The SAME thing holds true with building the puzzle that is our lives.

So…

How's YOUR puzzle building going?

Are you jumping ahead and trying to figure out the super-crazy-tricky parts of your life-puzzle before you've got your edge pieces all optimized?

Here's to clean, bright-line borders that make the rest of the puzzle so much more fun to build.

"I FOUND SOMETHING!"
THE "I LOVE YOU" GAME

One of my favorite things to do when Emerson was young was to curl up in bed and read together. It was an essential part of our PM Bookend and something we rarely missed.

As we've also discussed before, one of our all-time favorite series is called *The Magic Tree House* by Mary Pope Osborne. It features a brother and sister named Jack and Annie who demonstrate wisdom and courage and love on adventures to different times and places in history. (I highly recommend the whole series.)

So…

On one of their adventures (called *Good Morning, Gorillas*), our beloved Jack and Annie get swept away to the mountains of Africa where they spend some time with gorillas. The most memorable part of this adventure for us was when they taught the gorillas how to sign "I love you."

Which leads us to a little game Emerson and Eleanor and I like to play and to the point of this +1°.

Here's the game…

I'll be cruising around the house when, all of a sudden, I'll stop! And say…

Me: "Buddy! I found something for you."

Emerson: Looking at me in anticipation.

Me: Reaching into my pocket to pull THIS out:

334

Emerson: Smiling with that deep joy that shows he knows he's loved. Then laughing. Then reaching behind himself and saying: "Oh!!! I found THIS!!!"

Me laughing: "That's funny because these were EVERYWHERE this morning when I was working. Did you leave them there?!"

Emerson: Another big soul smile.

And the game continues many, many (!) times every single day. Somehow, it never loses its charm.

Two more things...

1. I found something for YOU!!!! Gimme a second. Where'd it go... Hmmmm... Oh! Here it is!!!

2. I wonder. Got any kids who might enjoy the "I love you" game?

From the Johnson house to yours, we love you.

WANT TO IMPROVE? MEASURE
THE POWER OF A PEDOMETER

Did you know that one of the easiest ways to optimize any aspect of your life is to simply measure it?

Yep.

In fact, this effect is so powerful that it's actually a big issue in research studies.

Get this: Simply asking people to pay attention to something IMMEDIATELY and SIGNIFICANTLY improves their behavior on that activity.

For example, giving someone a pedometer as part of a randomized, controlled study will increase their movement by an average of 27% and result in them walking *at least one extra mile* per day!

Crazy but true.

Makes you want to get a pedometer and start measuring your steps, eh?

While you're at it, think about what other areas of your life you'd like to improve.

Remember: MEASURING your behavior—whether it's how you eat or move or sleep or spend your time—can IMMEDIATELY and SIGNIFICANTLY improve it.

ZERO-BASED THINKING
WHAT GOES IF YOU STARTED AT ZERO?

B rian Tracy is one of my favorite old-school self-development teachers.

I can still remember listening to his CDs back in the day when I was first getting into self-development. The man is a Big Idea machine. Here's one of my favorites.

Brian tells us that it's often helpful to "zero base" your thinking.

Here's how he puts it in *Focal Point*: "To simplify your life, zero-based thinking is one of the most powerful strategies you can learn and apply on a regular basis. Here's how it works. Ask yourself, 'Is there anything I am doing right now that, knowing what I now know, I wouldn't get into again if I were starting over today?'"

Think about that for a moment.

Step back from everything you're doing and imagine you have an absolute blank slate in your life.

Knowing what you now know, is there anything you're currently doing that you *wouldn't* get into again if you were starting over today?

Hmmm…

(Yes, that can be painful. And, it can be equally powerful.)

That's Part I of the reflection exercise.

Here's Part II: *"If your answer is 'yes,' then your next question is, 'How do I get out of this situation, and how fast?'"*

THAT can be an even more challenging (and even more powerful!) exercise.

Your mission, should you choose to accept it, is to do Part I of our zero-based thinking exercise. And then proceed to Part II if you feel so bold. Then to Part III which, of course, is to take action on Part II.

Here's to the +1°s that often follow the zeros!

DIRECTION VS. DESTINATION
THE GOOD LIFE IS A PROCESS

We talk a lot about the idea that the good life is one endlessly evolving process, with us spiraling up into the next-best version of ourselves.

Here's another take on that theme.

Carl Rogers tells us: "The good life is a process, not a state of being. It is a direction, not a destination."

Isn't that beautiful?!

The good life is a *dynamic* PROCESS. Not a *static* state of being. It's a DIRECTION, not a destination.

Tal Ben-Shahar reflects on that in *The Pursuit of Perfect* in which he tells us that our ideals are more like "guiding stars" than "distant shores."

Important note: We can *follow* guiding stars. But we're going to run into problems if we think of those STARS as distant SHORES we're actually going to reach some day.

The "best" version of ourselves is asymptotic. It's a curve that never quite reaches the line it's approaching.

As hard as we work, we'll NEVER (!) actually "get there."

Therefore...

The wisest among us throw a smile on our faces and remember to ENJOY the process of being *and* becoming.

That's our +1°.

Let's step back from the non-stop optimizing and appreciate everything that's *already* AMAZING.

Three things, please.

What's amazing in your life RIGHT NOW?

1. _____

2. _____

3. _____

Celebrate that.

And, remember this...

As Tal Ben-Shahar *also* tells us: "The word appreciate has two meanings. The first meaning is 'to be thankful,' the opposite of taking something for granted. The second meaning is 'to increase in value' (as money appreciates in the bank). Combined, these two meanings point to a truth that has been proved repeatedly in research on gratitude: when we appreciate the good in our lives, the good grows and we have more of it. The opposite, sadly, is also true: when we fail to appreciate the good—when we take the good in our lives for granted—the good depreciates."

HOW WE ENDURE
WHEN LAST PLACE = FIRST PLACE

K elly McGonigal wrote a great book called *The Joy of Movement*. In addition to deepening my understanding of the science of why exercise/movement are so essential and so beneficial to our flourishing, I can't remember reading a book that brought me to tears so many times.

Kelly is both a brilliant scientist and a brilliant storyteller. She shares a bunch of stories about everyday people that are incredibly inspiring. She also tells us about one of the most inspiring moments in Olympic history.

Here's the short story.

It's 1992. The Barcelona Olympics.

Derek Redmond is the world record holder in the four hundred meters. He missed the last Olympics due to an injury so this is his big chance to win a gold medal.

The semi-finals begin. He starts off strong.

Then...

Sixteen seconds into the race, Derek hears a loud pop. Later he'd say that he thought he got shot in the back of his thigh. In fact, it was his hamstring separating from his bone. OUCH.

He clutches his leg. Hops a few times. And is brought to a painful stop. All the other racers finish the race.

But he's not done yet. He gets up. Determined to finish the race. He's painfully hopping on one leg.

That's Heroic enough but then something else happens.

A man comes bursting from the stands onto the track—pushing aside and waving away Olympic officials as he makes his way to Derek.

It's Derek's dad.

He embraces his son and supports him as they make their way to the finish line. His dad fiercely waves away more Olympic officials telling them: "I'M HIS FATHER!"

Derek sobs into his dad's shoulder.

They finish. Together.

Dead last in the race. First place in our hearts and souls.

(I hereby challenge you to watch the video of that moment—just search "Derek Redmond's Emotional Olympic Story"—and NOT get misty-eyed.)

Kelly tells us that many people find Derek's Heroic grit incredibly inspiring—which, of course, it is.

But what she thinks is the *deeper* reason why we all love that scene so much is the fact that, ultimately, we endure most powerfully TOGETHER.

We all need each other to show up as our best.

Period.

That's our +1°.

Let's be the ones racing onto the track to be there for our loved ones who might have stumbled and hurt themselves.

And…

Let's be strong enough to accept help from others when *we* stumble as we remember the fact that we endure best *together*.

THE LAST BARRIERS
& THE FRIENDS WHO HELP US BREAK THEM

On October 12, 2019, Eliud Kipchoge made history by doing what many thought was impossible. In fact, it's been called "the last barrier of modern athletics."

You know what he did?

He ran a marathon in less than two hours.

You know how fast that is?

Well, imagine running a mile at a 4:34 pace. And then holding that pace for 26.2 miles.

I got tears in my eyes as I watched a short video of him breaking the tape at the finish line.

When I showed it to Alexandra, she said: "Wow."

Then she said: "And there were so many people right behind him!"

I didn't even notice them on my first watch. When I looked closer I realized all those guys were on his TEAM.

And that's what I think is the most powerful part of this record-breaking event. You know how many professional racers ran alongside and in front of Eliud to create a perfectly paced aerodynamic bubble around him?

Thirty-five on the course. Plus six on reserve.

As the *New York Times* put it: "his flock of pacesetters… happened to include some of the best distance runners in the world, including former world and Olympic gold medalists."

And let's not forget about the "electric timing car driving 4:34 per mile (with a second car on standby)."

Individual human achievement?

It takes a lot of will power. Even more soul power.

And, most importantly, incredible friend power.

That's our +1°.

What seemingly unbreakable barriers in YOUR life are you looking to break?

Who's on your crew?

And…

What barriers are people on your crew looking to break?!

Are you playing your role well to support THEM?

Let's do this.

With friends.

TODAY.

P.S. Shout out to my right-hand guy, Michael Balchan, for the heads up on this history-making goodness. Team work makes the dream work. Love you, brother. Couldn't do what I do without YOU and our crew.

P.P.S. Search "Eliud Kipchoge Final Kilometre of the INEOS 1:59 Challenge" to check out the official video.

WANT TO BE GREAT?
FIND THE TIME, FIND THE ENERGY

B ob Rotella is one of the world's best mental toughness coaches. He wrote a great book called *How Champions Think*.

He kicks that book off with a story about LeBron James. It goes something like this.

Once upon a time, Rotella coached LeBron. He knew the basics about him. 6'8". A chiseled two hundred fifty pounds with explosive speed. A proven superstar. But it wasn't until they sat down and chatted that he REALLY got LeBron's power.

Rotella asked him about his goals. LeBron told him: "I want to be the greatest basketball player in history."

Rotella thought: "Beautiful. This is a truly talented guy."

He tells us what he was MOST impressed by: "It was not that he had physical gifts. It was LeBron's mind."

Specifically, it was the way he saw himself that most moved Rotella: "The vital importance of that sort of attitude is the foremost thing I have learned about exceptionalism in my decades of work with people striving to be great."

That's worth repeating. Rotella has worked with THE top performers for DECADES. The "foremost thing" he has learned about exceptionalism and people striving to be great? The vital importance of seeing themselves and their potential with such audacious (!) clarity.

Which begs the question: How do YOU see yourself?

Now, continuing our story… After LeBron told Rotella he wanted to be the greatest basketball player in history (!), Rotella asked him where he thought he stood in relation to that goal.

LeBron told him he thought he was doing pretty well but that he wasn't going to be the greatest if his teams didn't win championships and they weren't going to do that unless he became a better three-point shooter.

Long story short: Rotella told him to create a video montage of him nailing threes from every spot on the court. Set it to music. Watch it every night. FEEL it. Program his subconscious mind.

And, he told him to hire a shooting coach, work with him every day and make two hundred three-point shots off the dribble every day while imagining the best defender guarding him. Then make another two hundred catch-and-shoot three-pointers. "I told him I didn't care how many shots it took to make those four hundred three-pointers, or how long it took. If he wanted to be great, he would find the time and find the energy."

Rotella continues: "The actual number of shots I suggested was not as important, in my mind, as the idea that LeBron would set a practice goal for himself, commit to achieving it every day, and wait patiently for the results."

Fast-forward.

LeBron went from being a 29% three-point shooter in his rookie season to a 40% beast—collecting a few championships en route to his quest to be the greatest player ever.

Of course, this +1° has nothing to do with LeBron James and his three-pointers.

It has to do with YOU.

In what domain are you committed to being exceptional?

Where do you think you stand in relation to that goal?

And what do you think you need to do every day (!) to have a shot at being your exceptional best?

Find the time.

Find the energy.

Be an exception.

Be exceptional.

YOU, MICHELANGELO & YOUR POTENTIAL
WHAT'S IN THE WAY OF YOU BEING YOUR BEST?

L egend has it that when Michelangelo stepped up to a block of marble, he could *see* the finished statue in his mind's eye. His job was simple: Get rid of what was in the way.

That's a pretty powerful image.

Let's apply it to our lives now.

Step back from your current life for a moment.

Fast-forward five to ten years. Look within the block of marble that is you and your potential. SEE the best version of you within that block of marble. You at your best.

Now…

What's in the way of you expressing that best, most Heroic version of yourself more and more consistently?

What little habits do we need to chip away at to reveal the most beautiful version of you hidden within that marble?

As you think about that, know this…

The word *character* comes from the Greek word that meant "chisel" or "the mark left by a chisel."

Our *character* is formed by a *chisel*.

One choice at a time.

Moment to moment to moment.

Here's to sculpting a masterpiece you're proud of.

THE MOMENT OF DECISION
IS WHERE IT'S AT

I n our last +1°, we took a quick trip to Michelangelo's studio and saw the best, most Heroic version of you sitting there in the marble.

Then we did a little chiseling at some behaviors that might be getting in the way.

Here's another question for you…

Do you know what moment Michelangelo decided to capture when he created the statue of David?

Think about that for a moment…

What moment in David's Heroic life do YOU think Michelangelo chose to capture in his iconic statue?

Know this…

The moment Michelangelo chose to capture *wasn't* his moment of celebration right after he "officially" became a hero by defeating Goliath.

It was his moment of DECISION.

It was the moment David DECIDED to step up and do his best to serve profoundly and, ultimately, heroically.

Know this: In that moment, the outcome wasn't certain. In fact, the odds were against him.

That moment of decision (and I have goosebumps as I type this) was what Michelangelo (rightly) considered to be *the most Heroic* moment of David's life—the moment he DECIDED to step up and strive to be a hero.

Guess what?

We get to make those micro-decisions all day every day.

Here's to choosing wisely, Hero.

TODAY.

THE GOLDEN YOU
CHIPPING AWAY AT THE EXTRA LAYER

Alan Cohen tells a great story at the beginning of the documentary *Finding Joe*.

The story goes something like this...

A long time ago in a land far far away, there was a huge, bigger-than-life Buddha statue.

It was PURE GOLD.

It was astonishingly beautiful.

Then one day, an invading army was approaching. The monks knew the army would destroy the statue so they quickly covered it in mud and whatever else they could find to make it look less than golden before they evacuated.

The army conquered the land but didn't notice the statue. The trick worked. Much later, new monks returned to the temple. They looked at the statue and just thought it was a ho-hum Buddha statue.

Then one day, a crack appeared in their ho-hum statue. Something glimmered below the surface. What was that? Hmmmm...

They looked a little closer. They got some tools and chipped a little more away.

It was something golden.

They chipped a little more away. And then a little more. And then they splashed some water on it to clean it off and lo and behold!

Is that GOLD?

YES!!

It's a *priceless* GOLDEN statue.

Moral of the story: Somewhere along the way, we've all gotten covered in mud but we need to remember that we are ALL (more specifically: YOU are!) that golden Buddha.

You're solid gold.

Know this: We don't need to "do" anything per se to make ourselves INTO that golden version of ourselves.

We just need to chip away at the stuff THAT'S GETTING IN THE WAY of that radiant awesomeness.

So…

What's getting in the way?

Is today a good day to chip away?

THE GOLDEN YOU (PART II)
IT'S TRUE

I always thought that story about the golden Buddha was a beautiful parable about the fact that we're all already perfect and that all we have to do is chip away at the stuff that's gotten in the way.

But… Get this: The Golden Buddha is actually real.

I discovered that fact while I was reading Tim Grahl's book *Running Down a Dream*.

I loved the Golden Buddha story as a pure parable. I love the combination of the historical reality with the metaphorical lessons even more.

Here's the quick recap. The true story mirrors the parable— with the added bonus that it's true.

Somewhere around the thirteenth or fourteenth century, in what is now Thailand, Buddhist monks made an epic, giant, golden Buddha statue. Ten feet tall. Weighing over 5.5 tons.

Then, in 1767, Burmese invaders were approaching. They were destroying (and looting) all the temples so the monks covered our golden Buddha statue in plaster with some colored glass to conceal its true value. The trick worked. The statue was ignored.

The trick worked *too* well. Once the invaders were kicked out and the king reestablished order, the statue was moved around and relegated to an insignificant spot in an insignificant temple. It was even placed under a tin roof for 10 years.

Then, in 1955—nearly *two hundred years* after it was originally covered in stucco—the statue was being moved to a new location when the ropes snapped and the statue fell to the ground. Hard. Some of the plaster chipped off—revealing the golden surface beneath the stucco.

Lo and behold, our ten foot, 5.5-ton stucco statue is, in fact, nearly pure gold.

It's worth $250 million dollars.

And is now on prominent display.

Once again...

Remember: You're golden.

When/if you find anything that "Needs work!" today, follow Tim Grahl's advice and imagine that you're joyfully (almost breathless in anticipation!) chipping away at the stucco as you reveal more and more of your true essence.

Let the golden, most Heroically activated you shine!

5-MINUTE SWEATY CONVERSATIONS
HOW TO NAVIGATE CHALLENGING CHATS

You know those times when you *know* you need to have a tough conversation and you're kinda sorta dreading it and then kinda sorta avoiding it?

One of my old mentors once told me that you just need to move through what he called a "sweaty five-minute conversation" to get to the other side of clarity and resolution.

Most of us avoid the challenging conversations because we aren't willing to endure those few minutes of discomfort.

I definitely used to avoid them. Now, I remember that "Speed Is a Force" then I WOOP it, chant "Bring it on!" and "I'm excited!" and jump in.

It's become a really powerful practice for me as I've mastered it over the years.

But... Here's the funny thing. Once upon a time, I needed to have one of those "sweaty conversations" with that mentor of mine.

Guess how it turned out?

It was, by far, LITERALLY, the worst conversation I've ever had in my life.

(HAH. Seriously. I kid you not.)

As Campbell said, when you dare to go after bliss, there's always the chance for a fiasco.

So, today's mission, should you choose to accept it...

The next time you find yourself avoiding a challenging

conversation, see if you can recognize the fear and then get to work on it with one (or more) of our growing array of tools.

Perhaps you can remember that your infinite potential exists on the other side of that fear and chant "Bring it on!" to yourself.

I'd definitely recommend you WOOP it! Wave the wand. Create your Wish. See it going perfectly. Experience the benefits. Then anticipate the obstacles and make your plan to deal with them.

Then, if you feel that now's the time, jump in and move through those few seconds/minutes of sweaty palms and make it happen.

You'll win or you'll learn. And learning IS winning so we WIN or we WIN!

P.S. I know for a fact that if I had that challenging conversation from nearly fifteen years ago *today*, it would have ended so much better. But I never would have gotten to where I am without the pain of that fiasco. We win or we learn and learning IS winning so... LET'S GO, HERO!

BRING FORTH
HOW TO BE A WISE PARENT

A s you might have noticed, it's easy to stress ourselves out as we strive to activate our Heroic potential.

So…

We need to make sure we're approaching this whole thing with the right mindset. We need to simultaneously hold ourselves to heroically high standards AND we need to have a ton of warmth and kindness for ourselves as we inevitably fall short of those ideals.

Parenting experts tell us the same thing.

If you want to raise great kids, you need to simultaneously hold high standards *and* offer tons of warmth and love.

That's called Wise Parenting.

If you just have high standards but no warmth, you're Authoritarian. If you have low standards and high warmth, you're Permissive. And, if you have neither high standards nor warmth, you're Neglectful.

We need to parent *ourselves*.

Wisely.

Btw… Did you know that the word *parent* comes from the ancient Latin word that means "bringing forth"?

Here's to bringing forth *your* Heroic potential.

TODAY.

UNILATERALITY
THINK: EXTREME OWNERSHIP RELATIONSHIP STYLE

Once upon a time, Phil and I were having another great coaching session. In this particular chat, we were discussing how to optimize my relationship with Alexandra.

Phil told me to practice something he calls "unilaterality."

Short story: When you decide to take action without looking to what the other person is doing and/or waiting for someone else to do something before you do it, that's called a "unilateral" action.

That practice is SUPER important for any (and all) relationships.

Decide what the right thing to do is. Then do it.

Unilaterally.

THAT is *unilaterality*.

I told Phil it reminded me of the Navy SEAL wisdom of "*Extreme Ownership*" a la Jocko Willink and Leif Babin. Same basic idea. You take EXTREME (!) Ownership of any and every situation.

No complaining. No blaming. No excuses. Ever.

You do the right thing because it's the right thing to do. Period.

That's *unilaterality*.

That's how you make a relationship work.

With that in mind, think of one of your most important relationships.

Got it?

Now, think of one little thing you *know* you could be doing.

Got it?

Now go do it.

Do it without waiting for the other person to do something or doing it expecting some sort of return.

Remember *unilaterality*.

P.S. Fun fact: When I interviewed Leif Babin and we chatted about *Extreme Ownership* as applied to relationships he laughed and said something along the lines of: "Yep. Chat with my wife about that. Applying this to our intimate relationships is the hardest thing."

Indeed it is.

Let's.

HOW TO EAT STRESS LIKE AN ENERGY BAR
REAPPRAISAL & PARADOXICAL STRESS SWAP

A re you chronically stressed?

Of course, the good life has its fair share of challenges and our goal isn't to try to eliminate all the stress.

No pressure, no diamonds!

But ...

We want to get really good at using the energy of stress to our advantage and mitigating any potential harmful effects.

First, we need to remember that, according to Kelly McGonigal in *The Upside of Stress*, how we *perceive* stress is actually the largest determinant of how it affects us.

In short: If you think life is challenging you to step up and give your best, you'll use that energy to do your best and feel energized.

If, on the other hand, you think life is threatening you and your well-being, *that* stress will erode your health and you'll feel enervated.

Part I check in ... How are YOU perceiving the stressors in your life? As *threats* or as *challenges*? Choose wisely.

Now for Part II.

In addition to reframing your perspective on stress, here's a somewhat paradoxical way to alleviate any potential chronic stress: increase your levels of acute, *short-term* stress.

Two ways to do that: physical exercise and short-term projects.

For a variety of reasons, engaging in an intense little workout is one of the best ways to mitigate any lingering, chronic stress you may be experiencing.

And, remember: If you're NOT exercising, you're effectively taking a "Stress Pill" every morning. Not a good idea.

Deliberately "stress" your body with a quick, acute bout of physical stress (a.k.a. a workout!) and voilà. You made a dent in your chronic stress. Do that habitually and you might just wipe it out.

Then we have short-term projects as a means to mitigate chronic stress.

Feeling stressed about something at work (or life)?

Get busy on a short-term project with a well-defined, doable near-term goal. Create some opportunities for small wins. Celebrate them. Repeat.

Although you'll increase stress in the immediate term, you just might reduce it longer-term.

Let's eat stress like an energy bar.

All day every day.

Especially...

TODAY.

PLEASING VS. SERVING
CHOOSE WISELY

I n *Crazy Good*, Steve Chandler makes an incredibly powerful distinction between "serving" and "pleasing."

Here's how he puts it: "When I was a desperate, suicidal alcoholic and I came to your home and you made me a strong drink, you were pleasing me. If, instead, you took me to a Twelve-Step meeting you were serving me. There's a big difference between pleasing and serving."

Pleasing vs. Serving.

There's a big difference between the two.

Choose wisely.

TODAY.

WHEN THE FACTS CHANGE
WHAT DO YOU DO?

S aving the longer philosophical chat about economic theories, let's chat about a brilliant line from one of history's most influential economists, John Maynard Keynes.

He once said: "I change my mind when the facts change. What do you do?"

Before we proceed, let's pause and take a moment to reflect on that question.

Imagine facts changing in your life—whether those facts are related to your Energy or Work or Love…

The facts change. What do you do?

To state the obvious: The wisest and healthiest among us CHANGE OUR MINDS! (Hah.)

Interestingly, as you may have noticed, this is considerably easier said than done—which is why some of the greatest philosophers have consistently echoed this theme.

Nietzsche told us: "Shedding one's skin. The snake that cannot shed its skin perishes. So do the spirits who are prevented from changing their opinions; they cease to be spirit."

Ralph Waldo Emerson told us: "The other terror that scares us from self-trust is our consistency; a reverence for our past act or word, because the eyes of others have no other data for computing our orbit than our past acts, and we are loath to disappoint them."

Emerson continues by saying: "But why should you keep

your head over your shoulder? Why drag about this corpse of your memory, lest you contradict something you have stated in this or that public place? Suppose you should contradict yourself; what then? It seems to be a rule of wisdom never to rely on your memory alone, scarcely even in acts of pure memory, but to bring the past for judgment into the thousand-eyed present, and live ever in a new day."

Note: That's from *Self-Reliance*. The next paragraph is all about not being a hobgoblin.

Here it is: "A foolish consistency is the hobgoblin of little minds, adored by little statesmen and philosophers and divines. With consistency a great soul has simply nothing to do. He may as well concern himself with his shadow on the wall. Speak what you think now in hard words, and to-morrow speak what to-morrow thinks in hard words again, though it contradict every thing you said to-day.—'Ah, so you shall be sure to be misunderstood.'—Is it so bad, then, to be misunderstood? Pythagoras was misunderstood, and Socrates, and Jesus, and Luther, and Copernicus, and Galileo, and Newton, and every pure and wise spirit that ever took flesh. To be great is to be misunderstood."

All that to say…

Do YOU need to change your mind about anything?

Let's quit dragging around dead corpses (!) as we shed the skin that needs to be shed and have the courage to live what we believe to be true.

TODAY.

DEO VOLENTE & THY WILL BE DONE
WISDOM FROM APOLLO, THE PATRON GOD OF PHILOSOPHY

*D*eo volente.

It's Latin for "God willing."

The ancient Stoics told us that it's important to have clear goals but we need to qualify those goals with something along the lines of "if fate will have it."

"I will travel by ship to Athens. If fate will have it."

"I will do x, y, or z. If fate will have it."

They called it the "reserve clause."

It's one thing to be super clear on what we're after and super committed to making it happen. But (very important but!), we need to remember the fact that, ultimately, the *results* of our actions are always out of our hands.

We'd be wise to remember that the patron god of philosophy was Apollo. Apollo was an archer. The archer does his very best to shoot the arrow straight toward its target but, once he has released the arrow, he knows that the outcome is out of his control.

Same with us.

We need to focus on the process (pick a wise goal, shoot the arrow straight!) and let the outcome be what it is.

So, *Deo volente* in the beginning when we share our goals with ourselves and co-creators.

And then (for me, anyway), "Thy will be done."

We don't hit the target? OK. It is what it is.

Thy will be done.

It's time to love what is.

The Stoics called this part of the equation the "art of acquiescence."

Whatever is, IS.

As Byron Katie says, it doesn't make a lot of sense to argue with reality. We'll lose. But only every time.

Accept what is. (Love it!) Get clear on the next target. Shoot straight.

Enjoy the process.

TODAY.

Repeat.

F O R E V E R.

REPAIRING RELATIONSHIPS
A KEY PRACTICE FOR OPTIMIZING THE LOVE IN OUR LIVES

L eading mindfulness (and neuroscience and relationship) expert Dan Siegel tells us that when something inevitably goes wrong in a relationship we want to REPAIR it as quickly as we can.

One of the examples he uses to make his point is a story about a time when he, Mr. Mindfulness, "flipped his lid," turning off his prefrontal cortex and going full limbic-brain, yelling at one of his kids.

I laughed as I typed that as (a) It's always refreshing to see a world-class teacher and practitioner humbly reminding us that no one is perfect and (b) I very much know the feeling as the father of very energetic ten- and six-year-olds.

So, we have an interaction that we're not proud of.

Then what?

Then, you REPAIR the relationship as quickly as you can.

Something like: "Wow. I got really impatient / loud / fill-in-the-blank. I flipped my lid! I want you to know I'm sorry and that I love you and that I'm committed to getting a little better at handling those challenging moments in the future."

* insert potential hug *

We don't want those little micro-moments of negativity to stew into jumbo-resentments and unhealthy cauldrons of ick.

Take a deep breath. Drop into your heart. Label the emotion. Dan says: name it to tame it.

Use whatever tool you need to as you regain your equanimity. And then repair.

+1° check in …

Any repairs waiting for you?

Get on that.

NOW.

YOU'RE TELELOGICAL
START ACTING LIKE IT!

A s we've discussed, Brian Tracy is one of my favorite old-school, kick-your-motivation-into-high-gear gurus.

Back in the day—as in WAY back in the day when CDs in your car stereo system were a new, cutting-edge thing—I'd listen to his audios ALL. THE. TIME.

He asks some of THE most provocative questions. Reading his books has led to some long journaling sessions packed with insight.

Today we're going to talk about the fact that we're TELEO-LOGICAL beings.

Brian Tracy tells us: "Aristotle wrote that human beings are teleological organisms, which simply means that we are purpose driven. Therefore, you feel happy and in control of your life only when you have a clear goal that you are working toward each day. This also means that this ability to become a lifelong goal setter is one of the most important disciplines you will ever develop. We are teleological beings. We are purpose driven. We NEED goals that drive us. Or we suffer."

Now…

To be VERY clear

That's not modern self-help silliness.

It's a scientific fact and a deep philosophical truth.

Modern philosopher Tom Morris (who has a dual PhD in Religion and Philosophy from Yale) definitely agrees.

In his great book *The Art of Achievement*, he tells us: "Aristotle has taught me we all need a target to shoot at. We must have goals to guide our actions and energies. The Greek word for target was telos. Human beings are teleological creatures. We are hard-wired to live purposively, to have direction. Without a target to shoot at, our lives are literally aimless. Without something productive to do, without positive goals and a purpose, a human being languishes. And then one of two things happens. Aimlessness begins to shut a person down in spiritual lethargy and emptiness, or the individual lashes out and turns to destructive goals just to make something happen."

Know this…

The Heroic app has TARGETS we set for ourselves BE-CAUSE OF **ARISTOTLE**.

Happy, flourishing, eudaimonically joyful human beings have clear targets. The best among us know what they are and hit them—all day, every day.

Modern scientist Sonja Lyubomirsky agrees with Brian and Tom and Aristotle and influenced me and our Heroic app development as well (and did the research scientifically validating our Coach program).

In *The How of Happiness*, Sonja tells us: "In 1932, weighed down by the sorrows and agonies of his self-absorbed and aimless clients, an Australian psychiatrist named W. Beran Wolfe summed up his philosophy like this: 'If you observe a really happy man you will find him building a boat, writing a symphony, educating his son, growing double dahlias in his garden, or looking for dinosaur eggs in the Gobi Desert.' He was right. People who strive for something personally significant, whether it's learning a new craft, changing careers, or raising moral children, are far happier than those who don't have strong dreams or aspirations. Find a happy person, and you will find a project."

I repeat…

Happy people have TARGETS.

Happy people have GOALS.

What are YOURS?

And…

Are you taking consistent action to hit those target-goals every day?

Here's to the wisdom and discipline to know what we're here to do and then to actually DO IT.

Not someday…

TODAY.

HAPPY THE ROOSTER
ALCHEMIZING BREAD CRUMBS, DISHES & LEGOS

The other day, Alexandra walked into my office to tell me that she thinks our rooster, Happy, is dying.

Before we talk more about that … Yes, our rooster's name is Happy. Emerson and Eleanor are phenomenal pet namers. We have Happy the Rooster, Lovey and Floppy and Spikey and Longbeak and Goldie the chickens.

Then there's Zap—the dog that showed up on our property one New Year's Day a couple of years ago and adopted us. And don't forget Wags, another awesome dog who decided he wanted to move in one day as well.

If you've ever listened to one of my Zoom calls, you've probably heard a rooster in the background.

Sometimes, I have to admit, I find his crow charming while other times I find it distracting—whether it's on a Zoom or in my morning meditation when he's doing his thing RIGHT outside my office window.

But this rooster is truly an awesome rooster. We hatched him ourselves and he does his job protecting his hens Heroically well and he's not an ornery guy like his dad rooster.

So, when Alexandra came in and told me she thinks he's dying (while she does her country-nurse thing with him to try to save him!), I felt a deeper sense of sadness than I've felt when we've lost some other chickens and found other dead creatures on the property.

I always use those moments as another Stoic reminder of Memento Mori but this one hit me deeper.

I really like this guy!

Then I thought of a story Alexandra shared once. It was about bread crumbs.

I forget the relationship book from which she got the wisdom but the basic idea was this ...

In a significant long-term relationship with ANYONE (let alone a spouse or kids) there will INEVITABLY be things about that person that annoy you.

Maybe they leave bread crumbs on the counter (which irritated the author of the book who told the story) or maybe they leave the dishes out or maybe they leave their Legos all over the house if they're kids (which, in his less-than-enlightened moments can irritate the author of *this* book).

Or maybe they do any number of things people do because they're human and none of us are perfect.

It's easy to find those little things annoying.

Yet ...

What if ...

One day...

Those bread crumbs or dishes or Legos or whatever weren't there because that loved one was no longer there?

All of a sudden we'd MISS those bread crumbs or dishes or Legos or whatever.

That's what I thought of when I heard Happy might not make it. He hasn't been crowing for the last several days because he hasn't been feeling great. I already miss him.

And, I want to make sure I don't let those little things my kids and wife and others do that I might find annoying distract me from the fact that their presence in my life—with ALL the imperfections—is a profound GIFT.

In fact, what I try to do these days is use those VERY things I used to find annoying as THE TRIGGER for me to appreciate just how blessed I am.

I hope our rooster makes it so I can remind myself of this wisdom every time I hear him crow.

Cock-a-doodle-do!

THE TOILET PAPER ROLL
"WHY IS IT ON THE GROUND AGAIN?!"

I n our last +1°, we talked about our rooster, Happy. I'm afraid he passed away shortly after we tried to save him. I have some of his tail feathers on my desk to remind me of him.

I want to continue the theme we explored in that +1°.

Let's see if we can get better at using the things that currently trigger us to feel annoyed to, instead, trigger us to feel grateful.

Here's an example from the Johnson house to help you think of things YOU might want to reframe in YOUR house.

So...

My son Emerson is a wonderfully high-energy kid.

Note: I was going to say my "little guy" Emerson but he's almost eleven as I type this and he's NO LONGER little. It's shocking to see the speed with which he's growing!

When he wakes up, he kinda runs out of the room like Kramer from *Seinfeld*—all energy all the time.

It's FANTASTIC.

Except, of course, when it's not. (Hah.)

So...

Mundane example.

For some strange reason, when Emerson uses the toilet paper in the bathroom, he often rips it off the little horizontal bar on which it rests and the roll of toilet paper winds up unraveled and strewn across the bathroom floor. (Hah.)

Now...

I'm a parent AND a teacher so, of course, we've had some Conquering Toilet Paper 101 classes on how to gently roll the toilet paper and gently rip the amount you need from the roll while ensuring it stays in place at the end of the job. (10 Big Ideas, folks!)

And, let's just say that lesson hasn't stuck. (Hah.)

So…

After Emerson's done his thing, that toilet paper roll often winds up strewn across the bathroom floor.

And… I can choose to use that toilet paper on the ground (again!) as either a trigger for my annoyance (and yet another lecture on the mechanics of toilet paper)…

OR…

I can use that *same* trigger as an opportunity to appreciate the fact that, one day WAY too soon, that toilet paper roll is going to be perfectly and permanently affixed to its resting place—never to see the floor again.

And…

I just got tears in my eyes typing that.

I'm not ready for that day yet.

I want to fully enjoy the incredible enthusiasm of my not-so-little-boy who is becoming a wonderfully enthusiastic young man for as long as I can—knowing that it, like all the other wonderful things in my life, will not last forever.

That's our +1°.

Got a trigger?

Seriously.

Pause.

Think of ONE little thing a loved one does that, if we AC-TUALLY practiced our philosophy with a little more rigor, could EASILY be alchemized from annoying to charming...

Got it?

Fantastic.

Let's remember the fact that life is preciously short.

And...

Let's use everything we can as a reminder of just how precious it is.

-1° to +1°.

Let's live with *Areté*.

All day. Every day.

Especially...

TODAY.

EITHER/OR?
GET AS MUCH OF BOTH AS POSSIBLE

Ray Dalio shares a lot of powerful wisdom in his great book, *Principles*.

Here's an idea I come back to often in my coaching sessions and in my own strategic thinking.

It goes something like this…

When you're faced with an apparent either/or decision, slow down, step back, and think harder about how you can have as much of BOTH as possible.

For Dalio, it was achieving high investment returns with low risk.

Either/or, right?

Not necessarily.

Figuring out how to have a TON of both is one of the primary reasons he's achieved his success.

What is it for YOU?

Do you have any apparent either/or dichotomies in *your* life?

Slow down.

Write the challenge down on a piece of paper.

Step back. Stare at the riddle.

Think a little harder.

How can you have as much of BOTH as possible?

GOLDEN & PLATINUM RULES
HOW TO TREAT OTHERS & YOURSELF

We've all heard of the Golden Rule.

But... Do you know how ubiquitous it is across cultures? And... Have you ever heard of the Platinum Rule?

Most importantly: Are you practicing both?

First: The ubiquitous Golden Rule.

I love the way Dale Carnegie puts it in *How to Win Friends and Influence People*.

He tells us: "Philosophers have been speculating on the rules of human relationships for thousands of years, and out of all that speculation, there has evolved only one important precept. It is not new. It is as old as history. Zoroaster taught it to his followers in Persia twenty-five hundred years ago. Confucius preached it in China twenty-four centuries ago. Lao-tse, the founder of Taoism, taught it to his disciples in the Valley of the Han. Buddha preached it on the bank of the Holy Ganges five hundred years before Christ. The sacred books of Hinduism taught it a thousand years before that. Jesus taught it among the stony hills of Judea nineteen centuries ago. Jesus summed it up in one thought: 'Do unto others as you would have others do unto you.'"

Here's the quick tour of all those other cultures...

Zoroaster: "Whatever is disagreeable to yourself do not do unto others."

Confucius: "'Is there a single word which can be a guide to

conduct throughout one's life?' The Master said, 'It is perhaps the word *shu*. Do not impose on others what you yourself do not desire.'"

Lao Tzu: "To those who are good to me, I am good; and to those who are not good to me, I am also good; and thus all get to receive good."

Buddha: "Hurt not others with that which pains yourself."

Hinduism: "This is the sum of duty: do naught to others which if done to thee would cause thee pain."

A goldmine of Golden Rules!

Next up: The Platinum Rule.

In *Happier*, Tal Ben-Shahar tells us: "Why the double standard, the generosity toward our neighbor and the miserliness where we ourselves are concerned? And so I propose that we add a new rule, which we can call the Platinum Rule, to our moral code: 'Do not do unto yourself what you would not do unto others.'"

In *The Pursuit of Perfect*, Tal also adds this gem: "When the Dalai Lama was then asked to clarify whether indeed the object of compassion may be the self, he responded: 'Yourself first, and then in a more advanced way the aspiration will embrace others. In a way, high levels of compassion are nothing but an advanced state of that self-interest. That's why it is hard for people who have a strong sense of self-hatred to have genuine compassion toward others. There is no anchor, no basis to start from.'"

The Golden Rule AND The Platinum Rule.

Let's put them to work. TODAY.

WHOSE BUSINESS ARE YOU IN?
YOURS, SOMEONE ELSE'S, OR GOD'S?

Byron Katie tells us that there are three different businesses we can be in: our own business, someone else's business, or God's business.

She tells us that if we want to reduce our suffering, we'd be VERY wise to focus *exclusively* on OUR business.

You may have noticed that it's IMPOSSIBLE to control someone else. No matter how hard you try, you simply aren't going to be able to flip a switch and change someone. Period.

Therefore, get out of their business and quit trying.

Notice how you suffer when you focus on what *other* people should be doing. Flip that around and focus on what YOU should be doing. THAT's *your* business.

And…

You might've noticed that it's even *more* I M P O S S I B L E to control GOD's business.

A tornado strikes. An earthquake shakes. The markets collapse. That kinda thing. God's business. It's not within your direct control. Period.

Want to suffer?

Focus on trying to control those things and then complain about them.

Want to stop suffering?

Focus on what IS within your control: YOUR BUSINESS. How YOU show up in the world.

The thoughts you allow yourself to think. The actions you decide to take. The habits you decide to build. The Heroic quests you decide to pursue. The love you choose to embody.

Other people's business. God's business. Your business.

Whose business are YOU in?

THE SERENITY PRAYER
SERENITY + COURAGE + WISDOM = A WINNING COMBO

In our last +1°, we talked about Byron Katie's idea that you can be in one of three businesses: someone else's business, God's business, or YOUR business.

Quick recap: We want to stay *out of* other people's business and we want to stay *out of* God's business as we remain exclusively in our business—remembering that, ultimately, the ONLY things we have control over are our own thoughts and behaviors.

Of course, all great wisdom traditions remind us of the same truth.

The Serenity Prayer may capture it most succinctly.

"God, grant me the serenity to accept the things I cannot change, the courage to change the things I can, and the wisdom to know the difference."

Our +1° mission should you choose to pursue it …

Let's commit the Serenity Prayer to memory.

"God, grant me the serenity to accept the things I cannot change, the courage to change the things I can, and the wisdom to know the difference."

Learning 101-style, pause for a moment and quiz yourself—see if you can recall those lines now.

If you can't, try chunking it down and memorize the first line. Then the second. Then the third. Then put it all together.

"God, grant me the serenity to accept the things I cannot change, the courage to change the things I can, and the wisdom to know the difference."

And, most importantly, play it in your mind and embody its wisdom in those moments when you find yourself losing your serenity or needing a little more courage and/or a bit more wisdom.

TODAY.

A BRIEF HISTORY OF LAWNS
OUR HORIZON OF POSSIBILITIES

Yuval Noah Harari is a very smart man.

He has a PhD in history from Oxford and he's written a number of bestselling books including *Sapiens* (which provides "A Brief History of Humankind"), *Homo Deus* (which provides "A Brief *History* of the **FUTURE**"; emphasis mine), and *21 Lessons for the 21st Century* (no explanatory subtitle necessary).

If you want to dramatically upgrade the way you see the world, I encourage you to read those books. (And, check out the Philosopher's Notes for some of my favorite Big Ideas.)

For now, I want to talk about lawns.

Lawns? Yep.

First, know this: Professor Harari tells us that we should study history so that we can learn that our modern cultures are neither "natural" nor "inevitable" nor "immutable." As we recognize that fact, we can broaden our "horizon of possibilities" and reimagine a better future.

Now... Back to the lawns.

In *Homo Deus*, Harari shares "A Brief History of Lawns" to bring his point home.

First, pop quiz: Do you have a lawn? If you're a well-adjusted American, odds are you do. No matter *who* you are and *where* you are in the world, you've been exposed to lawns and you've probably never thought about its origin story.

Here it is.

Back in the medieval day, resources were scarce. Peasant people simply didn't have the spare land and water and labor to create a big piece of green turf.

But, you know who did?

King Francois I.

Enter: The first "lawn" in history in front of his epic chateau in the Loire Valley.

Then…

Enter: Dukes trying to show that THEY had a ton of extra cash to spend on a piece of green turf in front of THEIR chateaus.

Fast-forward to modern times and you see a lawn in front of the White House and, again, if you're a well-adjusted middle-class American, we'll probably see a well-manicured lawn in front of YOUR house.

So… What's *that* have to do with optimizing our lives and activating our Heroic potential?

Well, we want to realize that living in a culture that prizes things like "lawns" is not "natural, inevitable and immutable."

With that super-simple insight, we can step back and see just how much of our current culture is ALSO not "natural, inevitable and immutable."

For example, you know that vacation you're dreaming about? That's another example of a myth programmed into our "romantic consumerism" culture so deeply that we take it for granted.

Oh! And how about all that sugar and flour you eat?

Just because EVERYONE does it these days does NOT make it *either* natural *or* inevitable OR Heroically optimal.

As Krishnamurti put it: "It is no measure of health to be well adjusted to a profoundly sick society."

Of course, we'll ALWAYS have the constraints of our culture to deal with but we can expand our horizon of possibilities as we explore more options and strive to create a life of deeper personal meaning.

As Harari says: "There is no way out of the imagined order. When we break our prison walls and run towards freedom, we are in fact running into the more spacious exercise yard of a bigger prison."

But... "Some freedom is better than none."

All of which leads us to our +1°.

When you see a lawn today—whether that's in front of your house or in front of an important government building—remember its origin story.

Perhaps we can playfully wink at the lawn and know that it's just one of an infinite number of examples of the many things in our culture we take for granted that, upon slightly further reflection, is a bit silly.

Then, most importantly, from that more wisely spacious perspective, let's recommit to playing our roles humbly yet iconoclastically and Heroically well as we help create a world in which 51% of humanity is flourishing by the year 2051.

Starting with us.

TODAY.

110-YEAR-OLD YOU
READY FOR SOME TIME TRAVEL?

In his great book *Happier*, Tal Ben-Shahar tells us that we have all the wisdom we will ever need—as evidenced by individuals who undergo a traumatic life experience and then radically transform their lives.

He gives us a fun, powerful way to access our innate wisdom. Here's my take on it.

Let's imagine that NASA (or, more likely Jeff Bezos or Elon Musk and their teams) has invented a time traveling machine. (YES!!)

This machine can magically take you into the future where you can meet the 110-year-old version of you.

Let's hop in. Close the door. Get comfortable.

(Please keep your hands and body parts inside the time traveling vehicle at all times.)

And… BAM!!!

We're there.

Imagine the 110-year-old version of you standing in front of you. Radiating a grace and beauty and love and wisdom and presence that makes your heart open.

Ask them to share the most important lesson they've learned and give you a little perspective on your current life and its challenges and opportunities.

What do they say?

Seriously.

The 110-year-old most radiantly awesome version of you is standing in front of you *right now*.

Close your eyes.

See them.

WHAT DO THEY SAY?

Know this…

That wisest version of you is ALWAYS there.

Pay attention to what they have to say.

TODAY.

THE DREADED "U"
& HOW TO CONQUER IT

Imagine yourself at the start of a Heroic quest.

You're looking out across a canyon. You can see a shimmering oasis on the other side. It's epic. Super bright and shiny and awesome. And it's yours.

You know it. You can feel it.

Then you get to work.

You descend into the depths of the canyon to get to the other side. It's dark in here. The trees are thick. So thick that you've got to cut your way through them.

You look up. You can't quite see that epic vision anymore. Eek.

Enter: That whiny little voice in your head that wonders what the heck you're doing and questions why you're down here in the mosquito-infested forest in the first place.

Todd Henry calls this part of the journey "The Lag" in his great book *Die Empty*.

Here's how he puts it: "The lag is the gap between cause and effect. It's the season between planting a seed and reaping a harvest. It's the time when all the work you've done seems to have returned little to no visible reward, and there is little on the horizon to indicate that things are going to get better."

Ever been there?

Me, too. (Of course we have!)

What to do there?

Well, here's Todd again: "When you are in the lag, the only thing that keeps you moving forward are (a) confidence in your vision and ability to bring it to fruition, (b) a willingness to say no to other things that tempt you to divert from your course, and (c) daily, diligent, urgent progress."

Our +1°…

How's YOUR lag?

First, celebrate the fact that you HAVE a lag.

(And, if you don't ever experience a lag, try a little harder. Stretch yourself a little more. Feel the burn, baby!)

Second, how are your ABCs of dealing with the lag?

What can you do to boost your confidence, increase your focus, and make "daily, diligent, urgent progress"?

Fantastic. Get on that.

See you on the other side!

P.S. Todd is the one who also defined "mediocrity" for us.

As you may recall, the word *mediocrity* comes from the Latin *medius* + *ocris* which literally means to be "stuck in the middle of a rugged mountain."

As we discussed, mediocrity has a bunch of synonyms (average, middling, unexceptional, unexciting, lackluster, forgettable, amateurish, etc.) but it has only *one* antonym: EXCELLENCE.

So… If you want to make it to the summit and avoid getting stuck in the lag of mediocrity, you need to practice EXCELLENCE. Again and again and again. ESPECIALLY when you don't feel like it.

THE PURSUIT OF HAPPINESS
DON'T CHASE HAPPINESS—PRACTICE IT

Of course, we all know that Thomas Jefferson wrote these beautiful words in the Declaration of Independence:

"We hold these truths to be self-evident, that all men are created equal, that they are endowed by their Creator with certain unalienable Rights, that among these are Life, Liberty, and the pursuit of Happiness."

But…

When Jefferson wrote those words, "the pursuit of Happiness" didn't mean "to *chase* after" happiness and/or to "pursue it" in the sense we think about it today.

Back in the day of men wearing powdered wigs and writing with quill feathers, the "pursuit" of something meant the PRACTICE of it.

So…

I repeat: Happiness wasn't something you *chased after*.

It was something you PRACTICED.

Here's to appreciating the wise, disciplined, loving, and courageous effort of our founding mothers and fathers as we recommit to PRACTICING our philosophy.

Close the gap.

Live with *Areté*.

In service to something bigger than yourself.

TODAY.

THE LAST LECTURE
WHAT'S YOURS?

Have you seen Randy Pausch's "Last Lecture"? Over twenty-one million people have watched it and, if you're one of them, you know just how magnetically inspiring Randy was.

If you *haven't* seen the video yet and don't know who Randy Pausch was, here's the short story…

Randy was a Professor of Computer Science at Carnegie Mellon University. He was diagnosed with pancreatic cancer. When it became terminal, he gave his "last lecture." The talk was recorded. It went viral. He wrote a great book that extended the ideas from that talk.

That book, as you'd expect, is called *The Last Lecture*.

As we discuss in the Philosopher's Notes, the book features fifty-three micro chapters—each telling a different story from Randy's life. It's packed with wisdom.

In the introduction to his book, Randy tells us that he (at the time he wrote the book shortly before he passed away) was the father of three young children.

He recorded his last lecture and wrote the book as a way to teach his kids the things he wished they could have learned from him if he was able to be with them as they grew up.

(Goosebumps as I typed that.)

Our +1° is simple yet demanding.

If you have kids (and/or if you aspire to have kids and/or if you did have kids)…

What would YOU want to teach your kids if YOU only had weeks to live?

Seriously.

We don't need to go on a mini retreat to script the lecture or write the book per se (although that might be a wise idea)…

What IMMEDIATELY arises for you?

What one or two or three things would you DEFINITELY want your kids to know about how to live a good, noble, Heroic life?

Let's pause for another moment while you connect with your daimon.

And…

Let's consider those three things now…

If I only had a week to live, I'd want to make sure my kids knew THESE three things about what I think would help them live a noble life:

1. _____

2. _____

3. _____

Beautiful.

Bless you and your wisdom.

Now for the MUCH more challenging question…

Are you LIVING IN INTEGRITY with that wisdom?

Because…

As you know…

Our kids are "reading the book" that is our lives and learning how we think they should live ALL DAY EVERY DAY.

Note: If that isn't a sobering wake up call, I don't know what is.

Let's make sure we're giving them the lectures (by our embodied demonstration of the wisdom we cherish!) that we hope they embody in the years and decades ahead.

Memento Mori, Hero.

Today's the only day we're guaranteed.

Let's show up and act like we mean it.

For our kids and their kids and everyone we love.

Day 1. All in.

LET'S GO.

THE LAST LETTER
I WROTE MY BROTHER

S cience says that expressing our appreciation to others in the form of a "Gratitude Letter" that we read to them in person can be an incredibly powerful experience for both people involved.

Robert Emmons puts it this way in *Gratitude Works!*: "What was the effect of composing and delivering the letter for those who participated in the experiment? When their moods were measured after one week of doing the assigned exercise, participants were happier and less depressed. This boost in happiness and decrease in depressive symptoms were maintained at followup assessments one week and one month later. It turns out that a gratitude visit is one of the exercises that, to Seligman's surprise (he once confided to me, 'Bob, I don't do gratitude'), made people lastingly less depressed and happier than any other positive psychology intervention."

I happened to read this book on the power of gratitude shortly before my brother passed away from pancreatic cancer.

As I was reading the chapter on gratitude letters, I *knew* that I needed to write a letter for my brother.

So that's what I did.

I read the letter to my brother on what was, literally, his deathbed.

It was one of the most powerful moments of my life—one that I will cherish forever and one that I am so happy I experienced as it allowed me to end my relationship with him with a deep sense of connection and love.

I would like to share that letter with you as a tribute to my brother and, I hope, as an inspiration for you to consider doing something similar for someone in *your* life who you think would appreciate knowing you appreciate them.

I also shared this letter at my brother's end of life celebration.

A little more context: I am the youngest of five kids—good Catholic family. My mom got married to my dad at seventeen and had my brother when she was eighteen. Then they had three girls. Then, after waiting THIRTEEN years, my brother *finally* had a little brother.

The title of my letter was: "Love You, Brother Rick."

My Dear Brother Rick,

I want you to know how much I appreciate you.

Thank you for supporting me for the last forty-five years.

I know you waited a long time to have a little brother and I want you to know that I think you've been a great big brother.

I was reading a book on gratitude the other day (you know me!) and they talked about the power of writing a letter of gratitude to someone who has supported you and made your life better.

I IMMEDIATELY thought of you. Before anyone else.

Then they asked a bunch of questions, including: "Who taught you how to throw a baseball?" I laughed. Then I started to cry.

I'm not sure if you're the one who taught me how to throw a baseball (you probably did—so thanks!) but I'm pretty sure you were involved in making sure my first word was "Ball!"

(Not too long before I got the chance to help you with your newspaper route.)

As I thought about you and baseball and sports and reflected on their question, the image that came to mind was you helping me practice free throws before I entered a free-throw contest when I was in 8th grade. I don't know if you remember but I must have been 12 or so—which means you must have been around 25. If I'm remembering correctly, we cruised on over to Gisler Park (did we walk or drive in your sweet blue Celica which I had probably just waxed?!) and you rebounded countless shots and delivered bullet passes so I didn't have to move an inch as I took shot after shot after shot.

As I reflected on that memory, I thought to myself: "What twenty-five-year-old guy does that for his little brother?"

A good man. That's who.

(Btw: We crushed that free-throw competition—tying for first place with something like twenty-two or twenty-three out of twenty-five. Hah! Go us!!)

Then I thought of you coaching my Little League Baseball teams. Coach Rick before he was THE COACH RICK! I can still see you down there on the third-base line cheering me on as I made my strike zone invisible and tried to rip one down the line in your direction. I'm not sure if I managed to do much more than walk or bunt (then steal second!) but that wasn't because you weren't there to bring out my best.

Then I thought of all the weekend trips to your place over an hour away where we'd play darts all night long and drive back with the sunroof open and you brushing your hair in style! (Oh, the days when we both had hair!)

Then I thought about hanging off my big brother's arms—which were so superhero big and strong that I couldn't even wrap my hands around them.

Then I imagined watching you play softball and marveling at your booming home runs and gold-glove-like shortstop plays.

Then I thought of the honor of being your best man. How was that twenty-five years ago?!

Then I fast-forwarded through countless other moments of connection to the first chat we had about my second business. I was raising money. I got to the end of whatever my pitch was and you said: "Brother Brian. I don't care what you're doing. It's you. It's going to work. I'm in."

That was one of the most touching moments of my life—to feel 100% unconditionally supported and to know how much you believed in me.

All that to say: I love you. I appreciate you.

I want you to know that I wouldn't be who I am today without you and your support.

Thank you, brother.

Love,

- Your Little Brother Brian

GOALS: TELESCOPES & MICROSCOPES
HEROIC APPS TO DOMINATE THE DAY & DECADE

Not too long ago, we spent some time with Brian Cain and some of his wisdom from a couple of his little fables: *One Percent Better* and *The 10 Pillars of Mental Performance Mastery*.

I want to revisit some of his wisdom.

Let's talk about your goals.

We'll invite Cainer back to the party to help us check them out from a couple different perspectives.

In *10 Pillars*, he tells us: "Setting big goals is great, but they have to be the right goals or they become traps. Financial goals must be secondary to family goals or you won't have any family to set goals with. You also need to have telescope and microscope goals. Telescope goals that you can see off into the future, and then you must reverse engineer a process back to your microscope and execute on your microscopic daily goals. Telescope goals are one, three, or five+ years into the future and the microscope goals are what you will do in the next 24 hours to move towards your telescope goals. Remember, inch by inch, goal setting is a cinch and yard by yard, it's hard."

That's from a chapter on Pillar #2 of Mental Performance Mastery—which is about our Motivation and Commitment.

Cainer tells us (and all great peak performance teachers affirm) that one of the most important things we can do to get (and sustain!) elite levels of motivation is to set clear goals.

I just LOVE the way he helps us do that.

So... Let's bust out our Telescopes AND our Microscopes then the Heroic app and do some work.

First, the Telescope.

What are your most inspiring one, three, and five+ year goals? (Seriously. What are they?)

If you feel so inspired, let's do a quick inventory of your 5-year goals in your Big 3: Energy, Work, and Love.

Remember: If we don't prioritize our Love alongside our Work we may not have the opportunity to set and celebrate the achievement of our Work goals with the people in our lives who matter most.

And... If our Energy isn't where it needs to be, there's no way we'll show up powerfully in either our Work or our Love so...

Here's to the Big 3 for the win!

This is my #1 Five-Year ENERGY Goal:

_____

_____

This is my #1 Five-Year WORK Goal:

_____

_____

This is my #1 Five-Year LOVE Goal:

_____

_____

Now, it's time to bust out the Microscope.

I'm (clearly) biased but…

I think one of the easiest ways to get clarity on what you should DO TODAY to be in integrity with the best version of yourself that's capable of ACHIEVING those goals is simple…

Do some Target Practice on the Heroic app as we move from Theory to Practice to Mastery Together TODAY.

Step 0. Set up your Big 3 protocol by getting clarity on who you are at your best in your Energy, Work, and Love along with the virtues that best version of you embodies and what, SPECIFICALLY, you will actually DO TODAY to be in integrity with that best version of yourself.

Step 1. Commit to being that best version of yourself and doing those things TODAY.

Note: As we like to say (and I promise to repeat myself!)… New Year's Resolutions are nice and warm and fuzzy. New DAY's Resolutions are where it's at if you actually want to consistently perform at the highest possible levels.

Step 2. Hit your targets. ALL DAY. EVERY DAY. ESPECIALLY TODAY!

And even more importantly… Commit and hit them on those days when you don't (insert whiny voice) *feel* like it as you forge your invincible, antifragile confidence.

Step 3. Repeat. Forever.

See your moonshot goals with your Telescope. See the next steps in your Microscope. Dominate the day with your Heroic app. And give us all you've got, Hero. TODAY.

PROGRAMMING YOUR MIND
TO BE HEROICALLY ENERGIZED, PRODUCTIVE & CONNECTED

As you know if you've been following along and moving from Theory to Practice (en route to Mastery!) with the Heroic app, we architected the Big 3 protocol to help you get clear on who you are at your best in your Energy, your Work, and your Love.

We help you set your Identity for your "Heroic Big 3" and then we help you get clear on what VIRTUES you embody when you show up as the best, most Heroic version of yourself in your Energy, your Work and your Love.

THEN we help you get clear on what specific Behavioral Targets you hit when you are living in integrity with those Identities and Virtues.

Then, of course, we encourage you to spend a minute or three FIRST thing in the morning (EVERY MORNING!) recommitting to BEING that best, most Heroically Energized, Productive, and Connected version of yourself.

It may sound too simple (and/or boring) to be effective, but early research shows that spending even just a minute or three every day in the Heroic app "tap tap tap" recommitting to your Big 3 protocol and then hitting as few as THREE Heroic targets you set for yourself can lead to a 40% boost in your Energy, a 20% boost in your productivity, and a 15% boost in your connection.

Why? How is that possible?

When you set a clear INTENTION, your ATTENTION tends to follow and you are more likely to remember to (and find ways to) DO the things you KNOW are best for you after you recommitted to them in the morning.

Then, when you celebrate the micro-behavior WIN with a Target Swipe splash of dopamine, surprising goodness ensues.

Don't believe me though. Try it.

Here's one reason why it's so powerful.

Question: Have you ever bought a car?

If so, follow-up question: When you were thinking about buying that car and shortly after you bought it, did you suddenly see that type of car EVERYWHERE?

Of course you did. But why?

It's simple.

Your brain evolved to filter the EXTRAORDINARY number of stimuli you are exposed to in any given moment into a manageable load.

How does one of the most ancient parts of your brain filter all those inputs? It "decides" what gets into your conscious mind based on what you "told" it was "important."

Result: If you're thinking about buying a certain type of car, you'll suddenly see it everywhere.

Guess what…

That same idea applies to EVERYTHING you think about. Your brain (more specifically, your reticular activating system) is CONSTANTLY paying attention to what you're thinking about and will show you more of whatever that is—which is awesome, except when it isn't.

If you're thinking about all the things that are WRONG in your life (and the world), guess what? You'll see more of that.

On the other hand, without becoming a Pollyanna-ish idealist who ignores reality, of course…

If you think about the stuff you want to see MORE of in your life, you'll see more of it.

For example, IF YOU REMIND YOURSELF OF WHO YOU ARE AT YOUR BEST AND WHAT VIRTUES YOU EMBODY AND WHAT SPECIFIC BEHAVIORS YOU WANT TO ENGAGE IN ON A DAILY BASIS (via something like the Heroic app perhaps?!) guess what you're likely to see more of in your life?

You will see more opportunities to live in integrity with those Identities, Virtues and Behaviors.

And…

That's life changing.

And…

That's our +1°.

Here's to programming our minds with what we want to see more of.

And then seeing all the opportunities to show up as the best, most Heroic versions of ourselves.

TODAY.

THE WALKING STATUE
THAT IS YOU

We've covered a lot of ground together.

We started with The Big 3 origin story then we chatted about our Energy (start here!), our Work (time for some Genius Work!) and our Love (Heroically encourage one another!).

Then we multiplied that Big 3 by 2 as we chatted about our Identities (start with who!), Virtues (what virtues does that best you embody?), and Behaviors (what does that version of you DO?) before exploring a bunch of different ways to think about our Energy, Work, and Love.

Before we wrap up our time together with this objective, let's go back to Michelangelo's studio for another moment.

If you feel so inspired, imagine your heroically-best self right there in the marble in Michelangelo's studio.

Then...

Imagine yourself STEPPING INTO that statue.

Then...

Imagine yourself walking right out of the studio.

We are that living, breathing statue.

And the studio that is our lives *has no walls*.

We are (quite literally!) sculpting ourselves every single moment of our lives.

Seriously. Science is unequivocal on this fact. EVERY SINGLE little millisecond of a thought shapes your brain.

Moment to moment to moment we get to sculpt the always-evolving masterpiece that is our lives as we embrace the constraints of our imperfect marble while committing to giving the world all we've got.

How?

Areté.

When?

As always…

TODAY.

And… That's the focus of our next objective. It's time to create some masterpiece days.

TODAY'S THE DAY!
MAKE IT A MASTERPIECE

Welcome to Objective IV. We know the ultimate game we're playing. We're forging antifragile confidence and we're optimizing our Energy, Work, and Love.

Now, it's time to seize the day as we systematically architect our Masterpiece Days.

Before we go any further, let's summarize this objective in three simple words. We'll bring back the all caps and all bold so we don't miss it.

Here it is…

TODAY'S THE DAY!!!

I repeat: TODAY'S the Day to move from Theory to Practice to Mastery, Hero!

It's simple: If we want to make our LIVES a masterpiece, we need to make TODAY a masterpiece.

My intention with this objective is two-fold. First, I want you to *really* get the fact that TODAY is, in fact, the day to give us all you've got. Second, I want to help you get *really* good at making today awesome.

Before we get to work, here's a quick little thought exercise to make the point…

In *Die Empty*, Todd Henry tells us to imagine that from the moment we wake up to the moment we go to sleep we have a reporter following us around taking notes on every little thing we do. After tracking our behavior for the day, the reporter goes off and writes a report describing what we did, when, how, etc.

That little report they create will serve as the summary of *our entire lives*—which is a pretty good incentive to make *today* the day to live our deepest values, eh?

And…

Guess what?

That reporter *is* there every day.

Let's make them proud.

Today.

MASTERPIECE DAY CHECKLISTS
HOW TO REDUCE MORTALITY RATES BY 47%

Atul Gawande is a world-class surgeon.

In his great book *The Checklist Manifesto*, he walks us through the astonishing power of simple checklists.

I got the book after reading Teresa Amabile's *The Progress Principle* in which she raved about it.

Professor Amabile is the head of research at Harvard Business School. She says: "The results are astonishing. In a three-month experiment in eight different hospitals around the world, the rate of serious complications for surgical patients fell by 36 percent after introduction of the checklist, and deaths fell by 47 percent. Even Gawande himself, a highly trained surgeon with years of operating experience, found that his own performance improved notably after he started using the checklist. His point is that surgery, like any complex task, requires a regular check of all the fundamentals—to liberate the team to focus on the work and any unexpected circumstances that may arise."

The surgical checklist was *crazy* simple. So simple that many surgeons (who trained for decades to do what they do) thought it was laughably useless.

It included very basic things like each member of the surgical team introducing themselves and confirming which side of the body the surgery would be performed on.

But the results from that super simple checklist were astonishing. Deaths fell by 47%.

I repeat, this time in bold caps to make sure you don't miss the memo…

AFTER USING CHECKLISTS, MORTALITY RATES FELL BY FORTY-SEVEN PERCENT!!!

The research is clear…

You can (and should!) use checklists for any complex thing you do that you want to make sure you consistently do well— whether you're a surgeon, a pilot, or a Hero on a quest to create a masterpiece life.

Here's the short story on a good checklist: It's short. It's precise. And, most importantly, it's SUPER PRACTICAL.

For our Heroic purposes, we want to make sure we have a simple little checklist to reduce the fatality rate of our Masterpiece Days.

So… What's on your list?

Let's create a super simple v1 Masterpiece Day Checklist. Short. Precise. Practical. What THREE things do you do when you have your best days?

Think about that for a moment.

What are they?

1. _____

2. _____

3. _____

Figure out the few super-basic things you do to help you have great days. Create a checklist to make sure you do them.

And make TODAY a masterpiece.

P.S. We architected our Heroic app with this wisdom in mind. Set up YOUR Heroic Big 3 (checklist!) protocol today and watch your Masterpiece Day mortality rates drop by AT LEAST 47%!!

TIME BLOCKS
THE #1 POWER TOOL FOR GREAT DAYS

G ary Keller created the largest real estate agency in the world. He also wrote a great book called *The ONE Thing* in which he tells us how he achieved his extraordinary success.

As per the subtitle of the book, he shares: "The Surprisingly Simple Truth Behind Extraordinary Results."

That surprisingly simple truth?

FOCUS.

He tells us that we need to *ruthlessly* focus on what's most important. He takes the 80/20 principle to the extreme and has us tighten our focus until we get to the ONE Thing that drives the whole show.

Then he has you ruthlessly focus on what you need to do TODAY to make that ONE Thing a reality—knocking over the next domino in a chain of dominoes that inevitably leads to the outcome you're looking for.

Of course, just *figuring out* what your ONE Thing is (over the long run and for today) obviously takes clear thinking and demands some Deep Work to get that clarity.

Which leads us to the #1 practical tip Gary shares.

He calls it the #1 "power tool" of time management.

What is it? Time Blocking.

Basic idea: Create a block of time in which you eliminate ALL distractions. Focus on whatever you decided is THE most important thing.

Then we make a habit of doing that. Every. Single. Day.

Time Blocking. If you want to activate your Heroic potential, it's a must.

It's obvious how powerful this can be for Work. It's less obvious just how powerful this can be with Love.

I personally have a dedicated Deep Work Time Block EVERY SINGLE MORNING. Right after my meditation, I show up and hit my most important win in a 30-60-90-minute, creative-before-reactive Deep Work session.

It's my secret weapon for Heroic productivity. You couldn't pay me to not do it. With *rare* (but important) exceptions, I hit this every morning.

For Love, I like to create Time Blocks every weeknight after my shutdown complete to spend with the kids. No phone. No distractions. Just me and the family. I like to create even BIGGER Time Blocks on the weekends.

These are my secret weapons for Heroic connection.

How about YOU?

How can you step up your Time Block game in *both* your Work *and* your Love?

Get on that.

TODAY.

YOUR PRIOR BEST
= YOUR NEW BASELINE

It's time to put some pen to paper as we begin to architect our protocol. Our unapologetically ambitious target? We want to make your prior best your new baseline.

To do that, we need to spend some time thinking about you at your best.

Let's grab that flashlight of curious awareness and shine a bright light on those times in your life when you've shown up as your best.

If you feel so inspired, grab a piece of paper.

Put "ME AT MY BEST" at the top. Then draw a line right down the middle. At the top on the left side, put "I DO THIS." At the top on the right side, put "I DON'T DO THIS."

Now, write down some of the things you DO when you're at your best and some of the things you DON'T DO when you're at your best.

Don't over think. Just write down what comes to mind on your first pass. Make sure you write down what you do Energy, Work, and Love wise when you're at your best. And, what you *don't* do.

Got it? Good. Now, here's a Pro Tip: Want to feel *great* more and more consistently?

Do more of the "DO" stuff and do less of the "DON'T" stuff. It's not *easy* to do that, but it REALLY IS that simple. (Seriously.)

Now, take another look at all the behaviors on that piece of paper. What's the #1 thing you do when you're at your best that you're currently *not* doing that, if you *did* start doing it consistently, would most change your life?

Seriously. What is it?

Got it? Fantastic.

Circle it.

Now imagine your life with THAT habit installed along with all the other ones from the "Do" list. Then imagine deleting all (yes, all!) the bad habits from the "Don't Do" list.

We KNOW you can do that because you've ALREADY done it in the past.

Remember the science of self-efficacy?

As you may recall, one of the most important ways to build your confidence with your *current* challenges is to recall times in the past where you demonstrated mastery.

With that in mind, we just need you to make your prior best your new baseline.

I'll leave it at that for now as we'll spend our time in the next objective talking about the art and science of behavioral change so you can install and delete habits like a ninja.

For now, know this: It's impossible for me to overstate the power of having clarity on the things that help us activate our Heroic potential and then DOING THOSE THINGS whether we feel like it or not.

Make that: ESPECIALLY when we don't feel like it.

Here's to forging your antifragile confidence and making your prior best your new baseline, Hero.

CARPE DIEM
SEIZE THE DAY! (OR IS IT "PLUCK THE DAY"?)

*C*arpe Diem!

I don't know about you, but I get fired up just saying that. (Hah.)

Today we'll have fun looking at the ancient Latin roots of the phrase and see how we can apply that wisdom to optimizing our lives.

So... The Latin phrase *carpe diem* (seize the day!) comes to us via Horace's *Odes* written over 2,000 years ago.

(Well, technically, the phrase came to most of us via Robin Williams's character in *Dead Poets Society* but he got it from Horace's *Odes*.)

But...

Here's the thing.

"Seize" the day isn't quite the best way to capture the essence of the Latin word *carpe*.

Although it doesn't sound quite as cool, a more precise translation of *carpe diem* would be to "pluck the day." As in, pick today off the tree of life—it's ripe and ready to enjoy!

The difference is subtle but significant.

Imagine a ripe piece of fruit hanging from a tree. It's juicy and ready to be enjoyed.

We don't need to "seize" that fruit as if it's something we need to "take hold of suddenly and forcibly."

We want to "pluck" it. And then enjoy it.

THAT's the essence of what Horace was getting at.

Life is preciously brief. Today—and, more precisely, THIS MOMENT!—is something to be enjoyed and lived to its fullest.

So…

Our +1°…

Pluck the day!

Eat it like your favorite piece of fruit.

And, savor every bite.

CARPE PUNCTUM
YOU CAN'T SEIZE DAYS—ONLY MOMENTS

In our last +1°, we talked about the ancient roots of the phrase *carpe diem*.

We learned that a more accurate translation of the phrase would be "pluck the day"—as in, the day is ripe and ready to enjoy!

But … Here's the deal.

We can't actually pluck or seize a DAY.

We can only pluck or seize (or squander!) the MOMENT.

Therefore, as Dan Millman wisely tells us in *Everyday Enlightenment*, the phrase we *really* want to get fired up about is *carpe punctum*—"seize the moment."

Carpe punctum.

Moment to moment to moment we have the opportunity to close the gap between who we're *capable* of being and who we're *actually* being to activate our Heroic potential.

Carpe punctum.

Moment to moment to moment we have the opportunity to live with *Areté* and experience the joy of high-fiving our inner daimon.

Carpe punctum.

Our +1°…

Let's see how many of those moments we can pluck as we savor the eudaimonic joy of a life well lived.

ENLIGHTENED BEINGS
THERE AREN'T ANY

I n our last +1°, we talked about the fact that we can't seize the *day* per se—we can only seize the *moment*.

Enter: *Carpe punctum*.

In *Everyday Enlightenment*, Dan Millman makes another brilliant point. He tells us that there are NO enlightened beings. There are only *more* or *less* enlightened MOMENTS.

Here's how he puts it: "No one feels the same way all the time. Even if you are angry, depressed, crazy, afraid, or grieving, you'll have moments when you are distracted. There are no enlightened people, no nice, bad, smart, neurotic, or stupid people, either—only people with more (or less) enlightened, nice, bad, smart, neurotic, or stupid moments."

That's a really powerful (and empowering) distinction.

As wonderful as it would be, NO ONE gets to a place where they're exonerated from all future work. Period.

The issue isn't reaching that "I've finally perfected myself once and for all and isn't life great?!" state; it's about stringing together more and more enlightened MOMENTS in our day-to-day lives.

And guess when the best time is to practice your new enlightenment? Yep. Right NOW.

Close the gap. Live with *Areté*.

Remember: There are no enlightened people. Only more or less enlightened moments. So… *Carpe punctum!*

AM & PM BOOKENDS
GET THESE RIGHT & YOU'RE 80% THERE

As we set out to make TODAY a masterpiece, here's the first thing we need to know…

If you're like most people, you have more control over the beginning and ending of your day than you do the middle of your days.

In his great book *The Compound Effect*, Darren Hardy (the former publisher of *Success* magazine) calls those segments of your days "AM and PM Bookends."

I love that. That's what we call them as well.

Know this: If we can get our bookends dialed in, we're 80% there—which is why we focus a *lot* of our attention here in the Heroic app and Coach program.

We want to figure out how to integrate your highest-leverage Energy, Work, and Love wins into your AM and PM bookends to help you more consistently show up as that best, most virtuous version of yourself so you can be more energized, productive, and connected than ever.

We also need to know that, somewhat paradoxically, your day *actually* started the night before. Therefore, as we architect your masterpiece days, that's where we'll start: with your PM Bookends.

As we get better and better at more consistently executing our end-of-day protocols that make up our PM Bookends, we'll wake up feeling more energized.

Then we want to make sure we start the day strong by creating some early Big 3 wins.

For now…

Take a moment and imagine YOUR ideal day.

What's it look like?

What's ONE thing you *know* you could be doing to create a stronger PM ritual that would help you wake up feeling more energized and ready to have a great day?

Perhaps more importantly: What's one thing you know you could STOP doing at night that would help you wake up feeling more energized and ready to have a great day?

Then…

With that PM Bookend +1° more optimized, how would you START your day if you were ALL IN on making TODAY a masterpiece? And, again… What *wouldn't* you do?

Got it. Fantastic.

I repeat: Today's the day, Hero.

Let's move from Theory to Practice to Mastery as we get our AM and PM Bookends optimized and activate our Heroic potential.

TODAY.

LIMITLESS STEPS
EXPONENTIAL GAINS FOR THE WIN

R emember our chat about Team Sky and the power of "marginal gains"?

As you may recall, when we aggregate and compound a ton of tiny little gains over an extended period of time we get HUGE gains.

And…

What do you think would happen if we could tap into the power of not just "marginal" gains but SUPER-HIGH LEVERAGE gains?

Answer: We'd experience the power of *exponential* growth!

Let's invite Jim Kwik to the party to help unpack this idea. Jim wrote a great book called *Limitless*.

He's one of the world's leading experts on memory improvement, brain optimization, and accelerated learning.

The best part of Jim's story?

After suffering a brain injury in kindergarten, he was described by a teacher as the kid "with a broken brain." He struggled with learning for most of his life. Then he went antifragile on it and studied (and applied!) the science of how we learn.

Fast-forward a couple decades and he's now the "brain coach to a who's who of Hollywood's elite, professional athletes, political leaders, and business magnates." (Heroic Antifragility for the win!)

Jim tells us: "Moving forward incrementally is a significant sign of progress. Every step you can take in the process of becoming limitless is a step in the right direction. But what if you could move your genius forward exponentially? After all, if we take 30 normal steps forward, we'll wind up somewhere down the street. But if we took 30 exponential steps, we'd circle the Earth more than two dozen times."

Well, isn't that FASCINATING?

Let's think about that for a moment longer.

If we take thirty normal steps, we'll get about ninety feet down the street.

That's great. We're making progress. Go us!

But…

If we can figure out how to take thirty EXPONENTIAL steps, we'll be able to zip around the Earth two DOZEN TIMES!

That is *crazy* great. Now we're making *exponential (!) progress*. GO US!!

Note: Google calculator tells us that there are 5,280 feet in a mile. The Earth is about 24,901 miles around the equator.

If my math is correct, that's about 131,477,280 feet or, assuming three feet per step, 43,825,760 steps for one trip around our beautiful planet.

Two dozen trips around the Earth comes out to roughly 1,051,818,240 steps—which is just *slightly* more than the ninety feet from thirty "normal" steps, eh?

All that begs yet another practical question…

How do we take thirty metaphorically *exponential* steps?

Simple.

We want to figure out what we think might be THE highest-leverage optimizations we can make and then CONSISTENTLY execute those behavioral changes while aggregating and compounding the gains over an extended period of time.

Enter: Earth revolving MAGIC.

And, you know what? I don't think those highest-leverage optimizations are necessarily the big fancy things reserved for the blessed few. I think they're the crazy mundane, simple actions we can ALL take.

Stuff like turning off our electronics at night via a digital sunset so we can get a GREAT night of sleep. (Seriously. That ONE change can *literally* change your life OVERNIGHT.)

Then, what if you reduced/eliminated sugar and ultraprocessed food from your diet? (That ONE change can *literally* change your life.)

Then, what if you resisted the urge to get online right when you woke up and started meditating for one minute and built that up to eleven minutes and you did it every day? (That ONE change can *literally* change your life.)

Then, if you were REALLY feeling inspired, what if you took that amazing Energy you cultivated and focused it like a laser beam on the most important task for your day during an AM1 Deep Work time block? And you did *that* every day? (That ONE change can literally change your life.)

Then, what if you decided to keep your phone out of sight and out of touch when you were with your family so you could bless them with the power of your presence? (That ONE change can literally change your life.)

Then … What if you had fun adding a series of twenty-five additional exponentially powerful optimizing steps?!

Answer: You'd RADICALLY change your life. And you might just zip around the Earth a couple dozen times.

So, my dear Heroic friend …

What's THE #1 next-most-exponentially powerful step YOU can take?

As we consider that, let's keep Krishnamurti's wisdom in mind. He told us: "To go far you must begin near, and the nearest step is the most important one."

Let's take that next step.

TODAY!

HIGHER HIGHS & HIGHER LOWS
A RETURN TO THE FORGE

I t's officially time to return to the only place in which we can get our antifragile confidence to the levels we need to show up as our Heroic best.

It's time to return to The Forge.

As you (hopefully) recall, when we are *antifragile*, we are no longer *fragile*—breaking the moment life gets challenging.

Nor are we just *resilient*—more skillfully dealing with life's challenges and bouncing back a little faster when we get knocked around.

When we're ANTIFRAGILE, we use all those challenges as FUEL for our never-ending growth.

And… When we cultivate the ability to alchemize all those challenges into *fuel* for our growth by living from our Heroic-best Identities and doing what needs to be done whether we (insert whiny voice) *feel* like it or not, we create true, sustainable, INTENSE trust in ourselves.

That's the essence of antifragile confidence.

I repeat… We forge that antifragile confidence via one very simple formula: The *worse* we feel, the *more committed* we are to our protocol.

That, *very* importantly, presupposes we HAVE a protocol. And, of course, it presupposes we have the discipline to actually EXECUTE that protocol in those moments when we're feeling wobbly.

If you feel so inspired, please take a moment to feel the near-*invincible* power you will have when/if you can get to a place in which you're able to flip a switch in your brain such that the WORSE you feel the MORE committed you are to showing up as the best version of yourself. That ability is truly a superpower.

One more time: What do YOU *currently do* when you feel wobbly?

If you're like how I used to be and how most of us are most of the time, when things get hard, you forget to do the things that keep you plugged in and then you slip into doing the things you know don't serve you and … Eek.

We enter a vicious spiral DOWN.

But …

WHAT IF …

Going forward, when you felt those same fears and doubts and stress and wobbliness, INSTEAD OF spiraling DOWN you were able to get yourself to commit EVEN MORE POWER-FULLY to the practices that keep you plugged in?

Then, rather than spiraling down as you go off the rails (yet again!), you'd spiral UP. And, most importantly, you'd KNOW that you are now the type of person who can not only handle whatever life throws at you, but actually get stronger with every obstacle you face.

In short, you'd FORGE ANTIFRAGILE CONFIDENCE.

As we've discussed, when we get better at this, we'll still have "highs" and "lows" because of the simple facts that we are (a) human and (b) there are no perfect humans.

But… Our HIGHS will be HIGHER *and* our LOWS will also be HIGHER.

Personally, my "bad" days are now, in many ways, considerably better than my prior "best" days.

That's an EXHILARATING feeling.

From my perspective, there are few things more empowering than knowing that we're the kind of people who, when life kicks us around, GET STRONGER.

It's also *really* hard to have a series of *really* bad days when you run the "the worse I feel the more committed I am to my protocol" algorithm.

Don't believe me? Test it.

Seriously. Test it.

TODAY.

SPINNY FINGERS
HOW TO QUICKLY REGAIN YOUR EQUILIBRIUM

Here's a little exercise you may want to try.

Find a safe place where you can spin around and get yourself dizzy. (Obviously, don't do this if you're going to injure yourself.)

Spin around. And around. And around.

Get yourself nice and dizzy.

Once you (safely) get yourself nice and dizzy, I'd like you to stand still. Then look around the room—randomly looking up then down then around.

How do you feel when you aimlessly look around?

If you're like me and the thousands of people with whom I've done this exercise, you feel DIZZIER.

That's Part I of this exercise. Time for Part II. Regain your equilibrium and, if you're up for it, do it again.

Spin around. And around. And around.

Get yourself nice and dizzy.

Once you (safely) get yourself nice and dizzy, stand still again. This time, rather than looking around aimlessly, I want you to put your hands together like you're praying—with your palms and fingers touching one another.

Now, put your fingers RIGHT in front of your face then STARE right at your fingertips.

What happens when you focus your attention like that?

If you're like me and the thousands of people with whom

I've done this exercise, you quickly regain your sense of equilibrium.

Guess what? When life spins us around and we get dizzy, we'd be wise to FOCUS ALL OF OUR ENERGY on our protocol and simply do the things we *know* we could be doing.

It's astonishing how quickly we can regain our equilibrium while forging the antifragile confidence that makes us invincible.

The main point of focus?

Areté.

Close the gap.

Be your best self.

TODAY.

THE EQUANIMITY GAME
HOW TO PLAY IT LIKE AN EMPEROR

In our last +1°, we talked about spinny fingers and how to quickly regain our equilibrium when life gets us dizzy.

Hint/reminder: FOCUS ON YOUR PROTOCOL.

Here's another one of my favorite practices, inspired by Marcus Aurelius.

In his *Meditations*, Aurelius wrote to himself: "When force of circumstance upsets your equanimity, lose no time in recovering your self-control, and do not remain out of tune longer than you can help. Habitual recurrence to the harmony will increase your mastery of it."

(Now, remember: This was an *emperor* writing down a reminder for *himself*—he NEVER intended to publish those words. I find that incredibly inspiring.)

I call that The Equanimity Game.

When you (inevitably!) get knocked down and/or spun around, make it a game to see how fast you can recover.

Practicing it often makes you really good at it.

So… When (not "if" but "WHEN") you get knocked off center today, see how fast you can regain your equanimity.

Remember: When we're doing it right, it's all a big game.

Let's play it well.

TODAY.

SIMPLIFY THE BATTLEFIELD
WITH FRONT-SIGHT FOCUS

I n our last couple +1°s, we talked about how to quickly regain our equanimity when life spins us around. Here's another way I like to think about it.

I got this idea from Mark Divine.

Mark is a former Navy SEAL Commander and author of some of my favorite books on mental toughness and peak performance, including *Unbeatable Mind*, *The Way of the SEAL*, and *Staring Down the Wolf*. He's also a dear friend and Heroic investor. (Hooyah, CDR!)

Mark tells us that, in the chaos of war, elite SEALs are taught to "simplify the battlefield."

When the fog of battle rolls in and things are nowhere near as clear as they were just a moment before, Mark tells us that it's *absolutely* essential that we simplify *everything*.

He tells us that we need to identify THE next most important target and then put ALL of our energy into successfully executing that micro-mission by maintaining what he calls "front-sight" focus.

Simplify the battlefield. Identify the next most important target. Focus. Execute that micro-mission. Repeat.

TODAY.

CENTER YOURSELF
HOW FAST CAN YOU REGAIN YOUR BALANCE?

Now that we've discussed how a great Emperor-Philosopher and great Navy SEALs regain their equanimity, let's invite one of the all-time great martial artists to the party to learn how *he* approached the same challenge.

In *The Art of Connection*, Michael Gelb tells us how important it is to be able to regain our poise and equanimity when we lose it in our day-to-day social interactions. He shares a story about Morihei Ueshiba (the founder of Aikido) to bring the point home.

O-Sensei, as he was known, was one of the greatest martial artists ever. An absolute master.

One of his most senior students once said to him: "'Your techniques are perfect! You never make any mistakes. You never lose your center!"

O-Sensei replied, "I lose my center frequently. I just find it again so quickly that you can't see it."

How about YOU?

How quickly do *you* regain your center when you get a little wobbly?

The next time you get knocked off center, make it a game. See how fast you can recover.

As Aurelius says: "Habitual recurrence to the harmony will increase your mastery of it."

CONSTRAINTS ARE AWESOME
RULE #1 OF WHY GAMES ARE FUN

Here's Rule #1 for creating great days: We need to make it a game.

Pop quiz: You know what ALL games have in common?

Answer: All games have CONSTRAINTS—which is why Alan Watts once said: "Tennis is more fun with a court."

We tend to think that constraints are bad. But the wisest among us know that it's only when we draw those lines on the ground, make some rules (a.k.a. create CONSTRAINTS!), and say: "This is in… That's out!" that the *game* becomes a GAME.

Let's use the world's most popular game as an example: Soccer.

You know how many people love soccer?

FOUR BILLION.

The rules are almost laughable.

Here's the quick take.

Draw a rectangular line on a large field of grass. Make that rectangular box about two hundred and twenty feet wide by three hundred and fifty feet long. Put two posts about twenty-four feet apart in the middle of the smaller sides then add a cross bar on the top of those posts and attach a net. We'll call that the "goal."

Now, grab a ball. The circumference should be about twenty-seven to twenty-eight inches and the weight should be between fourteen to sixteen ounces. Inflate it between 8.5 and 15.6 psi at sea level. (Make sure you get it just right!)

Create two teams. Each team gets 11 players. The players can touch the ball with their feet and any other part of their body *except* their hands as they try to get the ball into the other team's goal.

Oh! Actually, the person protecting the goal for each team are the only ones who can use their hands. But they can only use their hands in THAT box right there.

Etc., etc., etc.

You know what happens when we create and embrace constraints like that? Everything gets A LOT more fun.

This is why great artists embrace constraints—whether they're writing a haiku poem (only three lines and seventeen syllables!) or creating a concerto (with its characteristic three movements).

It's also why the great composer Igor Stravinsky once said: "The more constraints one imposes, the more one frees oneself. And the arbitrariness of the constraint serves only to obtain precision in the execution."

What's that have to do with creating Masterpiece Days?

Everything.

THE PM BOOKEND
TODAY STARTED YESTERDAY

As we get ready to architect our Masterpiece Days within the idiosyncratic constraints of our reality, let's step back and take a moment to remind ourselves of the two key intentions for this objective.

First, we need to really get the fact that **TODAY** IS THE DAY to move from Theory to Practice to Mastery. Second, we need to get really good at actually making today a great day.

Here's a potentially life-changing idea as we become masters at creating Masterpiece Days...

TODAY *actually* started LAST NIGHT.

This idea is so simple (and so obvious) that you might want to skip ahead to the more interesting stuff. I totally get it. And, of course, feel free to skip ahead and around, etc.

Fun story: I recently had a chat with one of our Heroic Coaches. He was near the end of our 300-day training program, and we laughed about the fact that, as he was going through the Mastery Series lectures that are the foundation of the program, he actually *skipped* the one on the PM Bookend.

It was only later in the program that he came back to it and... As it turns out, getting his PM Bookends right was the missing link for him. Once he optimized his end-of-the-day rituals, his sleep improved, which means his Energy improved which means his Work and Love and, well, EVERYTHING improved.

So... I repeat: When most people plan their days, they start in the morning.

We want to start with the night before.

I want you to SEE the connection between your PMs and your AMs and how the decisions you're making at the end of your days are directly impacting the quality of your sleep which is then directly impacting the Energy with which you wake up the next morning which then cascades into that day which then affects your ENTIRE LIFE.

If Masterpiece Lives are created one Masterpiece Day at a time (they are!), the surprising truth is that it's the Masterpiece PM Bookends that drive the whole show.

+1 HOUR OF SLEEP
COULD BE LIFE CHANGING

How do you think you would feel if you got ONE more hour of sleep?

The reality is most people don't get the recommended seven to eight hours of sleep every night.

In fact, in his great book *Why We Sleep*, leading sleep scientist Matthew Walker tells us: "Two thirds of adults throughout all developed nations fail to obtain the recommended eight hours of nightly sleep."

He continues by saying: "I doubt you're surprised by this fact, but you may be surprised by the consequences. Routinely sleeping less than six or seven hours a night demolishes your immune system, more than doubling your risk of cancer."

Yikes.

Not only does routinely sleeping less than six or seven hours a night demolish our immune system while more than doubling (!) our risk of cancer, it ALSO demolishes our Zest-Energy which diminishes our ability to show up as powerfully (and joyfully!) as we know we can in our Work and our Love.

Personal question time: How many hours of sleep did YOU get last night?

Know this: If you're like the vast majority of people not getting the recommended seven to eight hours of sleep per night, then helping you get ONE more hour of sleep is my #1 intention with this objective.

BASELINE RESETTING
THE WORSE A PERSON IS...

You might be thinking... "I don't need the recommended seven to eight hours of sleep."

To which I would like to inquire: Do you know what the odds are that YOU happen to be one of the few people who can actually get by on less than the recommended 7-8 hours of sleep and still function at a peak level?

Our sleep science guru, Professor Walker, tells us that the odds of you being blessed with a rare genetic mutation that allows you to get by on less than the recommended amount of sleep are about the same as the odds of getting struck with lightning.

You know what those odds are?

About 1 in 12,000.

You know what percent likelihood that is when you round it to the nearest whole integer?

0%.

You: "Come on. It's not that bad. I feel fine with less sleep."

Professor Walker: "YOU DO NOT KNOW HOW SLEEP-DEPRIVED YOU ARE WHEN YOU ARE SLEEP-DEPRIVED."

Get this: He actually used all caps in the book. I repeat (with bold to make sure you don't miss it):

"YOU DO NOT KNOW HOW SLEEP-DEPRIVED YOU ARE WHEN YOU ARE SLEEP-DEPRIVED."

Walker calls this problem "baseline resetting" and tells us that: "With chronic sleep restriction over months or years, an individual will actually acclimate to their impaired performance, lower alertness, and reduced energy levels. That low-level exhaustion becomes their accepted norm, or baseline."

Another yikes.

He continues by telling us how MILLIONS of people around the world are unwittingly spending years of their lives "in a sub-optimal state of psychological and physiological functioning, never maximizing their potential of mind or body due to their blind persistence in sleeping too little."

Seneca comes to mind here as well.

2,000 years ago, he told us the same thing: "The worse a person is the less he feels it."

How about you?

SHUTDOWN COMPLETE
THE #1 PM BOOKEND WORK TIP

Remember those constraints on a tennis court (and on a soccer field) that make those games so fun?

Well, same basic idea applies to our Work. Something magical happens when we draw some lines around the edges of our workdays and decide what's out of bounds.

In *Deep Work*, Cal Newport tells us about his "Shutdown complete" ritual. At the end of his workday (around 6:00 p.m. for him), he does one last check to make sure everything that needs to get done is done then he ritualistically turns off his computer and says to himself: "Shutdown complete."

At that point, his workday is officially over. He won't be checking his email one more time or even thinking about stuff that he's working on. He turns his brain OFF.

He tells us: "When you work, work hard. When you're done, be done."

This isn't a new peak performance idea.

Two thousand years ago, Seneca was talking about the same thing. In *On the Shortness of Life*, he tells us about the importance of giving our minds time to rest.

Specifically, he says: "Our minds must relax: they will rise better and keener after a rest. Just as you must not force fertile farmland, as uninterrupted productivity will soon exhaust it, so constant effort will sap our mental vigor, while a short period of rest and relaxation will restore our powers.

Unremitting effort leads to a kind of mental dullness and lethargy."

According to Seneca, back in the days of the Roman senate they wouldn't introduce anything important after their tenth hour. Depending on the season, that "tenth" hour on the ol' sun dial corresponded to about 4:00 p.m. in the winter and 6:00 p.m. in the summer.

Now, if that policy was good enough for the Roman senate, I say it's good enough for our lives—which is why I follow the same basic rules with my own "10th hour" shutdown complete ritual.

With rare exceptions, no more hard work after 4:00 p.m. in the winter or 6:00 p.m. in the summer. PERIOD.

Again: We need to give our minds the chance to rest, and we need to do so at a reasonable time otherwise we're going to have a hard time FALLING asleep and an even harder time STAYING asleep.

Therefore…

End your workdays at a reasonable time.

Turn your brain off.

"Shutdown complete!"

That's the #1 PM Bookend Work tip.

WORK TO LOVE
MAKE THE PM BOOKEND TRANSITION

When we practice a solid "Shutdown complete!" ritual Work-wise, we not only give our brains a chance to fully recover while also setting ourselves up for a good night of sleep.

We ALSO give ourselves the best shot at creating *much* deeper levels of connection—which is why that complete shutdown from work is *also* our #1 tip for optimizing the Love in our PM Bookend.

We want to create a really powerful, rhythmic transition from Deep Work to Deep Love with that "Shutdown complete!" ritual.

Then we want to set the intention to be 100% present with our families.

To achieve this, I'm going to encourage you to create more and more pockets of time in which your smartphone is in airplane mode out of both sight and touch.

We'll talk about the negative effects of what researchers call "The iPhone Effect" in a moment.

For now, after your new "Shutdown complete!" ritual, set the clear intention to be 100% present with your family and know that your smartphone is your #1 obstacle.

That best, most Heroic version of yourself is connecting with your family, not staring at a screen.

THE IPHONE EFFECT
THE FASTEST WAY TO OPTIMIZE YOUR CONNECTION

Have you ever heard of "The iPhone Effect"? It's a powerful thing. Here's the short story.

Bring people into a lab. Split them into two groups. One group sits down and chats with someone they've never met while a *smartphone* is visible on the table next to them. The other group sits down and chats with someone they've never met while a *notebook* is visible rather than the smartphone.

Guess what? The group with the smartphone in sight reports a significantly diminished quality of interaction vs. the group that didn't have the smartphone in sight.

Know this: The phone wasn't blowing up. And, it wasn't even THEIR phone. The MERE PRESENCE of that smartphone diminished the quality of their interactions.

Enter: The iPhone Effect.

The next time you're spending time with someone (whether that's a colleague or a spouse or a kid!), remember The iPhone Effect and put your phone out of sight (and, ideally, out of touch!) so you can be fully focused and present.

But... Only do that if you want to enhance the quality of your interactions, of course.

P.S. If there's ONE *incredibly* high-leverage and equally easy way to IMMEDIATELY improve the quality of your connections with loves ones, this is it.

DIGITAL SUNSET
BEDTIME FOR YOUR BRIGHT LIGHTS

With our transition from Deep Work to Deep Love installed (and our smartphones in airplane mode, out of sight and out of touch!), here's the #1 Energy tip for our PM Bookends…

Turn off your electronics AT LEAST an hour before bed.

I call that a "Digital Sunset."

Your brain needs time to go from a super active ON state to a more relaxed OFF state.

The shutdown complete ritual work-wise is the first step. The second step is limiting the blue light stimulation from all those screens at least an hour before you go to bed.

Part of a longer chat that we'll save for an in-depth sleep discussion, but we evolved for MILLIONS of years *without* blue light at night. The sun used to be the only source of blue light. When it went down, your body knew it was time to transition to sleep.

You simply can't keep pumping your brain up with all that cortisol-inducing blue light stimuli and then expect to have a calm, relaxed, melatonin-filled brain such that when your head hits the pillow you drop into a deep, restorative sleep.

For most people, the very last thing they do before hitting the pillow is check their phone. We want to create AT LEAST a thirty- to sixty-minute window (ideally two hours) from our last check in and our head hitting the pillow.

Digital Sunset. It does a mind and body and soul good.

THE 10,008-HOUR + 36-MINUTE RULE
WHAT MAKES GREAT PERFORMERS GREAT

A t this stage, most of us are familiar with "The 10,000 Hour Rule" Malcolm Gladwell made popular in his book *Outliers*. The research that inspired Gladwell was conducted by Anders Ericsson.

Although it's a bit more nuanced than "go put in 10,000 hours of hard work and you'll be great!" his #1 finding in his research is clear: The best performers in any field have put in the most deliberate practice. Period.

This is exciting because that means that greatness isn't a matter of winning the genetic lottery. It's about using the gift of adaptability to tap into our ultimate potential growth-mindset style.

But… Get this: The insight into the power of deliberate practice was only ONE of the big findings from that research.

You know what the second most important variable was that differentiated the best performers?

How much they slept!

The best performers slept, on average, 8 hours and 36 minutes every twenty-four hours—significantly more than the not-quite-so-great performers.

(Btw: That included an average of 2.8 hours of NAPPING per week—two hours longer than the average. For the non-math majors, that's an average of a little more than twenty minutes of napping per day.)

Why is this important?

Well, deliberate practice is HARD WORK.

You can't sustain that level of attention to mastery if you're tired. And, you need to recharge your batteries when you crush it that much.

All of which begs the question ...

How's YOUR sleep?

Are you more like the best performers and getting 8.5+ hours of sleep per day? Or... Are you more like the average American who gets less than seven hours of sleep?

MAKE THE CONNECTION!!!

If you want to consistently perform at your Heroic best, you've gotta know that sleep really really really matters.

So... What's one little thing you can do TODAY to get a better night of sleep?

Quick Pro Tip: Here's the #1 thing most people can do: Turn off your phone, leave it somewhere other than your nightstand, and get some good sleep.

As we've discussed, research is clear: If you check your phone right before bed, it will take you longer to get into deep sleep and you'll spend less time there once you do arrive. So... Turn off your phone! *At least* an hour before your ideal sleep time.

Remember The 10,008 Hour and 36 Minute Rule and watch your performance soar.

TAKE A NAP!
& CHANGE YOUR LIFE

In our last +1°, we talked about The 10,008 Hour and 36 Minute Rule.

We learned that the best performers got the most sleep—8 hours and 36 minutes on average in any given twenty-four hour period of time to be precise.

We also learned that they took, on average, a twenty+ minute nap every day—which makes me want to talk about the science of napping.

Yes. There's a science of napping. You know what it says? In short: Naps are awesome.

Get this: We're the ONLY animal that tries to get all of its sleep in one cycle. Every other animal on the planet is "multiphasic"—meaning they have multiple phases of sleep.

We human animals *used to be* multiphasic as well. It was only recently that we eliminated the afternoon nap from our everyday lives.

As Sara Mednick, one of the world's leading sleep (and nap) researchers tells us in her great book *Take a Nap, Change Your Life!*, naps are *literally* written in our DNA.

They used to be written into our *cultural* DNA as well.

Did you know that back in ancient Roman times, they actually had a precise time when they were supposed to slow down, check out, and take a nap? It was their sixth hour—roughly noon for us. They called it "sexta."

Their practice of napping in the sixth hour of the day is the origin of our modern "siesta."

Of course, it's no longer the cultural norm in our modern society to take a nap around noon but we'd be wise to remember that this shift away from mid-day reboots is a recent phenomenon.

So, back to the research on the scientifically-proven power of naps.

Sara tells us that: "Learning after a nap is equal to learning after a full night of sleep."

And that: "Test scores of non-nappers deteriorated across the day."

In fact, Harvard research tells us that a nap as short as six minutes (yes, SIX MINUTES!) can significantly boost your brain power. (*Six* minutes! That's astonishing.)

All that to say…

Want to be a supercharged and joyfully Heroic human? Take a nap. And you just might change your life.

CIRCADIANS & ULTRADIANS
THE RHYTHMS OF LIFE

At this stage, we're all familiar with the idea of circadian rhythms.

The word *circadian* comes from the Latin *circa* + *dies* which literally means "around a day." An astonishing number of our biological processes are tied to twenty-four-hour cycles.

(Of course, most of us IGNORE the natural rhythms baked into a day but we'll save that for another discussion.)

Today's focus: Have you ever heard of "ultradian rhythms"?

Ultra means "beyond."

Ultradian is a word coined in the 1960's and means "beyond the frequency of circadian rhythms"—meaning, more often than every twenty-four hours. Specifically, ultradian rhythms refer to periods of about ninety minutes.

Here's what we need to know: Research shows that our upper threshold for peak performance in any given burst is about ninety minutes.

After ninety minutes without a break, our performance begins to atrophy. Of course, we can move past this point via caffeine or sugar or by turning on our own stress hormones but we'd be much wiser to recognize the natural limit and then take a break.

When we ignore our ultradian rhythms, we experience what researchers call "endurance stress."

Do that often enough and get ready for chronic fatigue and depression to go along with that reduced performance.

The +1° is simple...

Cap your work bursts at ninety minutes. Then take a break for fifteen to twenty minutes.

And, while you're at it, remember: Not all breaks are created equal.

When you're taking a break, take a real break! Get offline and go for a walk or just relax.

Hopping on Instagram or TikTok or checking your email or surfing the web does *not* give you the optimal recovery you need to come back strong.

Circadians.

Ultradians.

Let's remember the rhythms of life.

MAKING WAVES
RIDE THEM TO YOUR HIGHEST POTENTIAL

In our last +1°, we talked about the importance of honoring your ultradian rhythms—remembering the fact that our performance atrophies after about ninety minutes of work.

Unless we enjoy poor performance, chronic fatigue, and depression, we'd be wise to take regular breaks to reboot.

Let's talk about that some more.

Tony Schwartz is one of the world's leading authorities on managing our energy. He wrote *The Power of Full Engagement* and runs a company focused on energy optimization.

He tells us that life is rhythmic.

Think: High tide and low tide. Day and night. Winter and summer. That sort of thing.

If we want to activate our Heroic potential, we need to follow the natural rhythms of our world and "make waves"—oscillating between being ON and being OFF.

And, if we REALLY want to take everything to the next level, we want to *expand the amplitude* of those waves as much as we can—being intensely focused when we're on and then equally relaxed when we're off.

Waves. Oscillating. With big amplitudes.

In *Maximize Your Potential*, Tony tells us that most people are just kinda sorta in a steady state all day—free from highs and lows and never REALLY going all in and never really turning completely off.

As is often the case, doing what most people do is a fantastic way to live a mediocre life. Not so great for living an extraordinary life.

(On that note: I always laugh when I think of Mark Twain's quip: "Whenever you find yourself on the side of the majority, it is time to pause and reflect.")

So…

Our +1°…

How are *your* waves?

When you're on, are you REALLY ON or just kinda sorta going through the motions?

And, when you're recovering, are you REALLY recovering or just kinda sorta checking out?

Make waves. Big ones.

Ride them to your highest potential.

THE 4.5-HOUR WORKDAY
THE MAGIC NUMBER FOR GREATNESS

Continuing our theme of making waves and riding them to greatness, let's learn a little more about how Tony Schwartz applies this wisdom to his own life.

First, let's go back to Anders Ericsson and his research. Remember our path to mastery and peak performance?

It was paved with a ton of deliberate practice. Over ten thousand hours for those keeping track.

Know this: Going outside your comfort zone and doing the hard work required of deliberate practice en route to true mastery isn't easy.

It takes a *ton* of energy.

The reality is, you can't do *that* much of it in any given day.

In fact, Anders discovered that the best violinists in his study put in 4.5 hours of deliberate practice a day. That's it.

(Recall: They took more naps and slept more than the sub-elite performers. Hard work requires deep recovery!)

So… Tony used to try to work hard all day when he was writing a book—ignoring his ultradian oscillations and experiencing poorer performance as a result.

Then, he decided to write his next book in ninety-minute chunks. Precisely ninety minutes. Not eighty-five minutes or ninety-five minutes. Ninety minutes.

He'd focus DEEPLY for those ninety minutes. Then he'd recover DEEPLY for fifteen to twenty minutes.

Then he'd repeat.

How many times? THREE.

For how many hours total? 4.5.

And guess what? He wrote his book in a fraction of the time it took him to write his prior books.

It's funny because as I was tinkering with my always-evolving Masterpiece Day, I arrived at the same number. Three Deep Work time blocks for a total of 4.5 hours.

When I am *really* going for it, I'll target a floor of 5.1 hours and see if I can sustain peak performance for seven. But 4.5 hours is *definitely* a magic number.

How about YOU?

What's your #1 WILDLY important goal? (That should *always* be driving everything you do work-wise, right?)

Imagine your Masterpiece Day.

Now, if achieving that goal requires focused, solo effort, picture three Deep Work time blocks, ninety minutes each.

Where do they fit? What do you do?

Remember the magic number for greatness.

The 4.5-hour (genius!) workday.

I like the sound of that.

MIRACLE MORNINGS
S.A.V.E.R.S. & THE THREE U'S

Hal Elrod is an incredibly inspiring human being.

At twenty years old he was hit head-on by a drunk driver. At seventy mph. (Ouch.)

He was found dead. (Yikes.)

After six minutes of that (near-)death experience, he spent several days in a coma and awoke to discover he had suffered brain damage and was told that he may never walk again.

He defied the odds and proved that we're all capable of overcoming obstacles while creating the life of our dreams.

Years later, he found himself in a funk and discovered that if he could get his morning routines dialed in, he could activate his Heroic potential.

Then...

He wrote a book called *The Miracle Morning*, in which he shares "The Not-So-Obvious Secret Guaranteed to Transform Your Life Before 8 AM."

The book has been translated into thirty-seven languages and has transformed *millions* of people's lives. It's fantastic.

As you'd expect, Hal tells us that our AM Bookend is *really* important. Great lives are created one great day at a time. And great days are created one great MORNING at a time.

How do we make tomorrow morning a miracle?

Hal tells us we want to integrate six key practices: silence, affirmations, visualization, exercise, reading, and scribing.

Put those all together and you get a miracle morning. You also get the acronym *S.A.V.E.R.S.*

Check out the Philosopher's Notes and book for more on all that.

In this +1°, I want to focus on one of my all-time favorite habit-building mental frameworks. We want to have this wisdom in mind as we navigate the process of changing our lives.

So…

Hal has a GREAT chapter outlining the three phases of habit creation—each around ten days long.

He tells us that the process goes like this…

First, the new habit is UNBEARABLE.

It's a pain. We don't like doing it. At all. But we persist.

The second phase is UNCOMFORTABLE.

It's not quite as bad as the first phase but not quite awesome… yet!

The third phase is when we become UNSTOPPABLE.

We feel the benefits of engaging in the habit, don't need to use so much willpower to get ourselves to do it, and we are now UNSTOPPABLE.

Unbearable.

Uncomfortable.

Unstoppable.

Yep. That's about right.

I say: Let's have THAT in mind as we move from Theory to Practice to Mastery and make our *entire lives* a miracle, Hero!!

PROCRASTIPAIN
PAIN IS IN THE ANTICIPATION, NOT THE DOING

Barbara Oakley taught one of the largest classes in history called "Learning How to Learn." She also wrote a great book called *A Mind for Numbers*.

In it, she talks about procrastination and shares some fascinating research.

Did you know that you can take people who hate doing math and scan their brains and actually SEE their pain centers light up as they contemplate doing math?

It's true.

But here's the deal.

Those pain centers turn OFF the moment they actually start doing the math.

It was the ANTICIPATION that was painful. Actually doing it? Not so much.

All of which leads us back to you ...

Are YOU procrastinating on anything?

Of course you are. You're human. What is it?

Remember: The pain of waiting is MUCH greater than the pain of actually doing. It's the anticipation that's getting you stressed out.

With that in mind, go do that thing you've been avoiding.

Close the gap. Live with *Areté*.

Activate your Heroic potential.

NOW.

YOUR FUTURE SELF
MORE LIKE YOU OR A STRANGER?

In our last +1°, we had our brains scanned and learned that the pain is in the ANTICIPATION of doing something—not in the actual doing.

(Good to know!)

Let's stay tucked inside that fMRI and do a little more brain scanning.

Walter Mischel is one of the world's leading willpower researchers. (He's the guy who did the marshmallow studies with kids—which we'll talk about soon.)

Walter tells us that you can scan someone's brain and ask them to think about themselves. When you do, you'll see a distinctive pattern in their brain light up. Researchers call this the "self center."

Then, you can ask them to think about a stranger. You'll see a different pattern light up. They call this the "stranger pattern."

Then, you can ask them to think about their future selves—ten years in the future.

Guess what…

For *some* people, thinking about their future selves lights up the "self center."

BUT…

For *other* people, thinking about their future selves lights up the "stranger center."

Isn't that fascinating?

And… Get this: The people whose future self looks more like a stranger have LOWER willpower than those whose future self looks more like their current self. They're less likely to delay gratification and more likely to be impulsive and engage in unhealthy behaviors.

The trick?

We need to strengthen the connection between our *future* selves and our *current* selves.

How?

There are a lot of ways to do it, but for this +1°, let's appreciate the fact that the decisions we are making TODAY are laying the groundwork for the version of us who will show up tomorrow and next week and the year after that.

Take a moment to see the future version of you. Let's say, ten years from now. Smile as you see your future self waving at the current you, BEGGING you to do the things that will make their life (your future life!) more awesome.

You can ALSO imagine the future version of you TEN MONTHS from now. Or TEN DAYS from now. Or TEN HOURS from now. Or TEN MINUTES from now.

Will the choices you're making RIGHT NOW (!!!) be a gift to that future version of yourself or a curse?

MAKE THE CONNECTION between what you're doing NOW and who you're becoming in the days and years and decades in the future. Then close the gap.

And live with *ARETÉ*.

Today's the day.

LET'S GO, HERO!

YOUR ADDICTION CENTER
HOW TO TURN IT OFF

I n our last couple +1°s, we've been having fun scanning our brains and seeing some fascinating stuff.

Let's stay in that fMRI machine for one more study.

This time, we're going to look at how your brain lights up in different ways depending on the food you eat.

First, a little context…

David Ludwig is a professor and researcher at both Harvard Medical School and Harvard School of Public Health. He has both an MD and a PhD and is one of the world's leading researchers on the science of nutrition. He's overseen dozens of diet studies and authored over one hundred peer-reviewed articles.

In his great book *Always Hungry?*, he tells us about some fascinating research, including this study…

You can bring people into a lab and have them drink a milkshake that's identical in every way but one. One shake has "fast-acting" carbs, and the other has "slow-acting" carbs.

You have the people in the study drink their shakes, and then, a few hours later, you scan their brains.

Guess what…

Well, before we even get into that fMRI machine, we see that the individuals who consumed the fast-acting carbs are reporting more hunger and their blood glucose levels have dropped more than the ones who consumed the slow-acting carbs.

And…

When we look at their brains, we see something amazing.

The people who consumed the "fast-acting" carbs have a little part of their brain lit up that's called the "nucleus accumbens." The nucleus accumbens is the primary reward center of our brains. It's the part of our brains tied to addiction—addiction to stuff like alcohol, tobacco, and cocaine. It's what drives you to compulsively consume more of something.

And it LIGHTS up when you eat fast-acting carbs.

So, right as your blood sugar drops and your hunger increases, you have your nucleus accumbens screaming at you to have more of the sugary stuff. Not a winning combination.

The solution?

First, make the connection between your food choices right now and your future self in x minutes and hours (and days and months and years and decades) as per our last +1°.

And…

Reduce or eliminate those fast-acting carbs.

What qualifies as fast-acting carbs? Well, the obvious stuff like sugar (in all its forms!) needs to go. The less obvious stuff like bread and pastas should also be on the elimination list.

Let's cool off that nucleus accumbens as we optimize our nutrition one bite at a time.

-1° = +1°. -1° = +1°. -1° = +1°.

P.S. The EASIEST way to -1° = +1° here? Follow Food Rule #1 (that we'll talk about in Objective VI) and quit drinking your sugar. TODAY.

SACRIFICES VS. DECISIONS
THERE'S A BIG DIFFERENCE BETWEEN THE TWO

Georges St-Pierre is one of the greatest mixed martial artists in the world. Ever.

Of course, he wasn't always one of the greatest.

At one point, he was just a young guy *working as a garbage man* who DECIDED he was going to be the best in the world.

People around him thought he was crazy.

(Of course they did. Who says stuff like that? Hint: People who have a shot at making it happen.)

So, when GSP decided (!) he would be the best in the world at what he wanted to do, he also decided what he WASN'T going to do.

"Train instead of party. Work instead of play. Perfect practice instead of casual repetition."

ALL of his energy went into achieving his goal and making his dream a reality. (You should see the consistency in his schedule. Astonishing.)

In his great book *The Way of the Fight*, GSP makes the important distinction that all those things he was no longer going to do weren't *sacrifices*. They were *decisions*.

Sacrifices vs. Decisions.

There's a huge difference between the two.

One comes with a whiny little voice. The other comes with the calm confidence and grounded, authentic power of a Heroically committed human being.

Now for the +1° practical application…

Who are YOU committed to being?

What *decisions* do you need to make to focus your energy?

Remember: The Latin root of the word *decide* literally means "to cut off." When we make a true decision, we CUT OFF all other options and go ALL IN.

Let's do that.

TODAY.

GOOD BAD DAYS
MASTERING THE ART OF PLAYING BADLY WELL

J ack Nicklaus once said that the key to being a great golfer was "playing badly well."

More precisely, he said: "The greatest and toughest art in golf is 'playing badly well.' All the greats have been masters at it."

It's one thing to play well when everything's rolling. It's an entirely different thing to be able to play well when things *aren't* rolling smoothly.

Jim Afremow, one of the world's leading mental toughness coaches and author of *The Champion's Mind*, calls it being "ugly but effective" and having "good bad days."

We need to master the art of having good bad days.

How?

Well, first, expect to have some rough days and to do silly things on occasion.

I forget what golfer said it, but they *expected* to have x bad shots in any given round so when they had the inevitable bad shot, they didn't lose it. They just said, "Yep. There's one!" And then they moved on.

We need to do the same thing.

Expect mistakes. Expect the rough patches when we're not as connected as we'd like.

That's the first step. Then we don't fall into a destructive cycle of wondering what's wrong with us.

We just acknowledge we're not at our best and take the next baby step.

Then what do we do?

We work our protocol—remembering to run the algorithm: "The WORSE we feel, the MORE COMMITTED we are to our protocol."

Here's to forging antifragile confidence as we master the art of playing badly well.

DID I WIN?
HOW TO SINK A $1M PUTT

Gold-medal-winning mental toughness coach and author Lanny Bassham is all about focusing on the PROCESS of goal achievement.

He tells a great story about one of his clients who happened to be a professional golfer.

Now, this golfer was struggling a bit. He was setting his goals for the year, and Lanny told him not to think about winning tournaments but to put *all* of his attention on mastering the *process* of playing well—identifying the key components of a successful shot and then taking it, literally, one shot at a time.

This golfer embraced the wisdom. Early in the season, he's out on the eighteenth green in the final round of a big tournament. He's lining up his putt, following the process he and Lanny established. He makes the putt.

His playing partner shakes his hand and congratulates him. Then he realizes something must be up when his wife *runs onto the green cheering.*

"Did I win?" he asks.

Yep.

You just won the tournament and $1 million, Hero!

Imagine that.

Imagine being *so focused* on executing the next baby step in your process that you don't even know you're sinking a million-dollar putt.

And guess what? You are (of course) much more likely to sink the putt when every ounce of your creative energy is focused on doing your best and not leaking out in concerns about doing well enough.

Process vs. Outcome.

Where's *your* focus?

REBOUND DAYS
WHAT TO DO AFTER A SUBOPTIMAL DAY

You ever have the kind of day where you fall short of your super-high standards and wonder what just happened?

Me too.

Now, thankfully, as we evolve, those "bad days" become less dramatic than the prior *really* bad days, but they're still going to happen as we continue to challenge ourselves with higher and higher standards.

So, Step 1.

Remind yourself that growth does not occur in one beautiful, straight line from where you are to where you want to be.

Growth looks more like a jagged zigzag line than a straight, up-and-to-the-right line.

George Leonard tells us that as we negotiate our path of mastery and let go of old habits, we need to have a "willingness to take one step back for every two forward, sometimes vice versa."

Gotta love that "sometimes vice versa."

Sometimes (!) you don't take two steps forward and then slide back one. You slide back two or three steps and then *crawl* back one. (HAH!)

That's just how it is.

No big deal.

Knowing that's how it works, we simply dust ourselves off, check in on what "Needs work!" as we shine a flashlight on how we could have done things a little differently, then bring a hammer as we forge our antifragile confidence—making sure that the day *after* our subpar performance is AWESOME.

I like to call those days *after* a not-great day "Rebound Days."

We want THOSE days to be EPIC.

We want to wake up *even more* committed to the little things, embracing the path of the master and skipping the whole shaming process as we get back to rocking it.

Then, rather than spiral BACKWARD, we use that oops day as a catalyst *FORWARD*.

Imagine throwing one of those little rubber balls against the ground. What does it do? The harder you throw it the higher it bounces, eh?

Let's do that. Antifragile style.

That bad day made us better. Thank you, imperfections.

Remember to dominate the Rebound Days.

THE 4 DISCIPLINES OF EXECUTION
HERE THEY ARE: 1 + 2 + 3 + 4

S tephen Covey's son Sean wrote a great book with some other
brilliant guys from FranklinCovey (Jim Huling and Chris
McChesney) called *The 4 Disciplines of Execution*.

I got it after Cal Newport referenced it in his great book *Deep
Work*. It's fantastic.

So, the authors tell us that there are 4 Disciplines of Execution (The "4DX"). Here they are in a very small nutshell.

Discipline #1. We need to focus on what they call our Wildly
Important Goals. Emphasis on WILDLY.

As in: Super, jumbo important goals that really fire you up
and that will really make a difference in your life.

Note: Not ten or twenty. Not even three or five. Max one or two.

The structure of a good Wildly Important Goal (or "WIG")
looks like this: We will go from x to y by z.

Discipline #2. The 4DX guys tell us that our WIG is a "Lag
Measure." It *lags behind* other things you will do to make that
goal happen.

Those things that produce the results? They're called "Lead
Measures." You want to focus on them.

Discipline #3. Once you've defined your WIG and your
Lead Measure, it's time to keep score. You've gotta know how
you're doing.

The primary score you want to keep isn't how you're doing
on your Lag; it's how you're doing on your LEAD.

Most people obsess about the *outcome* Lag Measures. We don't want to be like most people. Obsess about the process goals that *create* the results.

Discipline #4. We're on a roll. We have a clear, Wildly Important Goal. We know what we need to do to have a shot at hitting it. We're keeping track of our Lead Measure. Now we need to maintain "a cadence of accountability."

We can't be all fired up for a weekend and then forget about it the next week.

So, there ya go.

The 1 + 2 + 3 + 4's of Executing.

How are you doing with them?

Where are you strong? What needs work?

And, as always, most importantly: What's ONE thing you can do TODAY to activate your Heroic potential?

+1° and high fours!

KEEP SCORE
& WATCH YOUR PERFORMANCE SOAR

In our last +1°, we had fun with a quick look at the 4 Disciplines of Execution.

Quick question: Can you recall the 4DX?

Quick answer: 1) Know your wildly important goal; 2) Focus on your lead measures; 3) Keep score; 4) Stay accountable.

Let's chat more about the importance of keeping score. As the 4DX guys point out, keeping score is important. In fact, they tell us that it's *super* important.

They tell us to imagine bowling into a curtain. It's not very fun to watch your ball disappear behind a curtain and not know how you did. You'd probably stop playing immediately if you couldn't see how you were doing. (Right?)

They also tell us to imagine Venus Williams playing her sister Serena. In one scenario they're hitting the ball back and forth just for fun. No score. In another scenario, they're keeping score and playing for a championship at Wimbledon. Which scenario has just a tad more energy? When they're keeping score and playing to win. (Right?)

Well…

Guess what?

That's why we need to keep score in our lives.

It's a REALLY powerful way to step up our intensity levels and give ourselves a shot at activating our Heroic potential.

Remember the +1° featuring the study in which people were split up into two groups: one group got a pedometer to measure their number of steps and the other group didn't. The group that "kept score" with the pedometer walked a mile more than the other group.

Another quiz: Remember WHAT the 4DX guys say we're supposed to keep track of?

We don't want to just keep track of whether or not we hit our goals (our "Lag Measures") but whether or not we did the things that will help us *achieve* the goals (our "Lead Measures").

So...

What's your Wildly Important Goal?

And, what's your Lead Measure to hit that?

KEEP SCORE!

Dial up the intensity.

And have fun activating your Heroic potential.

TODAY.

TWO SCORECARDS
ONE FOR THE LEAD & ANOTHER FOR THE LAG

While we're on a roll with the 4 Disciplines of Execution, let's spend another moment chatting about Lead vs. Lag Measures.

This is a REALLY important concept to master.

To recap: Our "Lag Measure" is the "Wildly Important Goal" we want to achieve. We need to clearly identify that target and know why we want to hit it.

AND... We need to know that, although we can *influence* the outcome-target we want to hit, we can't totally control it.

Imagine a professional golfer. Their lag goal is to score well enough to win the tournament. Fantastic. But... Exclusively focusing on THAT is not going to lead to the outcome they want. In fact, focusing on that when they should be focusing on their performance is a good way to increase the likelihood of choking.

Now, the LEAD Measure is what you do to give yourself the best shot to achieve the Lag Measure.

These behaviors are so powerful because (a) they are within our direct control and (b) executing these behaviors at a high level is what actually creates the results we want.

Back to our professional golfer. They want to get clear on the behaviors that, when they consistently execute them, give them the highest chance of success. Then, they want to KEEP TRACK OF how frequently they execute THOSE things.

In *Finding Your Zone*, peak performance guru Michael Lardon tells us that this is such an important concept to grasp that he has his golfers keep TWO scorecards.

One scorecard is for the Lag Measure or the actual score on the hole. And the other (much more important!) card is for whether or not they executed their process before each shot.

All of which brings us back to YOU.

What do *your* two scorecards look like?

Get clear. Know what you want to achieve. Know what you need to do to have the best shot at achieving that.

And have the discipline to execute.

TODAY.

P.S. This is where the Heroic app comes in. The Big 3 target protocol is a great (yes, I'm biased!) scorecard to measure the *lead* targets that will help us win the ultimate game of life.

That's why I personally hit 101 targets a day.

Research shows that you only need to hit three to five targets per day to have a shot at boosting your energy by 40%, your productivity by 20%, and your connection by 15%.

Here's another easy link and QR code if you'd like to get started today: Heroic.us/Activate

ROMAN MASTERPIECE DAYS
AM'S & PM'S FEATURING 45- TO 75-MIN HOURS

As we briefly discussed, the Roman Senate had their own "Shutdown Complete!" ritual.

Apparently, according to Seneca, they wouldn't introduce anything important after their tenth hour.

Now, I knew that the "sixth" hour was the time around noon (and was known as "sexta" back in the day, which is how we got "siesta" today); and, therefore, the tenth hour would be around 4:00 p.m.

But…

I was curious how the Romans actually set up their days, so I headed to my reliable friend, Mr. Google.

Google: "Roman time."

Enter: Some fascinating historical facts and insight into Roman Masterpiece Days (via Roman timekeeping on Wikipedia).

Get this: Apparently, WAY back in the day (as in, before sundials were introduced in 263 BCE!), the Romans split their days in two parts: before noon and after noon.

In their lingo: *ante meridian* and *post meridian*.

Ring a bell?

That's where we get "a.m." and "p.m."

Fascinating.

Then, when they adopted the good ol' sundial, they split their days up into twelve hours.

Sunrise to sunset = twelve hours.

But…

They didn't use sixty minutes per hour.

They adjusted the number of minutes in the hour depending on whether it was winter or summer (or fall or spring).

With a Mediterranean latitude, their winters only had nine hours of daylight from sunrise to sunset and their summers had fifteen.

So, their "hour" in winter was only forty-five minutes long, while their hour in summer was around seventy-five minutes long.

I find that awesome for a number of reasons.

First: As Yuval Noah Harari reminds us, many of the things we take for granted (like sixty-minute hours and lawns in your front yard) are neither natural nor inevitable (nor immutable).

Second: I've always thought it made WAY more sense to structure our days based on the sunrise and sunset, and I've been having fun leveraging this ancient idea for modern times in my own daily rhythms.

For now…

Have an awesome a.m. and p.m.

From sunrise to sunset.

TODAY.

THE ZEIGARNIK EFFECT
HOW TO USE IT TO YOUR ADVANTAGE

Today we're going to meet a woman named Bluma Zeigarnik.

Professor Zeigarnik was a Russian psychologist who did some fascinating research.

Back in the 1920s as a graduate student, her professor, Kurt Lewin, noticed that waiters who hadn't been paid for their orders had better memories for those orders than they had *after* they'd been paid. (Fascinating.)

Bluma conducted a bunch of research into that observation and quantified it into what is now known as the Zeigarnik effect.

Basic idea: We have stronger memories for uncompleted tasks.

Kurt Lewin described it as "task-specific tension." Until you get completion on something you've decided is important, a part of your mind is focused on the task until it is completed.

For our purposes, let's look at a couple ways we can use this to our advantage.

First, creatively: Knowing that a part of our mind will continue focusing on something important until it is completed, let's follow the lead of some of the world's great mathematicians and writers.

At the end of your day, spend a few minutes thinking about whatever is most important to you.

Or, as Jason Selk advises in *Organize Tomorrow Today*, simply make a list of your top priorities for the next day before you wrap up at the end of the day, and in the process, you'll be priming your subconscious mind to go to work on it!

Second, psychologically: Knowing that a part of our mind will continue focusing on something important until it is completed, let's notice how often things that are stressing us out will pop up in our minds until we resolve them. (You ever notice that?!)

Want to end the rumination? Get resolution!

If you feel so inspired…

1. At the end of the day today, think about the most important thing you plan to do the next day. See yourself doing it the following day and let your mind go to work on it subconsciously until then.

2. Do you have any negative, open-loop things popping up in your head these days? What can you do to get some resolution on it so you can quit chewing on that issue?

Have fun.

Make Bluma proud!

P.S. You know who else knows all about the Zeigarnik effect? The producers of all those shows you binge-watch. They're hooking your attention with those cliff-hangers.

Pay attention. Don't take the bait.

LION VS. JUNGLE
BE NICE TO YOUR LIMBIC SYSTEM, PLEASE

Alberto Villoldo tells us that we evolved to deal with one lion roaring at us at a time.

That lion's roar triggered a fight-or-flight response. We would fight or we would flee. And, hopefully, we would live to talk about the tale later.

The important thing to note is that the stress from that event, although extremely acute, is also extremely short-lived. We respond to the challenge and move on. Our nervous system resets itself, all good.

Dr. Villoldo tells us that these days we've created a very different environment for ourselves.

With our 24/7/365 media exposure, we can track every single horrific thing happening in the world.

Instantly.

And constantly.

Then, for some truly bizarre reason when you slow down long enough to think about it, we continue the assault by consuming fictional horrors on TV and in movies for "entertainment."

All of that REALLY compromises our primitive limbic system that evolved to deal with that single lion threatening us in that acute moment of stress.

Now it's as if the ENTIRE JUNGLE is threatening us ALL DAY, EVERY DAY.

That's extraordinarily enervating.

The consequences of it are serious.

Our limbic systems simply can't watch all that news and entertainment and say: "That's happening over there and not to me. I'm fine."

Your amygdala lights up and responds AS IF IT WAS HAPPENING TO YOU RIGHT NOW.

Get this: Did you know that individuals who watched more than six hours of news on the 2013 Boston Marathon bombing had *more* PTSD symptoms than someone who was actually there and experienced the trauma?

Think about that for a moment.

And give your limbic system a break.

TODAY.

50 POUNDS = A
HOW TO MASTER THE FEAR OF ART

I t's your first day of art class. You signed up for an intro class on pottery. The teacher does something a little weird.

She points to one half of the class and says: "On the last day of class, I'm going to bring in a bathroom scale. You will get an 'A' if you produce fifty pounds of pots. A 'B' for forty pounds. Thirty pounds gets you a 'C.'"

Then she points to the other half of the class and says: "You'll get an 'A' for creating an amazing pot. I just need one pot from you. Make it awesome and you get the 'A.'"

Fast-forward to the end of the semester.

Who do you think created the best-looking pots?

Answer: The group that produced the fifty pounds of stuff to get an "A."

Why is that?

Well, as the authors of *Art & Fear* put it: "It seems that while the 'quantity' group was busily churning out piles of work—and learning from their mistakes—the 'quality' group had sat theorizing about perfection, and in the end had little more to show for their efforts than grandiose theories and a pile of dead clay."

Question: How do YOU approach *your* creativity?

Are you trying to create the "perfect pot"? Or are you willing to lean in and produce a TON of stuff—learning from your mistakes and, eventually, getting better and better?

Our +1°...
Go create a bunch of proverbial pots.
Remember: Fifty pounds and you'll get an "A."

P.S. Maslow comes to mind. He tells us: "It seems that the necessary thing to do is not to fear mistakes, to plunge in, to do the best that one can, hoping to learn enough from blunders to correct them eventually."

THE 80/20 PRINCIPLE
WHAT WORKS? DO MORE OF THAT

Once upon a time (1897 to be precise), an Italian economist named Vilfredo Pareto was studying wealth and income distribution in England.

He discovered that a small percentage of individuals owned the majority of land and wealth.

In fact, 20% of the population controlled 80% of the wealth and income.

On further analysis, mythical lore says that he found that this principle held true not only in different countries and different time periods but also in places like his garden—where he discovered that 20% of his pea pods yielded 80% of the peas that were harvested!

Since our pal Vilfredo identified the trend, many researchers have been busy pointing out some additional modern applications.

Here are a few fun ones:

- 20% of your carpet probably gets 80% of the wear
- 20% of streets account for 80% of the traffic
- 20% of beer drinkers consume 80% of the beer

OK. So, all of that's nice, but how's it relevant to activating our Heroic potential?

Well, the same ratios tend to apply to the rest of our lives.

In short, for our purposes: 20% of your behaviors are *probably* accounting for 80% of the goodness in your life.

The trick?

IDENTIFYING which 20%!

As Richard Koch puts it in his great book *The 80/20 Principle*: "20% of what we do leads to 80% of the results; but 80% of what we do leads to only 20%. We are wasting 80% of our time on low-value outcomes."

Which leads to this recommendation: "Calm down, work less and target a limited number of very valuable goals where the 80/20 Principle will work for us."

So, what "vital few" things are you doing that give you the most benefit?

More specifically, what THREE things do you do when you're at your best? The stuff you do that makes it *really* hard to have a *really* bad day and considerably easier to have a GREAT day?

For example, I can identify the few key behaviors I engage in that keep me connected to my best self:

1. I'm in bed for nine to ten hours to make sure I get enough sleep. I simply CANNOT consistently show up as my best self when I'm tired; therefore, this is a nonnegotiable priority.

2. I train like an athlete every day as I have fun doing my "1 + 10 + 100 + 1,000 + 10,000": one sun salutation, ten pull-ups, one hundred burpees, one thousand meters of rowing, and ten thousand steps.

3. I'm creative before I'm reactive as I do some Deep Work on what I've decided is my #1 WIN.

+1. I make sure I create phone-free micro-moments of awesome with my wife and kids.

If ALL I did was *those* three (+1) behaviors, I'd have a pretty awesome day. Whether the math is precisely 80/20, it's pretty darn close.

How about YOU?

What are *your* THREE key behaviors that most help YOU show up as the best, most Heroic version of yourself?

Get clear.

Dominate.

TODAY.

P.S. Bonus points for putting those key behaviors on a checklist. Even more bonus points for putting them in the Heroic app and hitting them every day.

THE MOTIVATIONAL CALCULATOR
SOLVING THE PROCRASTINATION EQUATION

P iers Steel is a leading research scientist.

After analyzing hundreds of studies on motivation, he came up with an equation to capture the essence of motivation.

It's a little abstract on first blush but worth internalizing and using as one of our tools. I recommend keeping this ready at hand and using it often to see where your motivation may be waning and how to keep it strong.

Here's the equation: $M = E \text{ x } V / I \text{ x } D$

Motivation = **Expectancy** x **Value** / **Impulsivity** x **Delay**

First thing to notice for non-math majors: If you want Motivation to be big, you better have a really big numerator and a really small denominator.

In other words, we need to increase our Expectancy and Value while driving down our Impulsivity and Delay.

Expectancy. That's an awkward word for confidence.

You have to expect that you can bring your goal to life. You have to KNOW (!) that you *can* do it.

Now, you may or may not actually achieve your goal, but you have to know in your soul that it's not only possible but that you think you can do it.

If you don't feel that, then you either need to simplify your goal until you *can* believe it or you need to build up your confidence so you can believe it.

Value. If I were writing this equation, I'd start here.

Before we ask ourselves whether or not we really think we can have it, we need to ask ourselves whether we really (!) want it.

Our DESIRE needs to be extremely high. Napoleon Hill called this a "burning desire" back in the day.

So, quick pause. What do you want to achieve in your life? Like *really, really* want? Is your motivation high?

If it isn't, check in. Are you going after something you REALLY want? And, if so, do you REALLY believe you can have it? If not, science and common sense say that your motivation will be weak.

Tweak those two variables so you have a shot at a very high level of sustainable motivation.

Now for the things that erode motivation.

Impulsivity. Can you focus your attention on what's most important? Or do you find yourself constantly distracted by the latest push notification or email alert or other shiny object?

The higher your level of impulsivity, the lower your level of motivation. We need to get really good at reducing/eliminating all distractions and doing the Deep Work that will move us forward. Period.

Delay. Another great way to erode motivation is to make the goal super far down the road. That delay doesn't help.

Solution? Create micro goals (today! this week!) that give you the chance to create a constant stream of micro wins—which is the PERFECT way to fuel the fire as you show up with high levels of motivation day in and day out.

Again, that formula might sound too abstract to be useful but, in my experience, it's incredibly powerful.

When my motivation wanes, I love to bust out a piece of paper and write down the equation—looking for little ways to optimize each variable to jack up my motivation.

Try it.

It works.

MOTIVATION = ENERGY X (VALUE X EXPECTANCY / IMPULSIVITY X DELAY)
A MODIFIED LOOK AT THE SCIENCE OF MOTIVATION

In our last +1° we talked about our motivation equation:

Motivation = **Expectancy** x **Value** / **Impulsivity** x **Delay**

Quick recap: Our motivation will always be driven by how fired up we are about getting something (Value) and how confident we are that we can have it (Expectancy).

To the extent we REALLY, REALLY want something and REALLY, REALLY believe we can get it, we're more likely to show up and work hard.

Then we need to make sure we don't dissipate that motivation by being distracted by all the shiny push notifications, etc. (Impulsivity) and that we consistently hit micro goals so we're always making progress (Delay).

All of that is super powerful.

Throw your current motivation into that equation and look at the data to see where you can turn up the heat.

And…

I think that equation is missing a VERY important variable.

Here's what I think that equation should be: Motivation = **ENERGY** x (Value x Expectancy / Impulsivity x Delay)

Fact is, if your energy isn't great because of poor lifestyle choices, the whole equation falls apart.

When you're tired, you just don't see the world the same way. Literally.

Did you know that sleep-deprived people have bad memories for good stuff but good memories for bad stuff?

It's true.

Hence, our #1 priority: Get your energy Heroically optimized.

I repeat: If you have a hard time getting out of bed because of poor lifestyle choices, you're going to have a (very!) hard time activating your Heroic potential.

So…

What's the #1 thing you can START doing to Eat/Move/Sleep/Breathe/Focus better, starting TODAY?

And…

What's the #1 thing you're going to STOP doing TODAY?

Let's optimize our Energy.

It's time to activate your Heroic potential.

DIGITAL SABBATICALS
TAKING BREAKS FROM FOCUS, NOT FROM DISTRACTION

L et's revisit Cal Newport's *Deep Work* for another brilliant idea.

As we've discussed: In our modern world, Deep Work is simultaneously more RARE *and* more VALUABLE. Unfortunately, way too many people are spending way too much of their time flitting around in Shallowville.

One of the best ways to go deep, of course, is to unplug from all the nonsense-distractions by turning off the Wi-Fi and the smartphone.

But here's the thing.

Cal tells us that most of us take a sabbatical FROM technology to go deep—whether that's deep into Work or Love.

But...

And this is a BIG *but*...

What we REALLY want to do is take a sabbatical from going DEEP to going Shallow. Plugging into our technology should be the *exception*, not the rule.

We should take a sabbatical *from* our Deep Work and Deep Love (and Deep Living!) to jump into technology to use it for all it's worth—WITHOUT getting sucked into the vortex that threatens to (literally) waste our entire lives.

As Cal so perfectly puts it: "Don't take breaks from distraction. Instead take breaks from focus."

And he says: "I propose an alternative to the Internet Sabbath.

Instead of scheduling the occasional break *from distraction* so you can focus, you should instead schedule the occasional break *from focus* to give in to distraction."

Amen.

Our +1° is simple but not easy...

Go deep. In every aspect of your life.

TODAY.

*

BATTING .300
IS HALL OF FAME MATERIAL (IN LIFE & BASEBALL)

I don't know about you, but I'm still kind of attached to the idea that I should never make a mistake.

I mean, I get it intellectually.

We need to remember to have a growth mindset, that we can't do anything great without some setbacks, no movie was ever shot in one perfect sequence of scenes—there are always "mis-takes," yada, yada, etc.

But that's only GENERALLY true. When it comes to ME and YOU, we should be perfect, right? (Hah.)

Seriously. As I discuss in Conquering Perfectionism 101, I used to be such a perfectionist that I remember stressing myself out at my first job trying to make sure I got a *staple* perfectly parallel to the top of the page. (Laughing with compassionate joy at that twenty-two-year-old version of me.)

So… Let's just say I've come a long way.

Here's another little distinction that has helped me over the years. I loved baseball as a kid, so this metaphor really hits home for me.

Do you know how often a HALL OF FAME baseball player gets a hit? If you're a baseball fan, you know that if you're batting .300, you're C R U S H I N G it.

If you can get three hits out of every ten at bats over the course of your career, you'll be *historically* great and, perhaps, inducted into the Hall of Fame.

Here are some fun facts.

As of this writing, 270 players have been inducted into the Baseball Hall of Fame. Only 114 of them had a career batting average of over .300.

Ty Cobb managed to bat .368 over the course of his twenty-four-year (!) career—which is astonishing. Ted Williams had a .344 batting average, while Babe Ruth had a .342 average and Hank Aaron batted .305.

Look a little further down the list and you'll see a LOT of guys WAY below .300. (Including some Hall of Fame MANAGERS who couldn't hit much at all, including Tony La Russa, who was a middle infielder and whose batting average was a paltry .199 in 132 games over six seasons.)

All that to say: If you can get a hit in just THREE out of ten at bats, you're among the best *ever*.

You could strike out the other seven times, and you'd STILL be Hall of Fame material.

Three for ten. That's it.

And now we're arriving at the point of our +1°.

Guess what? The best creators and entrepreneurs have the same batting average.

In fact, in *Originals*, University of Pennsylvania professor Adam Grant tells us: "Whether you're generating or evaluating new ideas the best you can do is measure success on the kind of yardstick that batters use in baseball. As Randy Komisar puts it, 'If I'm hitting .300, I'm a genius. That's because the future cannot be predicted. The sooner you learn it, the sooner you can be good at it.'"

For those who may not know, Randy Komisar is a Hall of Fame entrepreneur and venture capitalist.

If HE thinks getting it right three out of ten times makes him a genius, I think we can consider embracing the same standard.

So… The next time you inevitably (!) swing and miss, remember our Hall of Famers.

Then get back up and give us all you've got.

P.S. Babe Ruth batted .342 over the course of his career. Which is kinda crazy epic considering the fact that he was also a pitcher.

And… As we've discussed… At one point, he led the league in home runs AND in strikeouts. That's just how it goes. You swing hard and you're going to miss. Let's stay antifragile and know those strikeouts are often just reverse indicators as we have fun wisely yet aggressively swinging for the fences.

PYTHAGORAS'S PM REVIEW
VIA HIS GOLDEN VERSES

As we've discussed, Donald Robertson is one of the world's leading practical scholars on Stoicism. He's also a practicing therapist and author of *How to Think Like a Roman Emperor*.

Donald is the guy who gave us the whole "Warriors vs. Librarians" distinction—reminding us that it's not enough to merely STUDY philosophy. The ancient philosophers PRACTICED it.

In addition to winning the award for best title ever and giving us a fantastic biography of Marcus Aurelius, the book is packed with a TON of Stoic practices.

Want to think like a Roman emperor?

Follow Pythagoras's advice and have a solid PM Review.

Donald tells us: "This famous passage from [Pythagoras's] 'The Golden Verses,' which Epictetus quoted to his students, describes the evening meditation:

Allow not sleep to close your wearied eyes,
Until you have reckoned up each daytime deed:
'Where did I go wrong? What did I do?
And what duty's left undone?'
From first to last review your acts and then
Reprove yourself for wretched acts,
but rejoice in those done well."

That's our +1°.

If you feel so inspired…

"Allow not sleep to close your wearied eyes,
Until you have reckoned up each daytime deed:
'Where did I go wrong? What did I do?
And what duty's left undone?'
From first to last review your acts and then
Reprove yourself for wretched acts,
but rejoice in those done well."

Here's to turning up the heat.
+1°. +1°. +1°.
Old-school style.
TODAY.

FIRST THINGS FIRST
SECOND THINGS? NOT AT ALL

One of Stephen Covey's *7 Habits of Highly Effective People* is "First Things First." He also wrote a whole book by the same name.

You know where he got that phrase? Peter Drucker.

It was Drucker who said: "Put first things first."

And you know what he said we should do with "second things." He said we should ignore them. Specifically, he said: "First things first—and second things not at all."

He also said: "If there is one 'secret' of effectiveness, it is concentration. Effective executives do first things first and they do one thing at a time."

He *also* said: "There is surely nothing quite so useless as doing with great efficiency what should not be done at all."

Fact is, in any given moment, there is only ONE most important thing to do. And that's what the best among us do. Over and over and over and over and over again.

Of course, this doesn't just apply to executives.

Here's how Michael Phelps applied this wisdom to his life. Over the span of five Olympics (which, in itself, is an epic achievement), he won twenty-eight medals—twenty-three of them gold.

In his great book *No Limits*, he tells us about one of the secrets to his success he learned from his coach, Bob Bowman.

It's a very simple question that happens to form a powerful word: What's important now? "W.I.N." for short.

What's important now? Micro W.I.N.

How about now? Micro W.I.N.

And now? Micro W.I.N.

Over and over and over and over again.

Phelps created little micro wins all day, every day during his training and before his races. And, well, those micro wins added up to a TON of Big Wins.

So…

Throughout the day today, ask yourself:

WHAT'S IMPORTANT NOW?

P.S. To be clear by stating the obvious: This doesn't mean working all the time or obsessively grinding in any aspect of our lives. It means seeing the big picture and knowing when the most important thing is NOT working but, rather, turning off your technology so you can connect with your family or your higher self or whatever is truly most important.

That's TRUE Winning. Remember: First things first. Second things? Not at all.

P.P.S. The great meditation teacher, Matthieu Ricard, also has an opinion on the subject. He tells us: "A third form of laziness is not having the determination to do immediately what you know to be the most important thing and wasting your time instead on minor activities. To remedy this, establish priorities among your projects, and remember that, while your days are numbered, ordinary activities are like waves on the ocean—there is no end to them."

T.I.M.E.
HOW KIDS SPELL LOVE

The other day Alexandra printed out a bunch of inspirational quotes. I loved one of the quotes so much that I printed out my own copy.

Here it is: "Children spell love … T.I.M.E."

That's our +1°.

Do you have children?

Remember: They spell love "T.I.M.E."

Let's put away our smartphones and our other "super important" stuff for an extra moment and simply be there, fully, for our kids.

TODAY.

Note: Of course, WE ALL spell love T.I.M.E.

So, let's put away our smartphones and our other "super important!" stuff for an extra moment and simply BE THERE for each human with whom we're blessed to interact.

TODAY.

EFFICIENT VS. EFFECTIVE
ONE'S GOOD FOR TIME, THE OTHER'S GOOD FOR PEOPLE

Here's another potentially life-changing idea from Stephen Covey's *The 7 Habits of Highly Effective People*.

Covey tells us that we can be *efficient* with time and tasks but that we need to focus on being EFFECTIVE with people.

Think about that for a moment...

Efficient vs. ***Effective***.

As you may have noticed, if we try to be *efficient* with people (especially with our kids—who, you might remember, spell love "T.I.M.E."), we can often find ourselves quite *efficient* AND equally INEFFECTIVE.

The fact is relationships can be messy. And they definitely take fully present time.

So... Let's show the people in our lives just how much we love them by giving them more time—of the fully present variety.

And, as always, let's remember that our greatest obstacle to giving that fully present time and creating effectiveness in our relationships is almost always technology.

Why the distracted rush with the people we love? So we can scroll through our smartphones ten more times?

Let's take those wasted moments (and minutes) and put them into our relationships.

TODAY.

MAKE IT A GAME
HOW TO TURN CHORES INTO GIFTS

Grandma and Grandpa got the kids Fitbits for Christmas last year. And... After Mommy's first attempt to get them synced up to her phone didn't work, those new Fitbits wound up finding a home in our kitchen drawer, and we didn't get them working until well into the new year.

After the first night Emerson wore his new Fitbit, he sprang out of bed to check on his sleep (he got nine hours and forty minutes!) and started tracking his steps.

"Wow! I'm already at twenty-seven steps!" he said by the time he had gone to the bathroom and headed into my office.

Me with a chuckle: "That's amazing, buddy. Nice work!"

Emerson: "I bet I'll get more steps than you today!"

Me: "I bet you will, too. That would be awesome!"

Then his sister rolled into my office and checked in on her sleep. (She had gotten ten hours and already had her steps rocking.)

Then... The fun began. The two of them started racing back and forth in the hallway. Then they headed outside, hit our trail, and came back in nearly thirty minutes later all sweaty.

Emerson: "We just did FOUR loops! We already have seven thousand steps. How many do you have?!"

Me: "Wow. That's impressive! I only have 1,487 so far."

Now... This is quite remarkable because, although he loves running around and playing games, Emerson just isn't *that* big of a fan of getting out and exercising unless there's a really good reason to do it. His sister Eleanor naturally enjoys movement more, but it's never really been his thing.

Until…

It became a GAME.

Which is the point of this +1°.

One of the consistent themes in my daily 1:01 p.m. CT coaching sessions with our Heroic community is the fact that showing up and hitting our Heroic Targets can often feel like a CHORE— things we (insert whiny voice) *have* to do.

As per our discussion on Michelle Segar's wisdom on the science of getting ourselves to engage in healthy behaviors, I stress the importance of turning those "chores" into GIFTS we are giving to our future selves.

We need to remember the fact that, by eating well and moving our bodies and making sure we get great sleep, etc., we are giving our future selves a MUCH better shot at activating our Heroic potential.

Ideally, we want to arrive at a place where we experience hedonic *eudaimonia* and KNOW the truth of Seneca's statement: *"How much better to pursue a straight course and eventually reach that destination where the things that are pleasant and the things that are honorable finally become, for you, the same."*

One of the best ways to do that?

Channel your inner enthusiastic kid and…

MAKE IT A GAME.

ALL OF IT.

TODAY.

CREATIVE VS. REACTIVE
CHOOSE ONE BEFORE THE OTHER

*C*reative vs. *reactive.*

Those two words have the same exact letters—with just a *slightly* different placement of that *c*.

But, alas, that *c* in the beginning of *creative* leads to a VERY important difference.

If we want to activate our Heroic productivity potential, from my vantage point we MUST be *creative* before we're *reactive.*

It may not sound like a huge deal, but I think this is the secret sauce to Heroic productivity.

People tend to think of me as a reasonably prolific guy—which, I suppose I am. And they usually assume I'm working all the time and must be in a near-constant state of rushing to hit deadlines. But I'm not.

The #1 reason? I never (seriously, NEVER) allow myself to be *reactive* before I'm *creative.*

Every single morning, I'm creative before I'm reactive.

I start my day dominating my most important W.I.N. in a Deep Work bubble right after meditation and before anything else.

Phone is in airplane mode, turned off, hidden in the back of the top shelf in my closet. No email. No news. I'm CREATIVE before I'm reactive.

ALWAYS.

Although any one Deep Work session might not be astonishingly awesome, many are. And, more importantly, I consistently, as Cal Newport would say, "accrete" value.

What happens when we aggregate and compound those little gains over an extended period of time? Magic.

So…

How about *you*?

What's REALLY (!) important to you?

What's your #1 WILDLY important goal?

Your mission, should you choose to accept it: Put in creative work on *that* most important project BEFORE you let yourself go reactive.

Caveat: We all have different rhythms. For example, my wife "reacts" to our two kids. Or, more accurately, raising our kids is her most important creative work right now.

Of course, you'll need to create your own rhythms to most effectively meet *your* life's obligations.

BUT…

You don't need to roll over and look at your phone first thing in the morning! (Right?)

Be CREATIVE!

Before you're reactive.

But only if you want to activate your Heroic potential.

PRACTICE WHAT YOU PREACH
A SERMON ON THE GOOD SAMARITAN

When we lived in Ojai years ago, Alexandra and I were on a walk with Eleanor when we saw a dog that appeared to be lost. It had a collar and was acting sweet but a little scared.

Of course, if it was our dog (Zeus!), we'd hope that someone would call us. Unfortunately, neither one of us had our phones (trade-offs of digital minimalism) so we couldn't call the owner. So, we decided to hang out with the dog, waiting for someone to walk by who might have a phone.

As luck would have it, a couple walked up. They were super helpful—calling the owner (voicemail) and then the Humane Society (closed because it was a holiday).

Long story a little shorter, as we were trying to figure out what to do, the owner of the dog arrived. Case solved! Happy reunion.

While we were waiting, we got a chance to chat with the couple. A perk of digital minimalism: Opportunities for micro moments of positivity resonance, Love 2.0 style!

One of our new friends had a tattoo on the inside of his right wrist: *oṃ maṇi padme hūṃ*—a sacred Buddhist mantra that captures the essence of a compassionate life.

I was appreciating them for embodying that compassion and shared a fun little study about seminary students on their way to teach a lesson on the Sermon on the Mount.

Have you heard it before?

Get this: Researchers set up a little study where seminary students were on their way to teach a class on the Good Samaritan—you know, the parable in which the super devout religious people ignore a person in need and the nonreligious Samaritan is the only one who takes the time to help.

Well, the researchers set it up so the seminary students were running just a little late to teach their class on being a nice person.

And...

The researchers put a shabbily dressed man who was moaning (and *clearly* in need) right in their path. The seminary students almost had to step over him to get to their class.

Guess what happened?

90% of our devoutly religious teachers—ON THEIR WAY TO TEACH ABOUT BEING A GOOD SAMARITAN—ignored the person in need.

Eek. Of course, we ALL do the same thing at times. That's part of being human.

Martin Luther King Jr. had a great line about this. He said: "The first question which the priest and the Levite asked was: 'If I stop to help this man, what will happen to me?' But... the good Samaritan reversed the question: 'If I do not stop to help this man, what will happen to him?'"

And...

That's our +1°.

Let's practice what we preach.

TODAY.

TIME MANAGEMENT, DRUCKER STYLE
THE 1 + 2 + 3 FOR EFFECTIVENESS

Peter Drucker is considered the greatest business thinker of the twentieth century.

In *The Effective Executive*, he tells us that TIME is our most precious asset. You can lose money and get it back. You can even lose some health and get it back. But once your time is gone, it's gone. Period.

Unfortunately, too few of us pay attention to Aristotle's admonition that "We should count time by heart throbs."

Drucker gives us a three-step process to optimize our use of time. Here's a quick look.

First, he tells us that we should start by TRACKING our time. We need to get more clarity on where our time is currently going.

As we've discussed, the simple act of tracking *anything* immediately improves the performance of that activity. For example, if you're tracking your nutrition, you're less likely to want to write down, "Three Twinkies for lunch."

Right? Same thing with our time.

We need to know where our time is currently going. Then we can immediately spot the time wasters and get clarity on the fact that, perhaps, we're doing considerably less focused, effective work than we thought.

Once we have clarity on where our time is currently going, we then MANAGE our time.

The #1 thing we do in this part of the process? We *ruthlessly* eliminate the time wasters.

Again, rule #1 of optimizing *anything*—whether it's your health or your relationships or your time—is to GET RID OF the stuff that's making you sick.

Twinkies? Gone. Yelling? Gone. Smartphone apps? Gone.

After eliminating the time wasters, we CONSOLIDATE our time. Drucker is ALL about creating what he calls "large quantums of time"—the largest possible blocks of time to do truly deep, important work.

For him, that didn't mean ninety-minute chunks. It meant "half days" and even *weeks* of uninterrupted time.

To recap:

1. Where's your time going? Track it.
2. What needs to go? Eliminate it.
3. How can you create large time blocks? Consolidate it.

That's the 1 + 2 + 3 of time management, Drucker style. Let's make every heart throb count.

TODAY.

MULTITASKING IS A MYTH
IT'S REALLY TASK SWITCHING (WHICH HAS A BIG COST)

Multitasking is a myth.

Our brains aren't like computers with parallel processors. We can't actually do multiple things at one time. What we do is not "multitasking" per se; it's more accurately called "task switching."

Here's why we should care.

Remember our handy-dandy Deep Work equation?

High Quality Work Produced = Time Spent x Intensity of Focus

Essentially: If you want to create a high volume of high-quality work without spending your entire life working, you want to increase the intensity of your focus.

Here's the deal: If you constantly papercut your attention by switching from one task to another, you've gotta know that you're paying a high cost as you diminish the intensity of your focus.

Researchers can look at this in a lab and see what happens to your performance on tasks when you switch from one thing to another. They've discovered that your performance goes down dramatically when you constantly switch from one thing to another.

One of the reasons this happens is that all that task switching creates something called "attention residue." Part of your attention is still hanging on to the *last* thing you did. There's a *residue* of attention from that task you just switched from that's negatively impacting your ability to crush it right now.

The solution?

Create a Deep Work time block—a period of time in which you focus EXCLUSIVELY on one task. Then focus ALL your attention on ONE thing.

When?

How about all day, every day.

Especially…

TODAY.

TASK SWITCHING IS EXPENSIVE
HERE'S HOW TO CALCULATE THE COSTS

L et's quantify the costs of task switching with a little exercise. Please grab a stopwatch.

First, time yourself as you say the alphabet from *A* to *J*.

Ready…

GO!

How long did that take you?

Now, time yourself as you count from 1 to 10.

Ready…

GO!

How long did *that* take you?

Now, time yourself as you switch back and forth and go from A-1 to B-2 to… J-10.

Ready…

GO!

How long did THAT take you?

If you're like me and professional futurist Alex Pang, who introduced me to this test in his great book *The Distraction Addiction*, it probably took you around 1.5 seconds to count from one to ten and another 1.5 seconds to do the alphabet from A to J.

And…

If you're like us, it probably took you *at least* ten seconds to do the A-1 to J-10 series.

Here's the Captain Obvious analysis:

You can do one super-simple task in 1.5 seconds.

You can do another super-simple task in 1.5 seconds.

BUT...

When you combine the two super-simple tasks (which should take you, in aggregate three seconds if you did them separately), it takes you over THREE times longer to complete.

And your brain hurts at the end, to boot. (Hah.)

Now, that's obviously a mundane example, but we'd be wise to know that task switching comes with an *enormous* cost in terms of efficiency—not to mention the failure to drop into an energizing state of flow as you blow your nervous system up with one enervating stimulus after another.

Remember the ABCs and 123s of task switching.

And...

FOCUS.

Today.

SMOKEYBOT
VS. THE TORTOISE & THE HARE

Grant Cardone wrote a great book called *The 10X Rule*.

In it, he tells us that we got the whole "Tortoise and the Hare" story wrong.

Of course, in the classic fable we have the tortoise, who slowly but persistently plods along and beats the hare, who dashes out from the starting line but then peters out.

Grant's question: What if you combined the best qualities of both into one new animal?

That guy—with the speed of the hare and the persistence of the tortoise—would SMOKE both of them!

He tells us the fable would then be called "Smoked."

That new fictional animal with the speed of the hare and the persistence of the tortoise?

I like to call him Smokeybot.

Smokeybot H-U-S-T-L-E-S. He has the lightning speed of the hare.

And…

Smokeybot knows how to stay in the game for the long run. He knows how to oscillate his energy to make sure he doesn't burn himself out.

Do you?

REST BEFORE YOU'RE TIRED
REMEMBER YOUR HEART & ITS BILLIONS OF BEATS

D o you know how many times your heart beats in a lifetime?

That obviously depends on a number of factors, but for the sake of discussion, let's say that your average heart rate is seventy beats per minute.

That's 4,200 beats per hour. Just over 100,000 beats per day. Over 35 million beats per year. And, assuming a nice, round number of you living to one hundred, your heart would beat over 3.5 *billion* times. All without you ever thinking about it.

So… Question: How does your heart do *that* much work for *that* many years without taking a break?

Note: That's actually a trick question.

Your heart is able to work *that* hard for *that* long PRECISELY because it takes so many breaks.

Get this: In *How to Stop Worrying and Start Living*, Dale Carnegie tells us about the importance of dealing with *fatigue* if we want to deal with *worry*.

He tells us about how the U.S. Army has its soldiers rest for ten minutes out of every sixty minutes they march—resting BEFORE they get tired to increase their overall efficiency.

Then he tells us about Winston Churchill, who worked up to sixteen hours a day in his late sixties and early seventies during World War II. One of his secrets? He liked to work from bed and took a bunch of naps.

Then there was Rockefeller—who lived to ninety-six and took a thirty-minute nap every day at noon. And we have Edison, who attributed his enormous energy and endurance to his habit of sleeping whenever he wanted to.

So, back to our heart.

Carnegie cites Walter B. Cannon, a Harvard doctor, who tells us that "Most people have the idea that the heart is working all the time. As a matter of fact, there is a definite rest period after each contraction. When beating at a moderate rate of seventy pulses per minute, the heart is actually working only nine hours out of the twenty-four. In the aggregate its rest periods total a full fifteen hours per day."

The secret to your heart's longevity?

Recovery.

It works. And it recovers. And then recovers some more. Fifteen hours of recovery for every nine hours of work.

How about YOU?

Are *you* resting before you're tired?

Prioritizing rest and recovery is a tough thing to do in a manic, always-on world, but it's incredibly important if we want to maintain sustainable levels of awesome.

Our +1°...

What's one little thing you can do today to rest *before* you get tired?

Get on that.

And...

Remember the secret to your billions of heartbeats.

SYNERGY
WHEN 1 + 1 = 3 (OR MORE)

*S*ynergy.

It's Habit #6 of Covey's *Highly Effective People*.

The Apple dictionary tells us that *synergy* is "the interaction or cooperation of two or more organizations, substances, or other agents to produce a combined effect greater than the sum of their separate effects."

It's when the whole is greater than the sum of its parts.

It's when 1 + 1 doesn't equal 2 …

It equals 3.

Examples abound in nature. Put two plants next to each other, and their roots commingle and improve the soil—helping each plant flourish more than they would if they were far apart.

1 + 1 = 3.

Put two pieces of wood together, and they can hold more than twice the weight.

1 + 1 = 3.

Dave Ramsey shares a great story in *EntreLeadership* to bring the point home. He tells us about Belgian horses.

Apparently, they are some of the strongest horses in the world. One Belgian horse can pull eight thousand pounds. Put two random Belgian horses together and they can pull twenty to twenty-four thousand pounds. Not two times as much as one but THREE times as much.

$1 + 1 = 3$.

But here's what's nuts. If you raise and train the Belgian horses together, they'll blow past the twenty-four thousand pounds and go all the way up to thirty or thirty-two thousand pounds—pulling not just *three* times as much but FOUR times as much weight as the horses that didn't know one another.

$1 + 1 = 4$.

Synergy.

It's a powerful concept.

How can you apply it to YOUR life TODAY?

DOMINATING YOUR LIFE
IT'S WHAT YOU DO IF YOU'RE POWERFUL

Stuart Wilde was a leading a figure in the self-help movement in the 1990s, when he was giving lectures with Louise Hay, Deepak Chopra, and Wayne Dyer.

He's also a really funny and equally wise guy who wrote a great book called *Infinite Self*.

One passage in that book jumped off the page and grabbed me.

Here it is: "Messy surroundings and an untidy life reflect a weakened metaphysical and psychological state. If you are powerful, you will dominate your life, you will find time to clean up and order things, and you will want to do that as a part of your personal discipline. Mess is the external manifestation of the ego's disquiet and laziness."

One more time: "Messy surroundings and an untidy life reflect a weakened metaphysical and psychological state. If you are powerful, you will dominate your life, you will find time to clean up and order things, and you will want to do that as a part of your personal discipline. Mess is the external manifestation of the ego's disquiet and laziness."

Now, I'm a reasonably neat guy, but I'm often lazier with the details of keeping things clean than I'd like to be, and Alexandra and I have chatted countless times about the correlation between our mental "disquiet" and how that is mirrored by our external environment.

Specifically, our kitchen. The more tired/lazy I am mentally at the end of the day, the more likely our kitchen is messy at the start of the next day.

All that to say, it's time to talk about dominating our lives.

More specifically, I want to talk about ONE area of your life that could use some dominating as a simple, metaphorical representation of you stepping into the next best version of yourself.

For me, it's my kitchen.

I hereby proclaim my dominance over you, kitchen.

What is it for YOU?

Here's to having fun making that practice a part of our personal disciplines.

I repeat: "If you are powerful, you will dominate your life."

AMBITION & ROUTINE
IN AN INTELLIGENT PERSON

M ason Currey wrote a great book called *Daily Rituals.*

The book features brief vignettes about the idiosyncratic habits of 161 of history's most iconoclastic writers, scientists and other great thinkers—ranging from W. H. Auden, Charles Darwin, and Carl Jung to Stephen King, Benjamin Franklin, and Mozart.

If you've ever wondered how some of the greatest creators in history showed up on a daily basis, I think you'll love it. The extraordinary variety of approaches is inspiring and, more than anything, feels like a permission slip to unapologetically own our unique styles.

But I've gotta say that the first line(s) of the book might have been my favorite.

Here's how Mason kicks off the party:

"'Routine, in an intelligent man, is a sign of ambition,' Auden wrote in 1958. If that's true, then Auden himself was one of the most ambitious men of his generation. The poet was obsessively punctual and lived by an exacting timetable throughout his life."

I repeat: "Routine, in an intelligent man, is a sign of ambition."

When I read that line, I immediately said to myself: "Hah. That's AWESOME." Then I thought of Robin Sharma's reflection that greatness is consistency on the fundamentals.

As we'll discuss, the specifics of your routine will differ depending on whether the domain you want to master is business or sports or parenting or philosophy or whatever, but your disciplined CONSISTENCY on your chosen fundamentals will be there—in proportion to your ambition, to use Auden's words.

Spotlight on YOU...

What's *your* greatest ambition?

Do your routines reflect the scope of your ambition and the depth of your intelligence?

Here's to activating our Heroic potential.

With a well-structured protocol.

TODAY.

WORK OR PLAY?
MASTERS IN THE ART OF LIVING

In our last +1°, we talked about W. H. Auden's (genius) quip that routine, in an intelligent person, is a sign of ambition.

Then we did a quick check-in on *your* routines.

And, hopefully, we turned the heat up a degree or three and made sure that your routines were reflecting both the depth of your intelligence and the scope of your ambition.

Today I want to talk about work and play.

It's time to, as Abraham Maslow said while reflecting on a hallmark of self-actualizing people: "dissolve the apparent dichotomy" between the two.

Here's my all-time favorite passage on the subject.

Lawrence Pearsall Jacks tells us: "A master in the art of living draws no sharp distinction between his work and his play, his labour and his leisure, his mind and his body, his education and his recreation. He hardly knows which is which. He simply pursues his vision of excellence through whatever he is doing and leaves others to determine whether he is working or playing. To himself he always seems to be doing both. Enough for him that he does it well."

Here's to mastering the art of living by pursuing excellence (*Areté!*) in everything we do.

Q: Are we working or playing right now?

A: For us, we're always doing both.

NEW DAY'S RESOLUTIONS
IT'S DAY 1 (AGAIN!) (ALWAYS!)

New Year's Day is one of my favorite holidays.

It's right up there with Thanksgiving (how awesome is a day of gratitude?!), Independence Day (I always love to celebrate by honoring those who gave their lives for our freedoms, while making my own Declaration of Independence from the tyranny of my bad habits), and Easter (remember: to have a resurrection, we must be willing to have a crucifixion).

As the New Year rolls into town, I absolutely love taking the plastic wrap off my big ol' wall calendar and seeing a fresh twelve months ahead of me.

And… It's a thrill to set New Year's resolutions to (FINALLY!) (!) show up as that next best version of ourselves. (Right?)

And…

Did you know…

According to some research done in 2016, only 9% of the 41% of Americans who make New Year's resolutions feel they were successful in keeping them.

For the non-math majors in the crowd, that means that according to that research, 91% of people who set a New Year's resolution FAIL to keep it.

Now… To be clear, it's not that setting resolutions in and of itself is a silly idea.

Get this…

Although only 46% of people who set resolutions consider themselves successful after six months, ONLY 4% (!) of people who set similar goals *without* a resolution consider themselves successful.

So… Get fired up.

Set some inspiring resolutions for the new year, Hero!

Get clear on who YOU will be in your Energy, your Work, and your Love. Get clear on the virtues you will embody and the targets you will hit to go to the next level and become more Heroically Energized, Heroically Productive, and Heroically Connected than ever before.

And… As nice and warm and fuzzy as New YEAR's resolutions are, as I like to say… What we *really* want to focus on are New DAY'S resolutions.

We don't want to wait another 360+ days for you to remember that TODAY IS THE DAY to show up as the best version of yourself.

Which is why, I REPEAT, we architected our Heroic app to help you RECOMMIT *to* being and then celebrate yourself *for* being your best self TODAY.

Which begs the question…

Whether you use your Big 3 protocol in our Heroic app or your own idiosyncratic approach…

Did YOU recommit to being your best self this morning?

Remember… Today's the Day to move from Theory to Practice to Mastery.

It's DAY 1.

ALWAYS.

P.S. Now that we've explored some ideas on how to play the ultimate game well by forging antifragile confidence, optimizing our Big 3, and making today a masterpiece, it's time to chat about the art and science of self-mastery. That's our next objective.

IQ VS. WILLPOWER
ONE IS A MUCH BETTER PREDICTOR THAN THE OTHER

Here's a fun fact...

Did you know that willpower outpredicts IQ for academic performance by a FACTOR OF TWO?

In other words, if you know both a kid's IQ and their willpower, knowing their willpower score will make you twice as effective at predicting how well they're doing in school than knowing their IQ.

Think about that for a second. (Isn't that astonishing?)

Willpower (a.k.a. self-discipline/self-mastery/etc.) is *also* the best predictor of pretty much *everything else* we want in life: great relationships, health, wealth, etc.

And...

Most importantly: self-mastery is teachable.

Which kinda begs a couple of questions.

First: How much time are your kids spending in Self-Mastery class at school?

And: How much time are YOU spending developing YOUR self-mastery?

WARRIORS VS. LIBRARIANS
MOVING FROM THE IVORY TOWER TO THE ARENA OF LIFE

As we've discussed, Donald Robertson is one of the world's leading thinkers and practitioners of Stoic philosophy.

He's written a number of great books including one called *The Philosophy of Cognitive-Behavioral Therapy*, in which he traces the philosophical roots of modern cognitive behavioral therapy to ancient Stoicism.

Donald tells us that the ancient philosophers weren't interested in merely *understanding* how to live optimally, they were committed to actually LIVING optimally.

In fact, he tells us that those ancient philosophers wouldn't recognize a lot of modern philosophers who are often exclusively focused on theoretical ideas in the comforts of their ivory towers.

The old-school philosophers knew it was *really* hard to live in integrity with our highest ideals. They told us we needed to be WARRIORS of the mind, not mere *librarians* of the mind.

To state the obvious: All of these +1°s aren't ideas to be cataloged in the libraries of our minds. These are ideas to be LIVED in the moment-to-moment experiences that determine our destiny.

So… What's ONE idea you've merely cataloged in your mind that you need to take into the arena of your life?

Let's do that.

TODAY.

P.S. As we've discussed a number of times, the metaphor of the warrior winning the battle between their higher and lower selves is present throughout the ancient traditions.

Let's revisit some wisdom from Socrates and Rumi and bring the Buddha in to share his perspective as well.

Socrates put it this way: "I desire only to know the truth, and to live as well as I can... And, to the utmost of my power, I exhort all other men to do the same... I exhort you also to take part in the great combat, which is the combat of life, and greater than every other earthly conflict."

Buddha tells us: "One who conquers himself is greater than another who conquers a thousand times a thousand men on the battlefield."

And Rumi offers: "The lion who breaks the enemy's ranks is a minor hero compared to the lion who overcomes himself."

And, I repeat, even Gandhi's bible, the *Bhagavad Gita*, was set on a battlefield.

Let's win the battle between vice and virtue.

Let's be Heroic warriors of the mind.

Let's move from Theory to Practice to Mastery.

Together.

TODAY.

3 FORMS OF DISCIPLINE
REACTIVE + STRUCTURAL + EXPANSIVE

P hil Stutz tells us we need to develop THREE forms of discipline: reactive discipline, structural discipline and expansive discipline. Here's the quick take on each.

First, we have reactive discipline—which is just what it sounds like. Something triggers you. Can you step in between the stimulus and your habitual, sub-optimal response with the DISCIPLINE to CHOOSE a better response?

Fantastic. That's reactive discipline.

Structural discipline is all about the daily habits that keep us plugged in—that give our lives the "structure" we need to connect to and express the best versions of ourselves.

And, of course, structural discipline is the foundation of that protocol we want to make sure we're executing—ESPECIALLY when we don't feel like it.

Then we have expansive discipline. This, Phil says, is both the most important and the hardest of the three.

EVERY SINGLE MOMENT we have a choice.

Will we step forward into growth or back into safety?

If we want to activate our Heroic potential and have a shot at experiencing all that we're capable of being we must more and more consistently shout, "BRING IT ON!" as we choose to expand, *expand*, **expand**!

In short: We need to make that expansion a discipline.

How about a quick inventory?

How are YOU doing with your reactive discipline? Your structural discipline? And, your expansive discipline?

What's awesome?

What needs work?

What's ONE thing you can do a little differently TODAY?

Here's to your disciplines.

All three of them.

THE MARSHMALLOW TEST
CAN YOU WAIT FOR TWO?

Walter Mischel is one of the world's leading researchers on the science of willpower. You may be familiar with his classic study called The Marshmallow Test.

Here's the quick story: Preschool kids are brought into a simple little room. An adult tells the child that they're going to leave the room for a bit and that she can have ONE treat (a marshmallow or pretzel or other treat) NOW or… If she can wait a little while, she can have TWO treats when the adult comes back into the room.

Then the adult leaves the room and the researchers watch the kids behind a one-way mirror to see what they do.

Some kids immediately go for the one treat while others make it through the twenty minutes to get their two treats.

But here's the fascinating part of the study: Mischel and his team followed those preschool kids for DECADES after that simple little experiment.

To their surprise, the children's low or high delay abilities as a preschooler predicted everything from their SAT scores as an adolescent to their BMI index at thirty years old. (Wow.)

We need to know two things:

1. Willpower is THE "master aptitude." It's the greatest predictor of all the things we want more of in our lives.

2. It's malleable. We just need to practice building it. Good news: That's basically what we're doing with all these +1°s.

P.S. Let's remember: Sometimes, of course, going for that one marshmallow NOW is the wise and enjoyable thing to do. But we want to have the self-control to wait for two when that's the optimal approach.

Here's to +1°ing your willpower/discipline/self-mastery a little more today and enjoying all the treats along the way!

WANT WILLPOWER?
PLAY OFFENSE, NOT DEFENSE

M ost of us wonder how we can have more willpower in those moments of temptation.

But Roy Baumeister—the world's leading expert on will-power—tells us that the people who use their willpower wisely don't actually use it to deal with that many temptations.

When we chatted, Roy told me that willpower exemplars play OFFENSE with their willpower not defense.

How? Let's say you don't want to eat sugary cookies any-more. (Good decision!)

The way to play offense is simple. Never buy the tempting cookies again. You want to, as Tom Rath says, "Buy your willpower at the store" so you don't need to use it at home.

The less effective "defensive" strategy? Buying those cookies and then trying not to eat them.

When are you most likely to eat that junk?

Answer: When you feel the worst and your willpower is at its most depleted state, of course.

That's how you play OFFENSE not defense.

Think about one of your bad habits. Now think about how you could play OFFENSE with your willpower to create an environment where you're simply not exposed to that temptation.

Got it? Fantastic.

Go run your offense and win the ultimate game, Hero.

ODYSSEUS CONTRACTS
RUNNING YOUR WILLPOWER OFFENSE

As we've discussed, willpower out-predicts IQ by a factor of TWO for academic performance.

(Have you fully let that sink in yet? Because when you do, my hunch is you'll dramatically step up your willpower game while figuring out how to teach your kids to do the same.)

We've also discussed the fact that, as per our chat with Roy Baumeister, the best willpower exemplars among us play OFFENSE with their willpower NOT defense.

For our purposes today, I want to connect that idea to a practice researchers call "Odysseus Contracts"—which happens to be one of the best ways to make what scientists call "precommitments" and also happens to be a key component to our willpower offense.

And… The kids and I recently read about Odysseus's encounter with the Sirens so this idea is fresh in my mind.

Here's the quick recap.

After Odysseus spends his *ten* years at the Trojan War, he *almost* gets home to Ithaca before being blown back by the winds. He eventually lands on the island of the goddess Circe who, after turning his men into pigs, winds up advising Odysseus. After sending him to the Land of the Dead to meet with a prophet there, Circe tells Odysseus that he'll have to get by the Sirens— beautiful ladies who sing to sailors as they go by.

Odysseus laughs. How could *they* possibly harm him?

Circe tells him to be VERY careful. Their seductive songs have killed countless sailors; in fact, he'll see bones lying on the shores of their island as he sails by!

Long story a little shorter, do you remember what Circe tells Odysseus to do?

She tells him to put beeswax in his sailors' ears. Now, Odysseus was too stubborn to do that as he *really* wanted to hear the songs so she advised him to have his men tie him to the mast of his ship so he couldn't escape.

THAT, my friends, is playing OFFENSE with your willpower.

Psychologists call those types of commitments "Odysseus Contracts."

You KNOW you will be tempted. So you make a PRECOMMITMENT to a certain course of action.

That's how you avoid the tempting call of the Sirens.

All of which leads us to the point of this +1°.

What Sirens are tempting YOU these days?

Is it your smartphone? Drinking too much? Watching too much TV? Eating too much of a certain food? No shame. We all have our idiosyncratic addictions. What are yours?

And, most importantly, how can you play a little more *offense* and make it a little easier to avoid crashing into the rocks?!

Get on that. Navigate your journey past the Sirens and see you in Ithaca, Hero!

SIRENS
WHAT SONG DO THEY SING TO YOU?

In our last +1° we talked about Odysseus and the contract he made with himself as he navigated past the Sirens.

As we discussed, willpower scientists call precommitment strategies "Odysseus Contracts" in honor of our old-school Hero.

As you may recall, Odysseus tied himself to his mast to avoid heeding the Sirens' seductive songs while his sailors precommitted by plugging their ears with beeswax.

Way to play offense with your willpower, guys!

For this +1°, I want to focus on those Sirens.

Of course, the whole reason Odysseus and his crew needed to be cautious in the first place was because those Sirens had a bad habit of seducing sailors with their songs—leading them to crash right into the rocks. We all know that.

But...

Did you know that the Sirens crafted their songs in such a way that each sailor heard a different tune?

Yep. The Sirens knew each of the sailors' weaknesses and spoke directly to THAT flaw.

All of which begs the questions...

What song do the Sirens sing to YOU that get *you* to crash into the rocks? Is today the day to figure out how you'll safely avoid their seductive call the next time they start singing?

Safe sailing, Hero!

JASON & THE ARGONAUTS
ANOTHER STRATEGY TO DEAL WITH THE SIRENS

Years ago, Emerson and I enjoyed some Greek mythology via *D'Aulaires' Book of Greek Myths*. It was fun to spend some time hanging out with Zeus, Hercules, and some of the other epic gods and goddesses and heroes and monsters.

One of the stories we read was about Jason and his band of merry heroes, the Argonauts. We'll skip the details of their chase for the Golden Fleece and focus on how they got by the Sirens. Their strategy adds yet another approach to our evolving array of ways to deal with our distractions and addictions.

First, quick context/recap.

As you may recall from our previous discussions on Sirens and Odysseus Contracts, Sirens are dangerous creatures.

The Sirens sing such enchanting songs that no mere mortal can resist crashing into the rocks. And, as we discussed, each Siren sings a different tune—one that most seduces that particular sailor. (What song do they sing to YOU?!)

So, as we discussed, willpower scientists tell us that the best way to deal with the temptations of the Sirens is to play OFFENSE with your willpower, not defense. We want to recognize where we get tempted and then, like Odysseus tying himself to the mast after putting beeswax in his men's ears, we precommit to virtuous action and have a much better chance of avoiding danger.

But... Sometimes our offensive plans may not pan out and we need to embrace a good willpower *defense*.

That's when Jason and his Argonauts come in.

They're sailing along. They didn't do any precommitment planning (oops) and find themselves right in the middle of a symphony of Sirens.

What do they do?

Well, thankfully our Heroes have the legendary musician and singer Orpheus on the boat with them. He senses the impending danger and starts playing louder and louder—overpowering the Sirens' songs with his own music.

Voilà. Saved. How's that relate to our lives?

Pema Chödrön comes to mind.

In *The Places that Scare You*, she tells us about a practice she calls "doing something different."

Here's her take on it: "Acknowledging that we are all churned up is the first and most difficult step in any practice. Without compassionate recognition that we are stuck, it's impossible to liberate ourselves from confusion. 'Doing something different' is anything that interrupts our ancient habit of indulging in our emotions. We do anything to cut the strong tendency to spin out… Anything that's non-habitual will do—even sing and dance or run around the block. We do anything that doesn't reinforce our crippling habits. The third most difficult practice is to then remember that this is not something we do just once or twice. Interrupting our destructive habits and awakening our heart is the work of a lifetime."

Yep. That's another *great* way to deal with our bad habits.

Notice that we're starting to go sideways—which is, I repeat, always the first and most difficult step. Then, we want to do something different. ANYTHING that doesn't reinforce our crippling habits.

Our +1°...

Perhaps you can channel Orpheus and sing and dance the next time you find yourself steering toward the rocks?

And, remember. We don't do this once or twice. We're never exonerated. "Interrupting our destructive habits and awakening our heart is the work of a lifetime."

Let's get to work.

Close the gap.

And live with *Areté*.

Today.

BRIGHT LINES
HOW TO MAKE GOOD CONTRACTS WITH YOURSELF

I dropped out of law school before a semester was over but I do remember one big idea from Contracts class.

Lawyers like to say that a contract is a good one when there are "bright lines"—when it's *super* obvious what everyone is agreeing to.

Fuzzy lines? Not so good.

We want super crisp, obvious, BRIGHT lines.

Research scientists borrowed that phrase to describe one of the key attributes of creating good deals with yourself as you architect your ideal life.

They tell us that when we're building new habits, we want to have VERY BRIGHT LINES about what is and what is not acceptable behavior.

For example, when I wanted to quit eating fast food over two decades ago, the fuzzy line I had of "Eat at McDonald's less often" wasn't particularly helpful.

Every time I'd drive by that McDonald's on Wilshire Boulevard on the way home I'd have to ask myself: "Is today the day I get to go there?"

And, when did I go?

On the days when I was feeling the worst, of course.

Then, one day, I got BRIGHT with my lines.

I decided I would NEVER eat at McDonald's again.

Period.

Now, of course, I broke that commitment a few times before it stuck, but—and this is an important distinction!—at least then I *knew* I was breaking a contract with myself.

Eventually I dialed it in and kicked the fast food habit.

I did the same thing with digital news and the iPhone in bed and countless other things.

Fuzzy lines? Didn't help.

100% BRIGHT LINES? Worked like a charm.

So, how about *you*?

What's the #1 bad habit you'd like to get rid of?

How can you move from fuzzy lines to BRIGHT LINES?

Think about that and get on it.

TODAY.

COMMITMENTS: 100% IS A BREEZE
99%? NOT SO MUCH

As per our last +1°, bright lines are super helpful in making deals with ourselves.

Here's another way to look at the same basic idea.

This is from Jack Canfield's classic *The Success Principles*.

Canfield tells us that when we make a commitment to ourselves, we need to know that making a 100% commitment is, somewhat surprisingly, WAY easier than making a 90% or a 97% commitment or even a 99.99% commitment.

There's something about just going absolutely ALL IN on a commitment that saves a ton of energy and makes it way more likely to stick.

Fact is, when we have anything *less* than a total 100% commitment, we've left room for that little whiny voice to come in and start negotiating with ourselves right when we can least afford it and most need to ignore it.

Going back to my last example, when I used to eat fast food and had a less than 100% commitment to not doing it, literally *every* time I'd drive by a McDonald's, I had a conversation with myself about whether I should go or not.

Not wise. Of course, I lost the negotiation on the days when I felt worst and could least afford to go off the rails.

100%!

That commitment is, again, somewhat surprisingly, WAY easier than anything less.

As Canfield says: "Successful people adhere to the 'no exceptions rule' when it comes to their daily disciplines. Once you make a 100% commitment to something, there are no exceptions. It's a done deal. Nonnegotiable. Case closed! Over and out."

So...

To what new habit do you need to make a 100% commitment?

Pick one thing.

(Not 100!)

And give it 100%.

TODAY.

RECOMMITMENT
WHEN YOUR COMMITMENT GETS WOBBLY

We've talked a lot about the importance of making a strong commitment (and precommitment!).

We know that making a 100% commitment is, somewhat paradoxically, way easier than making a 90% or 95% or even a 99.9% commitment.

And ... Even with a strong initial commitment (and the most well-intended and architected precommitments), we're *still* going to fall short of the standards we set for ourselves.

Then what?

Then we pick ourselves up, dust ourselves off, and RECOMMIT.

Think of it like this ...

Imagine an airplane. Let's say we're flying from Los Angeles to Tokyo. The pilots have (obviously) made a 100% commitment to getting us there on time and safely. And they've precommitted to a certain flight path and all that.

But guess what?

Although they have clarity on their ultimate destination and they're committed to getting there, they're also OFF TRACK *most* of the trip. The wind blows them a little this way. They drift a little that way.

No big deal. Slight adjustment. Back on track.

Again and again and again.

That's how we want to approach this.

Step 1. Get clear on where we're headed. We need to know our destination so we can fulfill our destiny.

Step 2. Commit. 100%. (Provided it passes your WOOP test, of course. Otherwise, keep WOOPing till you arrive at something worthy of your commitment!)

Step 3. Take action. A lot of it. Diligently. Patiently. Persistently.

Step 4. Recommit when you inevitably lose that initial burst of commitment.

Repeat.

Until you arrive at your destination.

Then start again.

YOUR DREAMER & YOUR DOER
HAVE BOTH IN MIND TODAY

Barry Michels wrote both *The Tools* and *Coming Alive* with Phil Stutz. Today we're going to chat about an incredible idea he shared with me in one of our chats.

It's all about the relationship between what he calls your "Dreamer" and your "Doer."

First, a little context.

The essence of *Coming Alive* is the fact that there's an eternal battle going on within you between the best version of you and the not-so-great version of you.

Phil and Barry came up with a name for that part of us that's constantly getting in the way.

They call it "Part X."

Part X is the voice that's *constantly* telling you what's impossible. "No, you can't fulfill that dream. Or that one. Nope, can't break that habit or build that one." Etc. Etc. Etc.

Now, one of the best ways to deal with Part X is to get *really* good at doing the little things *really* well. And, to STOP doing the little *bad* things you know aren't good for you.

In one of our interviews, Barry said that, although we might not see the connection, self-restraint is what creates true confidence. For a couple reasons.

First, if you don't have self-restraint and you allow yourself to get carried away by every impulse you have, you never know when your life is going to go off the rails. (Right?)

Second, if you don't have the discipline to do what you say is important, you never know if you'll actually follow through on the big dreams you have. (Right?)

That's where the Dreamer and the Doer come in.

Your Dreamer is the version of you that can see your infinite potential. It KNOWS you can do so much more than you're currently doing.

Your Doer is the part of you that actually DOES the things that are best for you.

Here's the deal: Your Dreamer needs to be able to trust your Doer. Your Dreamer needs to know that when it says you need to do certain things to activate your Heroic potential, that your Doer will actually do those things.

To put it directly: If your Dreamer doesn't have that trust in your Doer, you won't have (and SHOULDN'T have) the confidence you need to do what you're here to do.

I repeat yet again: The word *confidence* literally means "intense trust." In this case, we're talking about trust between your Dreamer and your Doer.

Here's the way Barry tells us to operationalize that wisdom: At every choice point today (yes, EVERY), ask your Doer if the Dreamer will appreciate what you're about to do.

That's it. Moment to moment to moment. We're either Doing the things our Dreamer will appreciate or not.

Here's the one-word plan to help your Doer high five your Dreamer today...

Areté.

HARD TO EASY
GOETHE ON SNAPPING & POOPING IN THE TOILET

According to Wikipedia, Johann Wolfgang von Goethe was "a German poet, playwright, novelist, scientist, statesman, theatre director, and critic."

According to the Heroic quote art Alexandra put on our fridge, he once said: "Everything is hard before it's easy."

And… That's what I thought of when Emerson came into my office not too long ago and told me he wanted to learn how to snap his fingers.

Him: "How do you make a sound when you rub your fingers together?"

Me: "You mean this… *SNAP*!!!"

Him: "YES!"

Me: "Well, you go like this and then do that and *SNAP*!"

Him: "That's really hard to do!"

Me: "Of course it is! Until it's not! Remember… Everything is hard before it's easy, right?!"

Him: "Yep!"

Me: "So… How are you going to get good at it?"

Him: "PRACTICE!"

Me: "EXACTLY."

Fast forward to the end of the day and…

Him: "*SNAP! SNAP! SNAP!*"

The little guy's fingers were sore from practicing so much (hah!) but he could snap.

Then we talked about ALL THE OTHER things that were super hard before they were super easy.

Whistling. Carving. Reading. Writing. Not sucking his thumb. Pooping in the toilet.

Our +1°…

Spotlight on YOU.

Is anything currently "hard" in your life?

Perfect. WOOP it and decide whether or not you are willing to pay the price to make it happen then… Get to work.

Remember: "Everything is hard before it's easy."

COMMAND & OBEY
NIETZSCHE SAYS: WILL IS THE JOY BRINGER

I have an old-school Timex Ironman watch on my desk.

It's set to beep at me every sixteen minutes and forty seconds (1,000 seconds).

That beep is my prompt/cue/trigger to stand up and, if I haven't done one hundred burpees yet, bang out a set of eleven burpees.

And…

That 1,000-second timer went off about ninety seconds before I started typing this. It's 7:15 in the morning. I just finished my meditation and first thirty minutes of Deep Work on this book.

So, I got up and, as I did my third set of eleven burpees for the day, Nietzsche's wisdom popped into my head.

In *Thus Spoke Zarathustra*, he tells us: "He who cannot command himself should obey. And many can command themselves, but much is still lacking before they can obey themselves."

As I banged out my burpees, I silently chanted to myself:

"COMMAND *and* OBEY."

"COMMAND *and* OBEY."

"COMMAND *and* OBEY."

Know this: It's one thing to tell ourselves to do something. It's an *entirely* different and infinitely more important thing to actually DO that thing.

Which is why Nietzsche *also* said: "Will—that is the name of the liberator and the joy bringer."

Mastering our will is the ONLY possible way we can achieve *another* one of his dictums: "I must perfect myself."

So…

What's ONE thing YOU KNOW you *could* be doing that, if you *started* doing it consistently, would *most positively* impact your life?

Got it?

Awesome.

It's time to (re-)commit to doing it.

And…

Much more importantly…

It's time to DO IT.

It's time to Command AND Obey.

Here's to perfecting ourselves and remembering that will is the name of the liberator and the joy bringer.

Let's move from Theory to Practice to Mastery.

Together.

TODAY.

FLOORS & CEILINGS
HOW TO BE AN IMPERFECTIONIST

Stephen Guise wrote a great little book called *How to Be an Imperfectionist*. As a still-recovering perfectionist, I found it very useful.

Stephen tells us that most of us with high standards set very aggressive goals.

Now, this is a VERY good thing as having high standards in life is a key aspect to living an extraordinary life.

But...

Those high standards can quickly work against us (and paralyze us) if we aren't careful.

So...

Here's one way to deal with it.

We want to have our "everything-goes-perfectly" goals AND we want to have a basic, "let's-make-sure-we-hit-this-target" goal.

Stephen calls that having a "floor" and a "ceiling."

You have your basic, let's-make-sure-this-happens floor. And then you have your everything-goes-perfectly ceiling.

You live happily between the two of those.

Know this: If your floor EQUALS your ceiling then you're in trouble. Where's the space to live in that world?

Answer: There ISN'T any space to live.

When your floor IS your ceiling, you get suffocated by

do-or-die standards and run the risk of falling into the perfectionist's procrastination trap of not doing ANYTHING.

Floors and ceilings.

How are yours?

CUCUMBERS & PICKLES
YOUR BRAIN ON ADDICTION

A dam Alter wrote a great book called *Irresistible* in which he walks us through how we become addicted to technology and tells us about the businesses built on hacking our brains to capture our attention and create those addictions.

It's a powerful read and goes nicely with the must-see *60 Minutes* special on *Brain Hacking*.

One of my favorite ideas from the book was about cucumbers and pickles.

Specifically, it was a line from an addiction recovery therapist. She told her patients: "Remember, once your brain has been pickled, it can never go back to being a cucumber."

That's a REALLY powerful line.

Once you've become addicted to something (and we ALL have our own little and big addictions), your brain has fundamentally changed.

It's as if our brain went from being a *cucumber* in that domain to being PICKLED. And, you know what? You can't UNPICKLE a pickle. Once your cucumber brain is pickled, it's pickled.

What's that mean, practically speaking?

Well, take a moment to think of one of your addictions. (And, as you do, remember our three-part lesson on The Science of Self-Compassion, starting with common humanity. Again, nothing's wrong with you. We ALL have issues. Welcome to humanity.)

So…

Got it? Good.

Now get this: You may THINK that you can completely move past your addiction in that area, but, confronting fact: You can't.

Your brain has been pickled.

And, you (and I and everyone) need to have a deep respect for that fact. It's a slippery slope right back into that toxic addiction pond.

Note: 100% commitments are super helpful here.

Adam also tells us that the most dangerous time for someone recovering from addiction is the moment they feel that they've beaten it.

Then? They forget the pickle and dip their toe back into their addictive behavior and… BAM. Oops. Slipped into the toxic pond.

So… Know where your pickle jars are.

And… Don't open them up.

ACTIVE LOVE
HOW TO GET OUT OF A MENTAL MAZE

Have you ever found yourself REALLY upset with some-one—replaying whatever they did that annoyed you OVER and OVER and OVER again in your head?

Phil Stutz and Barry Michels call that being caught in "The Maze."

They have a Tool to deal with it.

They call it "Active Love."

Here's how to practice it: The first step, as always (!), is to *notice* that you're off.

Note: Because *noticing* when we're off is SO IMPORTANT to the process, we want to (a) train our ability to notice when we're off and (b) get EXCITED about detecting this disconnection.

Then take a deep breath and imagine your energy going from your head (where you've been running around in a mental maze of negativity) to your heart.

Smile gently.

Take another deep breath to focus your energy into your heart region.

Then think of some awesome things about the person who is currently annoying you. You can also send compassion for the challenges they may be facing.

Then imagine beaming them love.

If you feel so inspired, really get into it and see energy shining right out of your heart and into the world toward them.

That's Active Love.

It's a powerful tool.

I highly recommend you give it a try the next time you find yourself caught in a mental Maze.

GOT A NEGATIVE THOUGHT?
DRIVE IT OUT WITH A POSITIVE ONE

T he great meditation teacher Eknath Easwaran has his own "Active Love" practice.

In *Conquest of Mind*, he tells us: "To give one small illustration, whenever somebody is unkind to me, I can immediately unroll the panorama of that person's good qualities. Instantly the balance is set right. As with most skills, this is a matter of practice. When you are having trouble getting along with someone, a simple first step is to sit down quietly and recall how many times that person has given you support. You are using positive memories to drive out negative ones before they have a chance to crowd together and form a mob, which is all resentment really is."

Brilliant.

He also makes the point by telling us: "The first strategy is literally 'changing one thought for another': a negative thought for a positive one, an unkind thought for a kind one. 'Just as a carpenter uses a small peg to drive out a bigger one,' the Buddha says, 'you can use a right thought to drive out one that is wrong.'"

Got a negative thought?

Drive it out with a positive one.

NOW WHAT NEEDS TO BE DONE?
REMEMBER: FEELINGS FOLLOW BEHAVIOR

David Reynolds wrote what might be the best book you (and most other people) have never heard of.

It's called *Constructive Living*.

David is a sort of East meets West Zen psychotherapist. (He was a huge influence on Dan Millman, who recommended I read the book years ago.)

The main theme of the book is that feelings FOLLOW behavior.

Most of us get that backward.

David tells us that most people ask themselves "How do I *feel*?" before they do anything and then they let *that* dictate what they do.

Not good.

The fact is (and science confirms this) that feelings FOLLOW behavior at least as much as the other way around.

Just simply getting yourself to take action CREATES the feelings you thought needed to be there to get you started.

David tells us that the most profound sense of confidence comes from being the type of person who can get him or herself to do what needs to get done whether they *feel* like it or not.

He gives us a very practical question to use in those moments when we're not quite feeling our best but need to act like we are.

It's super simple. And, in my experience, equally powerful. Here it is:

"Now what needs to be done?"

That's it. Doesn't matter how we feel. We just need to ask that question.

"Now what needs to be done?"

And then, of course, we need to do it.

In a moment of wavering commitment, ask yourself that remarkably simple yet equally powerful question.

And then do it.

TODAY.

P.S. That question is truly one of THE most powerful ways to close the gap and live with *Areté*.

Remember...

"Now what needs to be done?"

"Now what needs to be done?"

"Now what needs to be done?"

TEFLON VS. VELCRO
WE'RE WIRED TO HOLD ON TO NEGATIVE STUFF

Rick Hanson is a leading neuroscientist and mindfulness teacher who has written a number of great books including *Buddha's Brain* and *Hardwired for Happiness*.

In *Buddha's Brain* he tells us that our brains evolved to focus on the negative. He says that our brains are basically like Velcro for the negative and like Teflon for the positive.

Why?

Well, the good stuff is nice (and science shows how important it is) but, back in the day, the "bad" stuff could literally kill us.

That place where the saber-tooth tiger nearly got us? Yah. Better remember that.

Now, evolutionarily speaking, it made sense to be wired to hold on to the negative. It's our ancestors who paid attention to the stuff that could kill them that lived long enough to pass on their genes.

But these days it's easy to get locked into a negative mode all day every day if we bombard ourselves with news and toxic social media posts.

So…

Our +1° has three parts.

#1. Notice how quickly you can get wrapped up in the negative Velcro. And how sticky it can be in your mind once you're in it. (See it?)

#2. Eliminate one unnecessary source of negativity from your life. (What's on the way out?)

#3. Incline your mind to joy (as Rick would say) by thinking of one awesome thing in your life. (What's awesome?)

Here's to taking a nice, deep, relaxing breath as we release (at least) one saber-tooth tiger from our minds back out into the wild.

TODAY.

PARENTING: 3 TIPS
LESSONS ON HOW TO BE A GREAT DAD

After a keynote I gave to a group of venture capitalists and entrepreneurs in Los Angeles, one of the CEOs came up and asked me how to apply the wisdom I shared to his parenting.

Then another guy who was also waiting to connect said: "I'd love to hear your thoughts on that as well."

I was struck by how inspiring it was that these super-successful and ambitious guys were so committed to being great dads.

So… First, I briefly told them about the etymology of the word *parent*. The word means "to bring forth." I told them that, from my perspective, our primary job as parents is to help *bring forth* and help activate the latent (Heroic!) potential within our kids.

Then I shared three things that I think are the most powerful ways to help bring forth that awesomeness. Here's a quick take.

#1. Be an exemplar.

It's a truism, but kids don't listen to what we tell them to do, they model what we ACTUALLY do. Therefore, the most important thing we can do for our kids is to be a demonstration of what we hope they will aspire to be.

Important note: This is, by far, my greatest motivation as a human being, a man, and a father.

#2. Give presence.

The second thing I shared is also ridiculously obvious: be present. As often as possible, put your smartphone in airplane mode in another room when you spend time with your kids (and your spouse and, well, any human).

This simple act removes the greatest barrier to our presence and provides the fastest route to both connecting with our kids and modeling the style of connection (see #1 on being an exemplar) that will be so important for our kids in a more and more hyper-connected (yet paradoxically disconnected) world.

#3. Embrace challenges.

The third thing we talked about was the importance of embracing what Carol Dweck calls a growth mindset. Her book *Mindset* has been my go-to playbook for parenting. I HIGHLY recommend it. I've been *very* deliberate in following Dweck's advice to embrace challenges and always reward EFFORT not "ability."

For example, on the effort front, I say things like: "Nice trail running!" rather than "You're a great trail runner!" Or: "I saw how hard you worked to climb up that slide—and that you almost fell then caught yourself and kept on going. Love how hard you tried!" rather than "You're such a great climber!"

On the challenges front, Dweck tells us to talk about our own challenges and how we're facing them. She encourages us to "rub our hands together" with excitement when things are hard. I'm ALL ABOUT this. I literally rub my hands together any time something is challenging (on the most mundane things) and say, "Oh, wow! I love challenges."

Or when I watch the kids do something hard—whether that's build a Lego set or play a tough opponent in chess—I say: "AWE-SOME. That one's challenging. How fun!"

It's almost surreal how much the kids have embraced this. Emerson once asked his nanny: "Do you love challenges? I DO!"

So...

Back to me and the two dads.

And YOU and our +1°...

If you're a parent, what's working? What needs work? What are YOUR Top Three all-time most powerful parenting practices? What, *specifically*, can you do to bring forth the best in yourself and *your* kids?

Let's create the strength for two as we do the hard work to activate our and our kids' Heroic potential.

TODAY.

BALLET, ANYONE?
HEAD THREADS, POWER POSES & THOR'S HAMMER

Right after that chat with the dads, I had a fascinating chat with a woman who was a former Russian ballet dancer.

She told me that one of the first things she noticed when I began my presentation was my posture. It reminded her of one of the most important, fundamental lessons she learned as a ballerina: to simultaneously go *up* AND go *down*.

She said I did that so well that I looked like I could be a ballet dancer. To which I said: "Thank you!"

Important note: As flattering as her kind words were, I can assure you that I am neither a ballet dancer nor a dancer of any kind. Just ask my wife and kids. (Hah.)

With that out of the way, here are three tips to optimize our posture: Head Threads, Power Poses, and Thor's Hammer.

First, Head Threads.

Once upon a time, I studied the Alexander Technique on a tiny island in Greece. One of the main aspects of that training is to imagine having a thread that runs from the base of your spine all the way through the top of your head.

To create a dignified posture, we want to *gently* pull that thread *up*—lengthening (and widening) our spine. Practice doing that when you sit, when you stand, when you walk. All day every day. This is one of the keys to grace and poise.

Then we have Power Poses.

Although some of the details of her research have been

debated over the years, in her great book, *Presence*, Amy Cuddy (who was also a ballerina, by the way) tells us that one of the fastest ways to feel powerful is to strike a "power pose."

Basic idea: How does the best, most Heroic version of yourself sit and stand and walk? Act like that NOW.

Channel your inner Superman or Wonder Woman. When you sit. When you stand. When you walk. All day every day. Experts in this field of research say that this is one of the most effective ways to cultivate our presence and power.

Get this: Even blind athletes, who have never seen anyone else do it, will strike that victorious "V!" pose with arms triumphantly up in the air when they win a race.

Finally, we have Thor's Hammer.

Eric Goodman is one of the world's leading biomechanics experts. He wrote a book called *True to Form*. You know who wrote the foreword to his book?

Thor! Well, technically, it was Chris Hemsworth, but he attributes his superpowers to Eric's wisdom.

Every time I flip the switch to invite the best, most Heroic version of myself to join the party, I have Eric's voice in my head. He tells us that the fastest way to assume a proper (and powerful!) posture is simple: "Chest up. Chin down."

Try it now. Then do it all day. Every day. "Chest up. Chin down." Thor says: It does a Hero good.

That's our +1°. Let's (literally!) embody the idea of buoyancy by simultaneously having *levity* and *gravity*.

Remember: Head Threads. Power Poses. Thor's Hammer. Flip the switch. LET'S GO!

RELENTLESS SOLUTION FOCUS
60 SECONDS OF WHINING & THEN YOU'RE ON!

Jason Selk is one of the world's leading mental toughness coaches. He tells us that the best among us have a "relentless solution focus."

Note: RELENTLESS solution focus.

Here's the game he tells his elite athletes (and executives) to play: When something goes sideways, give yourself sixty seconds (that's it! Sixty seconds!) to feel bad about it, blame someone for it, etc.

Sixty seconds.

Tick tock. Tick tock. Tick tock.

DING!

Whining over.

Now, it's time to find a SOLUTION to your problem.

You don't need to solve the whole thing—and you shouldn't try to. Just find one TINY (!) thing you can do right now that would move you forward in a positive, constructive direction.

Relentless. Solution. Focus.

As in, I repeat: R E L E N T L E S S.

Let's do a quick check in with the dictionary:
relentless |rəˈlen(t)ləs| *adjective*
oppressively constant; incessant

Our +1°...

What's your #1 stressor right now?

Give yourself sixty seconds to whine.

Starting now...

And...

Time's up!

What's one little thing you can do RIGHT NOW to improve the situation by 1%?

Get on that and activate your Heroic potential.

DUST
A SECRET TOOL TO MASTER NON-ATTACHMENT

L et's chat about something called "Dust."

It's a secret tool I learned from Phil several years ago.

Basic context: Remember Apollo, our patron god of philosophy? He was an archer. Like him, we need to have a clear target at which we're aiming our life force. We're ALL IN on hitting the next target and, somewhat paradoxically, we're simultaneously not attached to hitting it.

We focus on choosing our target wisely and on shooting the arrow straight. Then we let go of any attachment to outcomes.

Obviously easier said than done.

This tool helps us master that fully-engaged yet non-attached focus. Here it is.

Imagine going to a Hollywood movie premiere. You're on the red carpet. You make your way to the bright lights where you pose and get your picture taken. Congrats. You've made it. Everyone loves you. You're a star!

Now, imagine going to an old decrepit house in the middle of nowhere. It's been abandoned for who knows how long. You make your way up into the attic. It's covered in *inches* of dust. Pick up a handful of that dust. And THROW IT ON THE BRIGHT LIGHTS from the prior scene.

Dust.

Why would we want to use that tool?

Well, one of our greatest challenges is thinking that something outside of us can E V E R make us feel a certain way.

Those bright lights? They symbolize something outside of you that has you hooked, that has you convinced that you need those external bright lights to make you happy.

Throw dust on those lights. Take control. Stand up tall and proud and strong and know that you are the ultimate arbiter of what matters. *Nothing* outside of you can shake you or disconnect you from the highest within.

When I find myself getting a little too attached to an outcome (or someone's opinion of me), I imagine leaning down in that attic, picking up a big handful of dust and throwing it on the object of my attachment.

I literally squeeze my hand around the imaginary dust and then make a throwing motion as I open my hand to release it.

I smile every time I (remember to) do that. It immediately dislodges my attention from the source of attachment. My power is back and I'm focused on this moment astonishingly quickly and easily.

Dust.

Need to sprinkle some on anything?

YOU, A FARMER & HIS HORSE
A ZEN FABLE ON GOOD & BAD LUCK

O nce upon a time in a land far away, there was an old farmer. This man had a horse. One day his horse ran away.

All the neighbors said: "Gah! What bad luck."

The man said: "Maybe. It is what it is."

Then, one day, the horse returned. And, lo and behold, the horse brought along a bunch of wild stallions with him.

All the neighbors said: "Wow. What good luck!"

The man said: "Maybe. It is what it is."

At this point in the story, I should mention that the man also had a son. This son was pretty excited about the new horses. Especially one particularly wild stallion he wanted to train.

So, he hops up on the horse and, WHAM! He gets slammed to the ground and breaks his leg.

All the neighbors said: "Ohhhhhhhhh, man! What bad luck. I can't believe that happened. Now your son can't work the fields. That's *really* bad."

The man said: "Maybe. It is what it is."

Then one day, the army came marching into the small village. There was a war and the king demanded that all able-bodied young men join them in their battle. Our man's son with the broken leg was spared.

All the neighbors said: "Wow. Your son has been saved! What good luck."

The man said …

Well, at this stage you know what the man said.

Here's the +1° check in …

How do YOU respond to life's events?

Is it all either "good" or "bad?"

Or, perhaps, is it just what it is?

P.S. Shakespeare must have had this Zen story in mind when he had Hamlet say that "there is nothing either good or bad, but thinking makes it so."

MAKE THE CONNECTION
WHAT'S WORKING? WHAT NEEDS WORK?

I f you were a fly on the wall in the Johnson house, you'd hear us using the phrase "make the connection" quite a bit with our kids.

For example, our son Emerson really doesn't like to get sick. Thankfully, he's never had an antibiotic and the worst he's experienced is a fever or a runny nose/cold, etc.

But, and I type this with a smile, he *really* doesn't like having a runny nose. At all. I love it because I love having the opportunity to help him *make the connection* between things he does and outcomes he experiences as a result.

We've done this so many times that he now coaches himself (and me!).

Emerson when he gets a runny nose: "Hmmm… That little cupcake at the coffee shop with grandma might not have been a great idea and then I forgot to wash my hands after playing at the park."

Me: "Ah. Yes, that might be it!"

Then we might "needs work" it and talk about what we could have done differently.

Our +1°…

Have any little hiccups in your life recently?

Can you *make the connection* between your behavior and the outcome?

What's working? What needs work?

Make the connection.

Make the connection.

Make the connection.

And have fun activating your Heroic potential.

TODAY.

FINGERS & LECTURES
REMEMBER: ATTEND YOUR OWN LECTURES

Please extend your pointer finger and shake it as if you're lecturing someone—saying something like: "You shouldn't do
this, this, and this! Do that, that, and that!"

Thank you. Now, look at your hand and count how many
fingers are pointing at the person you're lecturing and how many
fingers are pointing back at you.

Unless you're missing a digit, you should see one finger pointing at the lucky recipient of your lecture and THREE fingers
pointing back at you.

You may want to pay attention to that the next time you're
lecturing someone.

Debbie Ford tells us that this practice is a powerful way to
notice our "shadow"—the stuff we haven't integrated in our own
lives that, unfortunately, we tend to project onto others.

She tells us to "attend our own lectures" because, more often
than not, whatever lecture we're giving someone else is the one
WE desperately need to attend.

The +1°…

The next time you start telling someone all the things you
think *they* need to start doing more of or less of or whatever,
imagine you're a student diligently taking notes on the lecture
you're giving.

You might just find that the lecture you're giving *them* is what
YOU most need to hear.

CHILD-PROOF YOUR TRIGGER BUTTONS
ANNOYED? ASK: HOW AM I THAT?

While we're on the subject of attending our own lectures and dealing with some of our dis-integrated shadow issues, let's talk about a great idea from *The Power of Full Engagement*.

Jim Loehr and Tony Schwartz give us a fun little game we can play today.

Think of someone who's recently annoyed you.

Got it? Now…

Identify what it is about them that *really* annoyed you.

Are they impatient? Grumpy? Do they cut people off mid-sentence and never really listen? Not showing up with 100% intensity? Do they act like they know it all?

What, SPECIFICALLY, is it about them that irritates you so much?

Got it? Fantastic.

Now, ask yourself: "How am I that?!?"

And make that a practice. What you'll notice, if you're like me, is that we tend to be most annoyed by people who are demonstrating qualities that we're still working on.

Debbie Ford says it's kinda like having electrical sockets on our chest. If we've recognized and accepted our own greed / selfishness / impatience / whatever, it's as if we've put one of those child-proof covers over the socket and no one can "plug into" that energy—we may notice a certain quality in people but we're no longer *triggered* by them.

BUT...

Run into someone who demonstrates qualities we *haven't* integrated in our lives and yikes!

They "plug into" that open socket and we find ourselves shockingly (pun intended) frustrated.

Again, the solution is (relatively) simple: Notice when you're being super critical of other people and know that you're just observing something within YOU that you need to address.

Then celebrate the opportunity to grow as you count how many fingers are pointing back at you, attend your own lectures, and ask: "How am I that?!"

Then get to work NOT being like that.

THE WORSE A PERSON IS
THE LESS THEY FEEL IT

A couple thousand years ago, Seneca said: "The worse a person is the less he feels it."

Think about that for a moment...

"The worse a person is the less he feels it."

Guess what?

This corollary follows that truth: The worse a person is the less they feel it. And... The worse they are, the less they want to hear about it from YOU! (Hah.)

AND... The worse a person is, the more they're going to see the *worst* in YOU—which leads us to one of my favorite gems from Marcus Aurelius.

In *Meditations*, he tells us: "The approval of such men, who do not even stand well in their own eyes, has no value for him."

Translation: If someone doesn't even like THEMSELVES, why would I care whether or not they like ME?

Say it with me now...

The worse a person is, the less they feel it. And, the worse the person is, the less they're going to like themselves (whether they're aware of it or not).

And... The less they like themselves, the less they're going to like anyone else.

THEREFORE...

"The approval of such men, who do not even stand well in their own eyes, has no value for him."

Epictetus had something to say on the subject as well.

Here's how he playfully puts it: "Who are these people whose admiration you seek? Aren't they the ones you are used to describing as mad? Well, then, is that what you want—to be admired by lunatics?"

Let's keep that wisdom in mind today.

While you're at it, before we get too self-righteous, don't forget to flip it around.

Know this: The worse YOU feel, the more *you* are going to see the WORST in others.

So, if you're getting impatient and rude with the people around you, you might want to check in and see how you're feeling about YOURSELF.

Then recommit to doing the little things that help you stay humbly plugged in, dear Hero.

THE SPACE
BETWEEN STIMULUS & RESPONSE

Viktor Frankl was a remarkable human being.

He was a leading psychotherapist before suffering the horrors of Nazi concentration camps. He alchemized those experiences into an even deeper understanding of human behavior that he shared in the form of the therapeutic approach he developed called Logotherapy.

Frankl captured the essence of that philosophy in his must-read book *Man's Search for Meaning.*

Two interesting historical facts on that book before we get into the +1° wisdom.

First, Frankl wrote what became one of the world's greatest books in *nine* successive days shortly after his liberation.

Second, he originally intended to publish the book anonymously—using only his prison number (Number 119104) rather than his name. He had no intention to make it a "bestseller" and only reluctantly agreed to put his name on it as he felt that was important to have the impact he desired.

Now… One of the key ideas in his book (and philosophy) is the importance of recognizing our freedom to CHOOSE our response to any given situation.

As Frankl says: "Everything can be taken from a man but one thing; the last of the human freedoms—to choose one's attitude in any given set of circumstances, to choose one's own way."

Related to that wisdom is this: "Between stimulus and response there is a space. In that space is our power to choose our response. In our response lies our growth and our freedom."

Know this…

There's a GAP between a stimulus and our response.

In THAT (!!!) space is our power to choose our optimal response. In that response lies our opportunity to grow and to step into the next-best version of ourselves.

Stimulus. Space. Response.

( ) — ( )

So…

What "stimulus" is getting you triggered these days? What sub-optimal "response" needs some work?

Step into the space between that stimulus and response. Step forward into your growth.

Live with *Areté*.

Moment to moment to moment.

TODAY.

HOW TO 100,000X YOUR PERFORMANCE
2 AI'S & 100 ALGORITHMS

R ay Dalio is one of the most influential (and wealthiest) people on the planet. In his great book *Principles*, he walks us through HOW he created his success and wealth.

In addition to embracing his weaknesses and learning from his mistakes while executing his Five-Step Process to Get What You Want in Life, Dalio also used some Artificial Intelligence to achieve his extraordinary success.

In Principle 5.11, he tells us to "Convert your principles into algorithms and have the computer make decisions alongside you."

He tells us that if we combine human intelligence with machine intelligence, we can increase our efficiency and effectiveness by 100,000.

In Dalio's case, he created a supercomputer that comes astonishingly close to predicting markets—close enough to make him and his clients billions of dollars.

How'd he do that? Well, in addition to feeding tens of millions of pieces of data into that supercomputer of his, he wrote some algorithms.

What's an algorithm?

He gives us a super-simple example.

Imagine you want to keep your house at 68 degrees. What do you do? You set your thermostat with a simple if-then algorithm.

If it's less than 68 degrees and it's not between midnight to 5 a.m., then turn on the heater.

That's the easiest way to leverage the power of "Artificial Intelligence." And, again, when you do that enough times, you create HUGE efficiencies.

But I think there's another AI that's even more powerful for our Heroic activation purposes: Ancient Intelligence.

Rewind 500 million years ago when the basal ganglia showed up in vertebrates. Our basal ganglia is basically what helps us put certain behaviors on autopilot.

Programming our Ancient Intelligence to let THAT supercomputer run the show is the secret sauce to activating our Heroic potential.

Psychologists would agree.

They *also* tell us that we need to write algorithms, only they call them "Implementation Intentions."

Same basic model: If this, then that.

With that in mind ... Let's do some AI programming.

Step 1. Decide you want to activate your Heroic potential.

Step 2. Start programming your supercomputer.

Here are a few of the simple "if-then" implementation intention algorithms I've installed in MY life:

If I wake up in the morning, then I meditate and do Deep Work before going online.

If my thousand-second timer goes off while I'm working, then I stand up and move my body.

If I feel fear then I say, "Bring it on!" and do what needs to get done.

If the sun goes down, then all electronics go off.

If this … then that. Let's create a non-stop Heroic-AI party all day every day. That's the ultimate use of the ultimate AI.

As Dalio says, traditional AI programming can increase productivity 100,000-fold. Here's how I do that math with our Ancient Intelligence.

If you can make a decision to do the optimal thing ONCE, then you save the effort (and enormous amount of willpower) of deciding 1,000+ times.

If you make 100 wise decisions like that then you just increased your optimizing efficiency 100,000-fold.

I say we do that. In fact, in our Heroic Coach program, we challenge you (and help you) to create one hundred micro-algorithms.

Let's start by spending a minute or three thinking about the #1 algorithm you could install TODAY that would most positively improve your life.

What is it?

While you ponder that, know this …

The #1 most powerful algorithm we could ever install?

If I'm alive, then I will strive to close the gap between who I'm *capable* of *being* and who I'm *actually* being.

In a word … *Areté.*

P.S. One of the reasons Dalio loves working with his computer is that, unlike humans, it's unemotional. It just does what it's programmed to do. That's why we need to program our AI. On those days when we're feeling the worst, we need to let our well-programmed supercomputer run the show.

UPERSIST!
HOW TO BE UNSTOPPABLE

Alden Mills is a former Navy SEAL who wrote a great little book called *Be Unstoppable*. I read it years ago with Emerson. And, now that I type that, I realize I need to re-read it with both Emerson *and* Eleanor.

It's a fantastic parable about a young captain who meets a wise, older mentor-captain who teaches him how to activate his Heroic potential to become a "Master and Commander."

Emerson and I loved it.

The Master Captain (who goes by Persistent Pete), has eight actions he teaches his young protégé.

The actions form the acronym **UPERSIST**.

Emerson can rattle each of the eight actions off.

#1. **U**nderstand Your Why

#2. **P**lan

#3. **E**nergize to Execute

#4. **R**ecognize Your Reason to Believe in Yourself

#5. **S**urvey Your Habits

#6. **I**mprovise to Overcome Obstacles

#7. **S**eek Expert Advice

#8. **T**eam Up!

Time for the +1° spotlight on you…

Do **UPERSIST**?! Let's do a quick check in.

First: What's your #1 goal these days? It ALL starts with an inspiring goal that's firing you up, Hero!

Now for a quick inventory on those eight actions...

#1. What's your why?

#2. How's your plan?

#3. You energized?

#4. What reasons do you have to believe in yourself?

#5. How are your habits?

#6. You improvising to overcome obstacles?

#7. Need to seek advice from any experts?

#8. How can you team up a little more today?

There ya go.

A super-quick take on how to *Be Unstoppable*.

Go get the book and read it with your kids if you feel so inspired and remember...

WEPERSIST!

"NEGU!"
NEVER EVER GIVE UP

Let's chat about another fun idea from Alden Mills's great little fable on how to *Be Unstoppable!*

We actually made it the "9th Action" in the Johnson house to go along with UPERSIST. (Even Eleanor likes to shout it!)

It's another acronym. Here it is: **NEGU!**

Imagine a tiny little, almost-two-year-old Hero in training shouting "**NEGU!**" with her six-year-old brother and you have a glimpse into what's often going on in the Johnson House.

(Hah. That's definitely like us!)

"**NEGU!**" "**NEGU!**" "**NEGU!**"

NEGU?

Yes. "**NEGU!**"

As in: **N**ever. **E**ver. **G**ive. **U**p.

"**NEGU!**"

One of the reasons Emerson loved the book so much was that Alden represented this little handy-dandy Heroic mantra via a funny little statue in the book featuring a frog being eaten by a pelican but somehow reaching out of the pelican's mouth and grabbing it by the neck before it could eat him.

Ridiculous, I know. But... **NEGU!**

P.S. Are there times when you *should* "give up?" Of course. But, that's not the point of this +1°.

This is: One more time (say it with us): **NEGU!**

THE 5 SECOND RULE
5... 4... 3... 2... 1... BLASTOFF!

M el Robbins gave one of the most popular TEDx Talks in history. Over 50 million people have watched her talk called: *"How to stop screwing yourself over."*

She also wrote a super-popular book called *The 5 Second Rule*.

Now, I still haven't watched the TED Talk yet (I read books, folks) but I did happen to grab Alexandra's copy of this book off the kitchen counter before she had a chance to read it after she gave me the quick overview.

It's fantastic.

Basic idea: In any given moment (especially the ones that really matter—which are all of them), we pretty much always know what we *should* do. But, as you may have noticed, we often fail to DO what we *know* we *should* do.

Ever happen to you? (Hah.)

Which kinda begs the question: What gets in the way?

Mel tells us (and leading philosophers and scientists agree) that we think too much.

We check in on how we "feel" about doing whatever it is that needs to get done and, lo and behold, we go from inspired (albeit perhaps nervous) clarity to doing nothing in a matter of moments. In less than five seconds, to be precise.

Here's a little more backstory, then the practical application for this +1°.

Mel tells us that at forty-one, her life was falling apart. She was drinking too much, struggling in her marriage, and struggling with her finances. It was so bad she didn't even want to get out of bed in the morning—hitting snooze so many times that by the time she got out of bed the kids had missed the school bus.

Then one day she was watching TV and saw a commercial with the classic NASA pre-launch countdown:

5... 4... 3... 2... 1... BLASTOFF!

She said to herself: "That's what I'm going to do tomorrow morning. "5... 4... 3... 2... 1... I'm out of bed!!"

She woke up the next morning, was tempted to hit snooze, remembered her idea, thought it was stupid, but then did the countdown and the blastoff.

"5... 4... 3... 2... 1... BLASTOFF!"

She immediately got out of bed. And, it changed her life.

Since then, it's changed a LOT of people's lives.

She created something called "The 5 Second Rule." It does an astonishingly elegant job at weaving together a TON of scientific research on habit formation, activation energy, locus of control, small wins, and a bunch of other behavioral change ideas.

The +1°...

If you feel so inspired, the next time you find yourself pretty clear on what needs to get done but hesitating before doing it, give yourself a little countdown to blastoff.

5... 4... 3... 2... 1...

BLASTOFF!

"I LOVE PUH!" (YOU?)
PAIN, UNCERTAINTY & HARD WORK

One of the big ideas from Jonah Hill's Netflix documentary on our mutual coach Phil Stutz (appropriately called *Stutz*—have you watched it yet?) is the fact that we will NEVER be exonerated from THREE things…

Pain. Uncertainty. And hard work.

Most of us spend most of our lives trying to pretend that this isn't true and… that's the source of most of our frustration.

We need to radically accept the fact that life is challenging. Even the Buddha's first noble truth established the fact that life is full of pain/suffering.

And… When we learn to not only ACCEPT this non-negotiable existential fact of life but learn to LOVE it, everything changes.

Which is why, as we've discussed, Phil's first tool in his first book, *The Tools*, is what he calls "The Reversal of Desire."

The mantra he tells us to SCREAM in our heads EVERY TIME we feel even a niggle of fear/doubt/overwhelm?

"BRING IT ON!!!"

Followed by… "I LOVE PAIN. PAIN SETS ME FREE!!"

Why does "pain" set us free?

Because, as we've discussed, your *infinite* potential exists outside your comfort zone. How's it feel outside your comfort zone? By definition, it feels uncomfortable.

That's pain.

And … That's why embracing pain "sets you free."

Nobel Prize winner Elizabeth Blackburn and leading positive psychologist Kelly McGonigal echo this wisdom. They tell us that how we INTERPRET the stress and stressful moments in our lives determines how they affect us—all the way down to our telomeres.

They also tell us to say "Bring it on!" as we APPROACH rather than AVOID life's challenges.

Why? Because that's the ONLY way we can grow—using the "turds" of life (as Phil playfully says in the documentary) as fuel for our growth.

Which brings us back to pain and uncertainty and hard work. I've been thinking about how to make those three things into a practical tool and playful acronym.

Then it landed.

Pain. Uncertainty. Hard work. That's "PUH."

And … Yes. That's *definitely* pronounced "poo."

And that, my dear Hero, is our +1°.

Remember. It takes poo to make a seed grow. And it takes PUH to make an aspiring hero truly Heroic.

Say it with me now with a smile …

"I love PUH!!"

Day 1. All in.

With a laugh.

LET'S GO, HERO!

LITTLE BY LITTLE
THE BUDDHA ON HOW TO OPTIMIZE

O ne of my favorite gems from the Buddha is this wisdom: "Little by little one becomes evil, as a water pot is filled with water. Little by little one becomes good, as a water pot is filled with water."

The optimal way to optimize?

Drop by drop by drop.

+1°. +1°. +1°.

Back in the day, I used to get all fired up and want to change EVERYTHING once and for all *and* RIGHT NOW! (Technically, I wanted it *yesterday* but you get the idea.)

You ever have that feeling? You go to a weekend workshop (or read a book or whatever) and you say to yourself: "It's on. I'm snapping my fingers and changing it all. Check me out!"

Then a week later you fall back into your bad habits and wonder what happened.

Rather than patiently add another +1° drop to my optimizing pot, I used to turn on the fire hydrant and send the pot flying around the room—nearly breaking it in the process.

Not wise. Now?

Now I love those little drops.

You?

Remember: "Little by little one becomes evil, as a water pot is filled with water. Little by little one becomes good, as a water pot is filled with water."

HOW TO DELETE A BAD HABIT
HINT: REMOVE THE PROMPT

A lex Korb wrote a great book called *The Upward Spiral*.

It's all about "Using Neuroscience to Reverse the Course of Depression, One Small Change at a Time."

Today I want to connect one of the big ideas from his book to wisdom from BJ Fogg's great book *Tiny Habits*.

First, let's take a super-quick look at the three primary variables in BJ Fogg's Behavior MAP.

BJ tells us that: "A behavior happens when the three elements of MAP—Motivation, Ability, and Prompt—come together at the same moment. Motivation is your desire to do the behavior. Ability is your capacity to do the behavior. And prompt is your cue to do the behavior."

Now, know this: "You can disrupt a behavior you don't want by removing the prompt. This isn't always easy, but removing the prompt is your best first move to stop a behavior from happening."

BJ also tells us: "Prompts are the invisible drivers of our lives." And, most importantly for our purposes with this +1°: "No behavior happens without a prompt."

Thank you, Professor Fogg.

What does Professor Korb have to say?

Well, first, know that he calls a "Prompt" a "trigger." (James Clear and Charles Duhigg call it a "cue." Same thing.)

And…

Alex tells us: "Figure out your triggers. It is much easier to avoid temptation than to resist it. If you know what triggers a particular habit, sometimes you can get rid of that habit simply by removing the trigger from your life."

The +1°…

What bad habit do you want to get rid of?

Pick one.

No big deal. No shame.

Remember: We all have our kryptonites.

Approach it like a curious scientist. As BJ says: "Once you remove any hint of judgment, your behavior becomes a science experiment. A sense of exploration and discovery is a prerequisite to success, not just an added bonus."

Got that bad habit in mind? Perfect.

What's the trigger/prompt/cue for that bad habit?

Figure it out.

Remove it.

TODAY.

P.S. Practical example: If you struggle with alcohol, get rid of *every* bottle in your house. The trigger/prompt/cue is tempting you all day every day. Same thing applies with junk food. Throw it out and quit buying it!

PSYCHOLOGICAL FLEXIBILITY
A HALLMARK OF HAPPY HUMANS

Dan Siegel is a Harvard-trained psychiatrist who is one of the world's leading mindfulness/neuroscience/interpersonal neurobiology experts.

He's written a number of great books.

In *Mindsight*, Dan tells us that one of the hallmarks of a healthy human being is that we are psychologically flexible.

He says that we need to be kinda like a river flowing between two banks—on one side we have structure and on the other we have spontaneity.

Now, the trick to maintaining psychological flexibility is to make sure we don't flood one side or the other.

We want to have *just* the right amount of structure—too much and you get rigid. Not good.

On the other side of our river of flexibility we have spontaneity. Again, we need a certain amount but not too much. If we go over the top on spontaneity we can flood that side and wind up with chaos. Eek.

I repeat: The healthy human being is like the river of flexibility that runs between the banks of structure and spontaneity.

Structure + spontaneity = flexibility.

How's *your* river?

Are you flooding one side or the other?

What's one little thing you can do to optimize today?

HOW TO STOP BEING A HARDAHOLIC
THE MAGIC QUESTION: WHAT IF IT WAS EASY?

Alan Cohen tells us to quit being a hardaholic—making everything harder than it needs to be.

Quick check in…

Are YOU a hardaholic?

Alan tells us that one way we can deal with this tendency is to ask ourselves *this* question…

"What if this was easy?"

That's our +1°.

What if it was easy to do the thing you keep on telling yourself is so hard?

(Yah, that one!)

"What if it was easy to…

_____ ."

(Go on! Take another few seconds and fill in that blank!)

With true, wise confidence we know we'll face obstacles, of course. But what if it was a LOT easier to do the things we want to do than we're making ourselves believe?

Let's quit being hardaholics.

WOOP your #1 most important goal and go dominate the next steps with a smile, Hero.

(Seriously.) (Get on that.) (I'll be here when you get back.)

HOW TO AVOID HABIT SUICIDE
OK TO SUCK; NOT OK TO SKIP

A s you may have noticed, for a number of reasons, it's a LOT easier to build a solid habit when you decide to do it every day rather than to do it three times per week or every other day. It's just how our brains work.

The more consistent we are, the easier it is.

Now, let's say you have a little streak going.

Five days. Ten days. Fifteen days.

A W E S O M E.

Your little habit seed is taking shape.

WHATEVER YOU DO, DON'T SKIP A DAY!

And, if you happen to miss a day (it happens), then *DEFI-NITELY* don't miss two days.

In his great little book *Superhuman by Habit*, Tynan calls missing two days in a row "habit suicide."

If you miss a day (again, it happens), make getting your habit back on track your #1 priority for the following day. Schedule it. Dominate it.

The reality is, if you miss that *second* day in a row, you're in trouble and if you miss *three* days in a row you run the very strong risk of losing all the hard work you've done installing it and will basically need to re-start from ground zero.

Quick check in: How many times have you let a day slip "just because" and then another day and then another and then BAM!

Habit begone?

Our +1°…

The next time you're tempted to skip a day, remember this wisdom: "It's OK to suck. It's not OK to skip."

Even if you have what you think is a *terrible* meditation or a *terrible* workout or a *terrible* writing session or a *terrible* whatever, it's *way* better to *suck* than to *skip*.

Here's to keeping our habits alive.

One day at a time.

Especially…

TODAY.

DON'T BREAK THE STREAK
DO THE WORK EVERY SINGLE DAY

Seth Godin is one of the world's most popular bloggers and prolific authors. He's written a ton of great books.

One of my favorites is one of his most recent ones. It's called *The Practice*.

In that book, he tells us: "Build streaks. Do the work every single day. Blog daily. Write daily. Ship daily. Show up daily. Find your streak and maintain it."

You may have heard of Jerry Seinfeld and the story about his write-a-new-joke-a-day streak.

Now... Apparently it's not *actually* a true story (hah) but the moral of the story remains super powerful so let's suspend our disbelief for a moment and enjoy the short story...

Once upon a time, Jerry Seinfeld was just another up-and-coming comedian. Yes, as with all great masters, there was a time when Jerry Seinfeld *wasn't* **JERRY SEINFELD**.

Young Jerry wanted to get so good people couldn't ignore him. So, he wrote a new joke. Then another one. And another.

Every single day he'd write another new joke.

He'd put a big ol' X on his wall calendar when he wrote a joke that day. He liked seeing all those X's next to each other. He didn't want to break the streak.

Here's the +1° question: What's YOUR streak?

What's the ONE THING you KNOW you could be doing that, if you did EVERY. SINGLE. DAY, would most positively change your life THAT you (very importantly!) intrinsically REALLY WANT to do (no shoulding on yourself, Hero!) that you REALLY *believe* YOU CAN DO?

Seriously. What is it? What's the ONE thing that you'd like to build a streak doing?

Getting your Energy optimized by meditating for at least a minute a day? Walking at least 10,000 steps a day? Spending 8–9+ hours in bed every day?

Focusing on your #1 Work WIN first thing every day in a creative-before-reactive Deep Work bubble? Shutting down completely by a certain time every day to transition powerfully from work to love?

Optimizing your Love by connecting with your family WITHOUT your phone for at least a minute or thirty every day? Kissing your spouse every day? Hugging your kids every day?

I've set all of those Targets for myself in our Heroic app.

Not all of them have *perfect* daily streaks but (goosebumps) my goodness is it fun to create a streak and keep it going.

So…

What's YOUR new, non-negotiable, high-leverage streak going to be, Hero?

Day 1. All in.

LET'S GOOOO!

THE VARIABILITY OF YOUR BEHAVIOR
REDUCE IT TO INCREASE THE LIKELIHOOD OF ROCKING IT

As we've discussed, the wisest among us use their willpower to install habits that run on autopilot.

Here's a pro tip: If you want to install a new habit, reduce the variability of your behavior.

Let's say you want to install the habit of meditating. You're clear on the why. You've made it silly easy to do—opting for a floor of one minute rather than trying to go for sixty minutes out the gate. You've made a 100% commitment, etc.

Now, what do you think will be more effective?

Option #1: Doing your one minute or more of meditation whenever you can get around to it? Sometimes you meditate first thing when you wake up, sometimes right after your workout, other times before lunch and other times when you get home from work or before you go to sleep or…

Or…

Option #2: Doing your one minute or more at a consistent time each day? You decide that a certain time of the day (say, right after you wake up) is the best time for you to meditate and then you do your new habit at *that* time EVERY SINGLE DAY.

Option #2 for the no-brainer win, right?

Actually, it IS a no-brainer.

By reducing the variability of your behavior you GREATLY enhance the likelihood of installing that positive behavior so it can run on autopilot—moving from having to think about it (and using up some of your precious willpower on it) every day pre-frontal cortex style to letting your basal ganglia rock it for you without any deliberate, resource-intensive thinking.

So...

Got a habit you've been having a tough time installing?

Are you consistent with the time/place you do it?

Or, would you benefit from reducing the variability of your behavior?

Let's +1° it!

And, of course, repeat that process with any and all habits you'd like to see running on autopilot!

SPEED IS A FORCE
MAY THE FORCE BE WITH YOU

I have worked with Phil Stutz over four hundred times over the last seven years. My stack of notes on those sessions is a couple feet high and one of my most cherished possessions.

We had our first session on Friday, January 13th, 2017. I'm looking at my notes from that session now as I type this.

The very first thing Phil taught me in our very first session together was on "The Rules of Action."

The first "Rule of Action"? Phil says that "Speed Is a Force."

He told me that the longer we wait between knowing what we need to do and actually doing it, the more our confidence and self-respect erodes.

Below my notes on that wisdom, I wrote: "DO IT NOW!"

And: "It's possible to make an impact now."

And: "The bias is always to take action."

Of course, not *every* idea is worth pursuing in general let alone with speed, but…

Are you letting gaps creep in between the moment of inspired clarity and the moment you take action implementing that idea? And, is your confidence eroding as a result?

Remember the first Rule of Action: SPEED IS A FORCE. When you know what needs to get done, DO IT NOW.

Our +1°…

With that in mind, what do you need to take action on RIGHT NOW? Get on that. I'll be here when you get back.

THE LAW OF DIMINISHING INTENT
GOES NICELY WITH SPEED IS A FORCE

In our last +1°, we talked about Phil Stutz's first Law of Action, the idea that Speed Is a Force.

To recap: The VERY first thing Phil taught me in our VERY first session was simple: When you know what needs to get done, DO IT. Your confidence will erode the longer you wait to take action.

Jim Rohn said something similar.

He called it "The Law of Diminishing Intent."

The basic idea: The likelihood of doing something diminishes the further away you get from the initial moment of inspiration.

And, I will add, your confidence almost certainly erodes as well. Not a winning combination.

Jim Rohn's protégé, Tony Robbins, echoes this wisdom. He tells us that we must never leave the moment of inspiration without taking action. Then we need to follow that up with *massive*, sustained action.

I repeat…

When you have a moment of inspiration and you *know* what needs to get done, DO IT. Seize the moment. Take action. Then follow that up with massive, sustained action.

Our +1°…

With that in mind, what do you need to take action on RIGHT NOW? Get on that. I'll be here when you get back.

GETTING STARTED VS. GETTING FINISHED
HOW TO DEAL WITH PROCRASTINATION

I f you're feeling a little less than motivated and tempted to procrastinate on stuff, you might find this distinction helpful.

In his great book *Solving the Procrastination Puzzle*, Tim Pychyl tells us that there's a big difference between getting yourself *started* and feeling like you need to get it *finished*.

Here's another way to think about it …

Tal Ben-Shahar is a teacher and, essentially, a professional writer. Yet, many days when he sits down to write he doesn't *feel* like writing.

On those less-than-inspired mornings, he doesn't say to himself: "Oh, well. I'll just hop online and find something more interesting to do." (As tempting as that is.)

Nope. He practices something he calls his "five-minute ramp-up." He tells himself to just *get started*. For five minutes. That's it.

And guess what?

With that simple, non-intimidating, doable micro-action we create momentum. And, as we've learned from Sir Isaac Newton, an object in motion tends to stay in motion and those five minutes often turn into fifty minutes of some of your best work—all on a day when, if allowed to, that whiny voice that didn't "feel like it" could have derailed the whole show.

Don't just do it.

Just get started.

TODAY.

THE GIFT OF GREATNESS
HERE IT IS

Anders Ericsson was the world's leading authority on the science of what makes great performers great. If you've ever heard of the "10,000-hour rule," you have him to thank.

In his great book *Peak: Secrets from the New Science of Expertise,* Anders shares what he learned over the course of decades of research.

He tells us that THE most important thing he learned is the fact that we ALL have the gift of greatness.

The gift is wrapped in a very unassuming package. Nothing fancy. No shiny ribbons or big bows. Just a plain ol' little box. But inside that box is magic.

It's the gift of *adaptability.*

The ability to change. The ability to incrementally optimize our chosen set of skills and to aggregate and compound those tiny gains over an extended period of time such that we can make the impossible look easy.

The difference between the great performers and everyone else? They've simply fully taken advantage of this gift.

Good news: So can you.

Important note: Anders tells us that the biggest barrier between you and greatness might be your inaccurate belief that the people you most admire have "it" and you don't. He calls this "the dark side of believing in innate talent."

So...

Open up the box. Receive your gift.

And, remember: That gift of adaptability looks best in overalls—with you working hard.

HOMEOSTASIS & ADAPTABILITY
GET OUT OF YOUR COMFORT ZONE

We've talked a lot about how important it is to get out of our comfort zones. But *why* is it so important?

Two words: homeostasis and adaptability.

First: Homeostasis. Every cell in our body and brain is *constantly* working to maintain a sense of stability—adjusting everything from our blood pressure and heart rate to our pH balance and blood sugar levels.

What's exciting is that, when we consistently push ourselves out of our homeostatic-comfort zones, our bodies respond by *overcompensating* in pursuit of creating a new, higher level of homeostasis.

For example, if you go from being sedentary to running a few miles a few times a week, your body is going to say: "Hey now! What's this? You're pushing me out of homeostasis. Let me see what I can do to handle this new load and reestablish a new baseline of homeostasis!"

The same rules apply for EVERYTHING we do.

Lifting weights. Cultivating our courage. Meditating. Etc.

This is a *really* exciting feature of the human body and brain. In fact, as per Anders Ericsson's research, our ADAPTABILITY is our greatest gift.

We just need to use it wisely.

I repeat: Get out of your comfort zone.

It's the only way to grow.

DYNAMIC EQUILIBRIUM
YOU AS A TIGHTROPE WALKER

O sho said that, in life, there's really no such thing as "balance." Certainly not "static balance" where everything is totally (ideally, once and for all!) perfectly at equilibrium.

He tells us that balance is a VERB, not a noun.

"*Balancing*" not "balanced."

He says life is more like walking on a tightrope than standing still.

Imagine that.

Imagine you up there on a tightrope. You're a really good tightrope walker. You've put in your 10,000+ hours and you can masterfully move across the high wire.

But…

Notice the important fact that you're never actually "balanced" up there per se.

At one moment you're leaning a little to the left. Then with the next step you're leaning a little to the right. Then back. Then back again.

If you look closely, you'll see that your balance is DYNAMIC. You're never actually "balanced" in a *static* way. You're creating that *dynamic* equilibrium with every step you take.

Same with life.

Moment to moment to moment we find a new, dynamic sense of equilibrium.

In one moment we're a little "imbalanced" in one direction. Then a little "imbalanced" in another.

And that's exactly how it should be.

So, let's stop thinking that we're going to get our lives perfectly balanced.

Remember: Balance is a verb.

Balancing.

Let's embrace the wonderfully energized feeling of dynamic equilibrium as we walk the tightrope that is our lives.

TODAY.

SMILE!
A POWERFUL WAY TO BOOST YOUR MOOD

Get this: Scientists can bring people into a lab and have them hold a pen in their mouths in one of two different ways to elicit two very different outcomes.

One group holds a pen between their lips.

The other group holds the pen between their teeth.

(Try it to feel the difference!)

Guess what?

The group that holds the pen between their teeth (which, you may notice, creates a sort of smile) are HAPPIER at the end of the experiment than people who hold the pen between their lips (which, you may notice, creates a sort of frown).

That's nuts!

How could something *that* simple lead to a significant change in well-being?

Well, as we've discussed many times, FEELINGS follow BEHAVIORS.

And, as it turns out, even something as mundane as unknowingly moving your happiness muscles into the shape of a smile while part of an experiment can make you feel better.

So, the moral of the story is simple: Work with a pen between your teeth today. (Hah. Not really.)

But, DO remember that feelings follow behaviors.

And, remember that the little things you do matter.

Stand up tall. Act the way you'd act if you were feeling great even if you're *not* feeling great. You might just find that your feelings follow that behavior more than you can believe.

And...

Let's smile more today.

It's fascinating to feel how quickly your whole mood can soften and elevate when you shift from a serious (or negative) facial expression to a simple, soft smile.

If you feel so inspired... Try it right now!

And...

If you *don't* feel so inspired... DEFINITELY try it right now, Hero! (Hah.)

+1° Smile. +1° Smile. +1° Smile.

(I'm smiling as I type that.)

P.S. In *Peace Is Every Step*, Thích Nhất Hạnh echoes this scientific truth with a spiritual truth: "Wearing a smile on your face is a sign that you are master of yourself."

FEAR DOORS
WALKED THROUGH ANY LATELY?

W e've all had moments in our lives in which we pushed through our fears and did something we were afraid to do that led to something awesome.

I call those moments walking through "Fear Doors."

Today I'll share a little story from my life as we shine a light on a few of those moments in YOUR life.

Once upon a time, I was a twenty-two-year-old with a full head of hair and big dreams to leave my job as an accountant-consultant to go to a Top Law School.

To fulfill that dream, I studied (very) hard for the LSAT.

My score on the initial diagnostic was above average but not phenomenal. I think it was around the 68th percentile.

I was a hard-working lad even back then. So, I bought every single LSAT ever written (literally) and took every one of them when I wasn't studying with my private tutor for whom, I should note, I forked out a sizable portion of my net worth.

Now, I had a 3.71 GPA from UCLA and figured that a score of 173 on the LSAT (out of 180—which is in the 99th percentile) would give me a great shot at getting into a great school and, very importantly, would also look nice and symmetrical. (Hah.)

So… I hustled.

Every day after work I rushed home to study. I worked all weekend. Repeat. Week after week after week.

By the time test day arrives, I was feeling pretty good about my chances of crushing it. In fact, I might have been thinking I'd kinda like to get a perfect score.

Now, while I hadn't achieved a perfect score on any of the prior tests I'd taken, I'd taken so many prep tests that I felt like I could WRITE an LSAT let alone take one.

But… More importantly, I hadn't taken my own class on Peak Performance 101 and Conquering Perfectionism 101 yet.

So… It's test day.

I sit down to take the test. It's old school (1996!) so we're talking pen and paper here for the exam.

I open the first section.

And…

I can't even finish it. I totally choke. I have to bubble in the last four answers: (C) (C) (C) (C)

I'm sweating profusely.

My internal dialogue goes something like this:

"What just happened?"

"Did I just miss out on my opportunity to fulfill my dream of going to a great law school."

"OMG. Should I just walk out right now and spare myself the embarrassment of totally screwing up?!"

That was literally what was going through my head. (I get a little misty-eyed typing *that* feeling into that sheer panic I felt that day.)

Now, I'm not sure how I pulled it together but I did. Somehow I managed to get focused. I turned the page. I started the next section. And finished the test.

Weeks later I called the automated testing service to get my score. Can you guess what it was?

173.

Good enough to have a bunch of the Top Ten law schools I hoped to attend sending me letters asking me to apply.

I wound up deciding to go to the best public school on the list (half the tuition, folks!) and briefly attended UC Berkeley's Boalt School of Law. (Class of 2000!)

Why am I sharing that?

Because that test (and its score) changed my life.

I walked through the Fear Door and BAM!

Literally, a different life.

Our +1°…

Has something like that ever happened to YOU?

Have YOU ever walked through a Fear Door that changed your life? Feast on that Hero Bar. Know that courage isn't the absence of fear. It's the willingness to act in the presence of fear.

Make the connection between your fear and your willingness to act and your achievement of some of the things you're most proud of.

Most importantly…

Are you *currently* standing in front of a Fear Door that you need to walk through?

Open that Fear Door.

Walk through it.

TODAY.

FEAR DOORS (PART II)
GET TO A CHASM? JUMP!

Joseph Campbell once shared a bit of advice given to a young Native American at the time of his initiation.

The wise elder said: "As you go the way of life, you will see a great chasm. Jump. It's not as wide as you think."

That's the same basic idea with our Fear Doors.

We often just need to open the door and walk through it.

Here's another example of me walking through a Fear Door that changed my life.

(Important note: As I share this story, think about a moment in YOUR life in which YOU had the courage to act in the presence of fear as you make the connection between those courageous moments and the achievements in your life that have made you most proud. Then commit to making MORE of those decisions!)

So…

I walked through the Fear Door while taking the LSAT and wound up getting a good enough score to get me into a great school.

Only problem was, I knew I didn't want to actually go to law school. It was just an escape route from a job I disliked even more. I figured getting a stamp of approval from a top law school would be a good thing but… I *literally* threw up the day I moved into my apartment in Berkeley.

I dropped out of law school after a few months.

It was NOT a good time.

I had NONE of the wisdom and discipline I've worked so hard to cultivate.

The only thing I could imagine doing (when I wasn't imagining ending my own life) was coaching a Little League Baseball® team.

So, I moved back in with my mom and that's what I did.

I volunteered to help a neighbor friend coach his son's nine- and ten-year-old team, the Angels.

We were the Bad News Bears. I think we lost our first five games. But I learned something. I learned that the quality of a kid's experience in youth sports was shaped, in part, by the quality of the coaching he received. My neighbor friend and I had no idea what we were doing and it showed—not just in the standings but in the morale of the team.

Before law school, I was a consultant with Arthur Andersen and learned a few things about technology and databases.

I had an idea...

What if I could create an online system (the web was in its toddler stage at that point in early 1998) that could bring these teams and leagues online and create a community where new coaches like me could learn how to run a practice from the expert coaches—you know, the ones with the headbands and clipboards who kick everyone's butts...

And wouldn't it be cool if I could make it easy to put a picture of Johnny sliding into home that his grandparents could check out if they missed the game?

Out of this idea, I created my first company: eteamz.com.

My genius twenty-two-year-old partner and I (I was twenty-four) cracked open our piggy banks, invested $5,000 each and, from our living rooms, built a suite of tools in a matter of months that served thousands of teams from around the world.

We won the business plan competition at UCLA's Anderson School of Business, raised $1 million of capital from angel investors, grew from 2.5 employees to 45 employees in less than a year, raised another $4 million, hired the CEO of Adidas to replace me as the CEO (we also hired the eventual winner of *The Apprentice 2*), and, get this...

I HIRED the law firm I would have wanted to work for BEFORE I would have graduated. Then, we wound up selling the business to one of our competitors and I had enough money to figure out what I wanted to do when I grew up and all that led to where I am today.

And...

Although that's a nice demonstration of Joseph Campbell's admonition to "follow your bliss," and I talk about that story in the documentary *Finding Joe*, that's not quite the point of this story.

Here's the thing I left out.

You know that business plan competition at UCLA that we won?

Well...

I almost didn't show up for it because "we weren't ready/good enough."

I was so stressed out in the days leading up to my trip that I *literally* ripped off my closet door. (I can laugh now.)

Somehow I pulled myself together, invested what was a

HUGE amount of money for me at the time to fly out to Los Angeles and then to pay for color printouts of our business plan. I can still vividly remember standing in line at Kinko's deciding if I'd go ALL IN on the color business plans.

(Goosebumps and tears in my eyes as I type that.)

Oh … I should also probably mention the fact that I was SO TERRIFIED of speaking in public that I may have had a little accident that led to a trip to the bathroom (hah!) the day before my presentation right after I was shown the huge auditorium in which I'd be giving my talk. I kid you not.

(I share that story in Public Speaking 101, btw.)

The point of the story?

Multiple Fear Doors.

Somehow…

I crawled/clawed my way through them.

Result: We won.

A venture capitalist who was a judge for the competition gave me his card after my talk. I flew out to meet him in Silicon Valley shortly thereafter.

Then we raised that $5 million, hired the CEO of Adidas to replace me as the twenty-five-year-old CEO, etc … and MY LIFE COMPLETELY CHANGED FOR THE BETTER.

But NONE OF IT WOULD HAVE HAPPENED had I not somehow managed to muster the courage to act in the presence of fear.

Fear Door.

Went through it.

Life changed.

And … That's WAY more than enough from me.

I share those stories simply to shine a spotlight on YOU.

I repeat …

Have YOU ever walked through a Fear Door that changed your life?

Feast on that Hero Bar.

Know that courage isn't the absence of fear. It's the willingness to act in the presence of fear.

Make the connection between your fear and your willingness to act and your achievement of some of the things you're most proud of.

Most importantly…

Are you currently standing in front of a Fear Door that you need to walk through?

Open the Fear Door.

Walk through it.

TODAY.

P.S. I wish I could reach through this book right now and look you in the eye and tell you … "You got this, Hero. Go crush it and come back and tell us a good tale!"

THE AUDIENCE EFFECT
THE POWER OF EYEBALLS

Have you ever heard of "The Audience Effect"? It's fascinating. Here's the short story.

Researchers can bring people into a lab (or bring the lab to them) and test them on everything from how much weight they can lift to how clean they keep their cafeteria.

For example, you can put pictures of human eyeballs on a wall in a cafeteria and students will keep it cleaner. (Hah!) (Seriously.)

Or, you can test people on how much weight they can lift in different settings and what you'll find is that they'll lift more when doing it on a stage alone in front of an audience.

That's called "The Audience Effect."

In Matt Fitzgerald's great book *How Bad Do You Want It?*, he tells us: "The online *Psychology Dictionary* defines it as 'the influence of the presence of other people on an individual's behavior.' Psychologists believe that the audience effect is mediated by a so-called sociometer, a mechanism involving multiple regions of the brain, including the anterior insula and the inferior gyrus. Through this mechanism people notice and interpret the attention of those around them and use this input to adjust their behavior in ways that are likely to earn more positive attention."

That makes me think of some parallel wisdom from Angela Duckworth on the power of community.

In *Grit,* she tells us: "The bottom line on culture and grit is: If you want to be grittier, find a gritty culture and join it. If you're a leader, and you want the people in your organization to be grittier, create a gritty culture."

Now…

You know whose eyeballs we want to make sure you're aware of as much as possible?

Your daimon's.

P.S. That wisdom on the scientific fact that one of the fastest ways to change your life is to join a community with high standards is one of the reasons why I'm so excited about our Heroic social training platform. It's the perfect place to support one another with accountability "eyeballs" as we all elevate our standards and make our prior best our new baseline within a community in which the OPTIMAL behavior is the NORMATIVE behavior.

MOM SAYS: BE VIRTUOUS
ABIGAIL ADAMS & HEROIC MOTHERS UNITE

Abigail Adams was one of the Heroic Founding Mothers of the United States of America.

I'm certain that she and Benjamin Franklin and their families would be part of our Heroic movement if they were alive today.

Why?

Because they were intensely passionate about cultivating virtue in their lives and in the lives of their children.

Abigail once wrote: "These are the times in which a genius would wish to live. It is not in the still calm of life, or the repose of a pacific station, that great characters are formed. The habits of a vigorous mind are formed in contending with difficulties. Great necessities call out great virtues. When a mind is raised, and animated by scenes that engage the heart, then those qualities which would otherwise lay dormant, wake into life and form the character of the hero and the statesman."

After reading a version of that in Warren Bennis's great book *On Becoming a Leader*, I looked it up to find its source.

It's from a letter she wrote to her son John Quincy Adams in January 1780–almost 250 years ago. He was on a trip to France with his father to elicit support for our Revolutionary War. (Thanks again, France!)

I looked up how old John Quincy Adams was in 1780.

He was twelve.

Check out the letter online. It's worth reading.

As you'll see if you spend a few minutes reading her brilliant letter, Abigail starts out the letter by basically telling her son that she made him go to France with his dad and brother even though he was whining about it.

Seriously. It's so good to see this great woman talking to a future president like, well, he was acting like a twelve-year-old.

Then we get to the quote that made me find the letter.

But get this…

Bennis actually MISQUOTED Abigail.

He said that she said: "These are hard times in which a genius should wish to live… Great necessities call forth great leaders."

But that's not *actually* what she said.

She didn't say great necessities call forth great LEADERS.

She said: "Great necessities call forth great VIRTUES."

Which, for the record, MAKES THEM GREAT LEADERS.

Note: Both John Quincy Adams AND his dad John Adams would become future U.S. Presidents. Virtue for the win!

That struck me because everything we do with Heroic is focused on helping us operationalize the fact that ancient wisdom and modern science agree that the ultimate purpose of life is to express the best version of yourself (in service to something bigger than yourself!) by living with virtue.

And, of course, we believe the historically significant challenges we are facing DEMAND that each of us step up and show up as the best, most Heroic versions of ourselves.

Which is why I was even more struck by the rest of her letter.

When I read THIS passage, I could literally SEE Abigail and her husband John (who, in 1780, was the Ambassador to France in what was year five of an eight-year Revolutionary War) and their kids using Heroic to commit to and then hit virtuous targets together all day every day (especially when they were so far away from each other!):

"I cannot fulfill the whole of my duty towards you, if I close this Letter, without reminding you of a failing which calls for a strict attention and watchfull care to correct. You must do it for yourself. You must curb that impetuosity of temper, for which I have frequently chid you, but which properly directed may be productive of great good. I know you are capable of these exertions, with pleasure I observed my advice was not lost upon you. If you indulge yourself in the practise of any foible or vice in youth, it will gain strength with your years and become your conquerer.

"The strict and inviolable regard you have ever paid to truth, gives me pleasing hopes that you will not swerve from her dictates, but add justice, fortitude, and every Manly Virtue which can adorn a good citizen, do Honour to your Country, and render your parents supremely happy, particularly your ever affectionate Mother."

Then I smiled when I realized that another beloved Founding Father, Benjamin Franklin, would have probably created something similar to our app to track HIS virtues (with his friends and family!) if he was alive today.

Know this...

These are times in which Heroes would wish to live.

As we do the hard work to activate our Heroic potential, may we remember that it is not in the still calm of life, or the repose of a pacific station that great characters are formed.

Remember: "Great necessities call out great virtues. When a mind is raised, and animated by scenes that engulf the Heart, then those qualities which would otherwise lay dormant, wake to Life, and form the Character of the Hero and the Statesman."

With love, wisdom, discipline, and courage I say…

Heroes unite!

Day 1. All in.

LET'S GO.

YOU ARE A WEIRDO
AT LEAST I HOPE YOU ARE

I n our last +1°, we talked about Abigail Adams and her letter to her son, John Quincy Adams.

She admonished the twelve-year-old, who would become the sixth U.S. President, to LIVE WITH VIRTUE.

I mentioned the fact that I think she and her family would have been part of our Heroic movement—encouraging their kids to cultivate their virtue while doing the same on our Heroic app.

I also mentioned the fact that I think Benjamin Franklin would have either created something similar to our Heroic app to track HIS virtuous targets or joined the cause to help us win our current war between vice and virtue.

After writing that, I typed "Benjamin Franklin" into my Mac's search bar to see if I could find a Big Idea from a Philosopher's Note on him and his commitment to virtue.

I hit the jackpot.

And… Not only did I find a Big Idea featuring Benjamin Franklin and his idiosyncratic awesomeness, I also found a reference to John Adams in the same Big Idea. Fantastic!

The references were from my Philosopher's Note on Alan Cohen's *Spirit Means Business*. Franklin and Adams showed up in an idea about helping us embrace our inner weirdos.

Alan tells us: "Being a misfit is not a defect. It may be your key to success. When I hear that a person is well adjusted, I ask,

'Well adjusted to what?' Learning how to find your way around a mental institution does not make you sane. Real sanity rests in authenticity."

Alan continues by saying that maybe we're not so weird at all and maybe our weirdness is actually our greatest asset.

Then he proceeds to tell us that idiosyncrasies go with the package of iconoclastic greatness concluding by saying: "Normality and genius are rare bedfellows. As Walt Whitman proudly proclaimed, 'Not a particle or an inch of me is vile… I celebrate myself.'"

That wisdom is from a chapter in which we learn about some of history's most awesome weirdos.

Get this: Did you know that Benjamin Franklin started each day with an "air bath," standing naked outside for thirty minutes? Yep.

And, that fellow American hero John Quincy Adams swam nude in the Potomac River at 5:00 a.m. every morning, even in freezing weather? (Cold plunge for the win! Wim Hof would approve.)

Then we have Nikola Tesla and Steve Jobs with their whole array of idiosyncratic behaviors and genius inventions. And let's not forget about Albert Einstein. Did you know that he didn't even speak until he was three and, as an adult, would stop his car, pluck a grasshopper and eat it? Yep. That's normal.

Then we have YOU.

Own your idiosyncratic weirdo-ness.

TODAY.

IF...
BY RUDYARD KIPLING

Have you ever heard of the poem called "If" by Rudyard Kipling? It's extraordinary. Here it is.

If you can keep your head when all about you
    Are losing theirs and blaming it on you,
If you can trust yourself when all men doubt you,
    But make allowance for their doubting too;
If you can wait and not be tired by waiting,
    Or being lied about, don't deal in lies,
Or being hated, don't give way to hating,
    And yet don't look too good, nor talk too wise:

If you can dream—and not make dreams your master;
    If you can think—and not make thoughts your aim;
If you can meet with Triumph and Disaster
    And treat those two impostors just the same;
If you can bear to hear the truth you've spoken
    Twisted by knaves to make a trap for fools,
Or watch the things you gave your life to, broken,
    And stoop and build 'em up with worn-out tools:

If you can make one heap of all your winnings
    And risk it on one turn of pitch-and-toss,

And lose, and start again at your beginnings
 And never breathe a word about your loss;
If you can force your heart and nerve and sinew
 To serve your turn long after they are gone,
And so hold on when there is nothing in you
 Except the Will which says to them: "Hold on!"

If you can talk with crowds and keep your virtue,
 Or walk with Kings—nor lose the common touch,
If neither foes nor loving friends can hurt you,
 If all men count with you, but none too much;
If you can fill the unforgiving minute
 With sixty seconds' worth of distance run,
Yours is the Earth and everything that's in it,
 And—which is more—you'll be a Man, my son!

NOT GETTING WHAT YOU WANT?
HERE ARE TWO (POTENTIAL) REASONS WHY

I n our last +1°, we spent some time soaking our souls in wisdom from Rudyard Kipling's classic poem, *If*.

I let that +1° stand on its own as there was nothing for me to add to that.

Today we're going to talk about some more wisdom from Rudyard Kipling.

Kipling once said: "If you don't get what you want it is either a sign that you did not seriously want it, or that you tried to bargain over the price."

Let's slow down and re-read that and let it sink in ...

"If you don't get what you want it is either a sign that you did not seriously want it, or that you tried to bargain over the price."

How true is THAT?

Question ...

WHAT DO YOU WANT?

More specifically, what's your current #1, most wildly important goal in your life?

Of course, it could be an Energy target or a Work target or a Love target.

What is it?

(Remember: Happy people are teleological/they have projects and goals that inspire them. If you don't have one, GET ONE.)

Now...

If you haven't gotten what you want yet, is it possible that you didn't seriously want it or that you tried to bargain over the price?

If so...

Check in.

Do you REALLY want it?

What price are you willing to pay?

Get clear. WOOP it.

And go pay that price.

TODAY.

MUSTERBATION
& SHOULDING ON YOURSELF

Wayne Dyer coined the word "musterbation" to describe the tendency of doing things because you (insert whiny voice here) "have to."

Whiny voice: "I *must* do this." "I *must* do that."

Enter: Musterbation.

Tony Robbins has a fun way to frame the same challenge. He tells us that we need to quit "should-ing" on ourselves.

Whiny voice: "I *should* do this." "I *should* do that."

Tony's perspective: Do something or don't do it, but quit shoulding on yourself.

This isn't a new idea.

2,000 years ago, Seneca put it his way: "There is nothing the wise man does reluctantly."

2,500 years ago, the Buddha put it this way: "If anything is worth doing, do it with all your heart."

Modern scientists also have an opinion on the subject. They tell us that the happiest among us have "agency" and "self-concordant" goals. They're doing what they want to do.

So...

Quit musterbating and shoulding on yourself.

Heroic lovers of wisdom do nothing reluctantly.

If anything is worth doing, let's do it with all our hearts.

Close the gap. Live with *Areté*.

TODAY.

TWO EASIES
EASY TO DO & EASY NOT TO DO

Jim Rohn tells us that our success in life is all about the *two easies*.

In short: We need to make sure we're dominating the little things that are simultaneously easy *to do* AND easy *not to do*.

For example, it's easy for me to leave my phone in another room when I'm hanging out with my family. Obviously, it's not particularly hard to leave the phone in my office.

But...

And this is a big BUT...

It's also REALLY easy NOT to do that.

Same thing with choices I make in my Energy and in my Work. I can go to bed when I say I will go to bed. I can meditate for a minute or more when I wake up. I can choose to be creative before I'm reactive. I can choose to hit the trail and exercise for fifteen to thirty minutes.

None of those things are *that* hard to do.

All day, every day...

We're faced with a choice.

Easy to do.

Easy not to do.

Two easies.

+1° or -1°.

Remember the two easies like your destiny depends on it. Because it does.

P.S. Here's how Jim Rohn puts it: "It all comes down to a philosophical phrase: the things that are easy to do are also easy *not* to do. That's the difference between success and failure, between daydreams and ambitions.

Here's the key formula for success: a few disciplines practiced every day. Those disciplines have to be well-thought out. What should you spend your time doing? You don't want to waste your time on things that aren't going to matter. But a few simple disciplines can change your whole economic future. A few simple disciplines can change your future with your family, your business, your enterprise, your career. Success is a few simple habits—good habits—repeated every day...

You've got the choice right now of one of two 'easies.' Easy to do, or easy *not* to do. I can tell you in one sentence how I got rich by the time I was thirty-one: I did not neglect to do the easy things I *could* do for six years. That's the key. I found something easy I could do that led to fortune, and I did not neglect to do it."

EMOTIONAL STAMINA (PART II)
EXECUTE THE PROTOCOL

Years ago, not long after I first learned about emotional stamina, Phil Stutz and I were celebrating some exciting stuff.

We chatted about the details of what was going on. Then he asked me how I was sleeping.

To which I said: "Well, it's impossible to ever create systems to guarantee perfect sleep but I'm sleeping great."

Then I proceeded to tell him that his wisdom on emotional stamina *really* landed.

Recall: The *worse* we feel, the MORE committed we need to be to our protocol.

I told Phil that I had used that wisdom to iron out a lot of the remaining "I'm up!" / "I'm down!" wrinkles to create an even more robust sense of emotional stamina in my life.

I repeat (yet again!) (spaced repetition for the win!)…

When you ACTUALLY follow that algorithm "The worse you feel the more committed you are to your protocol!" it's *really* hard to have a *truly* terrible day let alone consecutive/multiple bad days.

Of course, it's not EASY to do what you know you need to do when you're not feeling like it but that's the whole point.

But… That's not the point of this +1°.

This is…

As a guy who used to be very up and then very down, I've learned to discipline myself on the ups *as well as* on the downs.

I added this addendum to the emotional stamina mantra:

The *better* I feel, the MORE committed I need to be to my protocol.

When we're on fire with life and all kinds of awesomeness is coming our way, we want to *make sure* we're honoring our basic fundamentals.

THAT's how we make the *highs* (sustainably) *higher* and the *lows* (significantly) *higher*—WITHOUT going off the rails in either direction.

Our +1°.

Emotional Stamina. Two parts.

Part I: "The *worse* you feel the *more* committed you are to your protocol."

And...

Part II: "The *better* you feel, the *more* committed you are to your protocol."

All of which, of course, begs the question once again: What's your protocol?

What do YOU do when you're at your best?

Get clear. Execute. Repeat. All day. Every day.

Especially when you're particularly *down* OR *up*.

STARVE FEAR
OF ITS FAVORITE FOOD

I n *The 10X Rule*, Grant Cardone tells us that we need to starve fear of its favorite food.

Pop quiz.

Do you know what fear's favorite food is?

Think about it for a moment.

What's your guess?

…

Answer: TIME.

Fear FEASTS on time.

Afraid to do something?

Just give it some more time and your fear will grow stronger—which is precisely why Phil Stutz says that our confidence erodes the longer we wait to take action after we *know* what needs to get done.

And…

Let's be honest.

We pretty much always know what needs to get done.

Our +1°…

Go do that thing.

NOW.

DELETE THAT APP
YES, THAT ONE

Manoush Zomorodi wrote a great little book called *Bored and Brilliant.*

The basic idea is that we need to unplug from our constant tech stimulation such that our brain can settle into what scientists call the "default mode" where all the magic happens.

In short: She tells us that we're wasting an *insane* amount of time (my words) on our smartphones.

We all KNOW that, of course.

But she provides some math that sobered me up to just how much of my life I'm wasting with every little unnecessary pick up of the phone and distracting/unproductive tap/swipe.

Here's the math.

Let's say that you spend twenty-five minutes a day doing things (on your phone or otherwise) that you just KNOW you didn't need to do and probably *shouldn't* have done.

Twenty-five minutes.

That's not a crazy amount.

But it adds up. Fast.

Get this.

Twenty-five minutes wasted per day is TWO YEARS of your life. Gone. Never to be recaptured.

I don't know about you but when I read that I did a quick mental tally of time wasters and was like: "THAT's gotta go!"

For me: It's my phone. Specifically, when I was reading the book years ago, it was *news* on my phone. I'm P I C K L E D.

What about YOU?

What's your #1 thing?

How do YOU waste time?

Here's something to think about to help you reclaim those lost minutes. Manoush gives people a Seven-Day Challenge to invite more boredom and more brilliance into their lives.

The challenge from Day #4 is pretty epic. It's the fastest way to add two years back to our lives.

She tells us: "Your instructions for today: Delete it. Delete *that* app… You know which one is your albatross. The one you use too much. The one you use to escape—too often, at the expense of other things (including sleep). The one that makes you feel bad about yourself. Delete said time-wasting, bad-habit app. Uninstall it."

Yep. THAT app.

Which one is it for YOU?

Want two years of your life back?

Delete it.

NOW.

P.S. Jim Rohn once said: "We will all experience one pain or the other—the pain of discipline or the pain of regret—but the difference is that the pain of discipline weighs only ounces while the pain of regret weighs tons."

Let's pay in ounces.

CONQUERING HERO
VS. SUFFERING MARTYR

Daydreaming. It's another thing Manoush Zomorodi talks about in her great book *Bored and Brilliant*.

There's actually a science to it. Here's the short story.

First, we need to know that daydreaming or "mind-wandering" is really important.

Why? Because this is our ticket to activating the supercomputer-like "default mode" in which we tend to come up with our best ideas, create a more coherent narrative for our lives and resolve a lot of unresolved stuff.

When we DON'T ever create the space for this processing mode, we suffer. Period.

(Longer chat, but this is one of the most terrifying things with the adoption of 24/7 screen time for our next generation of heroes. They rarely have a moment in which they're *not* on a screen and, as a result, have lost the precious connection to themselves and this powerful mode of processing.)

But, here's the deal.

When we flip the "off" switch to our activated/focused brain and enter the default mode, you might've noticed that we can do it in more or less optimal ways.

Sometimes we unplug and have super-positive thoughts. Other times, when we're not focused on something (or distracting ourselves with something!) the thoughts that bubble up can get more than a little negative.

Hence, our desire to run away from them even more and overstimulate/numb ourselves in a never-ending loop.

Science says there are a few different ways we daydream.

If you have "poor attention control," you may have a difficult time focusing on *anything*—including your daydreaming.

Then we have "guilty-dysphoric." When mind-wandering is "dysphoric," our thoughts drift to some negative places that aren't positive or productive. Perhaps we ruminate on things and drive ourselves a little nutty in the process. We want to notice this and bring our attention to something positive.

And, finally, we have "positive-constructive" daydreaming. THIS, of course, is where we want to spend our time.

In this healthy default mode, we integrate our sense of who we are, do what researchers call "autobiographical planning" (a.k.a. think about our future selves in relation to where we are and have been) and digest all the interpersonal and moral challenges we face all day every day.

Here's another way to think about it.

When your mind is wandering and you're kinda randomly thinking about your life, do you imagine yourself as the *conquering hero* of your own story (positive-constructive) or the *suffering martyr* (guilty-dysphoric) of the story?

It's a big distinction. We want to get really good at noticing when we're falling into the "woe is me" helpless Victim mode and shift into Heroic mode.

How? Targeted Thinking. What do you want? What do you need to do to get it? Get on that. TODAY.

TOLERANT WITH OTHERS
STRICT WITH YOURSELF

Our Heroic Coach program is an intense, 300-day training in which we challenge people to move from Theory to Practice to Mastery.

It's basically this book turned up another 2000°.

One of the most frequently asked questions from people going through our program goes something like this...

"I'm really into this stuff and I can already feel my life changing as I start to move from Theory to Practice to Mastery. It's amazing!"

Then they continue with...

"But..."

Then I often know what's coming...

"The problem is that my [wife/husband/kids/extended family/colleagues/insert someone other than them!] *really* needs to work on this stuff and..."

I laughed as I typed that. And I usually laugh when I start my reply.

After chatting about unilaterality and other such ideas, I encourage them to avoid proselytizing and simply focus on DOING THE WORK—letting our *example* be the primary lesson rather than the lectures we're all tempted to give when we're on fire with our own self-development.

Then I tell them about the fact that MY OWN WIFE doesn't want me to coach her. (Hah.)

Trust me, Alexandra doesn't want me to coach her unless she explicitly asks me for the support. After fifteen years, I'm *almost* getting that fact!

Here's another frame I like to use.

I lean on some wisdom from Ryan Holiday's great book *Discipline Is Destiny*.

Ryan tells us: "'I am prepared to forgive everybody's mistakes,' Cato the Elder said, 'except my own.' Ben Franklin, many generations later, would put forth an even better rule: 'Search others for their virtues, thyself for thy vices.' Or as Marcus Aurelius put it: Tolerant with others, strict for yourself.

That's our +1°.

Let's be tolerant with others—looking for their VIRTUES and forgiving their mistakes. Let's be strict with ourselves—looking for our vices and getting to work on them.

We have more than enough work to do on ourselves.

Let's do it.

TODAY.

THE COMMON DENOMINATOR OF SUCCESS
YOU KNOW WHAT IT IS?

In 1940, Albert E.N. Gray wrote a little booklet called *The Common Denominator of Success*—which has influenced many of the leading motivational thinkers and speakers since.

You know what he says is the common denominator of success?

It's pretty simple.

He tells us: "The common denominator of success—the secret of success of every person who has ever become successful—lies in the fact that he or she formed the habit of doing things that failures don't like to do."

He also tells us: "The successful are influenced by the desire for pleasing results. Failures are influenced by the desire for pleasing methods and are inclined to be satisfied with such results as can be obtained by doing things they like to do."

Plus: "It is easier to adjust ourselves to the hardships of a poor living than it is to adjust ourselves to the hardships of making a better one. If you doubt me, just think of all the things you are willing to go without in order to avoid doing the things you don't like to do."

And, he says: "Why are the successful able to do things they don't like to do while failures are not? Because the successful have a purpose strong enough to make them form the habit of doing things they don't like to do in order to accomplish the purpose they want to accomplish."

Our +1°…

Remember…

"The common denominator of success—the secret of success of every person who has ever become successful—lies in the fact that he or she formed the habit of doing things that failures don't like to do."

With that in mind…

What's ONE thing you KNOW you could be doing that, if you did it more consistently, would most change your life?

Close the gap.

Live with *Areté*.

Activate your Heroic potential.

Today.

EFFORT COUNTS THRICE
EMERSON ON MASTERY

In the first microchapters of our book, we had fun using Emerson's passion for chess and the inevitable glitches he faces on his quest for Grandmastery as the context for us to explore some important themes of our work together.

We talked about conquering fear and laziness while closing the gap between who we're *capable* of being and who we're *actually* being as we remember the fact that, as per the discussion about my tattoos on the trail… ARETÉ = HEROIC!!

I repeat: The *moment* we choose to do our best and live with *Areté*, we *are* Heroic. Period.

We don't need to wait twenty-five years until we check off all the "Heroic" things on our vision board.

One more time: THE MOMENT we close the gap and do our best to live with *Areté* (right in that moment!) we ARE Heroic. That's a really powerful truth that I hope you can feel, my dear friend.

Now…

Let's focus on another chat I recently had with Emerson.

This one was after Emerson played in the San Antonio City Chess Championships.

It was an amazing weekend. We had fun going on one of our epic boys-only adventures.

Stayed in a hotel—which is always epic for Emerson. Fell asleep holding hands—which is always epic for me.

Worked out at the Alamo before the first match of the weekend—which was amazing.

And … He did really well. In fact, he won his division and not only became the San Antonio City Champion but became a professional chess player—earning his first $200 playing the game he loves. (I just laughed with pure, proud dad joy.)

So… On the drive home, he and I had a great chat about *how* he is cultivating mastery in chess. I leaned on some Angela Duckworth wisdom from her classic book *Grit*.

Angela tells us that there's a formula for achieving great things. It goes like this:

$$\text{Talent x Effort = Skill}$$
$$\text{Skill x Effort = Achievement}$$

Angela tells us that "Talent" (which she defines as the speed with which you can pick up a skill) definitely matters.

And … EFFORT counts TWICE.

You can have all the talent in the world and still never develop any skill and never really achieve anything.

I repeat: EFFORT counts TWICE.

After sharing that with Emerson, I wanted to create a little video with him in which *he* shared the formula so we could share that with our community as we've gotten a lot of feedback that parents really love sharing wisdom featuring Emerson with their kids.

We did a take. Oops. Goof.

We did a second take. Almost there …

Then we did a third take.

And…

Emerson spontaneously came up with an additional line. He said:

$$Talent \times Effort = Skill$$
$$Skill \times Effort = Achievement$$

Then he continued, adding:

Achievement x *MORE EFFORT* = *MASTERY*

To which I say… "What he said!"

Effort, my dear Heroic master, counts not *once* not *twice* but *THRICE*.

Here's to maximizing our Heroic potential by leaning into our natural talents with a ton of joyful effort.

It's time to move from Theory to Practice to Mastery.

TODAY.

P.S. It's also time to dominate our fundamentals. That's our next objective…

YOUR SOCKS
COACH WOODEN ON HOW PUT THEM ON

John Wooden's UCLA basketball teams won ten NCAA championships in twelve years, including an eighty-eight-game winning streak. (Go Bruins!)

ESPN says that Wooden was the greatest coach of the twentieth century. That makes him, arguably, the greatest coach ever.

Couple things to note here.

First, quick question: You know how many years Wooden coached before he won his first championship?

Answer: He was at UCLA for 15 (!) seasons before he won his first title. And, he coached for a number of years before even showing up at UCLA.

As Seattle Seahawks coach Pete Carroll points out in *Win Forever*, it took Wooden quite a while to figure it out but, once he did, he could "win forever."

Keep that in mind when you think about Wooden's awesomeness. He wasn't *born* a great coach. He MADE himself a great coach, one incrementally optimized Masterpiece Day at a time, aggregated and compounded over an extended period of time, growth-mindset style all the way.

Second, another quick question: You know what Wooden did in the very first practice before he'd even let his players take the court?

He'd teach them how to put on their socks.

Imagine the *absolute best* players in the country coming to the *absolute best* program in the country and their coach won't even let them touch a basketball until they learned how to properly roll a sock over their foot and put it on *just* right.

Why'd Coach do that?

Because he knew that championships are built on a solid foundation. And there's nothing more fundamental for a basketball player than putting on your socks right. If you can't slow down long enough to do that right, you're in trouble.

Gotta make sure those wrinkles were out of the socks lest we might get a blister in practice. Get a blister and our performance in games will suffer. Therefore, put your socks on right, son!

… All that to arrive here: What are *your* "socks?"

You know, those super simple, mundane, unsexy "easies" that are too easy to overlook.

Which one are you going to +1° today?

Dominate the fundamentals.

And…

Win forever.

Starting…

TODAY.

WOODEN'S DECADES
BEFORE HE WON A TITLE

I n our last +1°, we spent some time with John Wooden. We're going to spend some more time with him today.

Wooden is one of my all-time favorite Heroes. In fact, his Heroic portrait is staring at me from my office wall as I type this— challenging me to do my best and make TODAY a masterpiece. ("I'm on it, Coach!")

We discussed some of the details of his career. I'm going to repeat a few of them as we make a very important point.

First, recall that ESPN says he was the greatest coach of the twentieth century. *The Sporting News* named Wooden the "Greatest Coach of All Time."

He's also the ONLY person to ever be inducted into the NCAA Hall of Fame as BOTH a player AND as a Coach.

And…

As we just discussed, Wooden coached for A LONG TIME before he won his first NCAA Championship.

More specifically, he coached at the collegiate level for SEVENTEEN (!) years before he won his first championship.

But…

Get this…

Before he coached at the *collegiate* level, Wooden spent ELEVEN years coaching *high school* basketball. Then, during World War II in 1942 (at thirty-two years old), he joined the United States Navy. He served until 1946 and left as a lieutenant.

It was only after all *that* that he coached college basketball for *another* SEVENTEEN years before he won his first NCAA Championship in 1964.

He was fifty-four years old.

By that point, he had been coaching for nearly THREE DECADES.

I always find it helpful to remember that our heroes weren't always the heroes we remember them as today.

Here's what's even more important for our purposes: Wooden didn't focus on winning or losing.

OF COURSE he wanted to win, but he knew that the only way to have the best shot at the big outcome goals WHILE winning the ultimate game of life (RIGHT NOW!) was to focus ALL of his and his players' energy on what was 100% within their control: their effort and their attitude.

That's our +1°.

Remember: Our heroes gave their ENTIRE lives to their pursuit of mastery.

And...

The greatest among them always kept their focus on winning the ULTIMATE game of life: showing up and doing their best.

Not someday.

But all day, every day.

Let's make our heroes and ourselves proud as we move from Theory to Practice to Mastery Together...

TODAY.

GREATNESS = CONSISTENCY
ON THE FUNDAMENTALS

R obin Sharma tells us that greatness is all about consistency on the fundamentals.

Look at any great performer and that's what you'll see.

Of course, a world-class artist will have different fundamentals than an athlete who will have different fundamentals than an entrepreneur who will have different fundamentals than a parent but the same rule applies in each case: mastery of the most basic fundamentals.

Which, of course, begs the question…

What are YOUR fundamentals?

I like to think of our fundamentals on two different levels: the universal and the specific.

We ALL share the need for mastery around the basic fundies: eating, moving, sleeping, breathing, focusing.

If we don't have those universal fundamentals dialed in then, from my perspective, there's simply no way we'll have a shot at activating our Heroic potential.

Then we have our specific fundamentals. The things that are unique to each of us and our particular crafts.

Our +1°…

How are YOU doing with YOUR fundamentals?

And…

How can you +1° it TODAY?

DIGGING FOUNDATIONS
WANT TO BUILD A SKYSCRAPER?

I magine you're at a construction site.

It's the first phase of the project.

If you wanted to guess how tall the building on that construction site was going to be and you couldn't look at the architect's plans or ask anyone about it, what's the best way to guess how tall the building will be?

Answer: Look at how deeply they're digging the foundation.

A shallow foundation will work for a single-story house.

A skyscraper with over one hundred floors? They're digging very, very deeply.

Our +1° spotlight on YOU...

Want to go high?

Then dig deep.

Create a solid foundation.

Dominate your fundamentals.

THE LIGHTHOUSE
GET YOUR WATTAGE UP

Joseph Campbell once posed the *kōan* question:

"What am I? Am I the bulb that carries the light, or am I the light of which the bulb is a vehicle?"

Hmmm…

Well…

What are you?

Are you the bulb that carries the light? Or are you the light of which the bulb is a vehicle?

I say: "YES!"

You?

Saving the longer philosophical-spiritual chat for another time, let's assume that, at the very least, we're the humble bulb through which the light shines.

If that's the case, then one of our main jobs in life (if not THE Job with a capital "J") is to get our bulbs optimized so we can handle as much of that divine light as we possibly can.

I mean… Would you rather be a 20-watt bulb that blows up the moment more light tries to get through or a stable 60- or 100-watt bulb that lights up the room?!

Or, for the spiritually ambitious among us…

Why not see if we can become great souls that shine like a 1,000-watt lighthouse bulb, lighting up our part of the world during these stormy times?

How do we do that?

I repeat…

We dominate our fundamentals.

PRACTICING WITH KOBE
AT 4:00 A.M.

A lan Stein is one of the world's leading peak performance coaches. He's worked with some of the most elite athletes (and executives) in the world and wrote a couple of great books.

In *Raise Your Game*, Alan tells a GREAT story about some time he spent with Kobe Bryant.

It goes something like this...

Once upon a time, Nike flew Alan out to Los Angeles to work the first-ever Kobe Bryant Skills Academy. At the time, Kobe was *the* best basketball player in the world.

Alan asked Kobe if he could watch him work out.

As Alan says: "That's how it is in my business. Everyone can see the game, but to really learn the secrets, you have to watch the practice. It's the difference between buying Jay-Z's album and sitting in the studio watching him write and record one."

So...

Alan asks Kobe if he can watch his workout.

Kobe says: "Sure. I'm going at four."

Alan says: "But don't we have a camp session at three thirty tomorrow afternoon?"

Kobe says: "I know. I'm working out at 4:00 a.m."

Alan's head explodes a bit at that moment.

Perfect.

Alan shows up at 4:00 a.m.

What did he see?

Well, first of all, by the time he arrives at 4:00 a.m., Kobe is already drenched in sweat.

He says: "For forty-five minutes I was shocked. For forty-five minutes I watched the best player in the world do the most basic drills. I watched the best player on the planet do basic ball-handling drills. I watched the best player on the planet do basic footwork. I watched the best player on the planet do basic offensive moves."

And: "Granted, he did everything with surgical precision and superhero intensity, but the stuff he was doing was so simple. I couldn't believe it."

Later in the day he thanked Kobe.

He didn't want to sound rude or condescending but couldn't resist asking him: "You're the best player in the world. Why do such basic stuff?"

Kobe's response?

Alan says: "He flashed that gleaming smile of his. 'Why do you think I'm the best player in the game?' he asked. 'Because I never get bored with the basics.'"

That's our +1°.

How are YOUR basics?

A.k.a.: Your FUNDAMENTALS!!!

Remember…

Greatness is ALL about consistency on the fundamentals.

Remember Kobe in the gym at 4:00 a.m. as you DOMINATE your fundamentals with superhero intensity today.

IF WE WORKED TOGETHER 1-ON-1
I'D ASK YOU THIS QUESTION

If you and I worked together 1-on-1, we'd have fun talking about a lot of things.

Of course, we'd obsess about you and your Heroic potential as we get more clarity on who you are at your absolute best in your Energy, Work, and Love. We'd chat about your wildly important goal(s) and what you need to do every.single.day in pursuit of those goals.

And...

I can assure you that there's *one* thing I KNOW we'd chat about: your fundamentals.

You know how when you go to the doctor, they tap your knee to check your reflexes?

Well, when you come to me, I tap your fundamentals.

It's super simple.

Me: "Eating. Moving. Sleeping. How are we doing? Where are we strong? What needs work?"

It's amazing how that simple question elicits some powerful distinctions.

Hero: "Well, my eating is pretty good. But I'm not moving as much as I'd like. And my sleep is just terrible. I really need to do X, Y, and Z."

Me: "Awesome. What's the #1 thing you KNOW you could be doing that would help you go to the next level if you started doing it consistently?"

Hero: "Oh. X. For sure."

Me: "Fantastic. What, *specifically*, will you do?"

Hero: "I will do THIS..."

Now, that #1 thing might not seem like a big deal.

But it is.

Your doctor gets nervous if your knee doesn't respond to his little tap.

We should get nervous if your fundamentals aren't dialed in.

So...

Your turn...

Me: "Eating. Moving. Sleeping. How are we doing? Where are we strong? What needs work?"

You: "_____."

That's our +1° coaching.

Get clear on what's working and what needs work.

And go dominate your fundamentals.

I look forward to seeing you and your funda-knee at our next appointment!

WORLD CHAMPION YOU
THE TRAINING CAMP

Josh Waitzkin is a fascinating guy.

You know that movie *Searching for Bobby Fischer* featuring a little chess prodigy kid?

Well, Josh was that kid. The movie was based on a book his dad wrote about his rise to the top of the chess world.

After dominating chess as a kid and young adult, Josh found himself a bit burned out and moved on to master the martial side of Tai Chi—becoming a world champion in the process.

Then he wrote a book on how he did it. It's called *The Art of Learning*, but I think a more appropriate title might be *The Art of Mastery*.

I rarely spend any time on the Internet but I wanted to see what Josh was up to these days so I cruised over to his site and clicked around. I wound up on a page for his 1-on-1 coaching services. He said he wasn't accepting new clients but you could apply and put yourself on a waiting list.

But, he said, only apply if you are committed to living like you're in a world champion training camp.

I thought that was brilliant.

Think about that for a moment.

What would YOUR life look like if you were in a WORLD-CHAMPION (as in, trying to be the absolute best at what you do) Training Camp?

Well, what would it look like?

In his book, Josh tells us we need to make a decision. We need to decide whether we want to be decent at what we do, good at what we do, great at what we do, among the best at what we do, or, THE BEST at what we do.

He tells us that if you want to go through life and be "decent," you have a high margin for error. You can have a setback like a job loss or whatever and sit on your couch eating Cheetos for a month or three.

But if you have REALLY high standards and aspirations, you've gotta step up.

Our +1°…

For the sake of discussion, let's assume you'd like to become THE best (most Heroic!) version of you.

You're stepping into a World Champion You Training Camp. As in, you just stepped into it a second ago.

What's your life look like starting TODAY?

What *immediately* gets dropped?

And what *immediately* gets dialed in?

Get on that. And go get 'em Champ!

CHAMPIONS DO MORE
GOT 10 REPS? GIVE ME 11!

Continuing our theme of stepping up and into our very own World Champion You Training Camp, let's have fun with a little practice of mine.

One of the common themes in sports-based mental toughness books is the fact that "Champions do more."

As Jim Afremow tells us in *The Champion's Mind*: "They outperform their contracts."

Every day. Every play.

For whatever reason, one day when I was doing my warmup for another trail workout, I was thinking of this idea and decided that my ten-rep wrist circle stretch thing was going to become eleven. My ten ankle circles? Eleven.

My side-to-side swings? Eleven. Arms swinging overhead forward and then back? Eleven plus eleven.

Sets of ten burpees? Eleven. Set of ten pull-ups? Eleven.

Of course, that's a totally ridiculous thing to do but I smile with a fierce joy every time I do one more rep and say to myself…

"That's like me. Champions do more."

That's our +1°.

Got ten reps?

Give us eleven.

BLISSIPLINE
BLISS + DISCIPLINE = SECRET SAUCE

Michael Bernard Beckwith coined one of my all-time favorite words: *blissipline*.

Two parts: bliss + discipline.

In *Spiritual Liberation*, Beckwith tells us: "The gift of self-discipline is that it has the power to take you beyond the reasoning of temporary emotion to freedom. Think of how empowered you've felt on occasions when you haven't given in to the 'I don't feel like it' syndrome and honored your commitment to yourself. What does not *feeling* like it have to do with it? The combination of love for something with the willingness to do what it takes to practice it—discipline—results in freedom."

I LOVE this line in particular: "What does not *feeling* like it have to do with it?" (Hah.)

You decided to do something. So DO IT!!

I think Seneca would've loved the idea of discipline leading to blissipline.

Here's how he put it a couple thousand years ago: "You have to persevere and fortify your pertinacity until the will to good becomes a disposition to good."

Translation: We need to have the discipline to stick with something long enough so we can create new habits that eventually lead to a new way of being where doing the right thing comes naturally.

Seneca also says: "How much better to pursue a straight course and eventually reach that destination where the things that are pleasant and the things that are honorable finally become, for you, the same."

Translation: Discipline leads to blissipline when what you *love* to do is what is *best* for you.

And, in fact, after we've used our willpower wisely long enough to install a habit that runs on autopilot, we get to a point where doing the less-than-optimal thing is harder to do because our basal ganglia is basically *forcing* us to do the right thing.

So…

How's *your* discipline?

Do what you've decided to do with a smile.

Here's to the blissipline that leads to our freedom.

P.S. Here's another Beckwith gem from *Spiritual Liberation*: "It's all well and good to read books, and to attend seminars, lectures, and workshops, and to say, 'Oh, that really resonates with me! It's now part of my life's philosophy.' Your philosophy may give you a temporary state of euphoria, but if you want to be anchored in reality, it takes practice, practice, practice. We are not here to be euphoric but to get free. Rudimentary spirituality is theory; advanced spirituality is practice."

P.P.S. This is worth repeating as we move from being librarians to warriors: "Rudimentary spirituality is theory; advanced spirituality is practice."

DILIGENTLY, PATIENTLY & PERSISTENTLY
& YOU'RE BOUND TO BE SUCCESSFUL

I n our last +1°, we talked about the power of *blissipline*. Bliss + Discipline = Boom!

When I think about bringing discipline to our lives, I immediately think of S.N. Goenka.

Anyone who has attended his ten-day silent Vipassana meditation (a.k.a. a ten-day bootcamp for your mind!) has this phrase permanently tattooed to their consciousness:

"Work diligently... Diligently. Work patiently and persistently... Patiently and persistently. And you're *bound* to be successful... *Bound* to be successful."

(Note: You need to imagine Goenka saying this with a beautiful, lyrical Burmese accent.)

I don't know how many times I heard him say that during the retreat Alexandra and I did together over fifteen years ago but it was a LOT.

"Work diligently... Diligently. Work patiently and persistently... Patiently and persistently. And you're *bound* to be successful... *Bound* to be successful."

Goenka would say that during our hour-long meditation sessions.

He was referring to the importance of working diligently, patiently, and persistently to cultivate a strong mind via our meditation practice, but, of course, the same rules apply to ALL aspects of our lives.

"Work diligently... Diligently. Work patiently and persistently... Patiently and persistently. And you're *bound* to be successful... *Bound* to be successful."

Our +1° spotlight on YOU...

How's *your* diligence?

How's *your* patience?

How's *your* persistence?

What's one little thing you can do to turn up the heat with each just a little more today?

I repeat, my dear Hero...

"Work diligently... Diligently. Work patiently and persistently... Patiently and persistently. And you're *bound* to be successful... *Bound* to be successful."

START AGAIN
& AGAIN & AGAIN & AGAIN...

In our last +1°, we spent some time training our minds with the renowned Vipassana meditation teacher S.N. Goenka as we repeated his wonderful mantra:

"Work diligently… Diligently. Work *patiently* and *persistently*… *Patiently* and *persistently*. And you're *bound* to be successful… *Bound* to be successful."

Goenka had another mantra that's worth chatting about. Here it is: "Start again."

As in, when your mind (INEVITABLY!) wanders—whether that's during your meditation practice or at any other point in the day—just start again.

Bring your attention back to what's important now.

No need to stop everything and psychoanalyze *why* your mind is wandering for the next month and a half.

Just say, as another mindfulness expert Herbert Benson tells us, "Oh, well." And, start again.

To recap:

Mind wander? Start again.

Focus on what's important now.

Mind wander? Start again.

Focus on what's important now.

Mind wander? Start again.

Focus on what's important now.

That our +1°.

If (or, should I say, "When?") you find your mind wandering a bit today, just start again. And again. And again.

Do that *diligently*, *patiently*, and *persistently* and you're *bound* to be successful, Hero.

STATES VS. TRAITS
HOW TO QUIT BEING A CANNONBALL

K en Wilber tells us there's a big difference between what he calls "states" and "traits."

It's pretty easy to have a "state" experience during which we feel super fired up. Think about the last time you attended a weekend workshop or got super inspired reading a book or doing whatever you do that fires you up.

Can you feel it?

That's a STATE experience.

You felt the presence of your higher self in a deeply moving, profound way.

Fantastic.

Now, unfortunately, what often happens when we get back from that weekend workshop high is that we crash. It's kinda like being shot out of a cannon. You fly wayyyyyyy up and briefly see the stars but... then... you fall right back to where you started. Ouch.

And, it hurts twice: You experience the pain of falling back down to reality AND you now know that something better exists but you don't know how to taste it again.

Here's what we need to know.

If we want that *state* experience to last, we've gotta do the work so that connection to our higher selves isn't just a fleeting *state* we chase after but a TRAIT—it needs to become who we are.

And there's only one way to make that happen.

A ton of hard work over an extended period of time. (Hah.)

We need to diligently, patiently, persistently create the scaffolding such that we can ascend to and consistently live from the heights we aspire to live from without all the cannonball-like ups and downs.

Which is why we come back to the fundamentals so often in Heroic Basic Training in the app and in our Heroic Coach certification program.

Eating. Moving. Sleeping. Breathing. Focusing.

I repeat: Want to see how high a building is going to be? Look at how deeply they're digging the foundation.

Want to LIVE from a place of connection to your highest self? Dominate your fundamentals.

Dig deep. Build up.

Make your states traits.

THE MIRACLE DRUGS
AKA, SLEEP, MEDITATION & EXERCISE

I always love it when conservative scientists present the power of their findings in the form of a miracle drug. Here are three of my favorites from three of my favorite scientists.

First, we have sleep researcher, Matthew Walker.

Here's how he puts it in his *brilliant* (must-read) book *Why We Sleep*: "AMAZING BREAKTHROUGH! Scientists have discovered a revolutionary new treatment that makes you live longer. It enhances your memory and makes you more creative. It makes you look more attractive. It keeps you slim and lowers food cravings. It protects you from cancer and dementia. It wards off colds and the flu. It lowers your risk of heart attacks and strokes, not to mention diabetes. You'll even feel happier, less depressed, and less anxious. Are you interested?"

(I'll take it! You?)

Matthew continues by saying that, although the results might sound hyperbolic, they're not. Over 17,000 (!) studies have PROVEN the astonishing power of sleep and that "most of us do not realize how remarkable a panacea sleep truly is."

Then we have Jonathan Haidt, one of the world's leading researchers on the psychology of morality and flourishing.

In his brilliant book *The Happiness Hypothesis*, he gives us a similar ad for meditation when he tells us: "Suppose you read about a pill that you could take once a day to reduce anxiety and increase your contentment. Would you take it? Suppose further that the pill has a great variety of side effects, all of them good: increased self-esteem, empathy, and trust; it even improves memory. Suppose, finally, that the pill is all natural and costs nothing. Now would you take it? The pill exists. It's called meditation."

(I'll take it! You?)

Then there's Harvard MD psychiatrist, John Ratey.

In his great book on the science of exercise called *Spark*, he tells us: "I tell people that going for a run is like taking a little bit of Prozac and a little bit of Ritalin because, like the drugs, exercise elevates these neurotransmitters. It's a handy metaphor to get the point across, but the deeper explanation is that exercise balances neurotransmitters — along with the rest of the neurochemicals in the brain. And as you'll see, keeping your brain in balance can change your life."

(I'll take it! You?)

To recap...

Sleep is a magic pill. So is meditation. And so is exercise.

The more of those metaphorical pills we pop, the less of the other ones we're likely to need.

KRYPTONITE DUST
BRING THE VACUUM

D ave Asprey is one of the world's leading biohackers. In fact,
he pretty much founded the movement.

He's written a bunch of great books including one called *Head
Strong* in which he tells us about kryptonite dust.

Here's the short story.

We all know that Superman is vulnerable to big chunks of
kryptonite. It immediately drains him of his power.

But... Asprey tells us that the *really* smart way for Lex Luthor
to diminish Superman's power without him even knowing about
it would be to sprinkle a little kryptonite *dust* all around his house
and office.

Then his powers would slowly ebb away and he'd get to a
place where he didn't even remember what it felt like to be powerful—accepting his diminished state as a new normal.

Asprey tells us that's *precisely* what's happening with us. Our
steady exposure to all the kryptonite dust in our lives—from the
unhealthy foods to the nonstop drip of adrenalin from all the
screen time—gradually erodes our power until our diminished
state of vitality feels like the new normal.

The +1° question...

What kryptonite dust have YOU allowed into your life?

Pay attention. It's diminishing your superpowers.

Vacuum it up.

TODAY.

YOUR VISCERAL FAT
HOW'S YOURS?

R obert Lustig is a researcher and professor at UCSF. He's also one of the world's leading endocrinologists. He wrote a great book called *Fat Chance*, sub-title: "Beating the Odds Against Sugar, Processed Food, Obesity, and Disease."

Let's get right to work.

Lustig tells us that: "When it comes right down to it, it's all about your middle. This whole obesity/health/longevity question centers on your abdominal, visceral, or 'big belly' fat—at least statistically."

He also says: "In a nutshell, your body fat is your biggest long-term risk for infirmity. Nothing correlates with diabetes, heart disease, and cancer better than your fat."

But it's not any kind of fat. It's your *visceral* fat—that fat around your middle. As Dr. Lustig says: "Visceral fat is the fulcrum on which your health teeters."

Finally, he tells us: "The simplest and cheapest surrogate for determining your health status is your waist circumference, which correlates with morbidity and risk for death better than any other health parameter. This is arguably the most important piece of information in your entire health profile because it tells you about your visceral fat. A high waist circumference translates into the 'apple' shape that tips physicians off to risk for diabetes, heart disease, stroke, and cancer."

That's our +1°.

How's your waist circumference?

We'll add some nuance in our next +1°, but Lustig tells us that the easiest way to get a sense of your waist circumference is via your belt size.

He tells us that more than forty inches for men and thirty-five inches for women is a likely indicator of visceral fat.

Private question time: What's YOUR belt size?

Time to close the gap?

HOW TO PREDICT YOUR MORBIDITY
HOW'S YOUR WAIST-TO-HEIGHT RATIO?

I n our last +1°, we talked about the fact that, as per Robert Lustig's *Fat Chance*, your visceral fat (a.k.a. abdominal/"big belly" fat) is "the fulcrum on which your health teeters."

Dr. Lustig tells us that a waist circumference of more than forty inches for men and thirty-five inches for women is a likely indicator of visceral fat.

But… Research shows that there's an even more powerful predictor of morbidity than a simple waist circumference measure.

In fact, this is arguably *the* most important data you and your doctor can know to assess your metabolic health and risk for all the things you *don't* want to experience.

It's called the waist-to-height ratio or WHtR. The optimal ratio between your WAIST and your HEIGHT? <.5.

For example, I'm six feet tall. That's seventy-two inches. My waist can be up to thirty-six inches to pass the <.5 test. It's less than thirty-two inches.

Our +1°… Another private question: What's your WHtR? Seriously. What is it?

If it's not <.5, we need to get to work on that like your life depends on it because, I say with Heroic love and a fierce commitment to supporting you in dominating this, it does.

NOTE: It's not possible to capture all the ideas I'd like to share with you on this important subject within the constraints of this book.

Check out our Philosopher's Notes on dozens of the best books on nutrition and our hour-long master classes on Optimal Nutrition 101 and Optimal Weight 101 for more.

Get instant access to that content and more at Heroic.us/Activate or scan the QR code at the bottom of this page.

Plus: Check out our Heroic Coach program for a deeper dive into the nuts and bolts of how to conquer any challenges you may be facing in this domain while learning how to empower others to do the same. An inspiring number of people have shared notes like this:

"There are so many ways that the Heroic Coach program has made a difference in my life. Probably the most noticeable changes have been in the energy area. I have lost twenty-five lbs. this year and I am at a weight I never thought I'd ever see again on the scale. My cholesterol numbers are pristine and I'm on the verge of the waist-to-height ratio being .5... Applying the eating/moving/sleeping tools have changed my life. Friends and family have been asking me 'hey man... what are you doing... you look great.'"

Learn more about Heroic Coach at Heroic.us/Coach or scan this QR code:

THE CASE AGAINST SUGAR
IS VERY STRONG

Gary Taubes is an award-winning investigative science and health journalist.

He's also the author of a number of great books including *Why We Get Fat* and *The Case Against Sugar*.

Here's the basic idea for *The Case Against Sugar*...

If you were a detective trying to figure out a series of crimes and you noticed a common pattern among those crimes, you'd be wise to put the pieces together and see if you could narrow your search down to a single suspect. (Right?)

Well, that's what Taubes does in his book. The crimes? All the chronic diseases wreaking havoc on our society—from diabetes and obesity to heart disease and cancer.

Short story: All those chronic diseases are associated with metabolic dysfunction. And the fastest way to make your metabolism dysfunctional? Sugar.

Enter: The case against it.

Let's bring in a couple of expert witnesses to prove our case.

We'll start with Nobel Prize winner Elizabeth Blackburn. She discovered telomerase—the stuff that replenishes telomeres.

Here's how she puts it in *The Telomere Effect*—the great book she wrote with Elissa Epel: "When we want to spot the parties responsible for metabolic disease, we point a finger at the highly processed, sugary foods and sweetened drinks.

(We're looking at you, packaged cakes, candies, cookies, and sodas.) These are the foods and drinks most associated with compulsive eating. They light up the reward system in your brain. They are almost immediately absorbed into the blood, and they trick the brain into thinking we are starving and need more food. While we used to think all nutrients had similar effects on weight and metabolism—a 'calorie is a calorie'—this is wrong. Simply reducing sugars, even if you eat the same number of calories, can lead to metabolic improvements. Simple carbs wreak more havoc on metabolism and control over appetite than other types of foods."

Blackburn is at UCSF. She references her colleague Robert Lustig when she makes the point above.

As discussed, Lustig is one of the world's leading endocrinologists. You know what he says about sugar?

He tells us that sugar is the "Darth Vader" of the nutrition world.

This little statistic might be THE most powerful one we'll ever read regarding just how dangerous sugar is. (I repeated it half a dozen times in Optimal Weight 101.)

"If you had any residual doubt about 'a calorie is not a calorie,' this analysis should remove it. Every additional 150 calories per person per day barely raised diabetes prevalence. But if those 150 calories were instead from a can of soda, increase in diabetes rose sevenfold. Sugar is more dangerous than its calories. Sugar is a toxin. Plain and simple."

I repeat…

"If you had any residual doubt about 'a calorie is not a calorie,' this analysis should remove it. Every additional 150 calories per person per day barely raised diabetes prevalence. But if those 150 calories were instead from a can of soda, increase in diabetes rose sevenfold. Sugar is more dangerous than its calories. Sugar is a toxin. Plain and simple."

That's crazy.

150 additional calories from any source? Not a big deal. 150 additional calories from a can of soda?

DIABETES GOES UP SEVENFOLD.

Did you get that? Let me repeat it to *make sure* the point lands... 150 additional calories from any source? No big deal. 150 additional calories from a can of soda?

DIABETES GOES UP SEVENFOLD.

Know this: "Sugar is more dangerous than its calories. Sugar is a toxin. Plain and simple."

Please tattoo that on your consciousness. (Right after throwing away your sodas!)

And... To be clear: This isn't just about the risk for diabetes. It's a *metabolic* issue—which is all about how every cell in our bodies produces energy—which means it affects EVERYTHING.

Our +1°... If you feel so inspired, go throw away all the sodas in your house. (Seriously.)

The Case Against Sugar is REALLY solid. If we're serious about optimizing our energy so we can activate our Heroic potential, reducing/eliminating sugar should be a top priority.

Case closed. Let's go, Hero!

THE HEROIC FOOD RULES
THE BIG 3 (+1)

I've been a professional optimizer for over twenty-five years. During that time, I'm pretty sure I've experimented with pretty much every single nutritional philosophy out there.

I've been vegan. I've been Paleo. I've been ketogenic. I was even a fruitarian for a few weeks decades ago. (Yes, I just laughed at myself.)

Although I no longer spend any time debating nutrition as we can only do so much cherry picking before we get nauseous, I do believe we can boil down the essential truths into a few general rules we'd be wise to consider following.

Here they are:

Rule #1: Quit drinking your sugar.

If you're currently drinking sodas or fruit juices or any liquid with sugar, this is arguably the fastest and easiest way to take your nutrition to the next level—and, as a by-product, make significant progress in optimizing your metabolism so you can optimize your energy and your weight.

Are YOU drinking your sugar? If so, STOP!

Note: Soda is obviously not a health food but... Parents: Fruit juice is NOT a health food either.

Rule #2: Eat real food and throw out the factory food.

Consider reducing/eliminating three different types of factory food including: factory-ultraprocessed foods with ingredients you can't pronounce, don't have in your pantry, and didn't evolve to consume; factory-farmed animals for ethical, health, and environmental reasons; and factory fat including vegetable oils like soybean, safflower, corn, and canola oils—none of which existed pre–Industrial Revolution and all of which disrupt our Omega 3:6 ratios and create inflammation.

Quick check in: How are you doing there?

Rule #3: Eat within a time-restricted window.

Research is clear that *when* you eat matters as much as *what* you eat. Give yourself at least thirteen hours between your last meal of the day and your first meal the following day.

As you know if you've been following along, we have a last-input "digital sunset." We need an "eating sunset" as well.

In fact, science says: We want to eat *at least* two hours before we go to bed and target *four* hours before we go to bed if we're playing the professional optimizing game.

(Note: It's *astonishing* for me to see just how much the timing of my last meal affects my resting heart rate and heart rate variability as measured by my Oura ring.)

So… When was your last bite last night? When was your first bite today? How many hours were there in between?

Let's get to 13+ and know that if you have a hard time going that long between meals, it's probably because we need to work on some metabolic flexibility issues. See Rules #1 and #2 for support there.

And, finally, my favorite rule…

Rule +1: Eat like your favorite philosopher (who lived at least three hundred years ago).

Perhaps the simplest, wisest advice is to simply eat like our great-great-great-great-great-great-grandparents ate before all the factories.

I like to tweak that a bit to have fun helping you channel your favorite philosopher or spiritual teacher—whether that's Jesus or Muhammad or Moses or Buddha or Lao Tzu.

For me? It's Epictetus.

Guess what? Our favorite old-school philosophers didn't (and couldn't) drink their sugar because it didn't exist. And all they could eat was non-factory-produced food because factories didn't exist yet. And most of them couldn't eat all day every day because those wonderful inventions we call the grocery store and the fridge didn't exist yet.

There ya go.

The Heroic Food Rules in a nutshell.

Here's to changing our lives (and our families' lives) one bite at a time.

TODAY.

GOT SEROTONIN?
HIDE & SEEK: BRAIN VS. GUT

*S*erotonin.

At this stage, most of us have at least a vague sense that serotonin is one of the primary neurotransmitters that makes us feel all warm and fuzzy and happy.

And…

As with most things, it's a bit more complex than that.

As Wikipedia tells us: "Serotonin or 5-hydroxytryptamine is a monoamine neurotransmitter. It has a popular image as a contributor to feelings of well-being and happiness, though its actual biological function is complex and multifaceted, modulating cognition, reward, learning, memory, and numerous physiological processes."

So…

Serotonin is a complex and multifaceted neurotransmitter that influences a NUMBER of important biological functions, including our sense of well-being and happiness.

But…

That's not quite the point of this +1°.

This is.

If you were going on a treasure hunt to see if you could find as much serotonin in your body as possible, where would you look?

(Insert *Jeopardy* music here.)

Treasure hunt.

Looking for serotonin.

Where do you look?

Well, duh...

Your brain, right?

Well, no.

Take a trip from your brain down your vagus nerve and wander down to your gut. THAT's where you'll find 80 to 90% of your body's serotonin.

NINETY PERCENT?!?!

YES.

80 to 90% of your serotonin is hanging out in your GUT.

Isn't that interesting?

(Answer: Yes.)

And that's yet another one of the many reasons why optimizing your NUTRITION is one of the most important things you can do to optimize your EMOTIONAL well-being.

I repeat: Your PHYSIOLOGY drives *a lot* more of your PSYCHOLOGY than you may think.

Optimize it.

TODAY.

EAT REAL FOOD
NOT EDIBLE FOODLIKE SUBSTANCES

M ichael Pollan wrote a book called *Food Rules* and another great book called *In Defense of Food*.

The basic theme of those two books? In short, Western diets create Western diseases; traditional diets do not.

He tells us that traditional diets vary—from high fat to high protein to high carb. There's no "single ideal human diet." But there is one singularly bad human diet: the Western one packed with ultraprocessed, edible foodlike substances.

In *In Defense of Food*, he "defends food" against what we *think* is food but is *really* just what he calls "edible foodlike substances." That "edible foodlike substance" (a.k.a. ultraprocessed food) is made in a factory with ingredients that literally didn't exist a couple hundred years ago.

It now constitutes 58% of our diet.

Reread that last line.

58% of our modern diet consists of "food" that DID NOT EXIST a couple hundred years ago.

Consuming that ultraprocessed food in *any* significant quantity, let alone in the quantities in which the average Westerner consumes it, is not a wise idea.

Hence, the second of our three Heroic Food Rules: Eat real food and throw out the factory food.

In *Food Rules*, he offers 64 rules to consider.

Rule #1? "Eat food."

And quit eating the "edible foodlike substances."

Lucky Rule #13 is a good one: "Eat only foods that will eventually rot."

As they say, the longer the shelf-life of the food you eat, the shorter *your* life will be.

Then there's Rule #57: "Don't get your fuel from the same place your car does."

Did you know that "American gas stations now make more money inside selling food (and cigarettes) than they do outside selling gasoline"?

Yep.

Our +1°…

What are YOUR food rules?

Are you following them?

WHEN TO EAT
THE POWER OF TIME-RESTRICTED EATING

A re you or a loved one struggling with losing weight? Or struggling with low energy or a low mood? Or battling a chronic disease? Or, perhaps, all of the above?

If so... I think you'll want to pay attention to this +1°.

Satchin Panda is one of the world's leading researchers in the field of circadian biology.

He wrote a great book called *The Circadian Code* in which he shares the research that establishes JUST how important it is for us to align our eating, moving, and sleeping with the natural rhythms of our world.

Check out the Philosopher's Notes for the full story.

Today I want to focus on ONE very Big Idea from his book. It's about time-restricted eating.

Here's the short story.

Actually... Quick question...

At precisely what time did you first put ANYTHING into your body other than water yesterday? And, at precisely what time did you put that last bite of anything other than water into your body yesterday?

That's your eating window.

For example, if you had a cup of coffee or tea at 6:30 a.m. and then ate breakfast and then lunch and then dinner and then a little snack at, say, 8:30 p.m. before going to bed at 10:30 p.m., your eating window would be fourteen hours.

You need to know that if your eating window is greater than twelve hours, you will be *significantly* less healthy than if you ate within an 8-10-12 hour window of time.

It's called "time-restricted eating."

The research on this is REALLY (!) powerful.

Know this...

We didn't evolve to force our bodies to work all day every day digesting every little thing we throw into our mouths.

Our +1°...

Restrict your eating window and give your body a break to do some important repair work. It will do your mind, body, and soul good.

Practically speaking: Make a note of when you had your first bite/sip of anything other than water today. Make sure you have your last bite/sip of anything other than water less than twelve hours after that first bite/sip.

This VERY simple practice might just unlock VERY significant gains in your and your loved ones' well-being.

Day 1. All in.

Let's go, Hero!

ISN'T THAT EXTREME?
NO, IT'S NOT—THIS IS

Susan Peirce Thompson wrote a great book called *Bright Line Eating.* She has a PhD in neuroscience and is one of the world's leading experts on the psychology of eating.

Before all that, Susan was addicted to cocaine and food and basically everything else—which gives her a very nice vantage point from which to talk about how to recover from addiction.

In her books and programs, she integrates the bright lines of willpower with the fundamentals of nutrition.

Her top two bright lines for eating?

Eliminate sugar and flour.

Don't reduce or eat them more moderately, she says...

E L I M I N A T E them.

Period.

Susan walks us through all the reasons those edible foodlike substances act more like *drugs* than food and she points out the havoc they cause in our bodies.

But I want to focus on a question she often gets asked when she encourages people to make a 100% commitment to those two bright line rules.

People often say (insert at least a slightly whiny voice): "But... Isn't that extreme?

"I mean, really? I have to say no to donuts and cookies and pastries and pizza and...?

"Isn't that just sooooo extreme?"

"NO!" she says.

Cutting off your limbs because you have diabetes?

THAT is extreme.

Going through life blissfully unaware that your >.5 waist-to-height ratio is like a ticking time bomb, then "suddenly" dying of a heart attack?

THAT is extreme.

Getting checked into the hospital one Tuesday afternoon, then losing half your stomach after having gastric bypass surgery because you have a malignant cancerous growth on your withered pancreas that will kill you within months?

THAT is extreme.

Note: That's exactly what happened to my brother. He had NEVER been to the hospital before. Death sentence cancer diagnosis on his first trip.

All of those things are happening all day every day to more and more people around the world.

Those are extreme.

Removing sugar and flour? Not so much.

Of course, we need to follow our own idiosyncratic pathways as we make decisions we feel are best for us and for our families.

And…

Our +1° is simple…

Reduce and/or eliminate the sugar and flour.

Unless, of course, you think it's too extreme and you'd prefer the alternative down the line.

ANIMAL NUTRITION
YOU AT THE ZOO

A few years ago, I was reading the latest *Zoo News* quarterly magazine from the local zoo we used to like to visit.

I flip it open.

I land on an article about Animal Nutrition featuring a virtual tour by the zoo's resident Animal Nutritionist.

There's a great little Q&A that made me laugh with joy at how perfect their zoo nutrition ideas are for our modern primate lives.

Question #1: "Do you ever change the animals' diets?"

Answer #1: "We have around 145 species of animals and are always learning new information about what is best to feed them. We partner with research programs and keep up with the latest trends, so animal diets are continually being adjusted to reflect this research."

Note #1: Insert first chuckle. I LOVE that. Optimizing nutritional approaches with new research for the win!

Question #2: "What is an example of a change?"

Answer #2: "Modern hybridized fruit contains more sugar and less fiber than fruit typically found in wild primate habitats, for example. Since we don't have access to that fruit, we utilize a commercially-produced biscuit that is low in sugar. Bananas and grapes are now occasional treats rather than mainstay gibbon diets."

Note #2: Remember: YOU are also a "wild" primate.

That modern hybridized fruit with too much sugar and not enough fiber that isn't good enough for those zoo monkeys? Perhaps it's not good enough for you either.

Question #3: "What are the biggest trends right now?"

Answer #3: "We are moving towards diets that are more nutritionally similar to those that an animal would consume in the wild."

Note #3: Well that sure makes a lot of sense, eh? (I repeat: YOU are also, essentially, a wild primate.)

Question #4: "How do the exotic animal food companies respond to special dietary needs?"

Answer #4: "Our gibbon Jasmine has diabetes and we can manage it just through her diet. The commercial 'glucose-free primate diet' we use comes as a powder that is mixed with water and sets up overnight, like Jell-O. We also limit sugary fruits, so instead of grapes and bananas, she now gets apples and pears."

Note #4: Yes, you can manage a primate's diabetes with nutrition alone.

Oh, if only (all) our doctor's offices and hospitals had their own Zoo Nutritionists.

SPRAY PAINTING LEAVES
VS. WISE GARDENING

The other day I was having a chat with Emerson about the importance of solving health challenges at the root-cause level rather than just treating the surface-level symptoms.

Leveraging the wise metaphors employed by functional medicine doctors like Alejandro Junger, here's our chat...

Me: "Imagine we have a tree and the green leaves are turning brown. We're not sure what's going on, we just know something's not quite right. So, we call in an expert gardener to see what he thinks we should do."

Emerson nods his head.

I continue: "So, this guy shows up, looks at the brown leaves, then reaches into his bag and pulls out a can of green spray paint."

Pause. Emerson's eyes are widening.

Me: "Then you know what he does? He paints the brown leaves green and tells you that should do the trick. Then he writes down the type of green spray paint we should get from Home Depot and tells us that all we need to do is spray a little bit of the green paint on the leaves every day and we'll be fine."

Pause. Emerson is looking at me in disbelief.

I ask: "What would you say to that guy?"

Emerson immediately replies with a laugh: "I'd tell him we want the tree to be ALIVE, not DEAD!"

(I kid you not. That was *precisely* his response.)

To which I laughed and said: "Right?"

He continued: "I mean, the green paint might make it LOOK GOOD but it's still not going to live."

What could I say other than: "Exactly, buddy. Exactly."

Then I asked him what *he* thinks would help.

He thought taking care of the soil and watering it and giving it good nutrients would help.

I agreed.

Our +1°...

How's YOUR health?

Are you spray painting any leaves?

EXERCISE VS. ZOLOFT
HERE'S YOUR EXERCISE PILL

In *The How of Happiness*, Sonja Lyubomirsky tells us about what I consider to be one of THE most powerful well-being experiments *ever* done.

The study compared the power of Exercise vs. Zoloft.

Here's the short story.

Bring clinically depressed individuals into a lab. Randomly assign them into one of three groups. The first group is assigned to four months of aerobic exercise while the second group gets an antidepressant medication (in this case Zoloft) and the third group gets both.

The exercise group does three forty-five-minute sessions per week of cycling or walking/jogging at a moderate to high intensity.

Fast-forward four months.

As Sonja says: "Remarkably, by the end of the four-month intervention period, all three groups had experienced their depressions lift and reported fewer dysfunctional attitudes and increased happiness and self-esteem. Aerobic exercise was just as effective at treating depression as was Zoloft, or as a combination of exercise and Zoloft. Yet exercise is a lot less expensive, usually with no side effects apart from soreness. Perhaps even more remarkably, six months later, participants who had 'remitted' (recovered) from their depressions were less likely to relapse if they had been in the exercise group (six months ago!) than if they had been in the medication group."

Sonja continues by saying: "No one in our society needs to be told that exercise is good for us. Whether you are overweight or have a chronic illness or are a slim couch potato, you've probably heard or read this dictum countless times throughout your life. But has anyone told you—indeed, guaranteed you—that regular physical activity will make you happier? I swear by it."

Now…

Any time one of the leading, conservative scientists in the field GUARANTEES *anything* I sit up straight and pay attention. And, in this case, I put on my shoes and hit the trail.

All that to say…

Don't forget to pop your exercise pill.

TODAY.

HOPE MOLECULES
WHY EXERCISE IS SO GOOD FOR YOU

Not too long ago, we talked about the fact that exercise is a great way to reduce chronic stress.

Why?

Well, Harvard MD psychiatrist John Ratey puts it brilliantly in his great book *Spark*, which is all about the *science* of how exercise changes our brain.

He tells us that exercising "is like taking a little bit of Prozac and a little bit of Ritalin because, like the drugs, exercise elevates these neurotransmitters."

The bottom line: "Exercise balances neurotransmitters—along with the rest of the neurochemicals in the brain."

Kelly McGonigal echoes this wisdom in her great book on the subject called *The Joy of Movement*, subtitle *How Exercise Helps Us Find Happiness, Hope, Connection, and Courage.*

She even tells us that those "runner's high" neurochemicals that make us feel so good after a great workout have a name.

Get this…

They're called "hope molecules."

Know this…

A bunch of research (like the study we just discussed) has shown that exercising is as effective as antidepressants in reducing depression.

Exercise changes your brain in remarkably positive ways. Unfortunately, exercise doesn't have quite the same ad budget as the pharmaceuticals, so we don't see these results advertised to us all day every day.

(And, equally unfortunately, for some weird reason exercise isn't the first thing prescribed by therapists. It should be. Longer chat we'll save for now.)

So...

Are YOU exercising?

One final thing here...

Tal Ben-Shahar tells us that when we choose NOT to exercise on any given day, it's as if we're popping a depressant pill.

We'd NEVER do that.

Right?

THE MAGIC # OF STEPS
HOW TO SIDESTEP DEPRESSION

D id you know that scientists have identified a threshold for your step count under which you make yourself more vulnerable for anxiety and depression?

It's true.

In her great book *The Joy of Movement,* Kelly McGonigal tells us: "The average daily step count required to induce feelings of anxiety and depression and decrease satisfaction with life is 5,649. The typical American takes 4,774 steps per day. Across the globe, the average is 4,961."

YIKES!

Let's repeat that.

The average daily step count required to induce feelings of anxiety and depression (and decrease satisfaction with life) is 5,649. (Gotta love that precision, eh?)

And...

The typical American falls BELOW that threshold at 4,774 steps per day. While the average human across the globe ALSO falls BELOW that threshold at 4,961 steps.

All of which begs the question...

How many steps are YOU getting on average per day?!

Let's sidestep depression and anxiety.

One step at a time.

TODAY.

SOLVITUR AMBULANDO
IT IS SOLVED BY WALKING

*S*olvitur ambulando.

That's Latin for "it is solved by walking."

How great is that?

Walking is so old-school awesome in helping thinkers think that our ancient friends had a Latin phrase to capture its power.

Nietzsche was a fan.

He said: "All truly great thoughts are conceived by walking."

Kierkegaard was a fan.

He said: "I have walked myself into my best thoughts."

Then we have Immanuel Kant.

He was so consistent with his daily walks that his neighbors could set their clocks to the time he passed their houses. They even named a street after him called "Philosopher's Walk."

Then we have Charles Darwin.

For nearly FORTY years he followed his schedule with "clockwork" precision. And, you know what made it on the schedule every day?

His walk.

He was so committed to it that he actually leased his neighbor's land just so he could do a complete loop on what became known as Sandwalk (although he preferred to call it his "thinking path").

Then there's Aristotle.

He and his followers walked so much as they thought and taught and philosophized that they were known as the "peripatetics"—which literally means "walking up and down."

Of course, modern scientists have proven just how powerful walking is for creativity—especially in nature.

All of which is why Emerson and I carved out a little half-mile walking trail on our property right when we arrived.

I repeat…

Ancient and modern philosophers agree: Walking is powerful.

But…

You know what *none* of those philosophers had on their deep-thinking walks?

SMARTPHONES.

Of course, none of them lived in a world with such a nonstop tsunami of digital distractions.

But no self-respecting, deep-thinking lover of wisdom would bring a device that would subject them to *other* people's thoughts on a walk intended to tap into *their* own thoughts.

How about YOU?

Go for a walk. Unplugged. TODAY.

Say hello to your deep thoughts for me.

MOVEMENT > EXERCISE
LET'S NOT BE ACTIVE & SEDENTARY

In her great book *Move Your DNA*, Katy Bowman tells us that we have TRILLIONS of cells in our body.

Think about that for a moment: T R I L L I O N S (Estimates range from 15 trillion to 70 TRILLION.)

And, get this: Nearly every one of those *trillions* of cells has a little receptor tied to your level of M O V E M E N T. (Or, of course, your lack thereof.)

Know this: Our bodies were designed to MOVE.

All day.

Every day.

Period.

Which is why some people call sitting the new smoking.

Katy tells us that we can be "active AND sedentary."

We can be the type of people who conscientiously get up early, drive to the gym on the way to work, bang out an hour workout, then hop back in our car to drive to work where we sit *all* day before driving home and sitting *all* night.

That person is "active."

They're exercising—which is, of course, awesome.

But...

They're *also* SEDENTARY because they're sitting too much.

Active AND sedentary.

The way to deal with this?

Katy tells us to draw a big circle.

Then draw a little circle inside of that big circle.

The big circle = Movement.

The small circle inside of that big circle = Exercise.

Movement transcends and includes exercise.

Note: That's a really big idea.

In short: To activate our Heroic levels of Energy and avoid being active and sedentary, we need to make sure we're moving more throughout the day.

Practically speaking: The #1 thing I changed when I realized that I was dangerously close to being active and sedentary was to set a 1,000-second countdown timer (16 minutes and 40 seconds) and GET UP and move every time it went off.

Sometimes that'll be a set of eleven burpees, other times I'll just stand up and shake out my body.

The key is simple …

Don't sit all day every day.

Remember the big circle.

And the little circle.

And move your body.

TODAY.

OPPORTUNITIES TO MOVE
LOOK FOR OTMS & THEIR SUPER-FIT COUSIN OTWOS

Continuing our movement-is-good-for-you theme, let's talk about how Michelle Segar looks at this.

You may recall that Michelle is one of the world's leading researchers on the science of actually DOING the things you know are good for you.

In her book *No Sweat*, she tells us that we need to find "opportunities to move" throughout the day. Her clients like to shorten that to OTMs.

OTMs.

Opportunities to Move.

If we want to make our TRILLIONS (!) of cells happy so we can shine with a deeper level of radiant, energized enthusiasm, we'd be wise to look for more OTMs throughout our day.

Simple stuff.

So mundane, unsexy, and seemingly unimportant that we can easily overlook them.

You know, like parking as far away from the store (or gym or whatever) as possible so you get a few more steps in. Or, even better if you can pull it off, just walking to the store and leaving your car at home.

Or, once you're in the store, using a hand-held shopping basket rather than a cart. Tiny little opportunities to move more for the win.

Or…

If you really want to go all in and be like one of the 100 Fittest People of All Time like Dean Karnazes, you can go from finding Opportunities to MOVE all day to basically *working out* all day every day.

In our interview, The Ultramarathon Man Dean told me that's how he likes to roll. Apparently, right before our chat he banged out a quick (twelve-minute) high intensity interval training workout. And, he planned to do another mini-workout right after our chat. Simple sequence of burpees, pull-ups, and sit-ups.

Repeat. All day. Every day.

That focus on moving his body has allowed him to do the seemingly impossible like run 350 miles at once and run 50 marathons in 50 US states in 50 days. (Wow.)

Our +1°…

Whether you're looking for Opportunities to Move (OTMs!) or Opportunities to Work Out (OTWOs!), let's move a little more today.

And tomorrow.

And the day after that…

+1°. +1°. +1°.

LET'S GO!

PULL THE THREAD
THROUGH YOUR HEAD

On June 8th, 2001, I was on the back patio of my apartment a block from the beach in La Jolla, California, reading Michael Gelb's *How to Think Like Leonardo da Vinci*.

I had just turned twenty-seven and had just left the business (The Active Network) that acquired my first business (eteamz).

As we've discussed, that book changed my life—particularly the 100 Questions Exercise which led to me asking myself: "How can I get paid to do what I love?"

So…

I'm reading about how to think like Da Vinci. Michael tells us that, in addition to being one of history's greatest artists, scientists, and military engineers, apparently Leonardo was also an incredibly strong athlete as well.

In the process of telling us how important it is to optimize both our minds and our bodies, Michael recommended something called the Alexander Technique. It's a technique originally developed for singers and actors that helps with your posture and poise.

I decided I'd do a little retreat hosted by an NYU dance professor in Greece that summer. So, I booked my one-way ticket and had a great time with a few Americans and a bunch of Greek students on the magical island of Tinos.

Which officially leads us to the point of this +1°.

Here's the #1 lesson I picked up from that experience:

Imagine a thread that runs from the base of your tailbone all the way up your spine through the top of your head.

Can you feel it?

Now gently pull it up.

We know how important good posture is for our power and for our breathing. Pulling that little thread is a REALLY good way to quickly find your ideal posture and the relaxed grace and poise it provides.

So, one more time.

Imagine a thread running from the base of your tailbone all the way up your spine through the top of your head.

Gently pull it up.

With a smile.

SLEEP BEFORE & AFTER EDISON
HOW MUCH YOUR GREAT-GRANDPARENTS SLEPT

Think back to life around 150 years ago.

It's 1875.

No iPhones. In fact, no phones at all. Just telegrams. Alexander Graham Bell won't get his patent for the phone until 1876.

No cars. We cruised around at 10 miles per hour on horses—with no air conditioning.

And … We had no light bulbs. Just candles and gas lamps.

A slightly different world, eh?

(Take a moment to imagine that. It's mind-boggling how far we've come and how easy it is to take it all for granted.)

Enter: Thomas Edison.

On December 31, 1879, he flipped the switch on the first public display of an incandescent light bulb and our world changed in countless ways.

Let's count one way: sleep.

Guess how many hours your great-great-grandparents slept during an average weeknight.

8 hours? 9 hours?

How about up to 10 hours.

(10!!!)

Today?

Today the average American gets 6.7 hours of sleep.

That's a SHOCKING drop.

Millions of years: up to 10 hours of sleep.

Last 150 years: plummeted all the way down to less than 7 hours of sleep.

That's just not natural.

Nor is it healthy.

We need to know that, in the words of Sara Mednick: "Studies have conclusively linked sleeplessness to irritability, anger, depression and mental exhaustion."

Our +1°...

Let's take a moment and think back to the days before Thomas Edison and his brilliant team gifted us with the power of light.

Feel into a life without blue light beaming at you from a screen in the middle of the night.

Of course, we don't need to become luddites and throw away all the technology. But, let's use our technology wisely.

What can (and will) YOU do today to prioritize your sleep just a little more so you can wake up feeling Heroically energized tomorrow morning?

Got it?

Awesome.

Get on that.

TONIGHT.

CIRCADIAN CHICKENS
THEY'VE GOT THE RHYTHM... DO YOU?

As we've discussed, we live on a little land out in the country outside of Austin.

One of the first things we did when we got here was get some chickens. They've been awesome.

We have a little chicken coop where they sleep.

The other day Alexandra and I were chatting about the fact that they show up ready to hop into that coop at EXACTLY the SAME time every single day.

You know WHEN that is? Right around sunset.

You know WHY that is? Because…

As Satchin Panda tells us in *The Circadian Code*, EVERY SINGLE LIVING CREATURE (and by that, I mean EVERY SINGLE LIVING CREATURE!) is programmed to respond to the rhythms of the day.

Plants? Check.

They "open up" in the morning to receive the sun's energy. And do the opposite at night.

Animals? Check.

Whether they're nocturnal or diurnal, their rhythms are connected to the day/night rhythms.

Chickens? CHECK!

You know what would happen if our chickens stayed out and partied all night while soaking in some artificial daylight?

Hint: THEY WOULD DIE.

Laughing. Seriously.

And...

Final, most important questions...

You know what OTHER living creature evolved to live in alignment with circadian rhythms?

Human beings.

More specifically: YOU.

So...

Are YOU living in integrity with circadian rhythms?

You know what would have happened if YOU stayed out all night without protection back in the day?

You would have died. (Hah.)

You know what will happen if you do that these days?

As Satchin Panda tells us: "The longer your circadian rhythm is out of sync, the greater the risk of developing a serious disease."

And: "If you are experiencing any physical discomfort, or changes to the way you think, don't ignore them: They are early warning signs of chronic illness."

Our +1°...

What's ONE practical little (or big!) thing you KNOW you could do to optimize YOUR circadian rhythms?

Let's get on that.

And get ourselves Heroically Energized.

TODAY.

A BRIEF HISTORY OF (BLUE) LIGHT
SAVE IT FOR THE DAYTIME

While we're chatting about circadian rhythms (and chickens!) and what gets in the way of those rhythms, how about A Brief History of (Night) Light?

Here's the very quick take.

For millions of years, the only light at night came from the stars and the moon.

(Think about that for a moment.)

Then we got creative and harnessed the power of wood fire somewhere between 230,000 and 1.5 million years ago, depending on who you believe.

(Think about *that* for a moment.)

Then we got even more clever and started using animal grease for light about 15,000 years ago. The Egyptians brought us the first beeswax candles about 5,000 years ago.

Fast forward to 1879 and Thomas Edison creates the first commercially practical incandescent light bulb. Then things start to speed up.

The first television showed up about 100 years ago. Smartphones started showing up less than 20 years ago.

At the same time all that night light got jacked up, our sleep went down—from 10 hours per night to 8 to less than 7.

To recap...

For millions of years, the only source of blue light came from the SUN during THE DAY.

Then, over the last century and *especially* over the last decade, we turned the NIGHT *into* the day.

Our +1°...

We have trillions of cells.

98% of them are super sensitive to circadian rhythms.

I wonder if flipping day into night by blowing our brains up with blue light is a good idea?

All that to say...

Turn off the blue light at night.

Save it for the daytime.

UNTIL ONE IS COMMITTED
ARE YOU COMMITTED? THE FIRST STEP

One of my all-time favorite quotes is from W.H. Murray's *Scottish Himalayan Expedition*.

I've memorized and recited it in my head well over 1,000 times as part of my sequence of four quote-prayer-mantras I silently repeat to myself when/if I get up in the middle of the night. It always comes right before I recite a Churchill quote and right after I recite a Ralph Waldo Emerson quote that comes right after I recite a Steve Jobs quote.

In our next +1°, we'll chat more about those quotes and the "IF I get up in the middle of the night and my mind starts wandering, THEN I turn my brain off by saying a quote" protocol I run to help me get a great night of sleep.

For now, let's chat about that W.H. Murray quote.

Here it is:

"Until one is committed, there is hesitancy, the chance to draw back, always ineffectiveness. Concerning all acts of initiative (and creation), there is one elementary truth the ignorance of which kills countless ideas and splendid plans: that the moment one definitely commits oneself, then providence moves too. A whole stream of events issues from the decision, raising in one's favor all manner of unforeseen incidents, meetings and material assistance, which no man could have dreamt would have come his way. I have learned a deep respect for one of Goethe's couplets:

Whatever you can do or dream you can, begin it.

Boldness has genius, power, and magic in it. Begin it now."

Now... As inspiring as that is, here's what I think is MOST interesting (and most powerful!) about that passage.

You know what Murray says RIGHT before that passage?

(Neither did I until I read Steven Pressfield's latest book *Put Your Ass Where Your Heart Wants to Be*.)

Right before that all-time classic wisdom gem, he tells us: "... but when I said that nothing had been done I erred on one important matter. We had definitely committed ourselves and were halfway out of our ruts. We had put down our passage money— booked a sailing to Bombay. This may sound too simple, but it is great in consequence."

Then Murray proceeds with his (goosebumps) epic line that: "Until one is committed, there is hesitancy, the chance to draw back, always ineffectiveness..."

I repeat: The commitment Murray made wasn't some huge thing. It was SIMPLY BUYING A BOAT TICKET.

As he says: "This may sound too simple, but it is great in consequence."

That's our +1°.

What do YOU want to create in your life?

Are you committed? WOOP it. Decide whether or not you want to pay the price.

If you do...

What's your boat ticket? Buy it.

TODAY.

WAKE UP IN THE MIDDLE OF THE NIGHT?
HERE'S WHAT I DO

You ever get up in the middle of the night? Me, too. Welcome to the 21st century, over-stimulated club.

Of course, we can have a VERY long chat about WHY we tend to get up with our minds in overdrive and how to mitigate that but... We'll save that for another time.

Today I want to talk about what I do when I inevitably find my mind a little busy in the middle of the night.

The first thing I do is quickly shine a flashlight on what I did that day that might have contributed to an overactive mind. The obvious things like poor oscillations and too many inputs are likely candidates. Or blowing through my digital sunset protocol. Or a number of other factors.

Whatever it may be, I say: "Perfect."

Then I quickly do a 1-2-3 and "Needs work!" protocol on it and see how I could have done things a little better while committing to using that data to optimize. (It's all data. We win or we learn so... Never waste a mis-take, Hero!)

Then...

I silently recite the quote-mantra-prayers I've memorized while enjoying some nice, deep breathing. It's 10x better than counting sheep.

I always start by inviting Steve Jobs to the party to tell me about the Crazy Ones. (Note: I imagine Steve himself reciting this in HIS voice—Google that when you get a chance.)

He tells me: "Here's to the crazy ones. The misfits. The rebels. The troublemakers. The round pegs in the square holes. The ones who see things differently. They're not fond of rules. And they have no respect for the status quo. You can quote them, disagree with them, glorify or vilify them. About the only thing you can't do is ignore them. Because they change things. They push the human race forward. And while some may see them as the crazy ones, we see genius. Because the people who are crazy enough to think they can change the world, are the ones who do."

Then, I invite Ralph Waldo Emerson to the party.

He tells me: "Enthusiasm is one of the most powerful engines of success. When you do a thing, do it with all your might. Put your whole soul into it. Stamp it with your own personality. Be active, be energetic, be enthusiastic and faithful, and you will accomplish your object. Nothing great was ever achieved without enthusiasm."

Then I bring in W.H. Murray for his gem:

He tells me: "Until one is committed, there is hesitancy, the chance to draw back, always ineffectiveness. Concerning all acts of initiative (and creation), there is one elementary truth the ignorance of which kills countless ideas and splendid plans: that the moment one definitely commits oneself, then providence moves too. A whole stream of events issues from the decision, raising in one's favor all manner of unforeseen incidents, meetings and material assistance, which no man could have dreamt would have come his way. I have learned a deep respect for one of Goethe's couplets:

Whatever you can do or dream you can, begin it.

Boldness has genius, power, and magic in it. Begin it now."

Then I invite Churchill to join me.

He tells me: "There comes a special moment in everyone's life, a moment for which that person was born. That special opportunity, when he seizes it, will fulfill his mission—a mission for which he is uniquely qualified. In that moment, he will find greatness. It is his finest hour."

That's my protocol.

It works like a charm.

How about YOU?

What do YOU do when you inevitably get up at night?

Any opportunities to optimize? Any quotes (or prayers) you may want to memorize to gently focus your mind and bring it back from any potential ruminating?

Day 1. All in.

Here's to a great night of sleep, Hero!

HOW CAFFEINE REALLY WORKS
& WHEN (NOT) TO HAVE IT

D o you know how caffeine actually works?

Most of us think that caffeine gives us energy. But what it actually does is *mask our fatigue*—making us feel more energized than we actually are.

Here's the quick story on what's going on behind the scenes.

One of the by-products of being awake and having your neurons fire is a neurotransmitter called adenosine. As adenosine accumulates in your brain, you get tired—cueing you to go to sleep to recover.

Caffeine is structurally very similar to adenosine. So similar, in fact, that it can actually sneak into those little adenosine receptors and block the adenosine from doing its job of letting us know we're tired.

And voilà!

You feel energized.

Obviously, that's pretty awesome. (Hah.)

But… Here's our +1°: Two things we want to consider as we optimize our caffeine intake.

#1. We want to know that when we use caffeine we're "borrowing" energy. Therefore, we'd be wise to consider using caffeine *strategically* rather than *habitually*.

If we need caffeine to get going in the morning, what we really need is more rest, not more caffeine.

#2. We also want to know that caffeine has a half-life of 5–8 hours—which means that if you have a coffee with 200 mg of caffeine at 2 p.m., half of that (or 100 mg) is still in your system as late as 10 p.m. (That's a lot!)

Bottom line: If you're going to use caffeine, do it strategically and do it earlier in the day.

Have a "caffeine curfew" to make sure you get a good night of sleep. Experts say no later than 2 p.m. and earlier if you're really serious about allowing your body to recover.

So…

How's YOUR caffeine intake?

How can you +1° it?

THE RULES OF BREATHING
THE BIG 3: NOSE + BELLY + EXHALE

You can live for weeks without food, days without water, and only minutes without oxygen—which makes breathing arguably THE most important fundamental.

Yet…

How often do you think about it? And, do you specifically train your breathing to make sure it's optimized?

If you're like most people, the answer to the above questions are: "Never." And: "No."

Now, we could talk about breathing for a very long time.

I've read basically every great book on breathing out there and distilled the essence of those great books into a series of Philosopher's Notes and an hour-long class called Optimal Breathing 101. (Check them out in the Heroic app.)

For now, how about a quick look at the THREE simple rules of optimal breathing?

Here they are:

Breathe in through your nose.

Down into your belly.

Exhale slightly longer than your inhale.

Let's do a quick inventory; then we'll take a closer look at each of those three breathing rules.

First, the quick inventory.

Are you breathing through your nose? Most people don't. Go look around and/or in the mirror.

Do you see a mouth gaping open? If so, we'll want to work on that.

Do you breathe deeply (yet calmly) into your belly? Most people don't—especially if you breathe through your mouth.

And, is your exhale slightly longer than your inhale? This is the fastest way to relax.

That's a super-quick look at the 1-2-3 of breathing.

How about a nice, deep, relaxing yet energizing breath RIGHT NOW.

Sit a little taller.

Shake out any tension that may be present.

Breathe in through your nose.

Down into your belly.

Lightly.

Calmly.

Quietly.

Now breathe back out through your nose.

Exhaling slightly longer than your inhale.

Ahhhh…

Repeat.

All day.

Every day.

Especially…

TODAY.

BALLOON BREATHING
FOR KIDS (& THEIR PARENTS)

Patrick McKeown is my go-to guy for all things breathing. He's the author of a number of books including *The Oxygen Advantage*. He also wrote a kids' book we've read with our kids. It's called *Always Breathe Correctly*.

With his inspiration, here's how I taught Emerson and Eleanor how to breathe properly when they were younger.

(Yes, they both breathe *exclusively* through their noses and take pride in being able to run 5Ks doing so.)

First, I made the case that breathing right is *super* important as I explained the fact that we can survive without food for weeks, without water for days, but only minutes without oxygen.

And ... I told them that, as with many things in our modern, hunched-over, digitally overstimulated world, most of us aren't doing it right.

Then I gave them a quick overview of proper breathing techniques. I told them there were three things to know.

1. Breathe in (and out of) your nose. (As Patrick tells us: Your mouth is for eating. Your nose is for breathing!)

2. Breathe deeply into your belly. ("Deeply" not "bigly." You want to be nice and relaxed. Your chest and shoulders shouldn't be visibly moving much.)

3. Exhale slightly longer than your inhale. (This will help you flip the parasympathetic nervous system switch.)

With that theory out of the way, it was time for practice. This is what we did …

We blew up belly balloons.

I showed the kids how to make their bellies expand nice and big as I breathed in gently through my nose—like I was blowing up a balloon in my belly.

Then I showed them how to let all the air out of the balloon as I exhaled nice and long (through my nose) and squeezed all the air out.

Repeat.

They tried it. Loved it. Rocked it.

Of course, I asked them how they'd get good at it and they said … "PRACTICE!"

The +1°…

Got kids?

Why not have fun blowing up some belly balloons?

TODAY.

THE MAGIC SPOT
IN OUR MOUTHS

Here's another pro tip from Patrick McKeown to get yourself and your kids to breathe right.

This one is from his kids' book called *Always Breathe Correctly*. The book features a wizard who teaches kids how to breathe.

Of course, he teaches us that the nose is for breathing and the mouth is for eating while teaching us to breathe gently into our bellies, etc.

And … He teaches us how to find what he calls the "Magic Spot" in our mouths. You can find it by gently placing your tongue on the roof of your mouth right before your front teeth. When we hit that spot, we tend to automatically close our lips and breathe through our nose.

Which is why if I ever see Eleanor or Emerson with a gaping mouth, I'll say: "Magic spot, buddy!" Or: "Magic spot, big girl!"

They'll immediately smile, close their lips, and proudly breathe through their noses as I give them a thumbs-up and a quick sign-language "Love you, buddy!" / "Love you, big girl!"

So… As you go through the day today, if you happen to find yourself with a mouth gaping open and air going in through the wrong hole, perhaps you can playfully hear me say to you: "Magic spot, buddy!"

Let's activate our Heroic energy one breath at a time.

TODAY.

HOW TO STOP THINKING
THE #1 TIP TO MASTER THIS LOST ART

When I interviewed Patrick McKeown years ago, he made a very interesting point. He said that we spend all our lives in school learning how to *think* but that we're never taught how to STOP thinking.

Fact is, most of our "thinking" isn't *thinking* at all.

We're simply looping the same unproductive thought over and over again.

Get this: According to a study done at the University of Southern California, the average person has 70,000 thoughts per day. And, according to some experts, 80–90% of those thoughts are useless.

That's crazy. (Literally.)

It's also *really* enervating.

We waste a *ton* of energy spinning our mental wheels—creating more stress and anxiety and fatigue while diminishing our performance and well-being.

(Not a winning combination.)

Learning how to STOP thinking is a very important skill.

Patrick's #1 tip on how to master the art of *not* thinking? Breathe.

More specifically, breathe through your nose.

Deeply (but lightly!) into your diaphragm.

Exhale. Slightly longer than your inhale.

Repeat.

Take another nice, gentle, deeply relaxing breath.

In through your nose, down into your belly, back out through your nose. Exhale slightly longer than your inhale.

Repeat.

Ahhhhh…

Our mind has slowed down.

All that wasted energy is recouped.

That's the #1 tip on how to master the lost art of NOT thinking. Let's practice it. TODAY.

P.S. Two other ways to stop that mental chatter? Put your attention on your body and/or immerse yourself in the present moment.

INSTANT WILLPOWER
HERE'S HOW TO GET IT

Kelly McGonigal wrote three of my all-time favorite books on the science of flourishing: *The Willpower Instinct*, *The Upside of Stress*, and *The Joy of Movement*.

They're all fantastic. Check out the Philosopher's Notes for some of my favorite Big Ideas. For now, I want to chat about an idea from *The Willpower Instinct*.

Kelly tells us: "You won't find many quick fixes in this book, but there is one way to immediately boost willpower: Slow your breathing down to four to six breaths per minute. That's ten to fifteen seconds per breath—slower than you normally breathe, but not difficult with a little bit of practice and patience."

Why does that work?

Well, Kelly continues: "Slowing the breath down activates the prefrontal cortex and increases heart rate variability, which helps shift the brain and body from a state of stress to self-control mode. A few minutes of this technique will make you feel calm, in control, and capable of handling cravings or challenges."

There aren't a lot of quick fixes in life, but this is one.

So…

The next time you feel your willpower getting a little wobbly and you're about to do something silly, notice what's happening (always the most important first step!) and…

Take a nice, slow, calming, deep breath.

Let's practice now.

Get out a stopwatch.

(Remember: What you measure improves.)

See if you can get your breathing down to four to six breaths per minute. That's roughly ten to fifteen seconds per breath.

Try some different counts…

Inhale for four seconds, hold for one, exhale for five. That's a breathing rate of six breaths per minute.

Or…

My personal favorite…

Inhale for six seconds, hold for one, exhale for eight. That's a breathing rate of four breaths per minute.

Find your optimal breathing pattern. And, remember to flip the switch when you need it most as you activate your parasympathetic nervous system so you can show up as the most calm, confident, Heroic version of yourself.

All day. Every day.

Especially…

TODAY.

A COLD SHOWER A DAY
KEEPS THE DOCTOR AWAY

Wim Hof.

Also known as "The Iceman."

As you may know, he holds multiple world records for his feats of endurance and exposure to cold—such as climbing Mount Kilimanjaro wearing only shorts and shoes, running barefoot half marathons in the Arctic Circle, and standing in an ice-filled container for more than 112 minutes.

As you may *not* know, the effectiveness of his methods—which are now practiced by millions—have been validated by eight university research studies.

We're going to talk about some wisdom from his book *The Wim Hof Method*. Specifically, we're going to talk about the idea that a cold shower a day can keep the doctor away.

First...

Did you know that our vascular system, "if laid out end-to-end, would stretch nearly two and a half times the length of the world"?

Yep.

And, get this: "There are approximately sixty-two thousand miles of veins, arteries, and capillaries in each and every one of us. The vascular system is constructed, after millions of years of evolution, with millions of little muscles that contract and open the veins and the vascular channels in reaction to the weather."

But...

In our climate-controlled modern world, we rarely give those *millions* of little muscles the workouts they so desperately need—which isn't a good thing.

Enter: That cold shower a day that keeps the doctor away by deliberately training those muscles to do what they need to do to keep us energized.

The Wim Hof Method has three pillars: Cold + Breath + Commitment.

In the book, Wim Hof walks us through a simple way to build a cold shower protocol.

Here's the short story you can start putting into action TODAY if you feel so inspired.

In Week 1, just turn the warm shower to cold for the last thirty seconds. Then in Week 2, make it one minute of cold water at the end of your normally warm shower. In Week 3, move it up to a minute and a half of cold at the end. In Week 4, make it two minutes of cold water at the end of a warm shower.

Boom. Done. Repeat.

Give those millions of muscles a workout WHILE working out your mind doing something you don't want to do.

When? How about TODAY?!

Target swipe: Cold shower!

P.S. I personally target swipe a two-minute cold plunge at 49° (nearly) every day in our Heroic app.

Cold: It does a Hero good!

VAGAL TONE
MEET YOUR 10TH CRANIAL NERVE

Your 10th cranial nerve starts at the base of your brain and goes from there down to your heart, through your lungs, all the way down into your gut.

It kinda wanders.

Which is why it's called the vagus nerve. (In Latin, *vagus* means "wanderer." It shares a root with words like *vagabond*.)

Why are we talking about your vagus nerve?

Because it plays a REALLY important role in regulating our parasympathetic nervous system.

Short story.

As you probably know, we have a parasympathetic nervous system and a sympathetic nervous system. The parasympathetic system takes care of the "rest-and-digest" side of things while the sympathetic is there for "fight-or-flight" stuff. In short, the relaxation response vs. the stress response.

We obviously need both.

But modern life has thrown us into a near-constant arousal state with our sympathetic nervous system working overtime which leads to all the stress and dysfunction and burnout we don't want.

So…

In light of this tendency to stray into Stressville all day every day, it's more important than ever to know how to flip the switch and drop into Relaxationville.

Which, after a little wandering (wink), brings us back to our vagus nerve.

Did you know you can actually measure the health of someone's vagus nerve via something called "vagal tone"? Yep. The healthiest among us have a six-pack-like vagal tone as measured by heart rate variability.

Why do we want to optimize our vagal tone?

Because it's an indicator of your nervous system's ability to flip the switch and shift from stress to relaxation.

And... Do you know the fastest way to flip the switch and take a trip to Vagus?

... What would you guess?

Hint: Take a deep breath.

A nice, calm, deep, quiet breath in through your nose down into your diaphragm followed by a gentle pause, then an exhale that's slightly longer than your inhale, is where it's at.

Try it now.

Sit up a little taller. Release any tension that might be present. Pull that thread through your head. Smile.

Now, breathe in through your nose, down into your belly. Calmly, deeply, quietly. Exhale back out through your nose, slightly longer than your inhale.

You just flipped the switch.

That deep, calm, rhythmic diaphragmatic breathing sends signals up your vagus nerve to your brain stem saying: "We're good. No need to stress. All systems relax."

And *that* is a powerful way to optimize your vagal tone to create calm, focused energy.

P.S. Optimizing your vagal tone is *also* an incredibly powerful way to deepen your capacity to love.

Here's how Barbara Fredrickson puts it in *Love 2.0*: "People with higher vagal tone, science has shown, are more flexible across a whole host of domains—physical, mental, and social. They simply adapt better to their ever-shifting circumstances, albeit completely at nonconscious levels. Physically, they regulate their internal bodily processes more efficiently, like their glucose levels and inflammation. Mentally they're better able to regulate their attention and emotions, even their behavior. Socially, they're especially skillful in navigating interpersonal interactions and in forging positive connections with others. By definition, then, they experience more micro-moments of love. It's as though the agility of the conduit between the brains and the hearts—as reflected in their high vagal tone—allows them to be exquisitely agile, attuned, and flexible as they navigate the ups and downs of day-to-day life and social exchanges. High vagal tone, then, can be taken as high loving potential."

WHY MEDITATE?
A FEW REASONS

Meditation.

At this stage, my hunch is you don't need me to tell you that it does a Hero's mind, body, and soul good.

But are you practicing it?

For millennia, wise spiritual teachers have been encouraging us to use meditation as a means to connect to our best selves.

The scientific research also unequivocally establishes the practical benefits that go along with the spiritual ones.

Here are a couple of quick highlights to make sure you're properly sold; then we'll chat about HOW to create a more consistent meditation practice.

In her great book *The Sleep Revolution*, Arianna Huffington tells us about Stanford science that establishes the fact that you can fall asleep TWICE as fast if you're a meditator than if you're not—going from taking thirty-three minutes to fall asleep to falling asleep in fifteen minutes.

That basically means you get an instant ROI on that fifteen minutes of meditation you do today on a pure time basis, before we add in all the other benefits.

Then we have Jonathan Haidt's miracle meditation pill passage from *The Happiness Hypothesis* in which he tells us about a metaphorical pill "that you could take once a day to reduce anxiety and increase your contentment."

The pill also increases "self-esteem, empathy, and trust; it even improves memory."

That pill is, of course, meditation.

I like to think of meditation as strength training for my brain. I know that the ability to put my attention where I want, when I want, for how long I want is a hallmark of flourishing people. And I know that meditation helps me train that ability. Therefore, I hit the mind gym.

Do you?

HOW TO MEDITATE
THE 5 D'S

Now that we've explored a few reasons *why* you may want to meditate, let's take a quick look at HOW you may want to consider meditating.

Let's chat about what I call "The 5 D's of Meditation." Check out Meditation 101 in the Heroic app for the full story.

For now, here's the quick take:

1. **D**o it with
2. **D**ignity and a
3. **D**efined anchor with strong
4. **D**etermination, then
5. **D**o it again

The first most obvious rule of meditation? DO IT!

It really doesn't matter WHAT you do (or how you do it) but THAT you do it.

After picking your favorite flavor of meditation, do it with DIGNITY.

I love Jon Kabat-Zinn's wisdom on the subject. Wonder how to sit? He tells us to sit with *dignity*. You and your daimon, sitting nice and tall (spine straight!) yet relaxed.

Then we want to DEFINE OUR ANCHOR.

What does a ship out at sea do when it wants to stay in the

same spot? It drops an anchor, right? Well, same with us. We need an anchor on which to focus our attention.

It can be your breath, a mantra, a prayer, or whatever you'd like. But... Define the anchor. Then, when your mind inevitably (!) wanders, just say "Oh, well" and get back to your chosen focal point.

Once we've decided to do it with dignity and have defined our anchor, we'd be wise to do it with DETERMINATION. Specifically, I like to do it with *strong* determination.

I got that phrase from SN Goenka during one of his organization's 10-day silent meditation retreats.

Basic idea: Once you commit to a time, set your timer, then assume your posture, then resolve not to open your eyes, your hands, or your legs for the duration of your session.

Feel an itch on your nose? Ignore it. Curious how much longer you have to go? Forget about it. Legs feeling weird? Unless something's truly wrong, ignore it.

That's strong determination.

The fifth D?

Do it again tomorrow.

Repeat.

Those are The 5 D's of Meditation.

Do it with Dignity and a Defined anchor with strong Determination, then Do it again.

Pop that miracle pill.

TODAY.

THOUGHTS & HEARTBEATS
MEDITATING? THOUGHTS ARE NOT YOUR ENEMY!

Emily Fletcher was a Broadway performer living the dream. Only… Her hair was graying at 27, she was always stressed and had chronic insomnia.

One of her fellow Broadway performers was always super calm and confident. Emily asked her how she did it. The woman told her that she meditated. Emily rolled her eyes. Then she decided to give meditation a try.

After ONE day of meditation, her insomnia was gone. She was hooked. Soon after, she quit Broadway, traveled to India to study more deeply, then became a meditation teacher and created something called the "Ziva Technique" which she's taught to thousands of people.

In her book *Stress Less, Accomplish More*, Emily walks us through the science of WHY meditation is so powerful and then introduces us to the "3 M's" of her "Z Technique": Mindfulness, Meditation, and Manifesting.

If you've been looking for a book that might help you get started on your meditation journey and/or take your existing practice to the next level, I think you might love it.

For now, know this: "The single most important piece of meditation advice you can hold with you as you dive in is this: Thoughts are not the enemy."

Have YOU tried to meditate but felt like a failure because you couldn't stop thinking?

Know this: You're not *supposed* to be able to stop your brain from thinking. Period.

Emily tells us that she's *never* had a session in which she didn't have a single thought bubble up. It's not going to happen. Ever.

Why? Because, and I just love this line: "The mind thinks involuntarily just like the heart beats involuntarily."

I repeat: The mind THINKS involuntarily just like the heart BEATS involuntarily.

Yes, you can slow your heart rate quite a bit by learning how to breathe deeply and training wisely and all that. BUT… You can't just flip the switch OFF. Same with our thoughts.

Yes, of course, we can learn how to slow our thoughts down (interestingly, via the same mechanisms we use to slow our heart rates down: deep breathing, good sleep, exercise, etc.) BUT… We can't just flip the switch OFF.

Knowing that, when our minds inevitably move away from our anchors during our meditation, we can just say "Oh, well" (like Herbert Benson recommends) and get back to focusing on our anchor—whether that's our breath or a mantra or a prayer or whatever.

One more time: Our thoughts are not our enemies.

In fact, a meditation in which we have a *lot* of thoughts bubble up is, potentially, one of our *best* meditations because the process of sitting and calmly bringing ourselves back to our anchor allows us to process those thoughts that would otherwise have remained locked up in our minds and bodies.

Just show up and hit the mind gym. TODAY.

WHY THE BUDDHA MEDITATED
EVEN AFTER HE WAS ENLIGHTENED

In *No Mud, No Lotus*, the late Thích Nhất Hạnh tells us that when he was a young monk he thought the Buddha never suffered.

Then, as he matured, he realized that OF COURSE the Buddha suffered.

He had a body so he had to at least *occasionally* get a headache or a stomachache. And, when a friend died, he'd feel sad. He was a human being. Therefore, he experienced pain and suffering.

Of course, he was also the enlightened Buddha so he was *very* good at regaining his equanimity.

Which leads to another interesting discussion.

If the Buddha was enlightened, Thích Nhất Hạnh asks, why did he still meditate *after* attaining his enlightenment?

(Fascinating question, eh?)

Answer: Because even the Buddha's equanimity was, like EVERYTHING else in the world, IMPERMANENT.

The Buddha needed to tend to his own well-being. Every day. Even after his enlightenment.

Now, if the Buddha needed to keep on dominating his fundamentals after he attained his enlightenment, I'm *pretty* sure that means we do as well. (Hah.)

So…

How are YOUR fundamentals, dear Hero?

Want to maintain your high levels of awesome?

Continue crushing your fundies—long after you think you "need" to.

P.S. I'm reminded of peak performance and mental toughness trainers Lanny and Troy Bassham.

They tell us that *average* performers practice something until they get it right. *Elite* performers? They practice until they can't get it wrong.

The *jumbo, uber-elite-enlightened*?

They never stop practicing.

FLOW
WHAT IT IS & HOW TO GET IN IT

Mihaly Csikszentmihalyi was one of the world's leading researchers studying the science of well-being.

He co-founded the Positive Psychology movement with Martin Seligman and has written landmark books on *Creativity* and *Flow*.

After surveying thousands of people, Csikszentmihalyi (pronounced "cheeks-sent-me-high") was able to shine some light on that elusive state in which we're at our best. In fact, he's the one who coined the word "Flow."

Here's the basic idea…

Imagine drawing two lines.

On the x-axis we have our Skill level. On the y-axis we have our Challenge level.

Now…

If the Challenge is *high* but your Skill is *low*, what will you experience? ANXIETY.

On the other hand, if your Skill is *high* but the Challenge is *low*, what will you experience? BOREDOM.

Now, what if your Skill level matches the Challenge? Enter: FLOW.

Let's do a quick, practical check-in…

Are you feeling Bored? Increase the level of Challenge. (For example, if you're doing a mundane, repetitive task, see how flawlessly you can do it or how quickly or both!)

Feeling Anxious? Decrease the Challenge a bit and/or increase your Skill.

Want to feel more Flow?

Bring more awareness to the whole process, set a goal that focuses your attention (that is ALWAYS the first step, btw!), eliminate distractions (go Deep!), and allow yourself to be fully immersed in the experience.

Repeat.

Enter: FLOW!

FLOW JUNKIES
HOW TO ATTAIN SUPERYOU MASTERY SANS MISERY

In our last +1°, we spent some time with the godfather of flow, Mihaly Csikszentmihalyi. Today we're going to spend some time with the world's current leading thinker on flow and how to get into it.

It's time to invite Steven Kotler back to the party.

In *The Rise of Superman*, he updates our thinking on the science of optimal performance (a.k.a. flow), walks us through the traditional models of attaining mastery, and tells us that we can attain it "sans the misery."

After establishing the existing frameworks (he calls them the "3 M's"), he encourages us to become "flow junkies"—fueled by our love for what we do as we enjoy the present moment while creating an even more awesome future.

Let's take a quick look at the traditional paths to mastery; then we'll have fun with a Heroically optimized approach.

First, our 3 M's of mastery.

Steven tells us that we have Mothers and Musicians and Marshmallows.

The "Mothers" orientation approach says that mastery is all about having a nurturing environment.

The "Musicians" perspective basically says that we need to be like Anders Ericsson's violinists and log in 10,000 hours of grueling deliberate practice before we can have a shot at the greatness Peak.

The "Marshmallows" approach leans on research done with kids who either could or could not delay the gratification of eating a marshmallow and says you better learn how to delay your gratification if you want to be great.

Kotler tells us that extreme sports athletes take an alternative path to their superhuman abilities—FLOW.

He tells us that a lot of these athletes came from broken families (sorry, Mothers), didn't have the "deliberate, well-structured practice" at the heart of the 10,000-hour hypothesis (sorry, Musicians), and were the kind of impulsive kids who DEFINITELY would have snatched the one marshmallow rather than wait for two (sorry, Marshmallows).

What they did have was an absolute LOVE of what they did and the feeling they got when they entered flow.

That's the first half of his alternative theory for superman awesomeness.

Now for the second. Kotler tells us that there are Presents and there are Futures.

Presents are the people who WANT.IT.ALL.NOW! They're the ones who snatch the one marshmallow for immediate gratification. They tend to be impulsive and they have a tough time with long-range planning, etc.

Futures, on the other hand, are the people who are able to delay gratification. They can make long-range plans and commit to mastery but because they're so future-oriented they tend to burn themselves out by not enjoying the process.

Enter the power of Flow to help us optimize for BOTH of those orientations.

Kotler tells us: "After three decades of research, Zimbardo found that the healthiest, happiest, highest performers blend the best of both worlds. The optimal time perspective combines the energy, joy, and openness of Presents, with the strength, fortitude, and long-term vision of the Futures."

Note: Seneca said the same thing a couple thousand years ago: "How much better to pursue a straight course and eventually reach that destination where the things that are pleasant and the things that are honorable finally become, for you, the same."

In other words, how AWESOME is it when what you MOST love to do is what is the best for you?!

Answer: Very awesome.

To make his point, Kotler tells us all about an extraordinary athlete named Shane McConkey—who was one of the best extreme sports athletes ever.

Here's how he puts it: "But once the sensation seekers jump on the flow path, they don't need to delay gratification to achieve success—gratification becomes their path to success. 'I'm doing what I love,' explains McConkey. 'And if you're doing what you want to do all the time, then you're happy. You're not going to work everyday wishing you were doing something else. I get up and go to work everyday and I'm stoked. That does not suck.'"

Precisely.

That's mastery sans misery.

LOVING WHAT IS
IT'S ALL FUEL

Byron Katie wrote a great book called *Loving What Is*. She tells us that when we argue with reality, we lose—but only every time.

At this stage, I've read a fair number of books. This is one of my all-time favorite lines:

"I realized that it's insane to oppose it. When I argue with reality, I lose—but only 100% of the time."

Katie also tells us: "How do I know that the wind should blow? It's blowing!"

Then there's this gem: "If you want reality to be different than what it is, you might as well try to teach a cat to bark."

And, finally, know this: "The only time we suffer is when we believe a thought that argues with what is. When the mind is perfectly clear, what is is what we want."

Whatever has happened has happened. Arguing with that reality makes no sense. It is what it is. The Stoics said the same thing. So, for the record, did every wise person ever.

Our +1°…

Are YOU arguing with reality?

(How's that going for you?)

Quit doing that. It is what it is. Do what you can to accept it. Try to love it. Even better…

Use it as fuel to activate your Heroic potential.

TODAY.

80/20 PRINCIPLE + PARKINSON'S LAW
= HEROIC PRODUCTIVITY

Unless you've lived in a cave somewhere far away for the last decade…

You almost certainly know that Tim Ferriss is one of the world's most popular podcasters, authors, and, as per Wikipedia, "lifestyle gurus."

In his old-school classic *The 4-Hour Workweek*, he introduced me to a practice that has helped me activate my Heroic productivity potential.

He tells us that we need to combine two productivity concepts: The 80/20 Principle and Parkinson's Law.

First, we have the 80/20 Principle.

As we discussed, we need to know that a few key behaviors drive our results. And, of course, we need to know what those behaviors are. Then, we need to focus on them while ignoring the other stuff.

Then we have Parkinson's Law.

Basic idea with this? The amount of time something takes will always expand to the amount of time you give it.

Here's the power move: combine them.

The 80/20 Principle
+ Parkinson's Law
= Heroic Productivity

It's astonishing to me how much I can get done when I apply *both* of those concepts *at once*.

So…

Spotlight on YOU.

What's THE most important thing you need to get done right now?

And…

What's THE most Heroically fast time frame in which you can get that thing done?

Got it? Fantastic.

GET TO WORK.

SUFFERING = PAIN X RESISTANCE
AN IMPORTANT LESSON ON HOW TO REDUCE SUFFERING

In her great book *Self-Compassion*, Kristin Neff shares a little equation that can help us reduce our suffering.

It goes like this: **Suffering = Pain x Resistance.**

Here's what we need to know:

Pain, as the Dalai Lama tells us, is inevitable.

Suffering, on the other hand, is optional.

The trick is to keep the pain "clean" so we don't suffer unnecessarily.

And the key to doing *that* is to reduce our RESISTANCE to the pain we're experiencing.

This is the essence of Byron Katie's *Loving What Is* and the Stoic philosophers' "Art of Acquiescence."

We need to remember the very important fact that we LOSE when we argue with reality. But, as Byron Katie puts it: only EVERY (!) SINGLE (!!) TIME!!!

Whatever is, IS.

We want to accept the facts of our current reality—no matter how much we may dislike them. Then… By eliminating our resistance, we've eliminated our unnecessary suffering and we're in a MUCH better place to take effective action.

Question: Are *you* resisting anything painful in your life and thereby increasing your level of suffering?

How can you love what is just a little more today?

One way to do that is to simply label whatever emotion you're feeling and then get to work on your relentless solution focus—finding something you can do to make the situation just a little bit better—moving from victim to creator to hero!

Remember: Reduce your Resistance to the Pain and you reduce your Suffering.

NAME IT TO TAME IT
WHAT TO DO WITH LIMBIC GREMLINS

In our last +1°, we talked about the fact that Suffering = Pain x Resistance.

I briefly mentioned one way to reduce our suffering: simply labeling the difficult emotion you may be experiencing. Let's talk about that a little more.

This is one of the key practices of mindfulness. Research shows that it works in reducing the negative effects of painful emotions.

Different mindfulness teachers give the practice different names. Some call it "labeling."

Dan Siegel tells us we need to "name it to tame it."

I like that: "Name it to tame it."

The basic idea: When you're experiencing a difficult emotion—whether it's anger or sadness or overwhelm or whatever—it's REALLY powerful to simply *notice* that you're experiencing that emotion and then simply label it.

"Anger."

"Sadness."

"Overwhelm."

What happens when we do that is that we switch from spinning around in mental loops (with an overactive limbic system/amygdala) as we move up into our prefrontal cortex—which is a really good idea if we don't want to get swamped with those primitive emotions.

Note: We're not talking about going into a long archeological dig every time you're experiencing a challenging emotion. That can quickly devolve into unproductive rumination. Nor are we suggesting that we ignore or repress the emotion.

Simply use a word or two to label the negative emotion. Take a deep breath. Move on.

Perhaps after that labeling work you can do some targeted thinking and ask yourself…

"What do I want?"

Followed by…

"Now what needs to get done?"

Then go do it.

RUMINATION
IT'S TIME TO QUIT CHEWING ON YOUR MENTAL CUD

S cience says that the unhappiest among us (and each of us in our least happy moments) tend to ruminate about whatever is bothering us.

I personally find it helpful to remember that the word *ruminate* comes from what a cow does to food.

Imagine a cow munching on grass in an open field. It chews and chews and chews and then swallows. Then the cow digests the grass a bit before regurgitating it back into its mouth for some more chewing. Repeat.

That's ruminating. Healthy for a cow, not so much for our mental health.

Again, science is unequivocal here: Habitually ruminating isn't a wise idea. In fact, here's how Sonja Lyubomirsky puts it: "If you are someone plagued by ruminations, you are unlikely to become happier before you can break that habit."

We have a ton of alternatives. We can simply label the emotion we're experiencing, we can drop into relentless solution focus mode, use a mantra, go for a walk, whatever. But whatever you do, don't ruminate.

Sonja again. She says: "I have found that truly happy people have the capacity to distract and absorb themselves in activities that divert their energies and attention away from dark or anxious ruminations."

Chewing on the same thought? Spit out the cud!

TURNING AROUND GLITCHES
TRUE CONFIDENCE & HOW TO BUILD IT

True confidence doesn't come from thinking everything will always go perfectly.

That's crazy.

In fact, as Phil Stutz pointed out in one of our early coaching sessions, the need for absolute *certainty* results in absolute *terror*.

Quite simply: We MUST be willing to tolerate high levels of uncertainty if we want to activate our Heroic potential.

So, I repeat: True confidence isn't about thinking it'll always be easy and/or that things will work out just the way we planned. True confidence comes from *knowing* that we will have challenges AND that we have what it takes to meet each and every challenge.

In fact, as we've discussed, the Latin root of the word *confidence* literally means to "have full trust" or to "have INTENSE trust."

But...

Again...

Intense trust in what?

INTENSE TRUST in your ability to respond powerfully to each challenge as it arises.

I love the way Phil frames it. He says we need to *know* that we will have what he calls "glitches." The trick is in getting REALLY good at recovering from them.

He calls the process "collecting turnarounds." You have a glitch—disconnecting you from your highest self.

Fine. It happens to all of us. All day every day.

The question is: How fast can you recover? How quickly can you regain your connection to your Highest Self?

Glitch. Recovery. Glitch. Recovery. Glitch. Recovery.

Let's get *really* good at collecting those turnarounds.

TODAY.

LINT ON A PROJECTOR'S LENS
GOT ANY ON YOURS?

In *Loving What Is*, Byron Katie tells us: "As you inquire into issues and turn judgments around, you come to see that every perceived problem appearing 'out there' is really nothing more than a misperception within your own thinking."

Katie gives us a little metaphor to help us wrap our brains around that reality.

Here it is.

Imagine you're in a movie theatre, about to start watching a movie. The lights dim. The movie starts.

And...

There's this huge, weird thing on the screen.

What IS that?

Hmmm...

Now...

If you felt super bold, you may consider walking up and trying to rub that weird thing off the screen.

But you'd try to rub and rub and nothing would happen. The "thing" would stay there.

Why?

Because there was nothing on the screen.

The issue was with the PROJECTOR.

The lens had a little lint on it and THAT is what made the screen look weird.

Alas, so it is with life.

Those weird things showing up on the movie screens that are our lives?

That's just lint on our mental projectors.

And that's our +1°.

Let's love what is a little more today and, rather than try to fix things "out there," start right at home with our own consciousness.

As Wayne Dyer put it: "If you change the way you look at things, the things you look at change."

JESUS ON MOTES & BEAMS
IGNORE ONE, FOCUS ON THE OTHER

In our last +1°, we talked about lint on the projector's lens and the fact that, as per Byron Katie, "every perceived problem appearing 'out there' is really nothing more than a misperception within your own thinking."

As I imagined us all finding a nice little cloth to clean up our own lens rather than trying to change things "out there," I thought of another great spiritual teacher.

He lived a couple thousand years ago. In the land of Galilee. His name was Jesus.

You know what he said?

Well, in our Note on *The Jefferson Bible*, we flip open to the Bible, Matthew 7:3 where we find this wisdom: "And why beholdest thou the mote that is in thy brother's eye, but considerest not the beam that is in thine own eye? Or how wilt thou say to thy brother, Let me pull out the mote out of thine eye; and, behold, a beam is in thine own eye? Thou hypocrite! First cast out the beam out of thine own eye; and then shalt thou see clearly to cast out the mote out of thy brother's eye."

Yep.

That's *precisely* it.

And, that's our +1°.

See any "mote" in thy brother's (or sister's or spouse's or child's or colleague's or…) eye?

Settle down, Hero.

Look in the mirror.

Work on the beam in your own eye.

P.S. For curious souls, a "mote" is "a tiny piece of a substance."
Think: Sawdust.

A beam? It's much bigger.

Focus on that big thing in your own eye.

SPIRITUAL ECONOMICS
YOUR NEW WEALTH VOCABULARY

E ric Butterworth was a Unity minister in New York City. He wrote a great book called *Spiritual Economics* that helped me integrate my spiritual and material ambitions. I HIGHLY recommend it.

As we discuss in Abundance 101, the primary theme of his book is the fact that our primary economic goal should NOT be to try to make a ton of money, per se.

As Butterworth so beautifully says: "The goal should not be to make money or acquire things, but to achieve the consciousness through which the substance will flow forth when and as you need it."

How do we do that?

We know the ultimate game and how to play it well. We forge antifragile confidence. We optimize our Energy, our Work and our Love. We make TODAY a masterpiece. We master ourselves. We dominate our fundamentals. We activate our superpower.

The by-product of *that*?

"The consciousness through which the substance will flow forth when and as you need it."

Butterworth also helps us redefine a few words in our abundance vocabulary. Let's take a quick look at the true meaning of the words *prosperity*, *affluence*, and *security* as we create a new wealth vocabulary.

We'll start with the word *prosperity*. Did you know the word literally means "to go forward with hope"?! Yep.

Therefore, prosperity "is not so much a condition in life as it is an attitude toward life."

Of course, the good news is that as we "go forward hopefully" with a "prosperous" attitude in all things, we are more likely to be rewarded with all the external (and internal!) fruits of true prosperity.

Now… When we think of the word *affluence*, we tend to think of "cars and houses and baubles of all kinds."

Know this: "Its literal meaning is 'an abundant flow,' and not things at all. When we are consciously centered in the universal flow, we experience inner direction and the unfoldment of creative activity. Things come too, but prosperity is not just having things. It is the consciousness that attracts things."

Then we have the word *security*.

Have you ever caught yourself saying that you'll feel secure when you have $x in the bank or have achieved whatever other milestone such that you can finally relax and feel OK?

Again, Butterworth encourages us to look at the ancient literal meaning of the word.

He tells us: "The word *secure* comes from two small Latin words: *se* meaning 'without' and *cure* meaning 'care'—being without care, freedom from anxiety."

That sounds a lot like true, antifragile confidence.

Want to feel secure? Do the hard work to create an intense trust in your ability to handle whatever life throws at you.

Boom. No need to wait.

You're now secure.

Prosperity.

Affluence.

Security.

Let's add those words and their true meanings to your Heroic Dictionary.

TIME AFFLUENCE
VS. FINANCIAL AFFLUENCE

Having enough money to take care of your basic needs is an important variable in constructing an optimal life.

And, of course, nice things are nice.

But...

Research shows that after a certain level of basic financial well-being, there's a diminishing return such that more money doesn't necessarily make you happier.

You know what kind of affluence DOES strongly predict your level of well-being?

TIME affluence.

A sense that you have enough time to do the things you want to do and to enjoy the process.

Ironically, chasing more and more *material* symbols of affluence often erodes our TIME affluence. We run the risk making a really bad trade if the ultimate currency we're after is eudaimonic happiness. (Which, of course, it is.)

Spotlight on you...

Part I: Are you spending a lot of time and money trying to acquire things you don't *really* need? Are you trading some of your precious time affluence on less-than-precious *stuff*?

And...

Part II: Are you simply wasting time on nonsense? You know—all those meaningless TV shows and news feeds and countless other distractions?

If so, you're squandering your time affluence.

Want a cure? As you engage in those time-wasting activities, imagine burning $100 bills of time to rid yourself of that problem. (Hah.)

Seriously.

How are YOU wasting time?

Put that time back into your life's overall affluence bank.

TODAY.

THE AFFLUENZA VIRUS
FOUR WAYS TO INOCULATE YOURSELF

Continuing our quick look at what science says about money, let's turn to one of our favorite well-being scientists again: Sonja Lyubomirsky.

In her great book *The Myths of Happiness*, Sonja tells us that one of the big myths of happiness is the idea that having a ton of money will make us happy. In fact, she says we run the risk of catching the "affluenza virus" if we excessively pursue the bling.

Specifically, she says: "Why are materialistic tendencies important to identify? A mountain of research has shown that materialism depletes happiness, threatens satisfaction with our relationships, harms the environment, renders us less friendly, likable, and empathetic, and makes us less likely to help others and contribute to our communities."

Alright. You've got my attention, Dr. Lyubomirsky.

So... What can we do to optimize our relationship to money?

Sonja gives us four practical tips:

1. Spend less money on "stuff"—you'll hedonically adapt to that—and more of your money on experiences and "on developing ourselves as people, on growing, and on investing in interpersonal connections."

2. Spend money on others, not yourself. Fascinating research here. If you give people $20 and have them spend it

on themselves they'll be less happy than if they spend it on others.

3. Spend money to create more time for yourself. As we've discussed, TIME affluence is a much better predictor of happiness than financial affluence. So, use your money to buy time for yourself to do meaningful stuff.

4. Spend money now but wait to enjoy it. There's a ton of happiness in the ANTICIPATION of something. So, for example, book a trip for six months from now, then look forward to it the whole time, enjoy it, then savor it. (Buy one, get two free!)

1 + 2 + 3 + 4.

Our +1°…

It's time for your affluenza shot!

How can you practice one of those principles today?!

COMPETE? NAH. CREATE!
A KEY TO THE SCIENCE OF GETTING RICH

In *The Science of Getting Rich* (best title ever?), Wallace D. Wattles (definitely the best name ever) tells us that if we want to enjoy the process of creating abundance in every aspect of our lives, we'd be wise to make sure we focus on CREATING not COMPETING.

Specifically, he says: "You are to become a creator, not a competitor; you are going to get what you want, but in such a way that when you get it every other man will have more than he has now."

I love that.

Which leads us to another etymological pop quiz.

Q: Do you know what the word *compete* literally means?

(Insert *Jeopardy* music here.)

A: It comes from the Latin *competere* which means to "aim at, seek" (*petere*) "TOGETHER" (*com*).

To seek TOGETHER.

Not *against*. TOGETHER.

Our +1°...

How would your life change if you left the whole zero-sum competitive world and entered a pure, joyful creative realm?

And... What's one little thing you can do TODAY to make that vision a reality?

Here's to your creative brilliance as you have fun playfully striving *together*!

P.S. We'd also be wise to remember that social comparison is super toxic. Let's go with William Faulkner's wisdom: *"Don't bother just to be better than your contemporaries or predecessors. Try to be better than yourself."*

ENVY
THE ULCER OF THE SOUL

S ocrates once said that "Envy is the ulcer of the soul."

Modern science agrees.

Sonja Lyubomirsky tells us: "You can't be envious and happy at the same time. People who pay too much attention to social comparisons find themselves chronically vulnerable, threatened, and insecure."

Yikes.

Once again, ancient wisdom and modern science agree…

I repeat: "Envy is the ulcer of the soul."

The antidote?

As Sonja says: "The happier the person, the less attention she pays to how others around her are doing."

Our +1°…

Focus on what YOU are here to do.

Close the gap.

Live with *Areté*.

Today.

HERO BARS
DAVID GOGGINS & HIS COOKIE JAR

D avid Goggins is a fascinating human being.

He's a former Navy SEAL (and Army Ranger) who, among many other things, used to hold a Guinness World Record for completing 4,030 pull-ups in seventeen hours.

Yes, you read that correctly. 4,030 pull-ups. In seventeen hours.

And here I am reasonably happy with my 4,015 pull-ups a *year* accumulated eleven reps per day every day. (Hah.)

These days Goggins is setting records as an ultra-endurance athlete. But he wasn't always Mr. Superhero.

In his great books *Can't Hurt Me* and *Never Finished*, Goggins walks us through his transformation from being a 297-pound exterminator to a "Who IS this guy?!" special forces operator/elite athlete.

His story is incredibly inspiring.

Goggins tells us that we're only using 40% of our potential and, in his page-turning autobiographical books, he shares a bunch of practices we can use to activate our Heroic potential.

One of my favorites? Creating a "Cookie Jar" filled with memories of you at your absolute best.

Here's the short story… David's childhood was brutal and filled with abuse and terror. One of his small pleasures was the fact that his mom always had a cookie jar filled with his favorite cookies. He'd pick one out, look at it lovingly, and then savor the goodness.

Fast-forward to him in the middle of trying to set the Guinness World Record for pull-ups (which he failed at twice before succeeding, btw) or in the middle of one of his insanely-long ultra-endurance events.

He's in a CRAZY amount of pain. What does he do?

He reaches into his mind's virtual Cookie Jar. He reminds himself of all the times he's endured pain, didn't give up, and achieved something A W E S O M E.

As he puts it: "That's one reason I invented the Cookie Jar. We must create a system that constantly reminds us who we are when we are at our best, because life is not going to pick us up when we fall. There will be forks in the road, knives in your back, mountains to climb, and we are only capable of living up to the image we create for ourselves."

Skipping the discussion on the metabolic consequences of consuming too much sugar and flour in highly-processed cookies (as we discuss in Optimal Weight/Metabolism 101), let's call our "cookies" "HERO BARS."

And … Let's make some HERO BARS right now.

Think of ONE moment in your life in which you had the courage to act in the presence of fear. You showed up as your absolute best when you needed to the most.

Got it? Awesome.

That's a HERO BAR.

Create a box of them.

Never forget who you are at your best. Have that box of Hero Bars ready at hand as you battle the dragons on your Heroic quest.

P.S. Now that we've explored some ideas on how to play the ultimate game well by forging antifragile confidence, optimizing our Big 3, making today a great day while mastering ourselves and dominating our fundamentals, it's time to chat about how to activate our superpower. That's our next and final objective.

(I) KNOW THE ULTIMATE GAME

(II) FORGE ANTIFRAGILE CONFIDENCE

(III) OPTIMIZE YOUR BIG 3

(IV) MAKE TODAY A MASTERPIECE

(V) MASTER YOURSELF

(VI) DOMINATE THE FUNDAMENTALS

(VII) **ACTIVATE YOUR SUPERPOWER**

MY ALL-TIME FAVORITE HERO
HERE'S THEIR (& YOUR!) SUPERPOWER

Quick question for you: Who's your favorite hero?

If you feel so inspired, take a moment and think about that right now. Who comes to mind?

I have a few of my favorite heroes in my studio and on my office wall behind me. Great teachers and leaders who inspire me to show up as the best, most Heroic version of myself.

Aristotle. Epictetus. Marcus Aurelius. Abraham Lincoln. Winston Churchill. Gandhi. Abraham Maslow. Martin Luther King, Jr.

My wife and I even named our kids after two of our favorite Heroes: Ralph Waldo Emerson and Eleanor Roosevelt.

So… Again… Who inspires YOU?!

What individuals—living or dead—embody the qualities you most admire?

What individuals showed up and lived in a way that deeply inspires YOU to show up and give us all you've got?

As you think about that, know this…

All those heroes showed up in their own idiosyncratic way—Gandhi was frail and would go days without talking while Churchill was portly and rarely STOPPED talking. And, those two guys didn't even *like* each other.

But… ALL of those heroes had ONE thing in common.

It's what Aristotle had and what he helped ignite in Alexander the Great.

It's what Epictetus had and what he helped Marcus Aurelius cultivate in his life.

It's what Gandhi had and is the force that freed his nation. (And, for the record, it was Gandhi who actually gave this power its name.)

It's what Martin Luther King, Jr. had and, inspired by HIS hero, Gandhi, is something he actually talks about in his "I Have a Dream" speech.

It's what Eleanor Roosevelt had. And Florence Nightingale. And Helen Keller and Anne Frank and COUNTLESS others who may have made it into our history books or may have just humbly made an anonymous yet indelible mark on our world by deeply inspiring their friends and families and communities.

So… What's the ONE thing ALL the great Heroes across all cultures throughout history have had in common?

Soul Force.

It's every hero's superpower.

Soul Force.

It's that ineffable power you can *feel* in human beings living in integrity with their highest ideals.

Soul Force.

It's the force that can (literally) change the world.

And guess what…

It's YOUR superpower as well. We just need to ACTIVATE IT. Not *someday*. TODAY.

And then, very importantly, we need to REACTIVATE our *Soul Force* ALL DAY EVERY DAY.

THAT, my dear friend, is how we will fundamentally and permanently change your life while fundamentally and permanently changing the world together.

I want to wrap up this +1° with one more question…

Ultimately, do you know who my all-time favorite hero is?

I'll give you a hint…

Go look in the mirror.

My all-time favorite hero is, unquestionably…

YOU.

You are the hero we've been waiting for.

And helping YOU activate your Soul Force is my ultimate mission in life.

Day 1. All in.

LET'S GO!

SOUL FORCE, AN ORIGIN STORY
GANDHI'S GREAT SOUL (& YOURS!)

In our last +1°, we talked about the fact that YOU are my all-time favorite hero. (It's true.)

We also talked about the fact that, although every hero expresses it in different ways, EVERY (!) hero has the SAME superpower.

We named it ... *Soul Force.*

Today I want to share a quick origin story on where I got that phrase.

It involves one of my heroes: Mahatma Gandhi.

(Btw: Did you know that *mahatma* means "great soul" in Sanskrit? Yep. Aristotle had a word for that in ancient Greek as well: *magnanimous.*)

We're all familiar with Gandhi's (paraphrased) admonition that, if we want to change the world, we each must be the change we want to see.

What you may not know is just how FIERCELY disciplined Gandhi was. He practiced his philosophy with a relentlessness that I find deeply inspiring. He was the living embodiment of *Areté.*

Of course, Gandhi liberated India via what we called "non-violent resistance" in the West. But "nonviolent resistance" is a VERY weak translation of the Sanskrit word he coined to capture the essence of his movement and practice.

The phrase he used was *satyagraha.*

That word comes from two Sanskrit words: *sat* and *graha*. *Sat* means "beingness" or "truth." *Graha* means "polite insistence" or "force."

Gandhi fiercely believed in and fiercely challenged his followers to stand in the power of truth. He knew that Britain's domination of India was morally wrong and that, if he and millions of others could stand in that truth without resorting to violence, he could liberate the country without having to go to war.

Now, like many ancient/foreign words that are difficult to translate into English (see: *eudaimonia* and *Areté*!), *satyagraha* can be translated as not just "truth force" but also as "love force" or...

Soul Force.

There's an ineffable and extraordinary power that is palpable in an individual who is standing in their truth—living with fierce integrity to their highest ideals.

THAT is what Gandhi cultivated within himself and was able to help cultivate within enough people to *literally* change the world.

It's also what every hero we've ever admired has embodied and what I am so fiercely committed to personally embodying and to helping you embody in your own idiosyncratic way such that we can *literally* change the world.

How do we do that? By showing up and living in integrity with our highest ideals.

Not someday.

TODAY.

SOUL FORCE, THE EQUATION
HOW TO ACTIVATE YOUR SOUL FORCE

*S*oul *Force.*

It's the superpower ALL of our favorite Heroes expressed in their own idiosyncratic ways.

Gandhi had it. In fact, as we just discussed, he NAMED it. Martin Luther King, Jr. had it—he even mentioned it in his "I Have a Dream" speech. Winston Churchill had it. So did Eleanor Roosevelt and Florence Nightingale. And Viktor Frankl. And Epictetus and Marcus Aurelius.

ALL of our favorite Heroes had Soul Force. And, most importantly… YOU HAVE IT!

We just need to ACTIVATE it—which, I repeat, is the ENTIRE point of ALL of our work together.

Here's the Soul Force equation that will help us figure out how to activate it:

Soul Force = (Energy x Focus x WIN)^ Consistency

From my perspective, if we want to activate our Heroic Soul Force superpowers, we need to do THREE things at the highest possible level.

First, we need to get our ENERGY to truly Heroic levels. Fact is, if we're not dominating our fundamentals (Eating, Moving, Sleeping, Breathing, Focusing!) and have a hard time getting out of bed because of poor lifestyle choices, we're going to have a REALLY hard time showing up at our best in any aspect of our lives.

Then, we need to FOCUS that Energy on what's *truly* most important right now—or, as we like to say, on "WIN"—which is short for "What's Important Now."

That's the first part of our Soul Force Equation:

(Energy x Focus x WIN)

Then we bring in the final and, BY FAR, the most important variable: CONSISTENCY.

KNOW THIS: If you can only get yourself to get your Energy Focused on What's Important Now *once in a while*, you will NEVER (!) actualize your potential.

But…

If you can get yourself to show up CONSISTENTLY… You can tap into your *infinite* superpowers.

Here's the quick math to prove the point.

Let's say your Energy/Focus/WIN/Consistency can be measured from 0 to 100. If you can get your Energy to 100 and your Focus to 100 and put that Focused Energy on What's TRULY 100-level most important, you'd have 100 x 100 x 100 = 1,000,000 units of awesome.

Nice work.

Now it's time to bring in the EXPONENTIALIZING power of Consistency.

To use an extreme example to make the point: If your CONSISTENCY is a 0 and you can only get yourself to show up at your best once in a while or, insert whiny voice *when you feel like it*, your 1 million units of power, raised to the power of 0, will be reduced to 1.

BUT…

If you can CONSISTENTLY Focus your Energy on WIN, you know what happens when we take the 100 x 100 x 100 = 1 million units of awesome and RAISE IT TO THE POWER OF 100?

I can still remember the morning I typed this into the Google calculator.

(100 x 100 x 100) = 1 million.

1 million raised to the power of 100 is… *INFINITY*.

Want to activate your Soul Force and tap into your *INFINITE* superpowers?

Dominate the fundamentals to get your Energy to Heroic levels. Eliminate distractions and learn to Focus that Energy like a laser beam on What's Important Now. Then do that CONSISTENTLY.

And YOU, my dear friend, will activate your Heroic potential.

Let's do that and change the world.

One person at a time.

Together.

Starting with you and me.

TODAY.

MORAL CHARISMA
YOUR VIRTUOUS SOUL FORCE IN ACTION

In our last +1°, we talked about the Soul Force equation and the fact that CONSISTENCY is the *exponentializer* that activates our infinite potential.

I repeat: We activate our Heroic superpower (*Soul Force!*) by getting our Energy Focused on What's Important Now *CONSISTENTLY.*

Today I want to talk about the fact that cultivating this superpower was, essentially, the whole point of ancient Chinese philosophy as well.

We talk about this in our Philosopher's Notes on Edward Slingerland's GREAT book *Trying Not to Try* in which he integrates ancient Chinese philosophy with modern neuroscience. It's fascinating stuff.

Here's the short story. Ancient Chinese philosophers (like Confucius and Lao-tzu) were all about helping people experience the state of *wu-wei* (pronounced *ooo-way*).

We translate *wu-wei* as "effortless action" or "spontaneous action" but it, like so many of the beautiful ancient words we explore, has a deeper meaning—something closer to effortless *noble* or *virtuous* action.

In other words, ancient Chinese philosophers wanted to help people get to a point where they *effortlessly* showed up as the best (most Heroic!) version of themselves.

(Sounds a lot like *eudaimonia,* doesn't it?)

How did they help people do that?

They focused on helping them cultivate what was known as *de* (pronounced *duh*, as in "no duh").

What is *de*?

As Slingerland says: "People who are in *wu-wei* have *de*, typically translated as 'virtue,' 'power,' or 'charismatic power.' *De* is radiance that others can detect, and it serves as an outward signal that one is in *wu-wei*."

(Sounds a lot like *Areté*, doesn't it?)

Slingerland also describes that felt sense of power as "moral charisma."

Virtuous, charismatic power. (What a beautiful phrase!)

Also known as… *Moral charisma.*

Also known as… *Soul Force.*

How'd you like some of THAT?!

Our +1°…

Think of the most radiantly alive person you know—the one you most respect and admire.

Imagine yourself in their presence.

You know that energy you feel from them?

That's their *moral charisma*.

Or… As we like to say, their *Soul Force*.

Now…

Imagine YOURSELF as the most radiantly alive version of you. See yourself going through your day EFFORTLESSLY expressing the best version of yourself.

Feel the *eudaimonia* and the virtuous, charismatic power of your Soul Force being fully expressed.

Got it?

Fantastic.

Go BE that best, most Heroic version of yourself.

TODAY.

WE ARE ONLY THE LIGHTBULBS
OUR JOB? STAY SCREWED IN!

R ichard Rohr is one of my favorite teachers.

Alexandra got me his book called *Falling Upward* after I told her how much I loved David Brooks's *The Second Mountain*. Apparently, it's recommended alongside that book on Amazon. With 1,400+ reviews, Alexandra thought I might like it.

Not only did I like the book, I loved it. And, I fell in love with Richard Rohr in the process of reading it as well.

Father Richard Rohr is a Franciscan priest.

In fact, he's been a Franciscan priest for FIVE DECADES.

This has particular resonance for me as I was raised Catholic and went to Catholic school for twelve years. At my elementary school and primary church, our priests were Franciscan.

The closest I've come to studying an integrated Catholic perspective thus far has been Anthony de Mello—a Jesuit priest. (Matthew Kelly is phenomenal as well.)

So, I found Father Richard's wisdom particularly resonant for a range of reasons.

Now… When I read a book, I use a blank note card as a bookmark. On that note card, I jot down related books and ideas I want to make sure we cover in the Philosopher's Notes I create.

After reading chapters in which Rohr connected Odysseus

and the Hero's Journey to Christianity and our modern lives, at the top of my bookmark-card, I wrote this description of him: "If Joseph Campbell was a Franciscan monk."

I laughed as I typed that but it's pretty darn close to being a great micro-bio. Throw in a little Ken Wilber and we have one of my all-time favorite spiritual teachers.

In this +1°, I want to chat about a fantastic line from the book that comes pretty darn close to capturing the intention behind ALL of our work together.

Here it is...

"As Desmond Tutu once told me on a recent trip to Cape Town, 'We are only the lightbulbs, Richard, and our job is just to remain screwed in!'"

How great is THAT?

We're only the lightbulbs.

Our job?

Remain screwed in.

Activate your Heroic light.

And shine.

TODAY.

THE PARADOX OF THE EGO
WE NEED A STRONG ONE TO LET IT GO

L et's spend another moment or three with Franciscan mystic-monk Richard Rohr. We're going to talk about what he calls "The Paradox of the Ego."

As we discussed, in *Falling Upward*, he integrates his Catholic faith with ancient myths and modern wisdom.

His book is all about the "two halves of life" or "the two tasks of life."

Note: The "two mountains" in David Brooks's great book *The Second Mountain* are, essentially, his take on this idea.

As Father Rohr says: "There is much evidence on several levels that there are at least two major tasks to human life. The first task is to build a strong 'container' or identity; the second is to find the contents that the container was meant to hold. The first task we take for granted as the very purpose of life, which does not mean we do it well."

So... Two tasks.

First, we build up a strong Identity by playing the normal games of society.

THEN...

We move beyond that to connect with our higher purpose and something bigger than ourselves.

It's basically moving from an "ego" level to a "soul" level.

But...

Here's the paradox.

As Rohr says: "You ironically need a very strong ego structure to let go of your ego."

He continues by saying: "In fact … far too many … have lived very warped and defeated lives because they tried to give up a self that was not there yet. This is an important paradox for most of us."

Father Rohr leans on the wisdom of Joseph Campbell and Ken Wilber to make his point. So, let's invite them to the party to hear what they have to say on the subject.

In *Pathways to Bliss*, Campbell tells us: "Of course, to reach the transpersonal, you have to go through the personal: you have to have both qualities there."

In *One Taste*, Ken Wilber tells us: "But 'egoless' does not mean 'less than personal'; it means 'more than personal.' Not personal minus, but personal plus—all the normal qualities, plus some transpersonal ones… There is certainly a type of truth to the notion of transcending ego: it doesn't mean destroy the ego, it means plug it into something bigger… Put bluntly, the ego is not an obstruction to Spirit, but a radiant manifestation of Spirit."

Nathaniel Branden offers another way to look at it. In *The Art of Living Consciously*, he tells us that we can't let go of something we never had a firm hold of.

Again, as Father Rohr tells us: "You ironically need a very strong ego structure to let go of your ego."

That's the Paradox of the Ego.

So… Richard tells us that building this "ego container" is the primary task of the first half of life.

Then we need to empty it in the second half of life.

And refill it with God.

I think the simplest way to think about it is to go back to Desmond Tutu and his *brilliant* reminder that we're just the light bulbs. Our job is simple: Stay screwed in.

To do that, we must have the wisdom *and* the discipline to create a *very* strong sense of self SUCH THAT the Divine Light can shine through us.

Rather than "delete" the small "self," it's more powerful to think about the fact that we're plugging our little selves into something much bigger than ourselves so it goes ALL CAPS.

Like this... self → SELF!

Let's plug in and do that.

TODAY.

A STRONG EGO
= YOUR TICKET TO THE DIVINE

In our last +1°, we talked about what Father Richard Rohr describes as "The Paradox of the Ego."

This is an important subject that is part of a much longer discussion. Let's spend another moment or three on it now.

It seems to me that a lot of/most "spiritual" people these days tend to think that we need to "get rid of" our ego or otherwise maim it if we want to tap into the most divinely spiritual within us.

I don't agree with that approach.

I prefer to think of it more like Richard Rohr, Joseph Campbell, Ken Wilber and Nathaniel Branden.

Campbell tells us that he doesn't understand why there's all this talk about annihilating the ego when, in fact, it's our egos that keep us in the game.

Wilber tells us that it's not "ego-minus" but "ego-plus." We need a strong ego that's plugged into something bigger than ourselves. THAT's when the magic happens.

Then we have Nathaniel Branden who, as we discussed, tells us that even if we think "letting go of" the ego is either desirable or possible (he and I don't think it's either), successfully *letting go* of your ego would, by definition, require you to have a firm grip on your ego before you could let it go.

(Think about it for a moment: How can you let go of something you never had hold of?)

All of which leads us to how I like to think about our ego.

Of course, there are so many different definitions of what the "ego" is that we can get dizzy trying to keep up. I prefer to think of the ego in a classic Western psychoanalytic frame a la Freud.

In that model we have three components: our *id*, our *super-ego*, and our *ego*.

Our *id* is, essentially, that impulsive part of us that wants everything right.this.second. It doesn't matter whether that thing we want is good for us or not. Just give it to us. NOW.

When your impulsive *id* is running the show, you're probably engaging in one or more of your addictive behaviors—whether they're digital ("Hi, smartphone!") or chemical ("Hi, sugar and flour and alcohol and…").

Our *superego* is basically the conditioned part of us that's constantly judging all those things your *id* just did and wondering what in the world you were thinking.

It also really (*really!*) wants people to like us and can lock us into conformity when it isn't shaming us for not being perfect.

Then we have our *ego*. In this framework, our *ego* is that part of us that keeps our *id* and *superego* in check.

Note: We NEED a STRONG EGO to make sure we don't spin out of control, alternating between a hyper-impulsive/addictive version of ourselves and a hyper-conforming/perfectionistic-ashamed version of ourselves.

All of which begs the question…

How do you get your *ego* to be strong enough to deal with the pulls of the *id* and the *superego*?

In short: You have the wisdom to know the ultimate game you're playing and how to play to play it well. And, you have the discipline to do what you need to do whether you feel like it or not.

BUT...

If you think your ego is a *bad* thing and that having a strong sense of self is an "un-spiritual" thing to desire and work to attain, then, as per Rohr's commentary, you're in trouble.

Recall his comments: "You ironically need a very strong ego structure to let go of your ego."

The good (spiritual) news is that, as we deepen our connection to our highest selves by more and more consistently showing up and doing our best, we naturally tend to plug in to something much bigger than ourselves.

In *Pathways to Bliss*, Joseph Campbell puts it this way: "What is it we are questing for? It is the fulfillment of that which is potential in each of us. Questing for it is not an ego trip; it is an adventure to bring into fulfillment your gift to the world, which is yourself. There's nothing you can do that's more important than being fulfilled. You become a sign, you become a signal, transparent to transcendence; in this way, you will find, live, and become a realization of your own personal myth."

That's worth a reread:

"What is it we are questing for? It is the fulfillment of that which is potential in each of us. Questing for it is not an ego trip; it is an adventure to bring into fulfillment your gift to the world, which is yourself. There's nothing you can do that's more important than being fulfilled. You become a sign, you become a signal, transparent to transcendence; in this way, you will find, live, and become a realization of your own personal myth."

In the same book, Campbell also tells us: "This gets back to Krishna's dictum: The best way to help mankind is through the perfection of yourself."

All that to say.

It's time to perfect ourselves.

It's time to become transparent to the transcendent.

It's time to do the hard work to forge the strength for two.

It's time to close the gap and live with *Areté*.

It's time to activate our Heroic potential.

TODAY.

WHO SHALL INHERIT THE EARTH?
WAS IT THE "MEEK" OR THE "DISCIPLINED"/"TAMED?"

O nce upon a time, an extraordinary teacher gave a little
Sermon on the Mount.

Among other things, we are told that he told us: "Blessed are the meek: for they shall inherit the earth."

But, alas, what did Jesus REALLY mean when he said that?

It's kinda tough to know for sure given the fact that Jesus spoke Aramaic and the Gospels were written in Greek long after he was gone but get this...

The Greek word that was used in that passage is *praeis*.

According to the great spiritual teacher Eric Butterworth (who was, among other things, Maya Angelou's spiritual mentor), the word *praeis* didn't mean "meek" per se. It translates more closely to "tamed."

He tells us to think of Niagara Falls.

Niagara Falls has always produced an ENORMOUS amount of potential energy. But, it wasn't until recently that it was "tamed" such that all the latent energy falling all day every day was captured and channeled such that it could light up a good chunk of the Eastern seaboard.

Butterworth tells us that Jesus was telling us that WE have a *ton* of latent potential power.

And... Very importantly, he was telling us that we need to "tame" ourselves such that we can be a powerful vessel for that limitless divine energy.

Here's how Butterworth puts it in *Discover the Power Within You*: "When Jesus says 'Blessed are the meek,' He doesn't mean a surrender to people but to God. The best conductor of electricity is the substance that is least resistant to the flow of the electric current. Likewise, the best conductor of divine power is the person who is nonresistant to the flow of divine power. This attitude comes from a conviction that God is always the answer to human needs, and a willingness to submit wholeheartedly to the flow of the Spirit in and through us."

Steve Chandler shares yet another slight tweak on the translation of *praeis*.

He tells us it means something closer to "disciplined."

Enter: "Blessed are the tamed and disciplined: for they shall inherit the earth."

Here's to the wisdom and discipline and love and courage that leads to your inheritance, Hero.

PANKRATION = FULL STRENGTH
WHAT KIND OF BOXER ARE YOU?

L et's talk about the sport of mixed martial arts.

We may think it's a new thing and, of course, the way it's currently marketed is new, but the essence of the sport has been around for over 2,500 years.

In fact, in 648 BC, the Greeks made something they called "pankration" an Olympic sport.

Get this… According to Wikipedia, *pankration* "was an empty-hand submission sport with scarcely any rules. The athletes used boxing and wrestling techniques, but also others, such as kicking and holds, locks and chokes on the ground. The only things not acceptable were biting and gouging out the opponent's eyes."

The word *pankration* literally means "all strength."

It was an Olympic sport for 1,400 years.

Why is that relevant for us?

As Ryan Holiday tells us in *The Daily Stoic*, these days we use baseball and basketball and football (American and international!) metaphors to bring philosophical points home.

In ancient Greece and Rome, our wise philosophers liked to use boxing, wrestling or *pankration* metaphors.

In fact, Epictetus puts it this way: "But what is philosophy? Doesn't it simply mean preparing ourselves for what may come? Don't you understand that really amounts to saying that if I would so prepare myself to endure, then let anything happen that will? Otherwise, it would be like the boxer exiting the ring because he took some punches. Actually, you can leave the ring without consequence, but what advantage would come from abandoning the pursuit of wisdom? So, what should each of us say to every trial we face? This is what I've trained for, for this my discipline!"

I like that. A lot.

What kind of boxer walks into a ring, gets hit, and then walks out? Likewise, what kind of philosopher walks into the arena of life, gets knocked about a bit, and then walks out?

That makes NO SENSE!

The whole point (!) of our training is to learn how to most effectively deal with life's challenges.

And, as much as we may sometimes wish that life was more like a beautifully orchestrated *dance*, it's often much more like GRAPPLING than ballet.

In *The Daily Stoic*, Ryan also tells us that "Seneca writes that unbruised prosperity is weak and easy to defeat in the ring, but a 'man who has been at constant feud with misfortunes acquires a skin calloused by suffering.' This man, he says, fights all the way to the ground and never gives up."

Let's be that man or woman. Let's dare greatly. Let's enter the arena. And let's be willing to grapple with life's challenges.

If (or should I say *when*?) you get a bit knocked around by life today, remember Epictetus and Seneca and *pankration*.

Remember: THIS IS WHAT WE'VE TRAINED FOR!

Close the gap. Live with *Areté*.

Give us all the strength you've got!

IN THE ARENA
DARING GREATLY DAILY

In our last +1°, we talked about being willing to enter the arena of life and getting up every time we get knocked down.

If that isn't the perfect segue into Theodore Roosevelt's wisdom from what is now known as his "Man in the Arena" speech, I don't know what is.

Quick context: It's April 23, 1910.

Fifty-two-year-old Theodore Roosevelt has already served two terms as the U.S. President. He's delivering a speech at the Sorbonne in Paris, France. Although we now think of it as "The Man in the Arena" speech, it was actually called "Citizenship in a Republic."

Here's the passage that's worth tattooing on our consciousness:

"It is not the critic who counts; not the man who points out how the strong man stumbles, or where the doer of deeds could have done them better. The credit belongs to the man who is actually in the arena, whose face is marred by dust and sweat and blood; who strives valiantly; who errs, who comes short again and again, because there is no effort without error and shortcoming; but who does actually strive to do the deeds; who knows great enthusiasms, the great devotions; who spends himself in a worthy cause; who at the best knows in the end the triumph of high achievement, and who at the worst, if he fails, at least fails while daring greatly, so that his place shall never be with those cold and timid souls who neither know victory nor defeat."

Know this…

That arena?

It's not an "enter it once in a while" kinda thing. It's a daily thing. In fact, more accurately, it's a moment to moment to moment kinda thing.

As Maslow said and we discussed when we did some Destiny Math, in any given moment, we can choose (it's ALWAYS a choice) to step forward into growth (a.k.a. into the arena) or back into safety.

All day every day, the question is:

Forward into growth or back into safety?
Forward into growth or back into safety?
Forward into growth or back into safety?

It's time to step forward into the arena, Hero.
Close the gap. Live with *Areté*.
Activate your Heroic potential.
Today.

RESURRECTIONS & CRUCIFIXIONS
CAN'T HAVE ONE WITHOUT THE OTHER

Joseph Campbell once said that we can't have a resurrection without a crucifixion.

Think about that for a moment.

If you want to be "resurrected" into the next, best version of yourself, you must first DIE to the current version.

And...

Last time I checked, crucifixions are painful.

It's especially hard to nail *yourself* up to your own cross.

But, alas, that's what we MUST do if we want to live heroically. We must be willing to leave the land of the familiar (a.k.a. our comfort zone) and reenter the forest of the unknown right at the darkest point (a.k.a. our discomfort zone)—letting go of the life we had planned for ourselves so we can create the life that is destined for us.

Campbell also tells us that the great life is one hero's journey after another. Therefore, we must be willing to go through that process of dying to the old and being born into the new AGAIN and AGAIN and AGAIN.

Although (if all goes well!) we get a little more graceful each time we go through the cycle, the process is still always a little (/a lot!) harrowing. As Campbell says: "There is no security in following the call to adventure."

Yet...

We MUST answer the call.

All of which leads to our +1° question ...

Do YOU need to die to an old version of yourself so you can be born into the new?

Of course you do. We all do.

Here's to being born into the next-best version of ourselves. TODAY.

REGRET, SCIENCE OF
& THE WISDOM OF MARK TWAIN'S TRADE WINDS

Mark Twain tells us that twenty years from now we will be more disappointed by the things we didn't do than by the things we did do.

So, he says, we should throw off the bowlines and sail away from the safe harbor—catching the trade winds in our sails.

Get this: Science agrees.

In *The Myths of Happiness*, Sonja Lyubomirsky walks us through the fact that we are surprisingly resilient in the face of adversity.

And, we consistently overestimate how bad we'll feel in the future if something goes wrong.

This is one of her "myths" of happiness.

In fact, this is such a common phenomenon that scientists actually have a name for it. They say we have poor "affective forecasting" abilities.

So, back to our quote to go for it.

If you go for it and fail, odds are you'll bounce back faster than you think.

But...

If you don't go for it, you run the risk of torturing yourself with an infinite number of scenarios where it could have worked out.

Enter: Regret.

Our +1°...

Do YOU have any dreams that you need to pursue?

WOOP it. Make sure you're being wisely antifragile about it, of course. And ... If it's time for you to answer the call to your next Heroic adventure then ...

Here's to sailing away from the safe harbors—knowing we have what it takes to bounce back from the inevitable storms (and occasional shipwrecks)!

Twenty years from now, let's look back with a smile at all the things we had the courage to do.

3:59.4
HOW TO DO "IMPOSSIBLE" STUFF

At this point, most of us know that Roger Bannister was the first person to break the four-minute mile. Very smart people of his era said that it was impossible. Period. End of story.

He, of course, wasn't so sure.

But here's what's awesome: Do you know *how* Bannister trained to do the impossible?

Hint: He broke down his goal into bite-sized pieces.

Here's how: First, he trained until he could run a quarter mile in a minute. (Nice job!)

Then he trained until he could run half a mile in two minutes. (Well done!)

Then he trained until he could run three-quarters of a mile in three minutes. (Exciting!)

Then he trained until he thought he could run the full mile in less than four minutes.

And, *voilà*!!

On May 6, 1954 at Iffley Road Track in Oxford, England, the timekeeper looked down and saw these magic numbers: 3:59.4.

Bannister achieved the impossible by breaking his "impossible" goal into little bite-size, doable pieces—which is always a very good idea.

As Henry Ford once said: "Nothing is particularly hard if you break it into enough small pieces."

Our +1°...

How about YOU?

What's YOUR jumbo-big exciting goal?

You know, the thing you would do if you *knew* you couldn't fail? (Yah. That one.)

Feel the power of making that dream a reality. WOOP it. Rub it up against reality. Know the price you'd need to pay and the obstacles you'd need to go over and under and through to give yourself a chance to achieve it. Modify as appropriate until you're ready to commit to going for it.

Write it down in a few words.

And...

Let's chunk it down and give you your next bite-size, doable target.

What's the very next micro-goal you need to hit en route to that big goal?! The thing that, once you achieve, will make it possible to hit the *next* target?

Got it? Awesome.

Now...

What's your next baby step?

And, most importantly...

Is NOW a good time to take it?

P.S. Want to watch Bannister break the four-minute mark and hear his commentary as he does it? Search for "First Four Minute Mile (Roger Bannister: 1954)" and watch that inspiring video.

DOMINOES
AMPLIFY YOUR LATENT POTENTIAL BY 2 BILLION

Are you familiar with the physics of dominoes?

It's fascinating. And wonderfully applicable to the power of lining up a series of micro-goals to generate a ton of momentum in the process.

One of my all-time favorite YouTube videos is a clip of a physics professor walking us through the underlying physics of dominoes. Search for "Domino Chain Reaction (geometric growth in action) video" and you'll find it.

Here's the short story… A domino can knock over another domino that is 50% larger than it.

Imagine setting up a chain of dominoes such that each one is 50% larger than the prior one. Let's say thirteen dominoes. The first domino is only five millimeters high and one millimeter thick—so small that you need a pair of tweezers to put it in place. The last domino is three feet tall and weighs one hundred pounds.

Push the first tiny little micro-domino over and BOOM!

More and more power is amplified as each domino in the chain topples over until we get to that thirteenth domino—at which point we have 2 BILLION times more energy in the *last* sequence than in the *first*.

That's what we want to do.

Step 1. Get clear on your big goal.

Step 2. Line up your micro-domino goals.

Step 3. Start with the tiniest one. Knock it over.

And…

Repeat.

Remember the physics of dominoes as you amplify your latent potential power.

TODAY.

P.S. If our physics professor had twenty-nine dominoes rather than thirteen, the last domino would be as tall as the Empire State Building. These things add up.

MAGIC PENNIES
THE POWER OF COMPOUNDING GAINS

I hereby offer you two choices: 1) I'll give you $2.5 million in cash *today*; or, 2) I'll give you a penny and then we'll double it every day for a month and give you whatever that is worth at the end of the month.

So...

Which one would you like?

The $2.5 million today or the penny that doubles every day for a month?

Hmmm...

Note: You'd be wise to ask: "What month are we talking about?"

Because if it's February (and it's not a leap year!), you'd be better off with the $2.5 million today. After twenty-eight days, your doubling penny is worth $1.3 million.

But...

If we're talking about a thirty-one-day month then you'd be wise to go for the penny.

Get this: That penny goes from one cent to two to four to eight to sixteen to thirty-two to sixty-four cents to over a dollar in eight days.

Then it gets a little bigger but still feels *really* small relative to $2.5 million for another few weeks. Then it starts to take off. We arrive at $1.3 million after twenty-eight days.

Then...

The magic REALLY begins.

We go from $1.34 million to $2.7 million on day twenty-nine. Then we go from $2.7 million to $5.4 million on day thirty.

Then, on that thirty-first day, we go from $5.4 million all the way to $10.8 million.

That's some pretty magical growth.

Moral of the story?

As Darren Hardy says in *The Compound Effect*, we need to remember that a good, Heroic life is all about "A continuum of mundane, unsexy, unexciting, and sometimes difficult daily disciplines... compounded over time."

It's the tiny, mundane little things that don't *feel* significant as you do them that have the most power when we aggregate and compound the gains over an extended period of time.

All of our little +1° choices?

Those are our pennies!!!

They add up IF (big "IF!") we maintain the momentum by showing up consistently and GIVING IT TIME!

So...

What are YOUR pennies?

How can you +1° your consistency and patience a little more today?

Let's aggregate and compound all those tiny gains and (echo!) GIVE THEM TIME to work their magic.

CLOCK VS. HORTICULTURAL TIME
HOW TO GROW YOURSELF

R elated to our magical doubling penny and its demonstration of the power of compounding growth, let's chat about clock time vs. horticultural time.

Question…

When you plant a seed, do you start your stopwatch and then go into your backyard an hour later to dig it up to see how it's doing?

Or…

Do you *know* that it takes time for the seed to germinate and then to sprout and then to grow and then, finally, to reach its fruit-bearing stage?

Of course (!) you honor the rules of horticultural time and give that little seed the time it needs to naturally move through its required stages of development.

Well, important news flash…

Our growth occurs on HORTICULTURAL time, not CLOCK time.

Epictetus comes to mind.

He tells us: "No great thing is created suddenly, any more than a bunch of grapes or a fig. If you tell me that you desire a fig, I answer you that there must be time. Let it first blossom, then bear fruit, then ripen."

Our +1°…

Remember clock time vs. horticultural time as we put our

stopwatches away and focus on giving our seeds of potential the right conditions to grow.

All day every day.

Especially...

TODAY.

THE PLATEAU OF LATENT POTENTIAL
ICE CUBES, STONECUTTERS & LOOOOONG COMMAS

As we've discussed, little things add up to big things. The problem is that it takes TIME for those little things to add up to those big things.

Unfortunately, too often for too many of us, we want our lives to change X days after starting the new diet or fitness program or whatever. And, when the results don't IMMEDIATELY show up, we stop doing the little things that would have led to the success we're after.

That gap between our effort and results?

In *Atomic Habits*, James Clear calls it the "Plateau of Latent Potential" and tells us: "It's a hallmark of any compounding process: the most powerful outcomes are delayed."

Darren Hardy wrote a whole book on a similar theme called *The Compound Effect*.

Remember our doubling penny?

When offered $2.5 million today or a doubling penny for a month, make sure you ask what month it is. Your doubling penny will be worth $1.3 million on day twenty-eight and $10.8 million on day thirty-one.

Jeff Olson also wrote a whole book on the same theme. His book is called *The Slight Edge*. He tells us that people want to go from "plant to harvest" without "cultivating."

He says: "Plant, cultivate, harvest. And that second comma, the one between cultivate and harvest, often represents a loooong period of time."

In *Atomic Habits*, James uses a couple of metaphors to bring his point home: an ice cube and a stonecutter.

First, the ice cube.

Imagine you and an ice cube hanging out in a freezing cold room. It's twenty-five degrees Fahrenheit. You can see your breath.

Your challenge: Melt the ice cube.

You figure out how to raise the heat to twenty-six degrees. Nothing happens to the ice cube. You work harder and get the temperature up to twenty-seven then twenty-eight then thirty degrees. NOTHING happens. The ice cube is still staring at you. Then, you get to thirty-two degrees and everything changes as the ice cube starts melting.

James says: "Complaining about not achieving success despite working hard is like complaining about an ice cube not melting when you heated it from twenty-five to thirty-one degrees. Your work was not wasted; it is just being stored. All the action happens at thirty-two degrees. When you finally break through the Plateau of Latent Potential, people will call it an overnight success."

(Btw: Of course, the same latent potential exists as we build up to the 212° and 451° activation points as well.)

Then we have the stonecutter.

Imagine a stonecutter hammering away at a HUGE rock with a sledgehammer. He pounds and pounds and pounds at that rock with his sledgehammer over and over and over.

And absolutely nothing happens.

Just a big rock. And a sweaty sledgehammer guy.

Then, apparently out of nowhere, on the next strike the rock splits.

Now…

If you happen to walk by *right* when he made the swing that cracked open the rock, you *might* think that the guy was either super strong and/or that splitting rocks was easy.

James tells us that the San Antonio Spurs have this quote from social reformer Jacob Riis hanging in their locker room: "When nothing seems to help, I go and look at a stonecutter hammering away at his rock, perhaps a hundred times without as much as a crack showing in it. Yet at the hundred and first blow it will split in two, and I know it was not that last blow that did it—but all that had gone before."

That's our +1°.

Remember the Soul Force equation and the fact that consistency is our exponentializer.

Embrace the latent potential inherent to your growth process. Don't give up right when you're about to make a breakthrough.

And…

Hit the rock.

How? Simple.

Close the gap. Live with *Areté*.

Moment to moment to moment.

Don't think about *when* the rock will split.

Just show up and take another swing.

TODAY.

GO 0 FOR 12 LATELY?
WHO CARES? WORK YOUR PROTOCOL, HERO!

One of my dearest friends and favorite human beings on the planet is a guy named Sean Casey.

Sean is the hitting coach for the New York Yankees. He's a 3x Major League Baseball All-Star who played first base.

He's also one of THE nicest guys on the planet. They called him "The Mayor" because he chatted up EVERYONE who made it to first base. He was SUCH a nice guy that *Sports Illustrated* declared him the friendliest guy in baseball.

Now...

If you know Sean, you know he's an incredible storyteller. Here's one of my favorite stories. It goes something like this...

Once upon a time, while playing with the Cincinnati Reds, Sean was having an insanely great season.

It was summertime and he was batting near .400—which, if you know anything about baseball, you know is an incredibly hard thing to do.

Then...

Sean went 0 for 12.

Now, going 0 for 12 is never a particularly great thing for a professional baseball player but going 0 for 12 after starting the season THAT strongly is especially painful.

So...

Sean called a guy named Harvey Dorfman. Harvey was that era's greatest mental toughness coach.

Sean tells Harvey that he's struggling: "I'm 0 for 12, Coach!!"

Harvey doesn't care about those stats. All he wants to know is if Sean is executing the protocol they committed to.

Sean tells him: "Yes! Of course. I'm doing exactly what we've talked about. I'm hitting the ball hard. And guys are just making great plays."

Dorfman listens a little longer then he says: "Why are you calling me?! We have nothing to talk about. Quit looking at the results and keep on dominating your protocol."

Click. Call over. (Hah.)

Of course, that story has nothing to do with Sean or baseball or batting .400.

It's all about YOU.

Are YOU going through a rough patch? Not feeling very energized or productive or connected?

Ultimately, I don't care about those things. What I do care about is this: Are you working your protocol?

Do you know who you are at your best in your Energy, your Work, and your Love? Are you recommitting to being that best version of yourself every morning?

Do you know what virtues that best version of you embodies? Are you recommitting to showing up with those virtues every morning?

Do you know what specific things you DO when you're most on fire? Are you recommitting to those things every morning and then *ACTUALLY* DOING those things every day?

I get it. Life can be incredibly challenging.

AND…

Life doesn't need to be THAT hard.

And the process of showing up as your best self is DEFINITELY not THAT complicated or THAT hard.

It all comes down to this…

Know who you are and what you do when you're at your best. Then recommit to being that version of yourself and doing those things you do when you're on.

Every. Single. Day.

Not someday. And definitely not only on the days when you really *feel* like it.

TODAY.

That's the only way to move from Theory to Practice to Mastery so we can change the world together.

Remember…

Consistency is the exponentializer.

Day 1. All in.

Let's go, Hero!

CONSISTENCY OVER INTENSITY
THE SECRET SAUCE

After selling my first business over twenty years ago, I had enough money to spend some time figuring out what I wanted to do when I grew up.

I read a lot, traveled a bit, and decided that, if I could get paid to do what I loved to do, I'd study how to optimize my life and activate my Heroic potential, strive to embody those truths, and inspire others with what I learned.

But the #1 thing I *immediately* knew was that I'd have a hard time reaching my potential if I had a hard time getting out of bed.

Even back then, I knew that it ALL started with energy.

So, I signed up to become a certified personal trainer—thinking that would be a good way to get some clarity on the basics.

The #1 thing I got out of that training?

That it's *all* about CONSISTENCY over INTENSITY.

When most people get started with a new training program and/or commitment to optimizing their lives they go *nuts* on the first day or two or three and then fizzle out.

For most, their sign of commitment is the level of INTENSITY they bring to that first workout or two. As is often the case, we don't want to be like most people.

Rather than start out as heroes in the beginning and then tip-toe out the backdoor when it gets a little hard to maintain motivation, we want to start *knowing* that it will get harder to maintain motivation.

With that in mind, we want to focus on CONSISTENCY rather than intensity.

Go micro on your habits. Create small wins. Train your brain to get used to you working out or eating better or writing more or doing a little more Deep Work or whatever.

In short, focus on CONSISTENCY over INTENSITY.

It's funny because even in my workouts these days, when I'm doing my high intensity interval training and moving closer to a max effort, I always have a voice in my head that says: "Smart max. Don't injure yourself. Be here tomorrow."

Repeat after me:

CONSISTENCY over INTENSITY.

CONSISTENCY over INTENSITY.

CONSISTENCY over INTENSITY.

Remember…

Consistency is our exponentializer.

THE VOICE OF CONSISTENCY
VS. THE ANGEL VS. THE DEVIL

Tony Horton created P90X. If you've ever done one of his workouts, you know who he is and you'll never forget his high-energy approach to getting better.

In addition to helping shape the fitness industry, Tony wrote a fun little book called *The Big Picture* in which he shares "11 Laws That Will Change Your Life."

The first law is based on his motto: "Do Your Best and Forget the Rest."

He got that from Don Miguel Ruiz's *The Four Agreements*—which is a great concept but not what I want to focus on today. I want to chat about Law #5: "Consistency Reigns Supreme."

First, Tony makes the point that there are simply no "cons" to consistency. Therefore, it should really be called *prosistency*. (Hah.)

But that's not quite what I want to talk about either. I want to talk about the voices in his head.

Here's a little more context...

Tony Horton is Mr. Jumbo Super Fitness. Do a Google Image search on him. The guy is in incredible shape and has the energy of an Energizer Bunny.

Now...

I have a question: Do you think he's always motivated to work out?

Answer: Not at all.

In fact, he tells us: "Here's a dirty little secret: I don't get all that fired up about exercise most of the time."

What? *Really*?

Mr. Health & Fitness All-Star isn't that fired up about exercise *most* of the time?

You mean he's just like you and me?! Yep.

Well, then... Hmmm... How in the world does he get himself to get at it?

Answer: He listens to the Voice of Consistency and ignores the other voices in his head.

Tony tells us that, on any given day, he'll hear from one of three voices in his head chiming in on whether or not he should work out: Devil Tony, Angel Tony, and Consistent Tony.

He even gives us a percentage for how often each of those voices shows up. It goes something like this.

Angel Tony is all about working out.

"YAH!!! Let's *crush* this!!" That voice, Tony tells us, is there about 21.35% of the time.

Then we have Devil Tony.

Devil Tony says: "Are you kidding me? I have zero interest in training today." That guy is yelling in Tony's ear 35.4% of the time. (Hah!)

Finally, there's Consistent Tony.

This guy is, as Tony says, "about as exciting as a wet dishrag." But he gets the job done. He's matter-of-fact about it and says things like: "All right, here we go, time to train."

Nothing flashy.

This guy just does what needs to get done whether he feels like it or not. He's talking 43.25% of the time.

Now… Put Mr. Angel + Mr. Consistent together and you have 64.7% on the side of the Good Guys—enough to outmuscle Mr. Devil and get the job done.

That's our +1°.

Three parts.

#1. Let's recognize the fact that we're not alone in not wanting to exercise consistently (and/or do all the other stuff we're talking about consistently).

Enter: Common humanity. Even the best among us don't always want to do what's best for them. The difference, of course, is that they do it anyway.

Enter: The Two Easies.

#2. Take an inventory of the voices in YOUR head.

#3. Make sure the Good Guys are winning the battle.

In sum…

Remember the fact that consistency is the exponentializer as you close the gap, live with *Areté*, and activate your Heroic potential. TODAY.

YOU THINK YOU'RE AT AN 8
BUT YOU'RE REALLY AT A 2

In our last +1°, we talked about Tony Horton and the voices in his head. Today we're going to talk about another fitness legend, Joe Manganiello.

You may know Joe from the *Magic Mike* movies. Yes, I just mentioned *Magic Mike*. (Laughing.)

And, I'm not sure what to say about the fact that *Magic Mike* was the first film Emerson ever watched. Granted, he was asleep as an infant on his mother's lap but still, I'm not sure what the long-term consequences of that will be. (Hah.)

With that important point out of the way, let's get to work.

Joe Manganiello is an actor who happens to be ridiculously jacked. He also wrote a great book called *Evolution*. It's packed with great ideas on his approach to fitness and to life.

Here's one of my favorite lines: "*Truth*: You think you're working out at an 8. You're actually working out at a 2. I don't care how long you've been training; that's just the reality. If that hurts your feelings, I'm sorry. It's time for you to reestablish your baseline in order to define intensity."

This is one of my favorite lines ever: You THINK you're at an 8. But you're really at a 2. In EVERY aspect of your life.

Hate to break the news to you and I'm sorry if that hurts your feelings. (Hah.) But that's actually (a) almost certainly true (right?) and (b) incredibly inspiring as it points to a ton of opportunities for optimizing.

The trick?

We need to step back, analyze our prior best, and make that our new baseline.

So…

Our +1°.

What's one area of your life that you *know* needs work?

Let's be honest. Are you operating at about a 2? No big deal. What would a truly 8-level of intensity look like for you?

Dial it up.

Evolve into the best version of you.

Then, most importantly.

Repeat that process.

Remember: You think you're at an 8. You're really at a 2.

Step it up, Hero.

It's Day 1.

LET'S GO.

CHARISMA 101
SCIENCE SAYS: PRESENCE, POWER & WARMTH

C harisma.

Most people think it's something you either have or you don't have.

But ... That's a myth.

As Olivia Fox Cabane tells us in *The Charisma Myth*, research shows that we can ALL learn how to dial up our charisma and become more magnetically connected to those around us. It's a skill we can learn.

How?

By practicing the three essential components of charisma: Presence, Power, and Warmth. Let's take a quick look at each.

Rule #1 of charisma?

Presence.

In fact, Stanford's Emma Seppälä tells us: "Charisma, simply put, is absolute presence."

Absolute presence.

Think about and feel into that for a moment.

Btw: As per our +1° on the iPhone Effect, guess what ISN'T present if you want THAT level of presence?

Your smartphone.

Your smartphone is basically kryptonite for charisma. Don't be the person constantly checking your phone for the latest push notification. You know what that tells the person with whom you're spending time?

That you just don't care that much about them. And, that's a great way to kill all connection and charisma.

(Another pro tip: Make eye contact.)

Our second facet of charisma?

Power.

Presence is the first step, but, according to Cabane, it's not enough by itself. People are constantly, subconsciously detecting power or a lack thereof. Therefore, if we want to dial up our charisma, we need to dial up our personal power.

Easiest way to do that? Your body language.

Stand tall, breathe deeply, smile. And, while you're at it, another great, quick way to boost your power before an interaction is to recall a prior success. Visualize it. FEEL the power you had when you crushed it. Soak THAT in, smile, and go connect.

The third facet of charisma?

Warmth.

We may be present and powerful but if the person with whom we're interacting doesn't think we'll use that power for their good then … no charisma.

So…

Dial up your presence and your power AND your warmth. How do we do that? Easy.

Truly care about the other person. Have a sense of goodwill for them. Want what's best for them. And beam that love their way.

That's Charisma 101: Presence + Power + Warmth.

Our +1°…

Where are you strong? (Celebrate it!)

What needs work? (Have fun getting to work on that!)

Remember…

Charisma is a skill.

You can dial it up at will.

Let's practice doing that a little more today!

DEATH AT THE CROSSROADS
MAKING DECISIONS IN LIFE

Here's yet another gem from my beloved coach and honorary godfather, Phil Stutz.

Phil tells us that when we come to a crossroads—a point in our lives when we need to make a choice between two or more options—we need to be willing to DIE to some of the options and go all in on one.

This is one of the reasons why people hate making decisions. They don't want to experience the pain of losing out on a not-taken path.

But, the fact is that there will ALWAYS (but only ALWAYS!) be trade-offs in every choice we make.

As such, if we want to get better at more confidently making decisions, we need to remind ourselves that the root of the word "decide" is *de + cir* which literally means "to cut" or "to kill."

We need to take a very sharp, decisive blade and make a choice at that crossroads—killing the other options.

We need to DIE at the crossroads.

And then we need to go ALL IN on our chosen path.

Phil has a great way to visualize this Tool. (As he does with pretty much all the Tools he's shared with me and as you know if you've seen *Stutz*!)

Draw a big ol' chunky arrow with, say, an inch-tall body heading to the right on your page. Then draw a splinter arrow that goes up and another splinter arrow that goes down representing other paths you could explore at your crossroads. (And know that you could draw an infinite number of those pathways.)

Then you use that pen-sword of yours and literally CROSS OFF AND KILL the other paths as you lean into the one you're choosing to go for.

You willingly choose to make the trade-offs. Then you focus all that energy you were dissipating chasing too many options as you go all in on your chosen path.

Death at the Crossroads.

It's a powerful perspective-tool to embrace as we take the next steps in activating our Heroic potential.

THE ROAD NOT TAKEN
BY ROBERT FROST

In our last +1°, we talked about "dying at the crossroads" of life and the power of focusing our energy on what we've decided is most important.

Robert Frost wrote a poem on the subject. You've almost certainly read it more than once. It's called "The Road Not Taken." Here it is.

Two roads diverged in a yellow wood,
And sorry I could not travel both
And be one traveler, long I stood
And looked down one as far as I could
To where it bent in the undergrowth;

Then took the other, as just as fair,
And having perhaps the better claim,
Because it was grassy and wanted wear;
Though as for that the passing there
Had worn them really about the same,

And both that morning equally lay
In leaves no step had trodden black.
Oh, I kept the first for another day!
Yet knowing how way leads on to way,
I doubted if I should ever come back.

I shall be telling this with a sigh
Somewhere ages and ages hence:
Two roads diverged in a wood, and I—
I took the one less traveled by,
And that has made all the difference.

That poem also reminds me of Joseph Campbell, and some of his wisdom from *A Joseph Campbell Companion*.

He tells us: "You enter the forest at the darkest point, where there is no path. Where there is a way or a path, it is someone else's path. You are not on your own path. If you follow someone else's way, you are not going to realize your potential."

Our +1°…

It's time to take the next step in our Heroic quests.

Together.

TODAY.

UTTER COMMITMENT
THE PSYCHOLOGY OF

The other day, Phil and I were chatting about the power of going ALL IN on ONE thing. We talked about how hard it is to do but how powerful it is once we do it.

Phil told me there's something special about what he called "the psychology of utter commitment."

The Psychology of Utter Commitment.

Isn't that a beautiful phrase?

Something magical happens when we focus ALL of our energy on whatever we've decided is most important to us.

Reminds me of Alexander Graham Bell and his great line: "Concentrate all your thoughts on the task at hand. The sun's rays do not burn until brought to a focus."

I repeat: The sun's rays do not burn until they're brought to a focus.

Have you ever grabbed a magnifying glass and tested that statement? It's a fun little experiment (kids love it!), and it's amazing to see how quickly you can burn a hole through a leaf when you focus the sun's rays.

There's SO MUCH latent potential in those rays, just waiting for us to focus them in a given direction.

Same thing with our lives, of course.

And… How do we tap into that power?

Well, one way is to focus via The Psychology of Utter Commitment.

Going ALL IN.

Focusing ALL your Energy on your ONE big, WILDLY IMPORTANT target.

Which begs the question…

What's WILDLY important to you?

The ONE thing that, if you achieved it over, say, the next year would have THE most Heroically powerful impact on your life?!

Are you clear on that and going after it with laser-like focus? Or are your goals kinda sorta fuzzy and your focus diffused in the whirlwind of distractions?

Let's get clear on what key things will make a difference in our lives. And then FOCUS our energy on that most important win.

Here's to concentrating our energy on what's most important now.

Remember…

Just like the sun's rays do not burn until brought to a focus, our Soul Force is not activated until we focus all of our energy on what's important now.

VISIONS OF A LIFETIME
MARCUS AURELIUS ON THE PRESENT MOMENT

Marcus Aurelius once wrote to himself: "Never confuse yourself with visions of an entire lifetime at once."

As a guy who used to have the habit of wanting to have it all perfectly figured out right now and forever, I remember being awestruck by that line when I first read it.

"Never confuse yourself with visions of an entire lifetime at once."

Do *you* ever do that?

Do you ever feel like you need to see every single step in your Heroic quest right from the beginning?

That's kinda like thinking you should be able to see the finish line at the start of your race.

Or thinking you should be able to see that turn you're going to take in 2,143 miles when you're driving from Los Angeles to New York City.

Of course, with a moment of reflection, we can see that's silly. We'd be much wiser to have a basic idea of where we're headed and then focus on the next step.

Then, when we're turned around or feeling a little lost, we bust out the high-level map and, most importantly, the inner compass that points to who we aspire to be.

We remind ourselves of who we are at our best and what virtues that best, most Heroic version of ourselves embodies.

Then…

We ask ourselves what that best, most Heroically virtuous version of ourselves would do in this moment.

Then…

We close the gap and live with *Areté* with these words guiding us…

"Never confuse yourself by visions of an entire lifetime at once… Remember that it is not the weight of the future or the past that is pressing upon you, but ever that of the present alone."

THE BIG PICTURE
ZOOM IN & ZOOM OUT

It's easy to fall into the trap of thinking that whatever challenge is capturing our attention in the moment is EVERYTHING!

If we aren't mindful, we can feel so attached to the outcome of that challenge that our success or failure on that one particular thing can easily feel like the only metric worth considering as we do our self-worth inventory.

Obviously, that's not a good idea.

So, here's one way to approach it.

Grab a piece of paper.

Draw a HUGE circle. Like, jumbo big—almost taking up the whole page.

Now, put a little pinpoint dot somewhere inside that circle. That little dot? That's your current challenge.

It may FEEL like it's the huge jumbo circle, but it isn't.

Of course, we want to be able to zoom in on that little dot and bring it into super-clear focus, so we can give our absolute best energy to rocking it moment-to-moment style, AND we want to be able to zoom out and hold the broader perspective and see that whatever is challenging us right.this.moment is just a tiny drop in the super big picture.

Our +1°…

If you feel so inspired…

Draw the big circle. Drop in the dot.

Zoom in to crush it and give it all you've got.

Zoom out to maintain perspective and know this is just one fun little adventure in the Heroic journey that is your multi-faceted life.

And, most importantly, let's enjoy the whole process.

Day 1. All in.

LET'S GO, HERO!

MICROSCOPES & TELESCOPES
ANOTHER WAY TO ZOOM IN & ZOOM OUT

In our last +1°, we talked about the power of drawing a huge circle and then a little pin-point dot. Zooming in to rock the current challenge. And zooming out to hold the bigger picture.

Here's another way to look at it.

The master warrior-of-the-mind Philosopher has a broad array of weapons/tools in his or her armamentarium/tool shed including these two: A microscope and a telescope.

We use the microscope to ZOOM IN on that little dot that is our #1 current challenge. We go ALL THE WAY INTO that challenge right down to TODAY. We can see a Masterpiece Day with vivid detail. Then we continue zooming down right into THIS MOMENT.

AND…

We can step back from the microscope and bust out our telescope. We consciously, deliberately step WAY back from that dot on a little piece of paper. We look to the super-big picture of our lives. Three years. Five years. Ten years. An entire lifetime. We KNOW (!) our future just keeps getting better and better Hope 101-style.

Microscopes. Telescopes.

Super simple metaphors. Super helpful ones as well.

Our +1°…

How are YOU doing with each of those? Use one more than another? Got some dust on either?

And, most importantly: What's one little thing you can do to optimize your scopes today?

Let's do that.

See you on Mars and … in the nanograms!

CHAMPIONS FINISH STRONG
SO DO HEROES. DO YOU?

Darrin Donnelly wrote a great fable called *Old School Grit.* It's the second book in his Sports for the Soul series.

This book features a retiring NCAA coach sharing wisdom with his grandchildren during his final March Madness.

Darrin has his Heroic guide share 15 Rules of Grit. They include the importance of embracing pressure, living for a purpose greater than yourself, and knowing that life is a series of wins and lessons.

Let's chat about Rule #4: Finish Strong.

Before their championship game, the coach says: "It's easy to start strong. Everybody can start strong. Whether it's a season or a game, everyone starts off excited, positive, and enthusiastic. Everyone starts off full of energy and optimism. But, fellas, after more than four decades of coaching, I've learned that, while everybody starts strong, only champions finish strong."

He continues by saying: "It's funny how quickly life can turn around if you keep pushing forward and expecting things to be most difficult right before they get drastically better."

Then he says: "You have to expect your most challenging moment right before your greatest victory. Remember this the next time you feel like you can't catch a break or you start questioning whether you have what it takes to accomplish your dreams."

To make his philosophical point with a hammer, he tells us: "Everybody starts strong, but champions finish strong."

I thought of a number of things when I read that.

I thought of one of my most influential mentors when I was running my first business. I thought of the Sanskrit word for being a hero in the beginning. And I thought of Napoleon Hill and his parallel wisdom on success coming RIGHT after we almost give up. Let's discuss each briefly now.

First, my mentor.

As we've discussed, way back in the day when I had more hair and less gray whiskers, I was a twenty-five-year-old Founder/ CEO running my first company. It was the 1999/2000 dot-com boom era. Our business was called eteamz.

We won the business competition at the University of California, Los Angeles's business school. We had raised $5 million. We were a pretty exciting start-up that blended sports and technology. Dartboard in my office. Ping pong table in the boardroom. The full deal.

We were blessed to hire the CEO of Adidas to replace me as the young CEO. Then the market crashed. Rather than going out and raising our next big round, we had to deal with some HUGE obstacles to survive—which is precisely when my mentor told me what Coach Flanagan told his players as they were getting ready for a March Madness NCAA game.

My mentor told me: "It's easy to START something. It's a lot harder to FINISH it strong."

I'm proud of how our team responded to those challenges as I earned my first batch of gray whiskers. We endured the tough times and wound up creating a positive return for our investors while ultimately serving millions of families involved in youth sports with our platform.

I'm even more grateful for my mentor's wisdom on the importance of finishing strong.

Then we have Eknath Easwaran.

He tells us that this idea of starting something strong and then tip-toeing out the back door when things get hard has been so common for so long that, THOUSANDS of years ago, the ancient sages of India came up with a word for it.

In Sanskrit, they call it *arambhashura*: "To be a hero in the beginning."

Not what we're looking for. Heroes finish strong.

Then there's Napoleon Hill.

In *Think and Grow Rich*, he tells us: "Before success comes in any man's life, he is sure to meet with much temporary defeat, and, perhaps, some failure. When defeat overtakes a man, the easiest and most logical thing to do is to quit. That is exactly what the majority of men do. More than five hundred of the most successful men this country has ever known told the author their greatest success came just one step *beyond* the point at which defeat had overtaken them."

That's our +1°.

Remember Rule #4 of Old School Grit.

Heroes finish strong.

Day 1. All in.

LET'S GO!

DOING THE DISHES
WITH BYRON KATIE

Byron Katie tells us that: "We never receive more than we can handle, and there is always just one thing to do."

She calls the practice of embodying that truth "doing the dishes."

Dishes need to be done? Do them.

Phone call needs to be made? Make it.

Kids are asking you to play a game? Play the game.

Fill-in-the-blank with whatever life presents. Complete. Repeat.

As we like to say: Get your Energy Focused on What's Important NOW. Consistently.

Some would say that's the essence of enlightenment.

Do the dishes. Chop wood. Carry water.

With a joyful, knowing smile.

Close the gap.

Live with *Areté*.

TODAY.

EDITING OUR LIVES
& THE QUEST FOR AUTHENTICITY

In a book called *Running Down a Dream*, Tim Grahl tells us about his experience working with some of the world's most elite authors and self-help gurus.

Quick context: Tim is a marketing genius. Specifically, he helps authors launch their books.

Tim is one of the best at what he does. To put it in perspective, at one point, FIVE of his clients were on the *New York Times* bestseller list at the same time.

But here's the thing…

He tells us that one of the biggest lessons he's learned over the years is just how much these luminaries "edit" their lives. There's the multiple bestselling author who didn't return his calls and emails for a while right before his launch.

Where was he?! In rehab again. But no one ever heard about it. Then there's the author who doesn't say anything about his divorce. And the one who doesn't say anything about that flaw. And that one who…

On and on and on.

EDITING. EDITING. EDITING.

It's not just self-help gurus, of course. In a world of social media, it's so easy to put up a facade of perfection.

EDITING. EDITING. EDITING.

Which is one of the reasons I spend PRECISELY ZERO time on social media sites (other than Heroic!). Period.

I know that social comparison is toxic and that social sites are cesspools for social comparison.

So...

Are you editing YOUR life to try to come across perfectly? How would it feel if you relaxed on the selfies (at the perfect angle!) just a tad and allowed yourself to enjoy the moment in all its (im)perfection?

And...

Can you see just how hard everyone else is constantly editing their lives? And, if you feel so bold, perhaps spend just a little less time on Instagram and Facebook and TikTok and wherever else all the cool kids are showing their best selves off these days.

This wisdom from Sonja Lyubomirsky's *The How of Happiness* is always worth keeping in mind: "You can't be envious and happy at the same time. People who pay too much attention to social comparisons find themselves chronically vulnerable, threatened, and insecure."

And, as we discussed but it's worth repeating: "The happier the person, the less attention she pays to how others around her are doing."

Here's to embracing our imperfections, caring less about what others are doing and always remembering the endless EDITING as we strive to create more and more authentic lives.

THE FOUR AGREEMENTS
IN LESS THAN FOUR MINUTES

Don Miguel Ruiz wrote *The Four Agreements*. His classic little book has sold over 15 million copies in the U.S. and has been translated into over 50 languages.

Let's have some fun unpacking those Four Agreements in less than four minutes.

The First Agreement: *Be Impeccable with Your Word.*

Ruiz tells us that the word "impeccable" literally means "without sin." In this context, we're talking about being in integrity with your highest self—to not "sin" against that best version of you, starting with how you communicate with yourself and others.

In short: No complaining. No criticism. No blaming. No gossiping. Ever.

Ruiz tells us that this is "the most important one and also the most difficult one to honor. It is so important that with just this first agreement you will be able to transcend to the level of existence I call heaven on earth."

The Second Agreement: *Don't Take Anything Personally.*

We need to know that, how someone responds to us, often says more about THEM than it says about us.

Imagine interacting with the same person in two different situations.

First, the person had an AWESOME day—they got a great night of sleep, won the lottery, and every other thing that could've possibly gone well for them unfolded perfectly. How do you think they're going to treat you?

Now, same person. This time, they got a bad night of sleep, lost their job, got in a car accident, and experienced every other annoying thing that could've happened. Not in such a good mood. How do you think they're going to treat us now?

Obviously those examples are (deliberately) hyperbolic and, of course, who we are and how we show up (obviously) impacts the quality of our relationships.

And… The important thing to note here is that WE were exactly the same in both situations. But if we base our opinion of ourselves on how someone else treats us, we're in trouble.

As Ruiz says: "Nothing other people do is because of you. It is because of themselves."

The Third Agreement: *Don't Make Assumptions.*

Want a quick way to get in trouble? Make assumptions about someone else's behavior. Notice how often we do that. And do we typically assume the best? No. We assume the worst.

The solution: "The way to keep yourself from making assumptions is to ask questions. Make sure the communication is clear. If you don't understand, ask. Have the courage to ask questions until you are as clear as you can be."

The Fourth Agreement: *Always Do Your Best.*

Ruiz tells us that it's the Fourth Agreement that brings the prior three to life. Want to ingrain your new way of being? Do your best. Moment to moment to moment.

(Sounds a lot like *Areté*, eh? Yes, my friend, it does.)

The important thing to remember is the fact that your best is variable—sometimes your best will be ridiculously awesome, and, at other times, it won't be so awesome.

But: "Under any circumstance, always do your best, no more and no less. But keep in mind that your best is never going to be the same from one moment to the next. Everything is alive and changing all the time, so your best will sometimes be high quality, and other times it will not be as good."

There ya go.

The Four Agreements in less than four minutes.

How can you use them to +1° today?

HOW TO PREDICT WHERE YOU'LL END UP
LOOK AT THE TRAJECTORY OF YOUR DAILY CHOICES

I've read a lot of books on how to create great habits. But *Atomic Habits* is the best. There's a reason it's the all-time best-selling book on habits. It's fantastic. I highly recommend it.

Here's one of the many brilliant ways James Clear establishes the power of little things to create big results.

Imagine you're flying out of Los Angeles. You want to go to New York City. Unfortunately, the nose of your plane is pointing just a *little* bit more south than it should be—say around 3.5 degrees more south than you want it.

What happens if the pilots don't correct it? Well, that 3.5 degrees is only about ninety inches off course (depending on the size of your plane), but even with just that *slight* shift in trajectory, you'll wind up HUNDREDS of miles off course. In fact, rather than land in NYC, you'll land in Washington, D.C.

I repeat: Ninety inches off equals hundreds of miles off when you give it enough time (and distance).

Know this: Little things matter. A lot.

Of course, that works in both directions for our lives.

As James says: "Making a choice that is 1 percent better or 1 percent worse seems insignificant in the moment, but over the span of moments that make up a lifetime, these choices determine the difference between who you are and who you could be. Success is the product of daily habits—not once-in-a-lifetime transformations."

Plus, going back to the trajectory of those planes and our lives, James tells us: "You should be more concerned with your current trajectory than with your current results… If you want to predict where you'll end up in life, all you have to do is follow the curve of tiny gains or tiny losses, and see how your daily choices will compound ten or twenty years down the line."

That's our +1°.

I repeat: Want to predict where you'll end up in your life?

"Follow the curve of tiny gains or tiny losses, and see how your daily choices will compound ten or twenty years down the line."

Here's to the curve that leads to the activation of your Heroic potential.

Little things matter. A lot.

Let's close the gap.

And live with *Areté*.

Today.

BONZAI TREES, GOLDFISH & YOU
HOW TO 100X YOUR AWESOME

L et's chat about bonzai trees and goldfish and you.

Alan Cohen puts it so perfectly (in his epically named book *Why Your Life Sucks*) that I'll let him take it from here:

"We have all been hypnotized into thinking that we are smaller than we are. Just as an undersized flowerpot keeps a mighty tree root-bound or a little fishbowl keeps goldfish tiny, we have adapted, adjusted, and accommodated to a Lilliputian life. But place the same tree in an open field or the fish in a lake, and they will grow to hundreds of times their size. Unlike the tree or goldfish, you are not dependent on someone else to move you. You have the power to move yourself. You can step into a broader domain and grow to your full potential."

Wow.

I never thought about it quite like that. You?

Think about that for a moment...

You can make what should be a HUGE tree super-dinky simply by keeping it in a tiny pot.

Same thing with a fish. Small bowl equals small fish. Big lake equals big fish.

Our +1° is simple.

Is it time to upgrade the size of your flowerpot/fishbowl?

Fantastic. Here's to 100x-ing your awesome.

PROVING YOURSELF RIGHT
VS. "I HOPE THIS WORKS OUT ALRIGHT"

When Hall of Fame NFL quarterback Peyton Manning was released from the Indianapolis Colts after fourteen seasons, a number of teams tried to recruit him.

He picked the Denver Broncos.

When he decided to go with the Broncos, he didn't say to himself: "I hope this works out alright."

He decided to PROVE HIMSELF RIGHT.

There's a huge difference between those two perspectives.

In one, you kinda sorta hedge and never really go all in—which, of course, is a great way to protect yourself from the risk of being wrong as you'll always be able to make a convenient excuse as to why things didn't work out, but it's also a great way to ensure you never move past mediocrity and do something truly great.

When you make a *real* decision, you, by definition, cut off all the other options and go ALL IN. Then you're not interested in hedging. You're interested in winning. So, you go to work, HUSTLING to make sure you prove yourself right.

Here's our +1°…

What's important to you right now?

As in, *really* important. If you could wave a wand and make THIS wildly important thing happen, what would it be?

Got it?

Fantastic.

Assuming you've WOOPed it and decided whether or not you're willing to pay the price to get it…

Are you hedging, or are you going ALL IN antifragile style?

Quit hoping it will work out alright.

Go prove yourself right.

TOUCHDOWN, JERRY RICE!
WHEN? EVERY TIME HE CAUGHT THE BALL

Jerry Rice was born in a small town in Mississippi. He was the sixth of eight kids. His dad was a bricklayer. He went to a small college (Mississippi Valley State) where he played football. Although he was an All-American, he didn't know if he'd be drafted when he watched the NFL Draft Day alone with his brother in 1985.

As it turns out, the football genius Bill Walsh saw something special in Jerry and traded a first, second, and third-round pick, so the Super Bowl Champion San Francisco 49ers could draft him with the 16th pick.

Note: His mom was cleaning houses and would have missed the draft if the woman whose house she was cleaning didn't insist she watch ESPN on her TV. His dad missed it because he was laying bricks.

So…

Imagine this…

After freaking out on the first airplane trip of his life, Jerry safely arrived in San Francisco. He shows up at his first practice as a rookie for the defending Super Bowl Champions.

He runs the first simple receiving route. He catches the ball. THEN HE RUNS FULL SPEED ALL THE WAY TO THE END ZONE.

"Touchdown, Jerry Rice!"

Repeat with the second receiving route.

Repeat again EVERY SINGLE TIME he caught the ball in EVERY SINGLE PRACTICE over his entire 20-year career.

Just to be clear in case you were wondering...

NO ONE DOES THAT.

It's crazy.

Seriously.

The veterans and other receivers thought he was crazy.

At first.

Then the other receivers started doing it, too.

(Funny how that whole leadership thing works, eh?)

Why would he run into the end zone every single time he caught the ball?

Well, as Jerry puts it in his great memoir called *Go Long!*: "How you practice = How you play. It's that simple. I don't care if we're talking about basketball or ballet, cooking or checkers. The way in which you prepare for a challenge is usually related to your success in that same challenge. If the level at which you practice is commensurate with the task, then on 'game day,' you'll be fine."

+1° time...

How are YOU going through the plays of *your* life? Are you showing up and playing the ultimate game with an ALL IN intensity or just kinda sorta going through the motions?

Here's to running our routes like we mean it.

"Touchdown, YOU!"

HOW TO BE LIKE MIKE
GO ALL IN

In our last +1°, we talked about the fact that Jerry Rice scored a touchdown every single time he caught the ball in practice.

I smile and get fired up every time I think of that story. It makes me work just a little harder. (In fact, I might have just banged out an extra set of burpees in Jerry's honor!)

Picture our hero Jerry Rice at his first practice as a rookie for the defending Super Bowl champions, the San Francisco 49ers. He ran a simple route, caught the pass. Then he went FULL SPEED for the touchdown.

He'd actually started doing that in college, a long time before he arrived in San Francisco.

I think Michael Jordan and Jerry Rice must have telepathically traded notes when they were young because they DEFINITELY played like one another.

Side note: I just Googled to see how old Michael Jordan and Jerry Rice are relative to one another. As it turns out, at the time I'm writing this they are both sixty years old—born within four months of one another.

In this +1°, we're going to look at Jordan in his early days.

More specifically, let's rewind the clock to the year Jordan infamously got cut from his varsity team. We've all heard the story at this point.

Jordan didn't even make his varsity team in high school?!

WHAT?

It's a true story. Jordan didn't make his varsity team as a sophomore in high school for a variety reasons—including the fact that there were a ton of returning varsity players, including a bunch of players at his position.

In any case, he didn't make the team—which DEVASTATED him. He cried. A lot.

And then...

He got to work.

In the great biography *Jordan: The Life*, Roland Lazenby shares a story about the day a varsity coach cruised into the gym while the junior varsity game was wrapping up.

Nine players were coasting. One guy (named Michael Jordan) was going OFF with *extreme* intensity.

The coach assumed his team must have been down by one point with a couple minutes to play. He looked at the scoreboard. Jordan's team was down by TWENTY points with a minute to go.

But Jordan? He was ALL IN.

Even at fifteen years old, Jordan was ALWAYS ALL IN.

That's what made him Michael Jordan.

THE GROWTH MINDSET
CAROL DWECK SAYS

In our last +1°, we talked about how to be like legendary Hall of Famers Michael Jordan and Jerry Rice.

Hint #1: BE ALL IN.

Hint #2: ALWAYS.

Hint #3: Have a growth mindset.

I briefly mentioned the fact that Jordan was DEVASTATED when he was cut from his varsity high school team. Then he used that failure as FUEL for his growth.

That reminds me of Carol Dweck. For two reasons. We'll talk about one now and the other in our next +1°.

Dweck is one of the world's most respected social psychologists. She is a Stanford professor who has dedicated her life to helping us understand the power of our mindset.

In her classic book *Mindset*, she tells us that we can live with either a "fixed mindset" or a "growth mindset."

We want to choose our mindset like our destinies depend on it because... they do.

Here's the super quick take.

If you have a fixed mindset, you think your abilities are "fixed." When you have this mindset, you avoid any and all challenges because you might fail, and that failure might prove to the world that you're not very awesome.

This is (obviously) a recipe for thwarted potential because, when you're locked in this mindset, you do everything you can to avoid looking bad—missing the fact that those challenges you're working so hard to avoid (that might result in failure and you looking bad) are PRECISELY the way you're going to have a shot at being GREAT.

People with the growth mindset, on the other hand, know that they can get better if they put in the hard work.

As Dweck says, they ACTIVELY SEEK OUT CHALLENGES. This mindset, when paired with the intense effort of a Jerry Rice or a Michael Jordan (or a Heroic you at your best!), leads to exceptional performance.

Now, let's go back to Jordan and that time he didn't make the varsity team. Dweck actually uses him as a case study multiple times to make some points throughout her book as he's such a PARAGON of the growth mindset.

She says: "Michael Jordan embraced his failures. In fact, in one of his favorite ads for Nike, he says: 'I've missed more than nine thousand shots. I've lost almost three hundred games. Twenty-six times, I've been trusted to take the game-winning shot, and missed.' You can be sure that each time, he went back and practiced the shot a hundred times."

That's our +1°.

How's YOUR mindset?

You can get a quick sense by checking in on how you deal with life's inevitable stressors.

Are you seeing them as THREATS to be AVOIDED?

Or, as CHALLENGES to be APPROACHED?

Choose your mindset wisely, Hero.

DEPRESSED? TWO WAYS TO RESPOND
SCIENCE SAYS: ONE IS BETTER THAN THE OTHER

In our last +1°, we talked about Michael Jordan and Carol Dweck and growth mindsets.

I mentioned the fact that, when I imagined Jordan crying after missing the cut for his varsity basketball team, I thought of Carol Dweck for two reasons. We just discussed the first reason. Here's the second.

Once again, let's imagine the great Michael Jordan (*before* he was the great Michael Jordan) missing the cut for his varsity team. Feel his heart SINK as he looked at the sheet on the wall and saw that his name was MISSING.

Of course, that shouldn't be hard to imagine (and feel) as we've ALL experienced exactly that sense of despair when we failed at something super important to us.

(Enter: Common humanity.)

Then, let's follow young Michael Jordan back to his house where he locked himself in his room and CRIED. And cried. And cried. Totally devastated.

That shouldn't be hard to imagine either as we've all experienced our own version of that as well, eh?

Side note: As Emerson and I were reading the *Odyssey* not too long ago, I was struck by just how often Odysseus and his men WEPT in response to the losses they experienced and the challenges they faced.

Yep. Heroes cry. A lot.

Remember Rule #1: It's NOT SUPPOSED TO BE EASY!

So… Our young basketball hero is devastated. Then what?

Then he embodied the essence of Dweck's growth mindset and WORKED HARDER THAN EVER—which is why she repeatedly comes back to him as a growth mindset exemplar.

Here's how Dweck puts it: "How do you act when you feel depressed? Do you work harder at things in your life, or do you let them go? Next time you feel low, put yourself in a growth mindset—think about learning, challenging, confronting obstacles. Think about effort as a positive, constructive force, not as a big drag. Try it out."

It's time for our +1° spotlight on you…

How do YOU act when you feel depressed?

We need to *really* get the fact that we *all* get knocked down and feel depressed at times.

And… We need to know that there are two *very* different ways to respond to that depression.

When fixed-mindset people get depressed, they tend to think that something's inherently wrong with them (and that they're the only ones who experience failure and its associated pain). Then they tend to STOP doing the very things that could help them rebound.

Enter: The dreaded downward spiral.

On the other hand, when we approach the exact same devastating failure with a GROWTH mindset, we respond in a VERY different way.

We KNOW we can get better. So, we work harder.

Let's remember that the next time we get knocked down.

SMALL WINS
ARE SURPRISINGLY POWERFUL

Teresa Amabile is the head of research at the Harvard Business School.

It's almost impossible to read a book on productivity without bumping into Professor Amabile and her decades of research on what makes people happy and productive at work.

In her *Harvard Business Review* article "The Power of Small Wins" and her book *The Progress Principle*, she walks us through her research on how to take our productivity and flourishing to the next level.

Here's what you need to know.

First, Amabile tells us that it all starts with our "inner work life." In other words, what's going on in our heads as we go through our days.

In short, if we're feeling good, we tend to be more productive and creative. If we're not feeling so good, well, we're not as productive and creative.

That's pretty straightforward.

What's *not* as obvious is *how* we get ourselves (and those who work with and for us) to feel good while at work to make sure we're consistently performing at a high level and enjoying the process.

With that in mind … Quick question: If you were managing someone and had to guess the #1 thing that would most boost their inner work life, what would you guess it to be?

Well… What's your guess?

Amabile has surveyed hundreds of top executives and managers. About 95% (!!!) of them get that question wrong.

They just don't know what motivates people.

What works?

Small wins.

Progress on meaningful projects.

People feel their best and perform at their best when they're *making progress on something that matters to them*.

It doesn't need to be a huge, Super Bowl-winning moment (which, by definition, happens very rarely). It's the TINY little wins we can create for ourselves day in and day out that make the most difference.

And yet, few managers prioritize this.

Our +1°…

As the CEO of your life, it's time to manage yourself as well as possible.

Two quick questions will help.

What's your #1 most Wildly Important Goal?

Got it? Great.

How can you make just a little bit of progress on it today?

Get your Energy Focused on What's Important Now.

And celebrate the small wins.

All day. Every day.

Especially…

TODAY.

INTERRUPTIONS?
THEY'RE OFTEN THE REASON FOR THE ROUTINES

This morning, I did my thing, dominating my Philosopher-mode protocol that featured a shorter (1,000-second) meditation, so I could get straight to work on this book.

I started working on a +1° when...

Emerson burst into my office with his joyful enthusiasm.

So...

I pressed pause on the writing and Focused my Energy on that moment's WIN... Emerson!

We chatted about his plans to prepare for his next big chess tournament. I ended our awesome chat with tears in my eyes as I told Emerson just how much I appreciate him and let him know how much fun I am having seeing him flourish.

I reminded him that nothing gives me greater joy than doing everything I can to support him in creating an amazing life.

It was a sweet, special moment.

Heroic app Target swipes...

- Respond to Bid from Emerson
- Micro-Moment of Awesome with Emerson
- Big Wrestle Hug with Emerson

Then...

As Emerson was on his way out of my office, Eleanor burst through the door and asked me to check out the house she built.

PERFECT!

Time to Respond to a Bid from Eleanor and create a Micro-Moment of Awesome with *her* as I shifted my Focus to the next WIN!

Heroic app Target swipes...

- Respond to Bid from Eleanor
- Micro-Moment of Awesome with Eleanor
- Big Hug with Eleanor

I'm typing this +1° an hour later after breakfast.

And... I'm reminded of Jim Mattis's wisdom from his great book, *Call Sign Chaos*.

In a very different context, he makes the same point when he tells us: "A former boss, Navy Captain Dick Stratto, who was held in the Hanoi Hilton for 2,251 days as a 'prisoner of war,' had taught me that a call from the field is not an interruption of the daily routine; it's the reason for the daily routine."

Of course, there are times when we need to be in deep, do-not-disturb-unless-it's-an-emergency mode and...

Those bids from our kids and loved ones?

They're not an *interruption* of the daily routine; they are the REASON FOR THE DAILY ROUTINE.

Let's remember our Soul Force Equation as we ACTIVATE our Heroic superpowers by Focusing on What's Important NOW.

Close the gap.

Live with *Areté*.

TODAY.

A BOWL FULL OF COFFEE BEANS
A LESSON ON FOCUSED ATTENTION

In our last +1°, we talked about some recent opportunities I had to practice my philosophy and activate my Soul Force by Focusing my Energy on some WINs with my kids.

As it turns out, I had another WIN Target swipe opportunity with Emerson from the same morning.

Quick context.

As you know at this stage, Emerson is REALLY into chess. He's also really into ChessKid.com. FunMasterMike, the primary teacher and Chief Chess Officer of the site/company is one of Emerson's Heroes. He plays kids in a live Zoom thing he does called "Beat FunMasterMike."

A LOT of kids are online trying to play him when he does these live Zooms. Emerson has tried to play him a BUNCH of times but never got lucky enough to be one of the kids who got through to play. Until… He got his lucky break!

So… Emerson plays FunMasterMike. Then he comes bursting into my office to tell me (with all the ineffable enthusiasm of the beautiful ten-year-old I absolutely adore!)…

"DADDY!!! I GOT TO PLAY FUNMASTERMIKE!!! I DIDN'T WIN BUT THAT'S OKAY BECAUSE I GOT TO PLAY HIM!!!"

To which I replied: "Dude. That's amazing!!!" Then I shifted my Focus AGAIN to this WIN as I knew it was a *really* important moment for him, and I wanted to savor it with him.

So… We go to the livestream and replay his game and watch him playing his Hero.

He tells me: "It was really hard to play him because I was listening to him talk about our game while I was playing."

To which I said: "DUDE!!"

Then I continued by saying: "It's IMPOSSIBLE to play him well when your attention is split between Focusing on playing your game AND listening to him talk to another person about what they're thinking!"

Then I knew we had a REALLY good teaching moment opportunity.

I celebrated how awesome it was that he was able to play him, *and* I celebrated how well he framed the experience as I hunted through our pantry to look for some beans, so I could make a point about the power of Focusing our attention on What's Important Now.

I couldn't find any open packages of normal beans, so I grabbed a bag of coffee beans. Then I grabbed two bowls.

I poured the coffee beans into one bowl, so it was full, and I left the other bowl empty.

I said: "You see this bowl full of beans? That's your brain FOCUSED ON ONE THING—playing chess."

Then I said: "You know what happens when you think about OTHER things BESIDES playing that game of chess—like listening to FunMasterMike talk while you're playing?"

Then I grabbed a handful of beans from the full bowl and put them into the empty bowl.

"Those beans go over here."

Then we talked about how being so excited and nervous and thinking about all that was going on was another scoop of beans in the wrong bowl.

Then we talked about the fact that, as he KEPT ON LISTENING to FunMasterMike narrate every move, he was taking ANOTHER SCOOP of beans out of one bowl and putting it in the other.

And then ANOTHER SCOOP of beans as he worried about his five-minute clock running out.

And ANOTHER SCOOP as they kept on talking until…

There were very few beans left in the Focus bowl.

Then I asked: "How well do you think you're going to play when all the beans are in THAT bowl of distractions?"

To which he replied with a big smile: "Not as well as I could if all the beans were in the other bowl."

To which I replied: "EXACTLY."

And… That's our +1°.

How's YOUR Focus?

Remember the coffee beans and keep them in the right bowl, Hero.

Activate your Soul Force.

FOCUS on WHAT'S IMPORTANT NOW.

All day. Every day.

Especially…

Today.

TO THINE OWN SELF BE TRUE
THE FIRST QUOTE I EVER MEMORIZED

William Shakespeare once told us (via Polonius in *Hamlet*)…

"This above all: to thine own self be true, And it must follow, as the night the day, Thou canst not then be false to any man."

For some reason, as a fifteen-year-old high school student, I decided *that* would be the very first quote I ever wrote down and committed to memory.

I can still vaguely see my handwriting on a little index card in my mind's eye. I smile with joy as I think of that awesome younger version of me thinking *that* was a quote worthy of my attention.

"This above all: to thine own self be true, And it must follow, as the night the day, Thou canst not then be false to any man."

To thine own self be true…

Are you?

Ralph Waldo Emerson echoed this wisdom centuries later when he said: "Trust thyself. Every heart vibrates to that iron string!"

Trust thyself…

Do you?

A GOLD MEDAL IN 1960
BUT NO MEAL IN YOUR HOMETOWN DINER

Muhammad Ali was born Cassius Clay.

In 1960, eighteen-year-old Cassius fulfilled his dreams and won the gold medal in the 1960 Olympic Games in Rome.

Then... He returned home to Louisville, Kentucky, and couldn't even eat in a restaurant in his hometown.

That experience changed his life.

Let's pause and reflect on that for a moment longer...

It's 1960. You're eighteen years old. Imagine training relentlessly to qualify and then go to the Olympics. You win the gold medal. You're incredibly proud of yourself and the fact that you just represented your country well. You come home and...

YOU CAN'T EVEN EAT AT THE RESTAURANT IN YOUR HOMETOWN.

As a white man, I can't even imagine that experience. And... That's exactly the world Muhammad Ali and millions of other Black men and women lived in as recently as the 1960s. And as insane as that reality was, go back just a few more generations, and those very same men and women and children were enslaved. Gah.

So... What would YOU do in that situation?

The young Cassius Clay threw his gold medal into the Ohio River. Then, a few years later, he threw away his name and became Muhammad Ali as he fiercely committed to doing something about the injustices his people were suffering.

P.S. In his autobiography *The Soul of a Butterfly*, Ali tells us about why he changed his name.

The short story is because he was named after his ancestors' slave master. Did you know the last name of slaves would CHANGE when they were bought and sold? (Again, it's impossible for me to even imagine that.)

He tells us that "Elijah Muhammad later gave me the name Muhammad Ali. Muhammad means 'worthy of all praises,' and Ali means 'most high.'"

P.P.S. As I read Ali's autobiography, I thought of my trip with Emerson to the Texas State Chess Championships. We dominated our pre-match protocol—eating, moving, sleeping, breathing, and focusing our minds like professional optimizers. Of course, I was proud of him for doing so well.

And… As I looked around and saw how many of the kids and their families were clearly struggling with their weight and their confidence and their overall well-being, my heart was broken.

What difference does it make if MY kid could compete at a high level in every area of his life if THESE kids didn't have anywhere near the same resources and advantages that he has?

Then I deepened my resolve to do everything in my power to help as many kids and their families as we can.

THE RIDDLES OF LIFE
GIRAFFES, SKUNKS & HEROES

L ast night, Emerson and I were having fun playing The Riddle Game while Mommy and Eleanor took a bath together (which might have been the cutest thing ever).

Riddles included:

Emerson: "What's spotted and tall?"
Me: "A giraffe?"
Emerson: "YES!"

Me: "What's striped and stinky?"
Emerson: "A skunk?"
Me: "YES!" (Hah.)

Me: "What has a face but no eyes?"
Emerson: "Hmmmm… I need another hint…"
Me: "In place of the eyes, the face has numbers."
Emerson: "A WATCH!"
Me: "Yes!"

Me: "What starts as an irritant and winds up a gem?"
Emerson: "A PEARL!"
Me: "Yes!!"

Me: "What's bigger than a tennis court but in your body?"
Emerson: "My soul?"
Me: "That's an amazing answer." (Wow.)
"Anything else?"
Emerson: "Hmmm…"
Mommy from the bath for the win: "Your small intestines!"

Me: "What virtue do heroes we admire most embody?"
Emerson: "Love."
Me (I was thinking courage, so I asked): "What else?"
Emerson: "Kindness."
Me: (I just realized he got it right) "You're exactly right."
"I love you, buddy."

Wisdom. Discipline. Courage.
They're essential to living a life of deep meaning and joy.
But… Love?
That's the answer to pretty much all of life's riddles.

WHAT'S 1 + 1?
IT DEPENDS

After Emerson gave me that answer to pretty much all of life's riddles (LOVE!), we went to visit the ladies in the bath to tell Mommy about his answer.

Which, of course, led to a whole 'nother round of riddles.

Including this one I got from Ellen Langer—the "mother of mindfulness" research and the creator of the "psychology of possibility."

I interviewed Ellen years ago.

During that chat, she asked me this riddle...

Ellen: "What's 1 + 1?"

[Before we carry on, what do you think? What's 1 + 1? Got it? Awesome. Now, back to the show...]

Ellen: "What's 1 + 1?"
Me: "Uhhh..."

For curious souls, here's the quick look inside my head in that moment: "I know the answer can't be two but..."

Insert thought from Part X: "At least, we're filming this, so I'll look ridiculous!"

Quick reply by my daimon: "That wasn't helpful Part X. Just have fun and answer the question, Brian."

Yes, that complete dialogue occurred in the span of a couple seconds. (Hah.)

Me: "Uhh… two?"

Ellen: "Nope. The right answer is 'It depends.'"

Then Ellen (in full Professor Langer mode) proceeded to school me on the importance of mindfully approaching life and its challenges.

"If you're adding two of the Arabic numeral ones together," she explained, "the answer is two."

"But… If you're putting two pieces of gum together, the answer is one."

And, after discussing this riddle with the ladies in the bath, the kids and Mommy and I had fun establishing the fact that if you're putting two 1's right next to each other, the answer is "11." Put a sperm and an egg together, and you get one baby (or maybe two!).

And…

You get the idea…

That's our +1°.

If you feel so inspired, have fun riddling your friends and family as we remember to approach life a little more mindfully.

All day every day.

Especially…

TODAY.

MOTIVATION (AGAIN)
WORK THE EQUATION

Whenever I'm working on a big project that I'm fired up about and equally committed to dominating, I, of course, pull out all my motivational tools from the ol' toolshed.

With that in mind, we're going to review our Handy Dandy Motivational Calculator.

Let's dust it off and apply it to whatever big project YOU are working on these days. (Which is… what?)

So… The Motivation Equation.

It's *really* good.

Another pop quiz: Can you remember what it is?

Recall: A leading researcher named Piers Steel did a meta-analysis of a *ton* of studies on the science of motivation. He came up with an equation to capture motivation, so you can "stop putting things off and start getting things done."

Here's what I like to write at the top of a blank sheet of paper when I'm applying this wisdom:

Motivation = Expectancy x Value / Impulsivity x Delay

Then I take an inventory of how I'm doing in each and find ways to optimize each variable to make sure my motivation is Heroically activated. (Then, btw, I almost always WOOP it.)

First variable: Value.

Also known as desire. Do you really, *really*, **really** want it? Like *jumbo* really? Awesome. Why?

The next variable: Expectancy.

Also known as confidence. Do you *really* believe you can get it? If so, awesome.

If not, recalibrate your goal so you do. No need to waste any more precious days of our lives going for something we don't even think we can get. That, of course, is a great way to lose motivation—which is why this is such an important part of your equation.

Alright. That's our numerator.

Want high motivation?

Make your Value x your Expectancy a REALLY big value.

Now, we're ready to deal with the things that will chip away at our motivation.

First variable for the denominator: Impulsivity.

Do you easily get distracted? Do you impulsively and addictively allow your attention to go from thing to reactive thing all day and fail to do what you *know* is the next most important thing?

Solution: Leverage the power of your desire to eliminate all the nonsense and FOCUS on what's important now!

Second variable for the denominator: Delay.

If your goal is a year from now (without smaller milestone goals), you're never going to maintain peak motivation.

We need to create a TON of micro-wins "Teresa Amabile *Progress Principle*" style. Make TODAY a Masterpiece Day by identifying What's Important Now and then WIN, WIN, WIN, all day every day.

With that in mind...

What's YOUR #1 Wildly Important Goal these days?

Important note: I'm asking you to identify YOUR #1 MOST WILDLY IMPORTANT GOAL RIGHT NOW.

Not your bucket list of one hundred things you want to do before you die. Or the ten things that would be super awesome to check off a list. Or even two or three exciting goals.

I want ONE super important goal.

What is it?

Important note #2: If you don't know what it is, how about we make figuring out your #1 most inspiring goal your #1 goal?

With *that* in mind...

If you feel so inspired, grab a blank piece of paper. Work the equation. Write this down at the top if the page...

Motivation = Expectancy x Value / Impulsivity x Delay.

Now, do the inventory...

What's working? What needs work?

Let's optimize those variables as we get your *energy focused on what's important now.*

Consistently.

TODAY.

UNFORTUNATE VS. UNFORGIVABLE
WASTED TIME & WAITING ANY LONGER

Here's another gem from Seth Godin's *The Icarus Deception*. If this doesn't turn up the heat, I don't know what will.

He tells us: "It's too bad that so much time has been wasted, but it would be unforgivable to wait any longer. You have the ability to contribute so much. We need you, now."

It's funny because when I first recalled that passage in my head while reflecting on it while walking on our trail, I thought Seth said: "It's *unfortunate* that so much time has been wasted. But it would be unforgivable to wait any longer."

Unfortunate vs. Unforgivable.

Unfortunate vs. Unforgivable.

Unfortunate vs. Unforgivable.

That phrase has become a bit of a mantra for me.

I thought of it the other day as I was reading notes from a journal I created over twenty years ago.

I found myself simultaneously inspired by the fact that I was talking about the same themes that guide my life today way back then and ... I found myself wishing I could reach back in time and GRAB that version of me and BEG HIM to WAKE UP and start living with a deeper sense of urgency.

Yes, it's unfortunate that we have all wasted so much time living at less than our best. And, it's simply unforgivable (goosebumps) to wait any longer.

Today's the day. Give us all you've got, Hero.

THE #1 SUCCESS PRINCIPLE
EVENT + RESPONSE = OUTCOME

Jack Canfield is the creator of the *Chicken Soup for the Soul* series. Fun fact: An astonishing 500 million copies of those books have been sold.

Canfield has been a leader in the self-development world for decades. He also wrote *The Success Principles* in which he distills "the sixty-four timeless principles used by successful men and women throughout history" to show us "How to Get from Where You Are to Where You Want to Be."

Let's chat about the very first Success Principle.

(Can you guess what it might be?)

Canfield tells us: "It is time to stop looking outside yourself for the answers to why you haven't created the life and results you want, for it is you who creates the quality of the life you lead and the results you produce. You—no one else! To achieve major success in life—to achieve those things that are most important to you—you must assume 100% responsibility for your life. Nothing less will do."

Important note: All the great teachers would agree. And, by "all," I mean ALL.

Canfield's #1 Principle is Covey's #1 Habit. It's also the essence of ancient Stoicism. It's Rule #1 of creating a great life.

We need to become the hero of our lives, and we simply can't do that if we're acting like a Victim. Period.

Canfield shares a formula to help us get the idea:

$$E + R = O$$
The Event + Our Response = The Outcome

An event happens. The event is, in itself, neutral. Buddhists would say that the event is "empty" of meaning.

We respond. We need to know that we ALWAYS have a choice as to how we respond, and it's ALWAYS (!) OUR RESPONSE that, ultimately, determines the Outcome.

Of course… When we're in Victim-mode, we think the equation goes $E = O$. Something happens, then there's an inevitable outcome. That, of course, is not true.

Canfield shares a simple story to bring home his point.

After the earthquake in 1994 in Los Angeles (I can still vividly remember being *thrown* out of bed while I was attending UCLA), one of the freeways took a beating. Traffic was at a near standstill. Some news reporters were knocking on commuters' windows asking them what they thought.

The first person was angry and complaining about the fires and the floods and the earthquakes and how much he hated California, whiny yada yada yada.

The second person was happy. Knowing there'd be delays, she hit the road early and brought some Spanish language learning tapes plus a book. Life was good.

That's our +1°…

Remember Success Principle #1 and the equation:

Event + Response = Outcome.

Choose the best response to the events in your life.

TODAY.

THE EMPOWERMENT DYNAMIC
VS. THE DREADED DRAMA TRIANGLE

As we discussed, David Emerald wrote a great little book called *The Power of TED**.

We had a quick chat about this in Objective II. We're going to practice some spaced repetition and revisit some wisdom from this book as it's a *really* powerful model that I use A LOT in my life and in my coaching work.

Know this: TED* stands for "The Empowerment Dynamic." David calls its opposite the "Dreaded Drama Triangle" or "DDT" for short.

He tells us that it's easy for us to live in DDT all day every day. We want to shift to The Empowerment Dynamic.

Here's the quick look at this super simple and equally powerful framework to optimize our interpersonal dynamics.

First, draw a triangle with a point at the top. Then draw a second triangle.

On your first triangle, put "Victim" at the very top. Then put "Rescuer" on the bottom left and "Persecutor" on the bottom right. That's your Dreaded Drama Triangle.

On your second triangle, put "Creator" at the very top. Then put "Coach" on the bottom left and "Challenger" on the bottom right. That's your Empowerment Dynamic.

Let's start on the top of that first triangle. In our Dreaded Drama Triangle, we start with a Victim orientation.

When we're showing up as a Victim, we're focused on what's

wrong, and we tend to feel Persecuted by life, and we look for things or people to Rescue us.

For example, let's say we lose our job. The Victim will complain about how their former employer or the economy or the world at large is constantly Persecuting them. They might look for someone to Rescue them from all their problems and/or turn to a substance that will numb them and temporarily Rescue them from those problems.

When we play in DDT, we tend to bounce around and play other roles in that triangle. When we're not playing the role of the Victim, we might step into the role of angry Persecutor or enabling Rescuer.

On the other hand, in The Empowerment Dynamic, we start with a Creator orientation.

When we live from this perspective, we aren't whiny Victims. We're empowered Creators. Therefore, we're not "Persecuted" by life. We're Challenged by it. And, although we're open to getting Coached, we're not looking to be Rescued.

And, very importantly, when we show up with the Creator mindset of The Empowerment Dynamic, we see *other people* as capable Creators as well, so we'll offer suggestions as a Coach or a Challenger without dropping into being a Rescuer or a Persecutor.

DDT vs. TED*.

Where do YOU tend to hang out?

The +1° for today...

High-five your new friend, TED*!

SINGER'S STOICISM
TRUE SURRENDER

Michael Singer is one of my favorite teachers.

He clearly practices his philosophy, and his philosophy is a good one. As I was reading his latest book, I was struck by the parallels between his wisdom and Stoicism.

Although they take different approaches to get there and describe the process in slightly different terms, they arrive at the same destination. Check this out...

Here's Michael Singer from *Living Untethered*: "One of the most amazing things you will ever realize is that the moment in front of you is not bothering you—you are bothering yourself about the moment in front of you."

Here's Marcus Aurelius from his *Meditations*: "If you are distressed by anything external, the pain is not due to the thing itself but to your own estimate of it; and this you have the power to revoke at any moment."

The wisest among us learn to have the wisdom and the humility to see the bigger picture and to ACCEPT REALITY.

That is what Singer would call "true surrender." Byron Katie calls it "loving what is." Phil Stutz calls it "radical acceptance." The Stoics called it "the art of acquiescence" and their ENTIRE philosophy is basically predicated on EXACTLY what Singer is describing.

Whatever you want to call it, let's practice it.

TODAY.

HEROIC ATHLETES UNITE!
JERRY RICE & OTHER GREATS FOR THE WIN

N early every morning, I start my day the same way.

First, important reminder…

My day started the NIGHT BEFORE with a solid PM Bookend protocol.

Last night, my workday was over ("Shutdown complete!") by around the tenth hour, followed by a digital sunset around the same time.

Then I transitioned to some Deep Love time that included playing catch with the kids while they jumped on the trampoline.

Then…

After a great night of sleep, I woke up and brushed the ol' teeth while I synced my Oura ring to see my data from last night's sleep.

THEN…

After reviewing my Readiness and Sleep scores and seeing how I can use the data to get just a little better (+1°!), I took an iPhone picture-grab of my scores and sent them to two of my dearest friends: Sean Casey and Brandon Guyer.

As we've discussed, Sean is a former 3x Major League Baseball All-Star who is currently the hitting coach for the New York Yankees. Brandon is another former MLB player who is currently the mental toughness coach for the Los Angeles Angels.

Note #1: They're also both Heroic Coaches.

Note #2: This practice of sending them my Oura scores has, unquestionably, made me a better human being. We might be a little competitive. (Hah.)

Remember The Audience Effect and the fact that the fastest way to change your life is to join a community with high standards—even if that "community" is just three people!

It's also a lot of fun and has made the three of us super close. So…

This morning, I sent them my Oura scores. As you know if you have an Oura ring, a "Readiness" and/or "Sleep" score over 85 earns you a crown and is considered optimal. I tend to get scores in the high 80s and low 90s.

Now…

Once upon a time, Sean got a pair of 87s and said: "A pair of Gronks (as in, the great NFL player Rob Gronkowski—who wore #87) for the win!"

I laughed. Brandon laughed.

Then…

After writing that +1° on Jerry Rice about how he scored a touchdown *every time* he caught the ball, I decided to use his number (80!) as a base number for my scores and then find the best athlete who wore the number for the difference between #80 and my score.

It's a fun way to channel my Heroic Energy Identity as a "Disciplined Athlete" by imagining an all-time great athlete and how THEY showed up to earn that status.

For example, this morning I got an 88 Readiness score and a 90 Sleep score.

That means I needed to find the best sports player to wear the #8 and the #10.

Enter: A quick Google search.

Kobe Bryant was #8. Pelé was #10. Perfect.

Here's my text: "Boys! I got a Jerry Rice + a Kobe and a Jerry Rice + a Pelé. I'm ready to dominate. Day 1. All in. Let's go!!"

And…

That's our +1°.

Remember: Activating our Heroic potential is more fun with friends and… when we make it all one big game.

It's Day 1.

Let's go all in like our favorite Heroic athletes.

TODAY.

A (TRUE) STORY ABOUT LA PIÑATA
WHEN DREAMS COME TRUE

In our last +1°, we spent some time with Sean Casey and Brandon Guyer and our Oura scores.

Let's chat about Brandon. He's the guy who inspired me to get my ARETÉ tattoo.

After going through our Heroic Coach program, he fell so in love with the idea of *Areté* that he told me he was going to get a tattoo.

To which I said: "Wow."

Followed by: "Not before I do!" (Hah.)

I booked my tattoo appointment for that week. We both have the tattoo on our right forearm in one-inch tall, three-inch long script.

Fun note #1: My dear friend Tom Morris (the guy with the dual PhDs from Yale in Philosophy and Religion), writes about those ARETÉ tattoos in his book *Stoicism for Dummies*.

Fun note #2: A bunch of other people now have ARETÉ tattoos—including my right-hand guy/Heroic Head Coach, Michael Balchan, and another guy on our team (what's up, Bryan?!).

Plus, the *very* first investor in Heroic, my dear friend and advisor, Matt McCall (who happens to be a Heroic Coach who also happens to run a venture capital firm called Forge Capital—yes, that's inspired by our wisdom on FORGING antifragile confidence) also rocks an ARETÉ tattoo.

Fun note #3: If YOU get an ARETÉ tattoo, send me a picture.

And, if you want the same font we all used, let me know. Just send me a note on Heroic social. I'll share your tattoo with our community, and we'll add it to our collection!

Now…

Tattoos aren't the point of this +1°.

This is…

Like ALL aspiring Major League Baseball players, once upon a time, Brandon was a minor league baseball player.

One day, after one of his *worst* performances, Brandon's Triple A manager brought him into his office. He was nervous about what his manager might tell him.

To Brandon's surprise, he was being called up to the Big Leagues. The VERY next day, he was going to play his VERY first game in the SAME stadium he grew up going to as a kid.

IMAGINE THAT for a moment or three.

It's his first at-bat. He steps up to the plate. And you know what he does?

He hits a home run in front of his friends and family—the first player to *ever* hit a home run in his first career at bat in Camden Yards.

IMAGINE THAT for a moment or three.

Actually, search "Guyer's first career homer" and watch that video if you feel so inspired.

I've watched Brandon hit that home run (in his first at bat!) at least a dozen times, and I've gotten tears in my eyes EVERY TIME. In fact, I just got misty-eyed watching it again.

So…

Our Hero hits a home run in his first at bat.

Then you know what Brandon does?

He strikes out in the next two at bats.

Then you know what happens?

He gets sent back to the minor leagues where he goes up and down for YEARS before making it stick in the Big Leagues.

And, you know how he navigated that whole process? With exactly the ideas that we come back to in this book.

Then you know what happened?

He made his dreams come true and became a seven-year MLB player who made some incredible plays in the playoffs and World Series—during which the announcer gave him the nickname "La Piñata" because he got hit by more pitches than anyone else in baseball.

He's now the mental toughness coach for the Los Angeles Angels and for the University of Virginia's baseball team (where he's a Hall of Famer). And, he created a program called Major League Mindset to teach young athletes how to win both ON *and* OFF the field.

How?

By living with *Areté*, of course.

He's the living embodiment of what it means to be Heroic.

Our +1°...

What dreams do YOU want to make come true?

It's Day 1. We're all in.

LET'S GO, HERO!

DISCIPLINED ATHLĒTĒS
WHAT CONTEST ARE YOU IN?

In our last couple +1°s, we've had fun hanging out with some of my all-time favorite athletes—from Jerry Rice and Kobe Bryant and Pelé to Sean Casey and Brandon Guyer.

I want to chat more about my Heroic Energy Identity and why I recommit to being a "Disciplined Athlētē" all day every day to get myself Heroically Energized, so I can show up, be Heroically Productive and Heroically Connected, so I can give my family and friends (and YOU!) and the world all I've got.

It's time for yet another etymology pop quiz.

(Yes, I was a nerd in school, and I continue to be *that* guy.)

Although I originally looked this up in my old-school, 2,084-page *American Heritage* dictionary, we'll go with the Apple dictionary for this one.

Flip open the virtual pages via a search, and we find that the word *athlete* is...

"from Greek *athlētēs*, from *athlein* 'compete for a prize', from athlon 'prize.'"

Actually, now that I type that out, I also want to include what my *American Heritage* dictionary has to say as well.

Here's what we find in there:

"from Greek *āthlētēs*, contestant, from *āthlein*, to contend, possibly from *āthlos*, contest"

Athlete.

"A contestant competing for a prize."

How AWESOME is that?

Now...

From my vantage point, with that etymology in mind and our shared commitment to WINNING THE ULTIMATE GAME OF LIFE, I say...

We are ALL athletes.

And...

That's why my Heroic Energy Identity is "Disciplined Athlētē"—with those beautiful lines above the "e" to remind me of the word's Greek origin story and my commitment to playing the ultimate game as well as I possibly can.

Our +1°...

It's time to get ourselves Heroically Energized, so we can be Heroically Productive *and* Heroically Connected, so we can give our families and our friends and the world all we've got.

It's time to close the gap, live with *Areté*, and activate our Heroic potential.

When?

As always...

TODAY.

High-fives, Heroic Athlētē.

See you in the arena.

LET'S GO!

MY SACRED (WORK) VOW
WHAT'S YOURS?

In our last +1°, we talked about my Heroic Energy Identity. As we discussed, I am committed to being a "Disciplined Athlētē" who wins the ultimate prize: activating my Heroic potential in service to something bigger than myself and experiencing the joy of *eudaimonically flourishing* in the process.

How will I win that game?

By living with *Areté*, of course.

How will I do *that*?

By living with virtue, of course.

Which is why I recommit to embodying the virtues of discipline, calm confidence, energized tranquility, and poise as part of my daily Heroic Energy protocol commitments.

But that's not enough…

I have to move from my aspired-for Identity and Virtues to the BEHAVIORS that are an expression of those Virtues that are an expression of that Identity.

Which is why I also commit to and then hit my top Energy targets that include being in bed for 9-10 hours to make sure I get my 7-8 hours of sleep, meditating for at least a minute and doing my 1 sun salutation, 10 pull-ups, 100 burpees, 1,000 meters of rowing, and 10,000 steps EVERY SINGLE DAY.

In this +1°, I want to talk about my Heroic WORK protocol.

We'll start with my Identity. I am committed to being a (and *the*) "Heroic Philosopher CEO."

As an expression of that Heroic Work Identity, I am committed to living with a number of virtues. I am fiercely ambitious, focused on WIN, unapologetically intense, antifragile, wise, disciplined, loving, courageous, grateful, hopeful, curious, zesty, humble, honest, competent, forward-looking, inspiring, and magnanimous.

Note: Each of those virtues has a deep meaning to me and could be their own +1°s. Check out my full protocol and videos on why I do what I do on our Heroic social platform. You'll find me @Brian.

AND…

After recommitting to that Heroic Work Identity and those Heroic Work Virtues, I commit to hitting my top Heroic Work behavioral targets every day.

My #1 Work target?

I recommit to my Sacred Vow.

I have recommitted to my Sacred Vow EVERY DAY for over two years. It has been an incredibly powerful practice for me, and I've been told by many people that it's inspired them to create their own Sacred Vows so… telling you about *that* and encouraging you to consider creating your own Sacred Vow is the point of this +1°.

But before I share it, a little more context.

As you know, if you've been part of our community, on election night 2020, I founded Heroic Public Benefit Corporation.

A couple days later, I learned that the crowdfunding regulations were changing such that startups like ours could go from raising a max of $1 million of investment capital from unaccredited investors via the existing crowdfunding regulations to raising a max of $5 million.

It was one of those moments in my life when I didn't *think* we could do it, I KNEW we would be the *very first* company to *ever* raise $5 million via the new regulations.

Of course, all that's nice and warm and fuzzy.

Then we had to actually do it. And long story a little shorter, after receiving $5 million of investment interest within 24 hours of our first email to our community (and $10 million of interest in the first 100 hours), we did it.

On March 23, 2021, with the support of 2,432 Heroic Founding Investors from 75 countries around the world, we made history as the very first company to ever raise $5 million via the new crowdfunding regulations.

Now...

Before it all became official, I needed to electronically sign some documents.

Before I electronically signed the documents, I went for a walk on our property—reflecting on the magnitude of the commitment I was making to our community.

It felt like I was making a lifetime commitment to our investors that was nearly on par with the commitment I made to Alexandra when we got married.

So... I decided that I should make a Sacred Vow.

This is what I wrote...

I, Brian Johnson, absolutely and fiercely commit to honoring your investment in me and in Heroic by doing my best to make you proud to be a part of our movement. I hereby make a sacred vow to YOU and to everyone else in our community to honor my fundamentals and to practice my philosophy. Of course, I will not be perfect and I cannot promise any particular outcomes and I will certainly make mistakes. But I promise you that I will show up day in and day out and do everything in my power to fulfill our Mission to change the world, one person at a time, together, starting with you and me, Today. With Love + Wisdom + Self-Mastery + Courage, I say: Heroes unite!

And... THAT's the vow I reread and recommit to every. single.morning.

But... Ultimately, this +1° isn't about me. It's about YOU.

Is there a Sacred Vow that you and your daimon would like to draft? Perhaps we can spend a moment or three thinking about that now...

I, [INSERT NAME] ...

_____

_____

_____

_____

_____

_____

_____

_____

_____ .

Target swipe: "ALL IN. LET'S GO!!"
Here's to our Sacred Vows, Hero!

P.S. If you would like to learn more about how you can invest as little as $100 (or as much as $1,000,000+) in Heroic Public Benefit Corporation, visit Heroic.us/Invest.

P.P.S. I dropped out law school before a semester was over. And… Our wonderful crowdfunding attorneys remind me that any time I mention a potential crowdfunding investment, we need to include some legalese so here we go…

These materials may contain forward-looking statements and information relating to, among other things, the company, its business plan and strategy, and its industry. These forward-looking statements are based on the beliefs of, assumptions made by, and information currently available to the company's management. When used in the offering materials, the words "estimate," "project," "believe," "anticipate," "intend," "expect" and similar expressions are intended to identify forward-looking statements. These statements reflect management's current views with respect to future events and are subject to risks and uncertainties that could cause the company's actual results to differ materially from those contained in the forward-looking statements. Investors are cautioned not to place undue reliance on these forward-looking statements, which speak only as of the date on which they are made. The company does not undertake any obligations to revise or update these forward-looking statements to reflect events or circumstances after such date or to reflect the occurrence of unanticipated events.

There ya go, Hero. Our +1° of legalese! (Hah.)

MY SACRED (LOVE) VOW
WHAT'S YOURS?

In our last couple +1°s, we've chatted about my Energy and Work protocols. It's time to talk about my Love protocol.

Let's take a quick look at my Top 3 Heroic Love targets, including ANOTHER Sacred Vow I make every day…

As I like to say, it's *really* hard to have a series of *really* bad days when I hit my Top 3 Heroic Energy targets and/or my Top 3 Heroic Work targets.

It's *even harder* to have a really bad day and *nearly impossible* to have a really bad *series* of bad days when I hit my Energy AND my Work AND my Love targets.

So…

These are my current Top 3 Love Targets:

1. Recommit to Sacred Vow (51st | BFFs | Papa)

2. Eat a Challenge Like an Energy Bar

3. Send Wifey a Love Note

(What are YOURS?)

Let's take a quick look at each while YOU think about what Love Targets help YOU stay connected to your best self!

1. Recommit to Sacred Vow (51st | BFFs | Papa)

As you may recall, my #1 Work Target is recommitting to my Sacred Vow to help create a world in which 51% of humanity is flourishing by the year 2051 as I get my Soul Force to 101 and strive to help one million people do the same.

I make a similar commitment to my *family* EVERY SINGLE MORNING.

I want to celebrate (and I am committed to doing what I need to do to celebrate—important addition!) being with Alexandra for fifty-one years. That's what the "51st" means. I want to be best friends with my kids when they are adults. That's what the "BFFs" means. And I want to be the "Papa" to my kids' kids. That's what "Papa" means for me.

Alexandra and I have been together for over fifteen years. Every morning as I recommit to being together for fifty-one years, I smile and commit to being worthy. Our kids are only ten and six. Every morning when I recommit to being close to them for our entire lives and then imagine THEM having kids, I smile and commit to being worthy. Not someday. TODAY.

It's hard to put into words just how powerful that 1-3-5-second intention-setting is for me. Highly recommend something similar if you feel so inspired.

2. Eat a Challenge Like an Energy Bar

My second target? I want to LOVE life and ALL of its inevitable Heroic challenges as I eat those challenges like the energy bars they are—which is why I commit to doing that every.single.morning.

Fun fact: I often immediately hit that target in the morning if I had a chance to contemplate a Heroic challenge in the middle of the night as I cooked a Hero Bar with my heroes.

3. Send Wifey a Love Note

This one is a new-er one. I've swapped out a lot in this spot including "Deep Love after Shutdown" and "Micro-Moments of Awesome with A + E1 + E2."

It's just what it sounds like it is. I commit to texting Alexandra a little love note. Then, I send it to her before I do anything else that day. This is another one of those tiny little things that takes 30-60 seconds that provides huge gains. HIGHLY recommend it.

Those are my Top 3 Heroic Love Targets.

I will repeat yet again … It's REALLY (!) hard to have a series of *really* bad days when I hit those three simple targets.

Which is precisely why I use the Heroic app to recommit to those targets every.single.morning and then strive to hit those targets every.single.day.

And … Again …

This +1° isn't about me.

It's about YOU.

What are YOUR Top 3 Love Targets?

What are three simple things you can commit to, to help you be at your best Love-wise? Seriously.

WHAT ARE THEY?!

1. _____

2. _____

3. _____

Fantastic.

Clarity is Step #1.

Now… Is TODAY a good day to commit to and then hit those targets, Hero?

Fantastic. Day 1. All in.

LET'S GO, HERO!

42%
TATTOOING GOALS

I'd like to chat about how I spent Father's Day 2022 with the kids.

Spoiler alert: We went to Blindside Tattoo in Austin, Texas, to add some Heroic targets to my forearm in permanent ink.

Before we go there…

The week before I got those tattoos, I read Admiral William H. McRaven's great book *The Hero Code*.

In that book, McRaven walks us through a series of virtues everyday heroes embody. One of them is perseverance.

He tells us about the fact that it was PERSEVERANCE that helped many of our favorite heroes weather the inevitable storms of their Heroic quests en route to the summit of fulfilling their missions.

Here's one of my favorite passages from the book: "George Washington was defeated on the battlefield more times than he won. Abraham Lincoln lost eight elections before he won the presidency. Thomas Edison failed ten thousand times before inventing the lightbulb. Henry Ford had two failed companies before he found success. J. K. Rowling was destitute before she got the first Harry Potter book published, and Oprah Winfrey had an extremely difficult childhood before finding her way. Martin Luther King once famously said, 'If you can't fly, run. If you can't run, walk. If you can't walk, crawl. But by all means, keep moving.'"

With that… It's time for that fun trip to Blindside Tattoo with the kids on Father's Day.

As you know, if you've been following along, I have "ARETÉ" tattooed on my right forearm to remind me to practice my philosophy as I strive to close the gap between who I'm capable of being and who I'm actually being in any given moment.

I tattooed "HEROIC" on my left forearm along with the numbers "51 | 2051" to capture the ultimate mission to which I've dedicated my life: playing my role as humbly yet heroically well as I can to help create a world in which 51% of humanity is flourishing by 2051.

The "51" also symbolizes being with Alexandra for fifty-one years.

On Father's Day 2022, the kids and I went on a little adventure to add "101 | 1M" next to the "51 | 2051."

The "101" represents my commitment to doing everything in my power to get my Soul Force to 101, so I can help YOU get YOUR Soul Force (as measured in the Heroic app) to 101.

The "1M" represents the first million people I'm committed to doing everything in my power to help get to a Soul Force score of 101, so we can have a shot at that 51 | 2051.

Did you know that science says we increase our odds of achieving our goals by about 42% if we write them down? Yep. Now, most people write their goals down on a Post-it note they put up on their bathroom mirror. I decided to write my most important goals somewhere I'd never miss them and let them serve as a constant reminder to PERSEVERE through all the inevitable obstacles we face on a good Heroic quest.

Every morning, I start my meditation by looking down at my arm and saying to myself: "Hero, I see a world in which 51% of humanity is flourishing by 2051. Let's get our Soul Force to 101 and help 1M people do the same so we have a shot at fulfilling our mission."

Our +1°....

How about YOU?

Although, of course, you don't need to get a TATTOO to remind yourself of your deepest commitments in life (although, maybe you *should* consider it?), what are YOU ALL IN committed to achieving in this precious life of yours?

Remember...

Science says you're 42% more likely to achieve that goal if you write it down.

Here's to knowing who we are and what we're committed to doing and then going ALL IN on giving the world all we've got as we take the next steps in activating our Heroic potential.

Let's go, Hero.

It's time to fulfill our Heroic missions.

Together.

TODAY.

STRENGTHS & WEAKNESSES
LINCOLN, GRANT, IOVINE & DR. DRE

Peter Drucker tells us that all great people have great weaknesses. Where there are peaks, there are valleys.

The best among us, he says, know that they can't be great (or even good) at everything, and they don't try to become "well-rounded" people. He says that's a sure path to mediocrity. Instead, we want to lean into our strengths so hard that we make our weaknesses irrelevant.

To bring the point home, Drucker shares a story about Abraham Lincoln and his leadership of Ulysses S. Grant. Grant was the first General who was willing to actually fight for the Union. This was exactly what Lincoln had been looking for. It was a great strength. Now, Grant also liked to drink. A lot. Oops. Weakness.

Lincoln's response to this weakness? He said: "If I knew his brand, I'd send a barrel to all my generals." (Hah!)

Peaks. Valleys. Great people have them. So do all of us.

When I read that story about Lincoln and his general who liked his whiskey, I thought of a modern duo—Jimmy Iovine and Dr. Dre.

In the jaw-droppingly inspiring documentary *The Defiant Ones*, we get a behind-the-scenes look at their creative process. At one point, the two are getting ready to sell Beats to Apple for a couple billion dollars. It's still a top-secret, confidential deal. And, as we know, no deal is done till it's done.

Then Dr. Dre busts open a barrel of Grant's favorite whiskey celebrating the deal with his friends and creates a little video that goes viral. Oops.

Iovine sees the video. He maintains his equanimity and says: "That's the horse I rode in on."

Peaks. Valleys. We all have them.

Our +1°...

What are YOUR strengths?

What are the things that you're *really* good at? What can you do relatively easily that most people can't do at all?

LEAN IN!

So hard that you make your weaknesses irrelevant.

Quit trying to be good at everything and choose to be great at being YOU.

P.S. Important note: Weaknesses that we DO need to take care of if they exist? Character and integrity issues. If you're wobbly with your integrity, work on it.

Otherwise, double down on your strengths. Every time.

MISTER ROGERS' CREATIVE NEIGHBORHOOD
WON'T YOU BE A CREATOR?

Have you seen the documentary on Fred Rogers (a.k.a. Mister Rogers) called *Won't You Be My Neighbor?*

It's an incredibly inspiring, behind-the-scenes look at his brilliant and heroically awesome soul. I highly recommend it.

There were a number of scenes that I found particularly powerful. Today we're going to talk about one related to Mr. Rogers' creative process.

Quick context.

Fred Rogers began his career in the very early days of television. He saw that it could be used in a much more constructive way than it was being used at the time.

After being ordained as a Presbyterian minister, he created *Mister Rogers' Neighborhood* as his ministry to serve kids and their families. Rather than outlandish cartoons and pie-in-the-face nonsense, he produced programming that helped kids show up as their best selves.

Over the course of THREE DECADES (!) he created over 900 episodes.

Pop quiz...

Do you think it was easy for him to write all those scripts and perform those 10 separate puppet voices show in and show out?

We'll let him answer in his own words via this journal entry he typed out to himself on yellow legal paper in April 1979.

"Am I kidding myself that I'm able to write a script again? Am

I really just whistling Dixie? I wonder. If I don't get down to it I'll never really know. Why can't I trust myself? Really that's what it's all about… that and not wanting to go through the agony of creation. AFTER ALL THESE YEARS IT'S JUST AS BAD AS EVER. I wonder if every creative artist goes through the tortures of the damned trying to create? Oh, well, the hour cometh and now IS when I've got to do it. GET TO IT, FRED. GET TO IT… But don't let anybody ever tell anybody else that it was easy. It wasn't."

Note: Fred was 51 years old when he wrote that little memo to himself. He had started his show 11 years earlier.

So… Answer: NO.

It wasn't easy for Fred Rogers to show up creatively. Nor has it been easy for any other creative artist—whether we're talking about a writer or a mother or an entrepreneur.

Nor will it be easy for *us* as we work hard to make our lives a masterpiece. And don't let anybody ever tell anybody else that it was or should be easy.

Know this: If the man who gave so many children such unconditional love experienced his own "tortures of the damned" trying to give his gifts to the world, perhaps we can embrace that as part of the process.

The next time YOU feel "the tortures of the damned," remember Mister Rogers.

The hour cometh and now IS when we've got to do it.
GET TO IT, MY FRIEND.
GET TO IT.

THE PARABLE OF THE TALENTS
ARE YOU USING YOURS?

We've all heard about the Parable of the Talents.

But... Do you know what a "talent" actually was?

Fun historical fact: Back in the day, a *talent* was a unit of money. In fact, it was a pretty good chunk of cash.

According to Wikipedia, a talent was worth about 6,000 *denarii*. A denarius was the usual wage for a day's labor. So, a talent was worth about 20 YEARS worth of work.

If you calculate that based on a modern annual salary of, say, $50,000, we're talking about $1,000,000 per talent in today's dollars.

Now, let's talk about that Parable.

Jesus tells us about a wealthy guy who leaves his servants with a bunch of cash—each according to his ability. One guy gets five talents ($5 million). Another guy gets two talents ($2 million), and the last guy gets one talent ($1 million).

When he comes back from his little trip, the wealthy guy is very pleased that the first two servants put the money to work and doubled it for him.

And... He's *not* so pleased with the last guy, who was so scared of losing anything that he buried it.

In fact, we're told that the Lord was FURIOUS with him and cast him "into outer darkness" to experience "weeping and gnashing of teeth."

Yikes. Tough boss, eh?

Moral of the story: The kingdom of heaven is just like that. If we want to get in, we better use our gifts wisely.

And, important note: We don't need to wait until we die to experience the joy or sorrows of failing to use our gifts.

The kingdom of heaven exists RIGHT THIS SECOND. Each moment we have a choice: Step forward into our highest selves or back into safety. Close the gap and live with *Areté* or... leave that gap and experience the inner "darkness" of despair.

Our +1°...

Don't bury your talents. Give them to the world.

I repeat: Close the gap. Live with *Areté*. And experience the eudaimonic joy of flourishing.

P.S. Recall that the word for happiness in ancient Greek (the language of the Gospels) was *eudaimonia*—which literally means "good soul." The kingdom of heaven exists when we are connected to the best within ourselves—giving our greatest gifts in greatest service to the world.

CAMPFIRES & CHAIRS
SPIRITUAL ONES NEED TO BE RE-CREATED EVERY DAY

L et's talk about campfires.

Campfires? Yep. Campfires.

You're out camping. It's nighttime. You light a fire. It keeps you warm. You wake up the next morning. The fire is out. You'll need to light another fire tonight to get warm again.

Now, do you complain about the fact that you need to create another fire? Or, do you just accept that that's how it is?

Unless you pretty much *exclusively* speak Victimese, you accept that reality and simply make another fire, right?

Well…

Steve Chandler tells us that the "human spirit" is JUST like that campfire. You need to relight it EVERY SINGLE DAY.

Most people don't like that fact.

They want their fire to burn all day every day from the moment they wake up until the moment they fall asleep (with pleasant dreams included as well)—with as little effort as possible.

That's called entitlement. You can also call it wanting to be exonerated from all future effort.

As it turns out, Phil Stutz says almost *exactly* the same thing. Only the metaphor he uses in our chats is that of a chair. He says that when you build a chair on the physical or material plane of life, it's there the next day.

BUT...

And this is another big "but!"

On the *spiritual* plane, that chair you built today WON'T be there tomorrow.

You need to get back to work RE-BUILDING it.

Every day.

Whether you like it or not.

Kinda like the campfire of the human spirit.

Here's the +1°...

At the end of the day today, use the wood from the chair you built to fuel the campfire you need to build every night—knowing that you'll need to build both again tomorrow morning.

And...

Know that when we *really* get this, we're nearly invincible. Why? Because we stop complaining when we inevitably feel a little off and simply get to work doing the things we KNOW will help us feel great.

THAT, I repeat, is the source of ultimate confidence.

We know we'll never be exonerated from pain, uncertainty, and hard work. The worse we feel, the more committed we are to our protocol.

Here's to your comfy chairs that act as kindling to activate our Heroic potential.

PERFECTLY IMPERFECT
OUR MARBLE & STUDIO

We've chatted about Michelangelo and his statue of David a couple times. Let's chat about some historical facts regarding his ACTUAL studio.

And, let's chat about that block of marble he used to carve what would become one of history's finest masterpieces. ("Hi, David!")

First, let's take a quick look at the statue of David.

It's one of the most perfect statues ever sculpted.

Only...

It's NOT perfect.

In fact, if you look closely, you'll see that his hands aren't quite proportional and his head is a little too big. (Gasp!)

And get this. At one point, of course, David was locked up in that block of marble.

Did you know that our beautiful 17-foot (!) David came from a block of marble that was REJECTED by two other sculptors because it had too many imperfections?

(I get goosebumps as I type that.)

One of *the* greatest statues ever created was sculpted out of marble that wasn't even good enough for two artists you've never heard of? Yah.

Finally, get this. It took Michelangelo TWO YEARS to sculpt David. (He finished it in 1504.)

Have you ever thought about what his studio was like?

Well, it wasn't inside with perfect climate control.

It wasn't even inside.

It was OUTSIDE.

And, you know what?

When it rained, Michelangelo got SOAKED as he worked.

Our +1° is simple…

IMAGINE **THAT**!

Imperfect block of marble. Imperfect creative conditions. Sounds a lot like what we have to work with, eh?

Let's, as Theodore Roosevelt would say: "Do what you can, with what you have, where you are" as we sculpt ourselves into perfectly imperfect masterpieces, shall we?

Day 1. All in.

LET'S GO, HERO!

THE BATTLE WITHIN
WOLVES & LAWYERS (WHO'S WINNING?)

We all have a battle within.

Winning that battle is the ultimate Heroic quest.

Let's explore a few great ways to think about it. We'll talk about wolves, lawyers, and bouncers, and angels and devils.

First, the wolves. You've almost certainly heard this story many times, but it's worth repeating.

Mark Divine wrote a whole book about it called *Staring Down the Wolf* while Marci Shimoff talks about it in her great book *Happy for No Reason*.

Here's how she puts it: "One evening a Cherokee elder told his grandson about the battle that goes on inside of people. He said, 'My son, the battle is between the two 'wolves' that live inside us all. One is Unhappiness. It is fear, worry, anger, jealousy, sorrow, self-pity, resentment, and inferiority. The other is Happiness. It is joy, love, hope, serenity, kindness, generosity, truth, and compassion.' The grandson thought about it for a minute and then asked his grandfather, 'Which wolf wins?' The old Cherokee simply replied, 'The one you feed.'"

In *Why Your Life Sucks* (best title ever?), Alan Cohen has another great way to describe the battle going on in our heads.

He tells us: "Imagine two lawyers in a courtroom inside your head. One is arguing for your possibilities and you achieving your goals. The other is arguing for your limits and why you don't deserve what you want. Who will win? The lawyer whom you pay the most. The way you pay these lawyers, however, is not with money; it is with your attention."

Brian Tracy uses the angel vs. devil on the shoulder perspective to make the same point.

In *No Excuses!*, he tells us: "Every day, and every minute of every day, there is a battle going on inside of you between doing what is right, hard, and necessary (like the angel on one shoulder) or doing what is fun, easy, and of little or no value (like the devil on your other shoulder). Every minute of every day, you must fight and win this battle… if you truly desire to become everything you are capable of becoming."

Demon vs. Daimon. Vice vs. Virtue.

All day. Every day. You. Me. Everyone.

The eternal internal battle continues.

As Steven Pressfield says, WINNING the battle once and for all isn't possible.

But we can (and MUST!) get better at *waging* the battle.

Let's do that.

TODAY.

THE (LUCKY) MASTER'S PATH
WALK ONE MILE & YOU'RE TWO MILES FARTHER AWAY

George Leonard was an aikido master who wrote a great little book called *Mastery*. It's one of my all-time favorite books. I highly recommend it.

Now… When you think of the path of mastery and the master who walks that path, what vision comes to mind?

How would you describe it?

Take a moment and think about that.

Got it?

Here's how Leonard frames it: "We fail to realize that mastery is not about perfection. It's about a process, a journey. The master is the one who stays on the path day after day, year after year. The master is the one who is willing to try, and fail, and try again, for as long as he or she lives."

That's mastery. It's a PROCESS.

When we commit to the path of mastery we stay on that path day in and day out. Month in and month out.

YEAR after YEAR after YEAR.

The alternatives to Mastery? Well, Leonard tells us we can be what he calls a "Dabbler" or a "Hacker" or an "Obsessive."

Here's the quick look.

The Dabbler: Gets really into something for a while and loves the quick results but the moment the newness fades, he or she is off to the next new thing—rationalizing that it just wasn't a good fit. Hence, no mastery.

The Obsessive: A bottom-line type of person who wants to get the tennis stroke right on the first lesson and, when results start to slow, pushes even harder to make it work, ignoring the fact that plateaus are part of the path of mastery—pushing and pushing mercilessly to create a continuing upward curve. Then? Injury/burnout/etc. Followed by a sharp, sharp decline. Hence, no mastery.

The Hacker: After sort of getting the hang of something, the hacker is content to stay at a plateau—never really improving his skills beyond the first basic level. Hacking, hacking, hacking. Hence, no mastery.

The Master. The Dabbler. The Obsessive. The Hacker.

And YOU.

How are *you* showing up these days?

As you reflect on that, here's one more piece of wisdom from the book that is permanently tattooed on my brain.

First, just a little more context.

Recall that Masters are ALL about the PROCESS of Mastery. They have goals that inspire them but that's not their primary focus. They are ALL IN on the PRACTICE of showing up day in and day out.

Now, when you get THAT engaged in the *process* and walk the path of life like a true master, you get to a point where you fall SO in love with the whole journey side of things that (and this is the tattoo on my brain), for every mile you walk toward your destination, you actually *hope* that your destination gets TWO miles farther away.

Think about that for a moment.

You're so in love with who you are and what you are doing and who you are becoming in the process of showing up day in and day out that you don't want to rush right up to your destination. You want to savor every moment and see just how far you can go in this precious journey of life.

I repeat: For every mile you walk toward your destination you *hope* that your destination gets two miles further away.

THAT's the master's attitude.

Let's let the master himself, George Leonard, describe it in his own words.

Here's how he puts it: "For a master, the rewards gained along the way are fine, but they are not the main reason for the journey. Ultimately, the master and the master's path are one. And if the traveler is fortunate—that is, if the path is complex and profound enough—the destination is two miles farther away for every mile he or she travels."

I repeat: "If the traveler is fortunate—that is, if the path is complex and profound enough—the destination is two miles farther away for every mile he or she travels."

Our +1°...

May we all be fortunate to have such a complex and profound path that our destination is two miles farther away for every mile we travel.

See ya on the trails, my dear Heroic master!

MAGNANIMOUS VS. PUSILLANIMOUS
WILL YOU BE A GREAT OR VERY SMALL SOUL?

Magnanimity might just be my favorite word. Do you know what it literally means?

Magna = "great" + *animus* = "soul."

A great soul? Sign me up! How do we become THAT?

Well, Aristotle's take on it is fantastic. Here's what he says in his *Nicomachean Ethics*: *"Greatness of soul, as the very name suggests, is concerned with things that are great, and we must first grasp of what sort these are."*

He continues by saying: *"Well, a person is considered to be magnanimous if he thinks that he is worthy of great things, provided he is worthy of them; because anyone who esteems his own worth unduly is foolish, and nobody who acts virtuously is foolish or stupid."*

Isn't that fascinating?

The first step to being a great soul is to THINK THAT YOU ARE WORTHY OF GREAT THINGS.

Now, of course, there's a vice of excess here. In Aristotle's words: *"The man who thinks that he is worthy of great things although he is not worthy of them is conceited."*

Got it. Definitely don't want to be conceited. Let's stay grounded and humble and committed to serving something bigger than ourselves.

And… Let's be clear that there's ALSO a vice of DEFI-CIENCY here.

Back to Aristotle: *"On the other hand the man who has too low an opinion is pusillanimous: and it makes no difference whether his worth is great or moderate or little, if his opinion of it is too low. Indeed the man whose worth is great might be regarded as especially pusillanimous."*

Wait …

Pusi-what?

Pusillanimous.

Dictionary, please.

pusillanimous | ˌpyōōsəˈlanəməs | adjective
showing a lack of courage or determination; timid.

Etymology, please.

ORIGIN late Middle English: from ecclesiastical Latin ***pusillanimis*** (translating Greek ***olugopsukhos***), from ***pusillus*** 'very small' + ***animus*** 'mind'

Magnanimous means "great soul."

Pusillanimous (I dislike even saying that word in my head) means "very small soul."

Magnanimous vs. Pusillanimous.

A GREAT soul or a very small soul.

Which would *you* like to be?

As we ponder that question, Eric Butterworth comes to mind. In *Discover the Power Within You*, he tells us: *"You may say, 'But*

I am only human.' This is the understatement of your life. You are not only human—you are also divine in potential. The fulfillment of all your goals and aspirations in life depends upon stirring up and releasing more of that divine potential. And there is really nothing difficult about letting this inner light shine. All we must do is correct the tendency to turn off our light when we face darkness."

Gandhi also comes to mind.

You know what they called him?

Mahatma.

You know what *mahatma* means?

"Great soul."

It's from Sanskrit *maha* ("great") and *atman* ("soul").

Sound familiar?

THAT's the kind of *great soul* we're talking about.

Our +1°…

I hereby challenge you, my dear friend, to step into the greatness of your soul. Here's to *your magnanimity*.

If you feel so inspired, let's flip the switch and invite the best, most Heroic version of ourselves to join us with a calm, confident, relaxing breath.

Bring to mind the most energized, radiantly alive, loving, kind, courageous, disciplined, virtuous version of yourself.

Now…

Go be that version of you today.

Let's get your energy focused on what's important now as we close the gap, live with *Areté*, and activate your *magnanimous*, Heroic potential.

A PSYCHOLOGICAL SUCCESS
MASLOW SAYS ANYONE CAN DO THIS

A braham Maslow died of a heart attack on June 8, 1970. He was jogging. He was only 62 years old.

As you can imagine, he left a lot of work undone.

In an extraordinary little book called *Future Visions*, we get an intimate glimpse into his thinking via a collection of his unpublished papers and private reflections.

That book is one of my all-time favorites.

In it, Maslow tells us: "Anybody, any person whatsoever, under any circumstance whatsoever, can be a psychological success—at least in the sense of doing the best that one can and doing fully what one can—to be himself or herself and to accept the reality of himself or herself."

That's our +1°.

I don't care who you are or what you've done or what you're currently doing. You can be a psychological success.

RIGHT. THIS. SECOND.

How?

Accept yourself.

Do the best you can and do fully what you can.

In other words, live with *Areté*.

Not someday.

TODAY.

WISDOM FROM MY MOM & THOMAS CARLYLE
GOD GAVE YOU GIFTS. GIVE THEM TO THE WORLD!

My mom and her husband, Tom, recently visited.

I was blessed to be the best man in their wedding. I especially enjoyed having the opportunity to thank my mom for helping shape who I am today and to thank Tom for being such a kind, good person and for taking such good care of my mom.

On her visit, my mom brought the local newspaper that she kept from the day I was born: May 22, 1974.

Watergate was (literally) front-page news.

But what caught my attention was the quote from Thomas Carlyle on the upper-left corner.

It's fantastic: "The man without a purpose is like a ship without a rudder; a waif, a nothing, a no-man. Have a purpose in life, and having it, throw such strength of mind and muscle into your work as God has given you."

Now…

I'm not much of a collector of things so the newspaper has been recycled—but not before I ripped off that corner quote and taped it to my whiteboard right above some strategic thoughts on the purpose to which I've dedicated my life.

But here's what's most interesting for me.

In my best-man speech at their wedding reception, I thanked my mom for seeing and supporting my potential and I shared a little story.

Once, when I was about 10 years old, I did something my mom didn't like. At all.

She sternly grabbed me by the shoulders and looked me straight in the eye (I can still feel it like it was yesterday) and said: "God gave you gifts. You must give them to the world!"

(I got goosebumps as I typed that.)

It's funny how my whole life and work can be summed up in those two sentences. And, how perfectly that quote from the day I was born captures the same point.

"God gave you gifts. You must give them to the world!"

"The man without a purpose is like a ship without a rudder; a waif, a nothing, a no-man. Have a purpose in life, and having it, throw such strength of mind and muscle into your work as God has given you."

That's our +1°.

If you feel so inspired, imagine me (or someone who believes in you) looking you straight in the eye and saying with a loving sternness…

"God gave you gifts. You must give them to the world!"

Let's make our moms and families and communities and selves proud as we go out and give life all we've got.

TODAY.

ARAMBHASHURA
LET'S BE HEROES ALL THE WAY TO THE SUMMIT

You're fired up.

Maybe you attended a weekend event or had an amazing insight about what you're here to do with your life. Or, maybe it's New Year's Day and you're about to embark on what you hope will be an epically great year—installing new habits and deleting the bad ones like an optimizing superhero.

(Or, maybe you're finishing a book like this!)

Fantastic.

You're fired up.

Cue your walk-on music.

Let's do this!

And…

Let's make sure you don't tiptoe out the back door X days later when things start getting a little tough and the whole process isn't quite as fun as it was on Day 1.

Get this: The phenomenon of starting out with a jumbo-ton of enthusiasm and then giving up shortly thereafter is such a common part of humanity that, thousands of years ago, they actually came up with a WORD for it in Sanskrit.

Arambhashura.

"To be a hero in the beginning."

Can you believe that? They actually had a word for that thing we've all done way more times than we'd like to admit. (Hah!)

Arambhashura.

"To be a hero in the beginning."

Captain Obvious here: Let's not be heroes in the BEGIN-
NING. Let's make it through those rough spots where we don't
feel like doing what we said we'd do and DO IT.

Be a hero.

All the way to the summit!

And...

Now's a good time to remember the ancient Romans had
a word for this as well. They told us we don't want to be heroes
just in the beginning or only halfway up the rugged mountain of
our Heroic quest.

Getting stuck in the middle (*medius*) of a rugged mountain
(*ocris*)?

That's *mediocrity.*

The key to summiting?

Diligent, patient, persistent excellence.

In a word...

Areté.

Cue the walk-on music.

It's Day 1. Always.

We're all in. In all ways.

LET'S GO, HERO!

VIRTUE DECLARATIONS
TO ACTIVATE YOUR HEROIC POTENTIAL

This is our final +1°.

I hope that you have been inspired by AT LEAST ONE idea from this book that can help you activate your Heroic potential.

As we wrap up our time together, if you feel so inspired, check out the back of your book.

There you will find the summation of this book in the form of declarations for each of the virtues that ancient wisdom and modern science tell us are essential to creating a life of deep meaning and joy.

Wisdom. Discipline. Love. Courage.
Gratitude. Hope. Curiosity. Zest.

I have silently recited the virtue declarations on the back cover of this book to myself THOUSANDS of times.

I've repeated the declarations during my daily AM and PM meditations, while taking a walk, while doing the dishes, while sitting in the cold plunge, and during countless other moments.

Why? Simple.

Operationalizing THOSE virtues is HOW we can live with *Areté* so we can close the gap and activate our Heroic potential.

WISDOM
I know the ultimate game and how to play it well.

DISCIPLINE
I forge antifragile confidence with every action I take.

LOVE
I am joyful, connected, and encouraging.

COURAGE
I am willing to act in the presence of fear.

GRATITUDE
I appreciate all the blessings and gifts in my life.

HOPE
I have inspiring goals, agency, and pathways.

CURIOSITY
I pay attention to what's working and what needs work.

ZEST
I dominate my fundamentals so I have Heroic energy.

It has been a sacred privilege to spend time with you.

With wisdom, discipline, love, courage, gratitude, hope, curiosity, and zest, I say…

HEROES UNITE.

It's time to change the world.

One person at a time. Together.

Starting with you and me and all of us.

Closing the gap and activating our Heroic potential by living with *Areté*.

TODAY.

HEROIC COACH
THE HERO BECOMES THE GUIDE

I have mentioned our Heroic Coach program a number of times throughout this book.

The program is, essentially, a distillation of the seven objectives we explored together in the form of a super-practical, guided 300-day program that has been scientifically shown to change lives.

It's such an important part of our mission to help create a world in which 51% of humanity is flourishing by 2051 that I'd like to take a moment to tell you a little more about it.

(You can also learn more at Heroic.us/Coach.)

Before we jump in... I want to start by saying that we have conducted research on the efficacy of our program with Sonja Lyubomirsky, PhD, and her well-being lab. In a moment, I will share the research memo she drafted describing the effects of our program.

For now, here's the spoiler alert...

Professor Lyubomirsky says: "I am not exaggerating when I say that the sizes of these pre-post effects were larger than I had ever witnessed in my own 35 years of research on well-being and human connection."

I'd also like to make sure you know that half the people who go through our program are professional coaches while the *other* half aren't "professional" coaches per se—they're people who are simply committed to showing up as their best selves while helping others do the same—whether that's their kids (and grandkids!), colleagues, and/or broader communities.

We've been blessed to serve individuals at the highest levels of corporate, military, and sports organizations, including executives at some of the largest companies in the world, commanding officers in the U.S. military and coaches of world champion athletes.

Here's the most important thing to know…

THE ULTIMATE HEROIC QUEST

Have you seen the documentary *Finding Joe*? It's all about Joseph Campbell and the modern hero's journey.

I happen to be in the movie along with great teachers and exemplars including Deepak Chopra, Sir Ken Robinson, Tony Hawk, and Laird Hamilton.

If you haven't seen it yet, you can watch the full movie for free on YouTube. Just search: "Finding Joe Free Movie."

The basic arc of the Hero's Journey goes like this…

The Hero (that would be YOU and me and all of us!) gets a "call to adventure." We realize that our current lives aren't *quite* what we know they could be. There's a nagging feeling that we're not *quite* doing what we're here to do.

We either ANSWER that call and begin our Heroic quest or… We ignore the call and suffer.

Let's say we answer the call. Then what happens? Then we meet a Heroic guide and some buddies who help us on our Heroic quest.

Then we battle the metaphorical dragons and win or learn (and win or learn some more!) before we finally conquer that quest's challenges and then…

It's time for THE most important part of the journey…

It's time for us to return back to our normal world with the treasures we discovered. The ultimate treasure, of course, is our transformed consciousness. THAT is the gift we give to the world.

ALL hero's journeys follow that basic arc.

Think of Harry Potter. He got Dumbledore as his Heroic guide and Hermione and Ron as his buddies.

Or how about Frodo? He got Gandalf as his guide and his buddies in the Fellowship of the Ring. Or what about Katniss Everdeen and her Hunger Games? She got Haymitch Abernathy as her guide and buddied up with her crew.

You know what happened after Harry Potter and his friends successfully completed their first few Heroic quests?

They became GUIDES to their fellow students at Hogwarts and taught THEM how to conquer *their* dragons and THAT is how they, together, won the battle between vice and virtue in their fictional world.

And THAT is what our Heroic Coach program is all about. We help you answer the call to adventure, and then we help you conquer your dragons and fulfill your potential, so *YOU* can help *OTHERS* do the same. And *that* is how we will change the world together.

Note: This isn't just mythology. This process of becoming your best self to help *others* become *their* best selves is a powerful spiritual and psychological ideal as well.

In Buddhism, the highest aspiration is to become what is known as a "bodhisattva." The bodhisattva works tirelessly to attain his or her own enlightenment for one reason: so they can help OTHERS do the same.

In Western psychology, Abraham Maslow is widely known for his research on the "self-actualized" human being. What is less discussed is the fact that there was something HIGHER than self-actualization on his hierarchy of needs. He called that highest state "self-transcendence."

Maslow and the Buddha and Joseph Campbell would all agree—we become the heroes of our own lives for one simple reason: so we can help others do the same.

I repeat...

The ultimate Heroic quest is simple: The hero becomes the guide. That, my dear friend, is what Heroic Coach is all about.

WHO'S IT FOR?

Since launching our inaugural class in early 2019, over 10,000 people from 115+ countries around the world have signed up for our Heroic Coach program.

What I always find fascinating is that almost exactly HALF of those who go through the program are professional Coaches who want to take their practice to the next level (or individuals who plan to become Coaches) while the *other* half "simply" want to use the program to become the best versions of themselves in service to the world.

We think of the two groups like this:

Masters: Individuals who want to live their most Heroic lives by mastering themselves and the Heroic perspective while integrating the wisdom gained from the program into their various leadership roles—from entrepreneurs, CEOs, professional athletes, venture capitalists, military leaders, and HR executives to therapists, addiction counselors, school principals, yoga teachers, and world-class moms.

Coaches: Individuals who want to live their most Heroic lives by mastering themselves and the Heroic perspective while integrating the wisdom gained from the program into their new or existing coaching practice.

Our program serves both of those groups. From my perspective, the most important thing we help everyone do to boost their professional success—whether that's the CEO or the Coach—is to become a radiant exemplar.

And, the fact is, we are ALL COACHES. At the very least, we have ONE client: ourselves.

Much more likely, we find ourselves in the role as informal "coach" a LOT more often than we may realize—whether that's in conversations with our kids, our colleagues, or others, there are ALWAYS opportunities to help bring out the best in those around us.

For individuals looking to create a coaching business (and/or to take their practice to the next level), we have training content in which we share best practices and offer additional resources, including interactive sessions with established, successful coaches.

You can check out hundreds of testimonials from *both* **Masters** *and* **Coaches** at:

HEROIC.US/COACH

For now, here are a few of my favorites…

HEROIC COACH

"I routinely tell those I serve that Heroic is where this coach goes to get coached. I use Heroic to ensure my own virtue alignment, deepen persistence towards my purpose, and find materials to help combat my own limiting belief systems. Heroic is an integral part of my own performance systems."

— **Brittany Loney,** Director of Elite Cognition and Human Optimization Program

"Brian Johnson and the team at Heroic have put together one of the most valuable assets in the area of personal development that exists on the planet. They've curated the best information, the best contributors, and the best luminaries, and carefully deliver it in a way that is impactful, easy to navigate, and can and will change the lives of millions of people. Instead of having to sort through and consume thousands of hours of books, courses, and podcasts, the Heroic Coach program boils it all down to what truly matters most. This is not another course with information overload. It is highly curated and actionable. I was blessed to be one of the first ever groups through the Heroic Coach program and still continue to come back every single week to this incredible resource."

— **Ben Pakulski,** "The Godfather of Intelligent Muscle Building," Former Mr. Canada, CEO of Muscle Intelligence

"Heroic has, quite simply, transformed our lives. My husband is so much more present and focused both at home and at work. I feel so much more empowered, confident, and able to manage the challenges that life throws at us."

— **Gisele Partaker,** Managing Director

"Heroic Coach is the most extraordinary education that I've ever received. For context: I went to the University of Pennsylvania for undergrad, I have a master's from the London School of Economics and a law degree from Berkeley Law School. However, the greatest education that I've ever received is actually the Mastery and Coaching certification program that I did with Heroic."

— **Isaiah Jacob**

"By far the best 'self-development' or 'life-coaching' investment I have ever made—at any price."

— **Nigel Brownjohn,** Software Executive

"Throughout my 12-year career in Major League Baseball, I was always on the hunt for mental tools that could give me an edge on my competition. I've experienced plenty of coaching programs over the years, but not a single one comes close to what Heroic Coach has to offer. The program has transformed my life. If you're ready to become the best possible version of yourself—as a coach, parent, spouse, coworker, or in any other role—then I encourage you to take a chance on

Heroic Coach. Trust me, it's the best decision you'll ever make. Grand slam!"

— **Sean Casey,** New York Yankees hitting coach, 3x Major League Baseball All-Star

"One highlight of Heroic Coach was connecting weekly with my Heroic buddy, who was my Naval Academy best friend and fellow closet philosopher who is also devoted to self-improvement, living a Heroic life, and making a difference. The Heroic Coach program was the perfect framework for us to connect and stay accountable to each other to reach higher levels of performance in Energy, Work, and Love. We completed the program months ago and our weekly calls continue and our friendship is better than ever. The program itself is outstanding and I recommend it regardless of your plan to become a Coach or simply master the material. Heroic Coach gave me the much-needed reps to fully adopt the wisdom. I've read countless great books, many twice, and still only implement 25% of the wisdom into habits. Brian integrates everything I've read (and more) into a coherent whole, and then recurrently hits you with the wisdom until it all sinks in. This program is a no-brainer!"

— **Jeff Everage,** President of Trident, former Navy SEAL

"I've been studying and practicing personal development for over 20 years, and Heroic Coach is by far the best program I've ever participated in."

— **Ron Reich,** Entrepreneur

"As someone with intellectual passions, I absolutely love how approachable Brian makes ancient wisdom and modern science. As a busy working mother, I have found Heroic Coach to be the one thing that helps me maintain balance in my work, health, and family life. It doesn't matter who you are or what your focus is, Heroic Coach can guide you to do whatever you dream of. It will make you smarter, more motivated, more optimistic, and more successful. And, most importantly, you'll want to motivate others to actualize their potential!"

— **Jessica Carew Kraft,** Mom, Naturalist,
Writer and Editor for Inspiring Achievers

"With full confidence, I can say that right now, I am the best version of myself that I've ever been. All for one reason: the Heroic Coach program. It truly has been life-changing. I am a better husband, father, son, friend, and coach than I've ever been. Of course I still get knocked down, have setbacks, feel fear, and have tough days. Only now I have the wisdom, the tools, and the self-mastery to eat those challenges up and come out stronger."

— **Brandon Guyer,** Los Angeles Angels mental toughness
coach, 7-year MLB player, founder of Major League Mindset

"I've seen the material offered by other certification programs. Many of them are good, but Heroic Coach is the best of the best. You and your team have really done a terrific job. The way the content is delivered, packaged, the energy of it all, the videos, the worksheets, all the PN's, the guest teachers like Cal Newport, the mobile app and site. It goes on and on. It is the most complete and simply the best."

— **Jonathan Bennett,** CTO at a health coaching company

"The program kicked my ass—in a good way! Being an experienced coach, I thought Heroic Coach would be a nice addition to my coach resources, but not a 'rock my world' kinda thing. Instead, I've found that I'm being rocked at a very foundational level, and have noticed big shifts in my life and my coaching."

— **Ian Stakiw,** Coaching Lead at large software company

"I already had two coaching certifications, but Heroic Coach was indisputably the most valuable I have taken."

— **Barb Ostrander,** Human Potential Coach
and Certified Functional Medicine Coach

HEROIC COACH RESEARCH
A MEMO BY SONJA LYUBOMIRSKY, PHD

In early 2019, my team and I were presented with an opportunity to evaluate a brand-new program in self-development: the Heroic (formerly Optimize) Coach program. The question we sought to answer was the following: What benefits—or drawbacks—would participants going through the 300-day Heroic Coach program experience?

To answer this question, we developed an extensive pre-post questionnaire to measure the impact of the Heroic Coach program on both behavior and well-being. To this end, we adapted several validated scales (e.g., Balanced Measure of Psychological Needs [BMPN], Comprehensive Inventory of Thriving [CIT], Integrative Self-Knowledge Scale, and Woodard Pury Courage Scale), combined with internally created measures, and administered the survey to the inaugural class of Heroic Coach participants.

Fast forward to the Spring of 2020: Just as the pandemic was exploding around the world, we received the hot-off-the-presses dataset. These data turned out to be a gift—both because analyzing and interpreting them was a welcome distraction and because the results were so exciting.

The 262 coaches participating in the research reported massive—yes, massive—positive shifts in their behaviors (e.g., meditating and exercising more, using their phones less) and in their feelings and states of mind (e.g., feeling more connected, focused, energized, etc.).

I am not exaggerating when I say that the sizes of these pre-post effects were larger than I had ever witnessed in my own 35 years of research on well-being and human connection.

To offer some examples, the Heroic Coach program saw more than a doubling in the percentage of coaches who felt productive (rising from 37% to 81%) and excited (from 41% to 83%); who meditated every single day (from 43% to 89%); and who were not distracted by their phones (from 29% to 74%). Furthermore, the results revealed a dramatic tripling in the proportion of coaches who felt energized in the afternoon (from 21% to 65%); who reported a bring-it-on mentality in the face of challenges (from 23% to 79%); and who put their phones away while working (19% to 62%). Incredibly, the number of participants who felt connected to the best version of themselves saw a three-fold increase (from 29% to 93%) after they finished the program.

A powerful testament to the strength of these effects lies in the very weakest finding in the dataset: before the Heroic Coach program, 78% confessed to sitting continuously for periods of longer than 45 minutes each day; after the program, that percentage decreased by (only!) a third (to 52%).

When we consolidated the data into three "buckets" or themes, labeled Love, Work, and Energy, we found that participating coaches reported gargantuan gains—with twice as many, on average, showing benefits on these metrics after the program than before. Future assessments employing rigorous designs and larger sample sizes will be critical to extend and replicate these data. But, for now, hats off to Heroic Coach!

SONJA LYUBOMIRSKY
Distinguished Professor of Psychology at the University of California, Riverside, bestselling author of
The How of Happiness and *The Myths of Happiness*

ABOUT HEROIC
PUBLIC BENEFIT CORPORATION

Heroic is a social training platform that integrates ancient wisdom, modern science, and world-class, scientifically proven behavioral design tools to help you show up as the best, most Heroic version of yourself.

We're also a history-making, crowdfunded Public Benefit Corporation committed to helping create a world in which 51% of humanity is flourishing by the year 2051 as we strive to run our business the way we think our heroes would—with wisdom, discipline, courage, and love.

It's always Day 1 at Heroic.

Learn more and join us today at:

HEROIC.US

WANT TO INVEST IN HEROIC?
LET'S CHANGE THE WORLD TOGETHER

I have mentioned the fact that Heroic is a history-making, crowdfunded Public Benefit Corporation.

We're on a mission to help create a world in which 51% of humanity is flourishing by the year 2051 and we are blessed to have the support of over 3,000 investors (just like you!) from over 75 countries around the world.

Would you like to help us change the world as a Heroic Investor? You can invest as little as $100 or as much as $1,000,000+ when we have an offering open.

Go to **Heroic.us/Invest** to learn whether we are raising funds, and the details of any offering.

And…

Any time we talk about crowdfunding, our attorneys remind us that we need to include this bit of legalese so here we go…

We are blessed to have the support of the following people, quoted in this book, as investors in Heroic Public Benefit Corporation: Phil Stutz, Sean Casey, Susan Peirce Thompson, Tal Ben-Shahar, Mark Divine, Brian Cain, Brandon Guyer, Scott Parsons, Jeff Everage, Ron Reich, Ian Stakiw, and Jonathan Bennett.

Note: None of these individuals received any incentive or consideration of any kind in exchange for their comments relating to, or endorsements of, Heroic.

Their comments, endorsements, and/or likenesses are included with their express permission.

Their comments and/or endorsements are not, and should not be regarded as, investment advice. Individuals considering an investment in Heroic should consult an investment professional before making an investment decision.

We also need to add this wonderful bit of legalese:

These materials may contain forward-looking statements and information relating to, among other things, the company, its business plan and strategy, and its industry. These forward-looking statements are based on the beliefs of, assumptions made by, and information currently available to the company's management. When used in this book, the words "estimate," "project," "believe," "anticipate," "intend," "expect" and similar expressions are intended to identify forward-looking statements. These statements reflect management's current views with respect to future events and are subject to risks and uncertainties that could cause the company's actual results to differ materially from those contained in the forward-looking statements. Investors are cautioned not to place undue reliance on these forward-looking statements, which speak only as of the date on which they are made. The company does not undertake any obligations to revise or update these forward-looking statements to reflect events or circumstances after such date or to reflect the occurrence of unanticipated events.

Once again, if you would like to invest in our Heroic movement/Public Benefit Corporation, you can learn whether we are raising funds along with the details of any potential offering by visiting:

HEROIC.US/INVEST

THANK YOU
THANK YOU, THANK YOU, THANK YOU

Gratitude. Science says it's one of the most powerful virtues to help us flourish.

As I reflect on just how many people have supported me over the last five decades to be in a position to write this book, I am overwhelmed with gratitude and intimidated by the challenge of making sure I properly thank everyone who has played such an important role in helping me be here with you today.

Bless every single one of you and please forgive me if I do not mention you by name. Know that I love and appreciate you deeply and hope that I am able to give back to you in equal measure for all that you have so generously given to me.

Where to begin?

This is a book with 451° Ideas to activate your Heroic potential so let's start there. I want to thank the hundreds (and hundreds!) of authors, teachers, and leaders who have shaped my thinking.

We featured over 200 wise human beings who have had an impact on me, but I still just scratched the surface of those who have deeply influenced me.

To each of you I featured: I want you to know that I wrote each chapter featuring your wisdom as, in part, a sort of thank-you note. I hope I have adequately captured and amplified the essence of your wisdom.

Special thanks to the (living) teachers I referenced the most often and who have had the deepest impact on me and my think-ing: Phil Stutz (we'll be coming back to you, Father!), Steve Chandler, William Damon, Tal Ben-Shahar, Tom Morris, Sonja Lyubomirsky, Mark Divine, Cal Newport, Pilar Gerasimo, Ryan Holiday, Patrick McKeown, Martin Seligman, Angela Duckworth, Nasha Winters, Ray Dalio, Steven Pressfield, James Clear, BJ Fogg, Byron Katie, Kelly McGonigal, Michelle Segar, Michael Singer, Barbara Fredrickson, Carol Dweck, Dan Siegel, James and Suzie Pawelski, Bob Rotella, Richard Rohr, Lanny Bassham, Matthew Walker, Teresa Amabile, Steven Kotler, Ken Wilber, Alan Cohen, Yuval Noah Harari, Robin Sharma, David Emerald, Kristin Neff, Admiral William H. McRaven, Eric Maisel, and Dan Millman.

Next, I would like to thank the 3,000 (!) Heroic Founding and Early-Stage Investors who have so generously supported our Public Benefit Corporation.

I am profoundly humbled by your support. I think of you every morning as I recommit to my sacred vow to make you proud to be a part of our movement.

This book is YOUR book and I sincerely hope that I made you proud and that this book helps catalyze our movement as we continue to do our best to help create a world in which 51% of humanity is flourishing by the year 2051.

It's Day 1. I have never been more all in and committed to serving YOU and your families and communities as powerfully as I can. Bless you for believing in me and in our team and giving us the resources we need to fulfill our mission.

Special thanks to...

Matt McCall for the countless strategic chats that preceded

and have followed the very first investment dollars into Heroic. You are a wise sherpa and I am blessed to have your support.

Zac Zeitlin for the near-instantaneous responses to the near-infinite bat signals. Your wisdom has deeply impacted me and Heroic.

Marty and Cheryl Bicknell for your astonishing support.

Brett Johnson for leading our first Wefunder crowdfunding round.

Katherine Collins for your incredible blend of spiritual wisdom, business acumen, thoughtfulness, pure moral goodness, warmth, and celebratory joy. Your presence in my life is a gift. You have made me a better person and our Public Benefit Corporation stronger.

John Mackey for so deeply studying, articulating, and embodying the ideals of conscious capitalism and for so generously taking the time to share your wisdom with me as you show us what an iconoclastic, wise, joyful, and impactful leader looks like.

Kelly Perdew, Chris Stappas, Randy Eisenman, Jon Miller, Joe Okleberry, Mark Divine, Jeff Everage, Andy Smith, Jim Phillips, Brad Schwartz, and Michael Garvey: Thank you for always being one text away from helping me improve my thinking and clarify our vision for Heroic while also celebrating each micro win along the way.

Michael Liftik for your friendship and extraordinary advocacy of Heroic at such a critical juncture in our business. Bless the Heroic gods for helicoptering you and your team in on our Everest quest.

Cal Newport for our friendship, your practical wisdom, our strategic chats, and your demonstration of what deep living and a commitment to excellence looks like.

Joe De Sena for showing me how to eat obstacles like energy bars and for celebrating the process of getting our cleats muddy in the arena together.

Mike Magaraci for showing me what it looks like to serve Heroically with such profound humility.

Jason Viyar and Scott Parsons for the sacred opportunity to share Heroic with the Cadets, faculty, and staff at the United States Military Academy at West Point and for our soul brotherhood.

Daryle Cardone for the sacred opportunity to be a part of your life.

Brittany Loney for your friendship, humble commitment to service, and generous (special!) support.

Brandon Guyer and Sean Casey for the incredible support and inspiration. Love you, HB's! Plus Brian Cain for connecting us and for all the inspiration and support.

Who next?

Our publishing team. Josh and Stephanie Stanton: You two and your team at Blackstone have been such wonderful partners. I'm thrilled we have created a publishing imprint together (Heroic Blackstone!) and I am inspired by all that we can do together in the years ahead. And, thanks for supporting me in breaking pretty much every rule in publishing. (Hah.)

And...

Our team at Heroic. It's simply not possible for me to do what I do without YOU and your support. I know I get all the public recognition, but I want you to know how much your Heroic heart and hustle and commitment to our movement means to me. Tears in my eyes as I type that.

Special shout-out to the team that helped bring this book together (and who do a bit of *everything* to help us fulfill our mission): Jana Dybinski, Patrick Buggy, and Calman Hilkert. You three are such good human beings and I am blessed to have your support.

Bernardo Fanti for your leadership as our Chief Technology Officer and for your pankration skills—both literal and metaphorical.

Alex, Ali, Brett, Bryan, Filo, Fred, Jesse, Joshua, J.T., Kach, Karthik, Nat, Paulina, Rosey, Seth, Sonia, Tania, Yssa, Yuva, Zak and everyone else: BLESS YOU.

And…

SPECIAL shout-out to my right-hand guy and our Heroic Head Coach, Michael Balchan. Being worthy of your fierce commitment to me and to our movement is one of my deepest motivations in life. I admire how committed you are you to EVERY aspect of your life—especially your commitment to Kristen and Dylan and Cameryn. You're a good man. I love you like the younger brother I never had.

And…

My *infinite* gratitude to the man who has had, by far, the most indelible imprint on my Soul: Phil Stutz. The Heroic gods had a very good sense of humor to wait forty-one years before introducing me to my spiritual Father but the wait was worth it. Words cannot capture how deeply grateful I am for you, your belief in and support of me. I love you so much.

I am also grateful to my dad, who passed away over fifteen

years ago. I know how hard you tried to do your best and I am so grateful that you gave so much of your heart and soul to me and to all of your kids. I wish we had the chance to celebrate many more moments. I love you and appreciate you.

And then there's my mom. What a wonderful human being you are. Of course, you were right when you said that God gave me gifts that I needed to give to the world. But the greatest gift God ever gave me was YOU and your devotion to and support in making sure those gifts were fully manifested in your youngest son. I love you so much and I am so committed to making you proud.

And…

My wife and kids. I'm typing this with tears in my eyes as I think of you, Alexandra. Our kids are *so* extraordinarily blessed to have YOU as their mother. One day they will know just how lucky they were. And, so will the rest of the world as you continue to share your extraordinarily bright light in your own humble, iconoclastic way. You're such a good person. I'm lucky to be your husband. And our community is lucky to have you leading beside me and guiding every step of our journey. I look forward to celebrating our fifty-first anniversary and enjoying the moments between here and there. Love you, Babes.

Emerson and Eleanor: This book is for YOU. I love you more than you will ever know. Being a Heroic dad for you is my biggest challenge and deepest aspiration. You two are already such beautiful human beings and my goodness I can't wait to see all that you will become and all the gifts you will joyfully give to the world in the decades ahead. I love you and I look forward to celebrating a lifetime of joyfully Heroic moments together.

HEROIC RECOGNITION
THANK YOU, THANK YOU, THANK YOU

I want to give a special shout-out to the extraordinary members of our community who supported the creation of this book. Bless ALL of you. I am deeply moved by you and your incredible support.

SPECIAL THANKS

Marty & Cheryl Bicknell,
Mariner Wealth Advisors

Roger Whitney

Randy Eisenman, Satori Capital

Jim & Beth Frey

Ava Amelia & Jason John

Ben Pakulski

Zac Zeitlin

Shaun Emmerson

Dudley Logan

Blair & Deborah Anderson

Todd Dickson

HUGS, HIGH FIVES & FIST BUMPS

The AmSty Team

Preston D. Arroyo

Fabián Badilla

Grant Ballard-Tremeer

Jake Beaman

Gieta R. Beckmann

Benevolent Capital

Michael Bennett

Teddy Bichon

Raymael Blackwell

The Blue Courage Team

Marc & Angie Bowker

Gwen Brehm

The Brinkmann Brown Family

Timmy B. Brown

Tony & Anna Bushong

Kevin B. Cahoon

Nathan Camp

Mark C. Carey

Aurora, Jaci & Tomas

Dr. Vivian H. Carrasco

Gina Cass

The Centrum Dental Team

Certas Energy

Frank Chang

Leo Chiang

Socratis Christoforou
Michael Cleveland
Martin J. Cole II
VC & Wendy, Jess,
Tara & Chase Coleman
Brian C. Cook
Patrick & Deborah Conner
CoreFitinc
Troy Mikulka & Anely Curiel
Joseph Croskey
D4M International
Alexis D'Amours
Louise Alexandra Daw
Laurie Dickey
Allie Diliberto
Graeme Richard Drew
Daniel C. Dreher
Christopher & Dachelle Duffy
The Duhon Team
Emilio Duran Molinari
Matt Eaton
Soren Eilertsen
Jeffrey A. Ernst
Helen Fjærvik Stortiset
Carey Folk
Danielle Forde
RJ & Mary Kay García
Trevor Gere
Amer Ghanem
David Glossberg
Eva Goldstein
Joselo González
Eugene R. Grass
@Guacamole_Is_Delicious
Chris Gulbrandson
Happy Manufacturing, Inc.

Shane Harbin
Dan Hegerich
Robert John Henry
Robert J. W. Herold
Dr. Jonathan Hoistad-Natalis
Wendy W. Holt
Sylvia Holtslag
The Honcharuk Family
Chris Hunsicker
Dr. Thaddeus Edward Jacobs
Mark Jacobson
Matthew Jakstis
The Jepsen Family
Robert Jewett
Hussein Jinnah
Justin Kane
Kristin Joys
Mark & Mary Keele
Bahar & Kevin Khakshouri
Debbi & Henrik Kjällbring
Joe Knight
Adrian Cunanan
& Kayo Kudo
Laura Larsen-Strecker
Damaris Lasa
Alycia Lee
Jackie & Aaron Lieberman
Kevin James Loder
Robin D. Love
The Love Family
Cassidy & Matt
The Lugsch-Tehle Family
Lori Mage
Maynard Manzano
Diane L. Martin
Janice Gail McCune

Hadley & Nash McFarland
Cameron Miller
Joe Mitchell
Dr. Tiffany Mitchell, NMD
Mixed Media Creations
John Allen Mollenhauer
Lu de la Mora
Chris & Laura Mueller
Johnathon, Joshua & Emma
Barnabas Nagy
Zsofia Kurko Navarro
Michael Nila
Rion Noone
Thomas Brent Norwood
Angel A. Ocana
Rick O'Neal
Carl Oxholm
Jocelyne Daw & Bob Page
James A. Parejko
Diane & Mark Parnes
Shelly Passios
Jim Phillips, MD
Angelina Popova
Christina Powers
Nazirah Premji
Katie Rangel
Erik Rankin
Ron Reich
Caroline K. Roberts
Michael A. & Ellen D. Robinson
Lisa Rothney
Lisa Royal
Jochen Schmiedbauer

Stephanie S. Scott
Jan Schulze-Feldmann
Todd & Stacey Schuster
Rhonda Schuttloffel
Michael Sherman
David Simon
In memory of Shirley M. P. Smith
Kathryn Soraiz
In memory of Daniel Sorum
Hellen Spanjer
Laura Sprinkle
Nancy & Chuck Stahl
David Stanford
Stoic Solutions Coaching
Grant Strachan
Rebecca Begelman Strub
Chiraag & Urvashi Swaly
James Will Szigeti
Cameron Terry
George Thorman
Holly, Maya & Daniela Tilbrook
Shane Tomes
Dr. Dane Treat
Jett & Sloane Uto
Signe Vaughan
Phil & Walden Ohana
Bill Weidacher
Kelly Wenzel
Matt Willcocks
Anthony Joseph Wilson
Dina Wilson
Kelly Dean Yagelniski
Yes with Kimmy

TOP 451 PHILOSOPHER'S NOTES
AS VOTED ON BY THE HEROIC COMMUNITY

In this book, we have featured wisdom from over 200 of the best self-development books. We have Philosopher's Notes on 500+ Notes in the Heroic app. Here are the Top 451 books we feature as voted on by the Heroic community.

1. *Deep Work: Rules for Focused Success in a Distracted World* by Cal Newport
2. *Atomic Habits: An Easy & Proven Way to Build Good Habits & Break Bad Ones* by James Clear
3. *The Tools: Transform Your Problems into Courage, Confidence, and Creativity* by Phil Stutz & Barry Michels
4. *Grit: The Power of Passion and Perseverance* by Angela Duckworth
5. *The 7 Habits of Highly Effective People: Powerful Lessons in Personal Change* by Stephen R. Covey
6. *Meditations* by Marcus Aurelius
7. *Tiny Habits: The Small Changes That Change Everything* by BJ Fogg
8. *Man's Search for Meaning: An Introduction to Logotherapy* by Viktor Frankl
9. *The Daily Stoic: 366 Meditations on Wisdom, Perseverance, and the Art of Living* by Ryan Holiday
10. *Rethinking Positive Thinking: Inside the New Science of Motivation* by Gabriele Oettingen
11. *Mindset: The New Psychology of Success* by Carol Dweck
12. *Principles: Life* by Ray Dalio
13. *The ONE Thing: The Surprisingly Simple Truth Behind Extraordinary Results* by Gary Keller & Jay Papasan
14. *The 5 Second Rule: Transform Your Life, Work, and Confidence with Everyday Courage* by Mel Robbins
15. *Flourish: A Visionary New Understanding of Happiness and Well-being* by Martin Seligman
16. *The Obstacle Is the Way: The Timeless Art of Turning Trials into Triumph* by Ryan Holiday

45 (+1) OPTIMAL LIVING 101 CLASSES
OPTIMIZE EVERY ASPECT OF YOUR LIFE

I've distilled the best Big Ideas from the best books across dozens of topics into hour-long master classes which are available in the Heroic app. Each class features 10 potentially life-changing Ideas. Here are 45 (+1) of the classes you may enjoy.

1. *Abundance 101:* How to Create True Wealth by Wisely Investing in You, Inc. (& The Best Way to Become a Billionaire!)
2. *Antifragile 101:* How to Use Everything to Fuel Your Heroic Growth
3. *Confidence 101:* How to Create Indestructible Trust in Yourself
4. *Conquering Anxiety 101:* How to Tame Anxiety and Live with Confidence
5. *Conquering Cancer 101:* How I'm Helping My Brother Fight Cancer & What I'd Share with You as Your Friend & Coach
6. *Conquering Cancer 102:* Rethinking Cancer: Theory & Therapy
7. *Conquering Depression 101:* Tame Your Gremlins and Create an Awesome Life
8. *Conquering Digital Addiction 101:* To Sculpt or to Get Hacked? That Is the Question
9. *Conquering Fear 101:* How to Alchemize Fear into Excitement & Use the Energy as Fuel to Reach Your Potential
10. *Conquering Perfectionism 101:* How to Quit Being a Perfectionist and Start Being an Incremental Optimizer
11. *Conquering Procrastination 101:* How to Quit Putting Your Life on Hold
12. *Cooking 101:* How to Optimize Your Nutrition in an Easy and Practical Way
13. *Energy 101:* How to Give Your Soul the Energy It Needs to Live Your Greatest Life
14. *Fatherhood 101:* How to Win Dad of the Year While Doing Your Life's Work
15. *Food 101:* How to Feel Empowered Around Food and Fuel a Great Life (Special Guest Teacher: Alexandra!)
16. *Goals 101:* How to Set and Achieve Goals That Will Help You Flourish
17. *Greatest Year Ever 101:* Make This Year the Greatest Year of Your Life

INDEX

ABOUT THE AUTHOR

Brian Johnson is the Founder & CEO of Heroic Public Benefit Corporation. He's 50% Philosopher + 50% CEO and 101% committed to helping create a world in which 51% of humanity is flourishing by the year 2051.

As a Founder/CEO, he's made crowdfunding history and built and sold two social platforms. As a Philosopher/teacher, he's helped millions of people from around the world, trained 10,000 Heroic Coaches from 100+ countries, and created a protocol that science says changes lives. He lives in the country outside Austin, Texas, with his wife, Alexandra, and their two kids, Emerson and Eleanor.

JOIN THE MOVEMENT
LET'S CHANGE THE WORLD TOGETHER

Learn more about *Areté* and Heroic by visiting:

HEROIC.US/ACTIVATE

Sign up for a daily email and download the app to get more wisdom in less time and to connect with me and our community from around the world.